Gospel According to Luke

Gospel According to Luke

Major Themes for Interpretation

Jayasree K. B.

Christian World Imprints

First Published in 2025 by

Christian World Imprints
Christian Publishing & Books from India
A-71 Group, Wazirpur Industrial Area
Delhi-110052
cwidelhi2017@gmail.com
www.ChristianWorldImprints.com
Phone: +91 11 41526079

ISBN: 978-93-6065-474-0

Printed in India.

Contents

Preface

I thank and praise God for His abundant grace and manifold blessings, which have guided me throughout the journey of completing this work. His strength and wisdom have been my anchor during moments of challenge and inspiration. I dedicate this work to the glory of God, with the hope that it will serve as a humble offering to further His Kingdom. May this endeavour bring encouragement, understanding, and edification to all who engage with it.

The Gospel of Luke stands out among the four Gospels as a vivid, compassionate, and detailed account of Jesus Christ's life and ministry. Written by the only Gentile author of the New Testament, Luke's narrative invites readers to explore the universal impact of Jesus' mission, emphasizing themes such as mercy, justice, and God's love for all people, especially the marginalized. This book was born out of a deep appreciation for Luke's distinctive contribution to the New Testament and the rich theological tapestry woven throughout his Gospel.

Over the years, I have been struck by the power of Luke's account to resonate with readers from all walks of life. Luke's Gospel doesn't merely recount historical events, it challenges us to rethink our perspectives on wealth, power, community, and God's Kingdom. From the earliest scenes of the infancy narratives to the climactic passion and resurrection, Luke's story is filled with compassion and conviction, offering a vision of God's Kingdom that is both inspiring and radically inclusive.

In preparing this book, I aimed to provide readers with a comprehensive exploration of Luke's major themes, distinctive features, and theological insights. Each chapter is devoted to a specific element of the Gospel, examining its historical context, literary characteristics, and relevance for today. Topics include the infancy narratives, the ministry of John the Baptist, the beatitudes and woes, parables, miracles, and Luke's perspectives on discipleship, leadership, and the Kingdom of God. This study also includes an overview of recent scholarly perspectives on Luke's Gospel, engaging with contemporary debates to enrich our understanding of Luke's message and to highlight how it continues to speak to us in new and profound ways.

My hope is that this book will serve as a guide for students, pastors, and lay readers who seek a deeper engagement with Luke's Gospel. I believe that Luke's portrait of Jesus, his interactions with people on the margins, and his teachings on the Kingdom offer timeless insights into discipleship and mission. I am especially grateful for the ongoing conversations with colleagues, students, and mentors who have inspired this journey, as well as for the contributions of recent scholarship that have brought fresh perspectives on familiar texts.

As you read, may you encounter the compassionate heart of Jesus, the divine vision of God's Kingdom, and the powerful invitation to embody these truths in our world. It is my prayer that this book will not only deepen your understanding of Luke's Gospel but also inspire you to live out its message with courage and faith.

I hope and pray that this book may bring Glory to the Trine God who took me from the miry clay and put me in the solid rock by His Amazing Grace and led me thus far.

Jayasree

Introduction

The Gospel of Luke, often described as the most universal of the four Gospels, offers a unique portrayal of Jesus Christ and his ministry, emphasizing themes of compassion, social justice, and divine inclusivity. Luke's Gospel, with its careful attention to detail and comprehensive narrative style, serves as a rich theological document that addresses both the historical context of Jesus' life and the broader implications of his mission for humanity. In the chapters that follow, this book explores the distinctive themes, teachings, and theological contributions of Luke's Gospel, with an emphasis on how these elements shape our understanding of discipleship, leadership, and Christian mission.

Beginning with the **Infancy Narratives**, we delve into the unique features of Luke's birth stories, including the angelic visitations, the prophetic responses of figures like Mary and Simeon, and the proclamation of Jesus as the bringer of joy and salvation. The infancy narratives in Luke present Jesus not only as the promised Messiah but also as the fulfillment of God's plan for all people, highlighting the inclusivity and hope that mark his mission.

In **The Ministry of John the Baptist**, we examine John's call to repentance and his message of radical transformation, which set the stage for Jesus' own ministry. Luke's account of John's call to an alternative lifestyle challenges readers to consider the social and spiritual dimensions of repentance, calling individuals to live in a way that reflects God's justice and mercy.

As we shift to **Recent Studies on Luke's Gospel**, we provide an overview of contemporary scholarship, identifying key trends and critiques that illuminate the complexities of Luke's narrative. This survey helps to situate our study within ongoing academic conversations, offering readers a broader perspective on Luke's literary and theological approach.

The **Beatitudes and Woes** in Luke provide a distinct critique of wealth and poverty, contrasting with Matthew's version and underscoring Luke's concern for the marginalized. This chapter explores the social and ethical implications of Jesus' teachings on wealth, challenging readers to consider how the values of the Kingdom contrast with worldly priorities.

Luke's **Parables** are essential to his storytelling, and here we examine the characteristics of these parables, with their vivid imagery and emphasis on God's mercy, forgiveness, and the invitation to transformation. Luke's parables, including the Good Samaritan and the Prodigal Son, offer insights into the heart of God, calling readers to a life of compassion and grace.

The **Theology of Miracles** addresses the miraculous acts of Jesus, which in Luke's account serve as signs of God's Kingdom breaking into the world. This chapter explores the theological significance of Jesus' healings and exorcisms, demonstrating how these miracles underscore his authority and compassion while also revealing God's concern for the vulnerable and oppressed.

In **Luke's Model of Discipleship and Leadership**, we discuss the lessons Luke offers through the examples of Jesus and his followers. This model emphasizes servant leadership, humility, and a dedication to God's will, offering timeless principles for Christian life and ministry.

The **Passion and Resurrection Narratives** represent the culmination of salvation in Luke's Gospel. This chapter examines Luke's unique portrayal of Jesus' suffering, death, and resurrection, emphasizing themes of forgiveness, divine purpose, and ultimate victory over sin and death. Luke's Passion and Resurrection narratives remind readers that Jesus' sacrifice is the foundation of the Christian hope.

Finally, **Current Discussions in the Gospel of Luke** focuses on significant themes such as table fellowship, hospitality, the role of women, and the reversal of social expectations. Luke's emphasis on table fellowship and inclusion, for example, highlights his vision of the Kingdom as a place where all are welcome, while his portrayal of women underscores their important roles in Jesus' ministry and in the early Christian community.

This book seeks to illuminate the Gospel of Luke as both a theological work and a practical guide to living out the Christian faith. By examining the various elements of Luke's narrative, readers are invited to encounter the Gospel anew, discovering its relevance and power for modern discipleship and mission. Whether you are a scholar, student, or seeker, it is our hope that this exploration of Luke's Gospel will deepen your understanding of the life and teachings of Jesus Christ and inspire a transformative engagement with his message.

1

Distinctive Features of the Lukan Infancy Narratives

Introduction

The Lukan Infancy Narratives refer to the stories surrounding the birth and childhood of Jesus Christ as found in the Gospel of Luke in the New Testament of the Christian Bible. These narratives contain several distinctive features that set them apart from the Infancy Narratives found in the Gospel of Matthew, offering a unique perspective on Jesus' early life. In the Gospel of Luke, the infancy narratives are situated between the prologue and the main body of the text, seamlessly blending into the broader context of the Lukan gospel. This integration means that any examination of them should consider the overall framework of the Gospel of Luke. From a narrative criticism perspective, this approach is not only important but also essential, as focusing on the coherence of the text is a fundamental principle of narrative criticism. Therefore, this chapter aims to analyze the essential literary aspects of the Lukan infancy narratives within the context of the entire gospel, emphasizing how these early stories contribute to the overarching narrative and themes presented by Luke.

Topics to be addressed include elucidating the term "infancy," examining the literary genre of the Lukan infancy narratives, engaging in a comparative analysis with the infancy narratives in Matthew, and investigating their interrelationship with the broader narrative of Luke-Acts. The objective of this chapter is to establish a comprehensive interpretive framework for the subsequent socio-narrative analysis of characters within the Lukan infancy narratives. The accounts of Jesus' birth are exclusively found in the Gospels of Matthew and Luke. Each Gospel employs distinct sources, with Matthew primarily emphasizing Joseph's perspective, whereas Luke provides a more nuanced depiction of Mary's experiences, along with those of her relative Elizabeth, the mother of John the Baptist. It is widely accepted that Luke's intimate knowledge of these events, which could only have been acquired directly or indirectly from Mary herself, augments the depth of the narrative. This chapter aims to explore these dimensions, offering a rigorous foundation for comprehending the unique contributions of the Lukan infancy narratives to the overall gospel and their significance within the corpus of early Christian literature.[1]

1. The Term Infancy[2]

The infancy of Jesus refers to the period of his life from birth to childhood, as recorded in the New Testament of the Bible, primarily in the Gospels of Matthew and Luke. These accounts provide details about Jesus' birth, his family's flight to Egypt to escape King Herod's persecution, and his upbringing in Nazareth. According to the Merriam-Webster Dictionary, the term "infancy" refers to early childhood; a beginning or early period of existence and the legal status of an infant.

To make a review of some areas of Infancy narrative look in Jaini Mariyam James, Voice of the Voiceless: A Contextualized Reading of Mary's Magnificat - The Salvific Proclamation In Luke 1:46-55 And Its Implications to the Marginalized Communities In Pathanamthitta District of Kerala, Thesis Unpublised, ETS, Ayur, 2022.

Two of the four Gospels, Matthew and Luke, commence with accounts of Jesus' conception, birth, and childhood. While each narrative coincidentally consists of two chapters, the Lukan narrative is more than twice the length of the Matthean. Although the term "infancy narrative" is commonly used in English, it is somewhat inaccurate and inadequate. Only Matthew chapter two and Luke 2:1-40 describe Jesus' infancy, while the first chapter in each Gospel recounts the period preceding Jesus' birth, and Luke 2:41-52 portrays Jesus at the age of twelve. Despite comprising only four out of eighty-nine Gospel chapters, the infancy narratives possess an importance far surpassing

[1] I. H Marshall, A. R Millard, J. I Packer, D. J Wiseman eds., *New Bible Dictionary Third edition* (Hyderabad: Authentic Books, 1996), 565.

[2] cf. Janiny Mariyam James, Voice of the Voiceless: A Contextualized Reading of Mary's Magnificat – The Salvific Proclamation in Luke 1:46-55 and Its Implications to the Marginalized Communities in Pathanamthitta District of Kerala, MTH Thesis, Ebenezer Theological Seminary, vengoor, Ayur, Unpublished, 2022.

their length.[3] They have provided ample material for reflection to both Christians and non-Christians, saints and skeptics alike.

These narratives are not merely historical accounts but also serve theological and literary purposes. They set the stage for the entire Gospel message, establishing key themes such as divine intervention, fulfillment of prophecy, and the humble beginnings of the Messiah. Additionally, the infancy narratives highlight the roles of Mary and Joseph, emphasizing their faith and obedience, which are exemplary for believers. The inclusion of angelic announcements, dreams, and prophecies underscores the divine nature of Jesus' birth and mission, enriching the reader's understanding of his unique identity and purpose from the very beginning of his life.

As an alternative, some critics have begun to use either the term "birth" or "Nativity."[4] However, both of these terms are also found to be inadequate because they overlook the prenatal period of Jesus' life as well as his infancy. Another option has been to combine the two terms "birth" and "infancy." But even in this case, the combined term "birth and infancy" still excludes the prenatal period of Jesus' life as portrayed in the first two chapters of the Lukan Gospel. Therefore, the popular term "infancy" will be retained and used throughout this work, acknowledging the limitations it carries while also recognizing its widespread usage and familiarity.

This decision underscores the necessity of a term that encompasses the entire early life narrative, from conception to childhood. The term "infancy," despite its limitations, serves as a practical and familiar reference point for discussing these pivotal events.[5] This work will explore the theological implications and narrative significance of the infancy narratives, delving into how they frame the identity and mission of Jesus from the outset. By retaining the term "infancy," we align with established scholarship while critically engaging with its nuances to provide a comprehensive analysis of these foundational Gospel chapters.

There are several key events from the infancy narratives that are crucial to understanding the early life of Jesus. The angel Gabriel visits Mary, informing her that she will conceive a child by the power of the Holy Spirit and that she is to name him Jesus (Lk 1:26-38). This moment highlights Mary's unique role and sets the stage for the miraculous nature of Jesus' conception. Jesus is born in Bethlehem, a town in Judea, during the reign of King Herod. Mary and Joseph find no room in the inn, so Jesus is born in a

[3] R. E. Brown, *The Birth of the Messiah* (New York: Doubleday, 1993), 25.

[4] B. J. Syiemlieh, *God's Favorites: A Socio-Narrative Analysis of the Characters in the Lukan Infancy Narratives (Lk 1:5-2:52)* (Delhi: ISPCK, 2005), 13.

[5] P. Winter, 'Some Observation on the Language in the Birth and Infancy Stories of the Third Gospel,' *NTS* 1 (1954): 111.

stable and laid in a manger (Lk 2:1-7). This event underscores the humble beginnings of the Messiah and fulfills the prophecy of Bethlehem as the birthplace of a ruler.

Angels appear to shepherds in the fields outside Bethlehem, announcing the birth of Jesus. The shepherds then visit Jesus and spread the news (Lk 2:8-20). This visit emphasizes the accessibility of Jesus to the common people and the joy his birth brings. Mary and Joseph bring Jesus to the temple in Jerusalem, where they meet Simeon and Anna, who recognize Jesus as the Messiah (Lk 2:22-38). This event connects Jesus to Jewish traditions and highlights his recognition as the Savior by devout individuals.

Wise men from the East, following a star, come to Jerusalem seeking the newborn king of the Jews. They find Jesus in Bethlehem and present him with gifts of gold, frankincense, and myrrh (Matthew 2:1-12). This visit signifies Jesus' universal significance and the fulfillment of prophetic symbolism through the gifts. Joseph is warned in a dream about King Herod's plan to kill Jesus, so the family flees to Egypt until Herod's death (Matthew 2:13-15). This event highlights the dangers Jesus faced even as a child and reflects the family's obedience to divine guidance.

After Herod's death, Joseph and his family return to Israel but settle in Nazareth instead of Bethlehem to avoid Herod's son Archelaus, who ruled over Judea (Matthew 2:19-23). This relocation fulfills the prophecy that Jesus would be called a Nazarene and further emphasizes the humble circumstances of his upbringing. These narratives emphasize the miraculous nature of Jesus' birth, his significance as the Messiah, and the fulfillment of Old Testament prophecies. They also highlight the humble circumstances of Jesus' early life and his family's obedience to God's will despite facing challenges and dangers. The infancy narratives thus provide a foundational understanding of Jesus' identity and mission, setting the stage for his later ministry and the salvation narrative that unfolds in the Gospels.

2. Narrative Structures

The prologue (1:1-4) serves as a metanarrative of the Gospel, guiding readers on the utilization of prior sources in composing the gospel, depicting the character of the gospel, and expressing the author's intention to assure readers of the reliability of his testimony. A transition to the infancy narratives of John and Jesus is evident, marked by a distinct change in style in Luke 1:5. The infancy narrative, spanning from Luke 1:5 to 2:52, alternates between John and Jesus, detailing their annunciations, births, circumcisions, and coming of age. Moreover, both Mary and Zechariah dedicate hymns, the Magnificat (1:46-55) and the Benedictus (1:67-79), respectively, to their offspring foretold by Gabriel, underscoring the significance of these events in the narrative's development.[6]

2.1. Geographical Details: Luke's Gospel provides specific geographical details that add depth and authenticity to the narrative. For instance, the mention of Nazareth as the hometown of Mary and Joseph establishes Jesus' Galilean roots, a fact that becomes significant throughout his ministry. Bethlehem's inclusion as the birthplace of Jesus fulfills Old Testament prophecy regarding the Messiah's lineage from the house of David. The reference to Jerusalem, particularly in the context of Jesus' presentation in the Temple, underscores the religious significance of these events within the Jewish faith. These geographical details are not incidental but are intricately woven into the narrative to emphasize the fulfillment of prophecy and the divine orchestration of events.[7]

2.2. Cultural Practices: The infancy narratives in Luke's Gospel depict various cultural and religious practices of first-century Judaism. The presentation of Jesus in the Temple and the subsequent rituals of naming and circumcision reflect Jewish customs and traditions. These practices were deeply ingrained in the social and religious fabric of Jewish life, highlighting Mary and Joseph's adherence to their faith.[8] The narrative's attention to these cultural practices serves to ground the events in a realistic historical and cultural context. It also underscores the continuity between Jesus' life and the Jewish tradition from which he emerged. By incorporating these cultural elements, Luke's Gospel bridges the gap between the ancient world and the readers of his time, providing a glimpse into the religious and social milieu in which Jesus was born and raised.

2.3. Chronological Sequence: Luke's Gospel presents a clear chronological sequence of events related to Jesus' birth and early life. The narrative begins with the Annunciation to Mary by the angel Gabriel, followed by Mary's visit to Elizabeth and the birth of John the Baptist. The journey to Bethlehem, the birth of Jesus in a manger, and the subsequent events such as the shepherds' visit and the presentation in the Temple follow in a logical progression. This chronological framework helps readers understand the sequence of events leading up to and following Jesus' birth. It also highlights the divine timing and orchestration of these events, emphasizing their significance in the unfolding of God's redemptive plan.

[6] D. A. Carson, *The Pillar New Testament Commentary* (Michigan: W.E. Eerdmans, 2015), 10.

[7] Pope Benedict XVI, *Jesus of Nazareth: The Infancy Narratives* (London: A&C Black, 2012), 64.

[8] Mark Allan Powell, *Introducing the New Testament: A Historical, Literary, and Theological Survey* (Grand Rapids, MI: Baker Books, 2018), 165.

2.4. Cultural and Social Context: The social and cultural context depicted in Luke's infancy narratives provides valuable insights into the daily life and customs of first-century Judea. The emphasis on family, marriage, and religious rituals reflects the values and practices of Jewish society during that time. For example, the importance of family ties is evident in Mary and Joseph's journey to Bethlehem for the census, a journey that underscores their obedience to civic duties and their familial connections. The naming and circumcision of Jesus, as well as his presentation in the Temple, showcase the religious significance placed on these rites of passage within Jewish tradition.[9] The narrative's attention to these cultural and social aspects adds depth and realism to the story, enabling readers to immerse themselves in the historical context of Jesus' birth and early life.

2.5. Fulfillment of Prophecy: One of the central themes in Luke's infancy narratives is the fulfillment of Old Testament prophecies regarding the Messiah. The mention of Bethlehem as the birthplace of Jesus fulfills the prophecy of Micah 5:2, which foretold that the Messiah would come from Bethlehem. The genealogy of Jesus traced back to David fulfills the Messianic expectation of a descendant from David's line. The inclusion of these prophecies and their fulfillment in Jesus' birth and lineage establishes a theological continuity between the Old Testament promises and the events of Jesus' life.[10] This emphasis on prophecy fulfillment serves to authenticate Jesus' identity as the long-awaited Messiah and reinforces the theological significance of his birth within the narrative framework of salvation history.

3. Historical Record

The historical context in Luke's infancy narratives is crucial for understanding the significance of Jesus' birth. The mention of Caesar Augustus and the census decree places Jesus' birth within the broader historical context of the Roman Empire's administrative activities. This historical detail aligns with known records of the Roman Empire's activities during that time. The inclusion of Caesar Augustus not only provides a timeframe for Jesus' birth but also highlights the political and social realities of the time. It demonstrates that Jesus was born during a period of Roman dominance and bureaucratic organization, setting the stage for the broader implications of his life and teachings within the Roman-occupied Judea.

One primary purpose is to provide an historical account of the birth and early life of Jesus. Luke, the Gospel writer, demonstrates a commitment

---

[9] Frank Ramsperger, *The Literary Form and Theological Content of Luke's Infancy Narratives* (Toronto: Regis College, 1965), 20.

[10] C. Lee Foreman, *Luke's Use of the Old Testament in His Infancy Narrative* (Portland, OR: Western Conservative Baptist Seminary, 1979), 30ff.

to historical accuracy by mentioning specific historical figures (e.g., Caesar Augustus, Herod the Great, Quirinius) and events (e.g., the census) that serve to anchor the narrative in its historical context. This historical grounding was important in the ancient world to establish the legitimacy and credibility of the Gospel message.[11] One of the key purposes of the Lukan Infancy Narratives in the Gospel of Luke is to serve as a historical record of the birth and early life of Jesus. Luke's Gospel distinguishes itself through its meticulous attention to historical and chronological details, offering readers a rich contextual understanding of the events surrounding the life of Jesus. The narrative carefully places the occurrences within a specific time and place, contributing to the Gospel's credibility and historical significance. What has been said about the difference of the infancy narratives from the rest of the Gospel material has implications for historicity which must now be pursued.

The Gospel of Luke begins by referencing rulers of the time, notably Caesar Augustus and Herod. This deliberate inclusion of political figures serves to anchor the narrative in a historical context, providing readers with a broader understanding of the social and political landscape during the period of Jesus' birth. Caesar Augustus, the Roman Emperor, is mentioned in connection with the decree for a census, a historical event widely recognized outside the biblical narrative. This decree becomes the catalyst for Joseph and Mary's journey to Bethlehem and plays a pivotal role in fulfilling the prophecy regarding the Messiah's birthplace. Additionally, the mention of Herod the Great further solidifies the historical grounding of Luke's Gospel. Herod's reign as a client king under Roman authority is well-documented in historical records. His presence in the narrative, particularly in the account of the Magi seeking the newborn king, adds layers of historical authenticity.

Luke's deliberate inclusion of these rulers, along with other historical and chronological details, reflects an intent to ground the Gospel in the reality of the times. The careful attention to historical accuracy enhances the Gospel's credibility and helps readers situate the life of Jesus within the broader historical and political context of the first century. This emphasis on historical details in Luke's Gospel aligns with the author's purpose to provide an orderly and accurate account of the events surrounding Jesus' life, as stated in the opening verses of the Gospel (Lk 1:1-4). The historical and chronological precision in Luke contributes to the Gospel's unique

[11] Mark Coleridge, *The Birth of the Lukan Narrative: Narrative as Christology in Luke 1-2* (London: Bloomsbury Publishing, 1993), 231.

character and its significance as a historical record of the life and teachings of Jesus Christ.[12]

The Gospel of Luke establishes a historical connection between the birth of Jesus and the Roman Empire, particularly through the decree of Caesar Augustus mentioned in Luke 2:1-2. This decree, calling for a census, reflects the historical context of Roman rule during the first century. Caesar Augustus, the adopted son of Julius Caesar and the first Roman Emperor, reigned from 27 BC to 14 AD. Historical records, including the works of Roman historians such as Tacitus in his "Annals" (Book 1, Chapter 11), mention Augustus's role in conducting censuses for administrative purposes. Suetonius, in "The Twelve Caesars" (Augustus 41), further supports the notion of Augustus employing censuses to regulate the population and taxation.

Censuses in the Roman Empire served the dual purpose of efficient tax collection and maintaining accurate population records. Augustus, as a ruler keen on administrative order, instituted periodic censuses, requiring individuals to return to their ancestral homes for registration. This aligns with the biblical narrative in Luke, where Joseph and Mary travel to Bethlehem for the census. The Gospel's emphasis on the census underlines the meticulous record keeping of the Roman administration. Scholars and historians frequently consult Roman historical sources, such as Tacitus and Suetonius, to corroborate and comprehend the historical context within the Gospel of Luke.

In addition to Tacitus and Suetonius, other historical sources, such as the works of Josephus, a first-century Jewish historian, provide insights into the Roman practices of taxation and censuses. Josephus, in "Antiquities of the Jews," offers a broader historical perspective on the events and circumstances surrounding the Roman Empire during this period. The mention of Caesar Augustus and the census in Luke 2:1-2, when examined in conjunction with various historical sources, enhances our understanding of the geopolitical backdrop in which Jesus' birth is situated. This connection underscores the Gospel's integration of historical realities into its narrative, emphasizing the significance of Jesus' life within the broader context of Roman rule in the first century.[13]

[12] Pope Benedict XVI, *Jesus of Nazareth: The Infancy Narratives* (London: A & amp; C Black, 2012).

[13] Cf. Mark Coleridge, *The Birth of the Lukan Narrative: Narrative as Christology in Lk 1-2* (London: A&C Black, 1993), 10ff.

3.1. The Problem of Corroborating Witnesses

The main body of Gospel material has a claim to be anchored in the memories of those who accompanied Jesus from shortly after his baptism until his death (Acts 1:22) and to whom he appeared after his resurrection (Acts 10:41; I Cor 15:3). If the readers of the Gospel ask how do they know that Jesus was baptized, or that he preached in Galilee, or that there was a supper on the night before he died, or that there was a death, burial, and resurrection, one can reply that there was a tradition passed on about such things (I Cor 11:23; 15:3). But how do we know what happened at Jesus' birth? Certainly none of the apostolic preachers of the Jerusalem community who accompanied Jesus during his ministry and whose tradition is at the basis of the Gospel stories of the ministry was present at the birth. Indeed, the body of the Gospel shows that the people among whom Jesus had been reared knew nothing about an extraordinary infancy (Matt 13:53-58; Luke 4:31-32, 36-37).

A common *guess* has been that the tradition about Jesus' infancy came from Joseph or Mary. Yet Joseph never appears during the ministry of Jesus and seems almost certainly to have been dead by that time, so that it is pure speculation to posit him as a source. Mary does not seem to have been close to the disciples of Jesus during the ministry (Matt 12:46-50; Mark 3:31-35; John 2:4), although there is New Testament evidence that she was part of the post-resurrection community (Acts 1:14). While there is no *a priori* impossibility that she was the source of the material in the Lukan infancy narrative which describes experiences for which she would be the most plausible witness, there is an *a priori* unlikelihood that she was the source for the material in the Matthean infancy narrative which centers upon Joseph and in which she figures only on a secondary level. In the second century, James the "brother of the Lord" who lived into the 60s, was thought to be a plausible source for information about Jesus' infancy, but the resultant Protevangelium of James is highly legendary, makes elementary mistakes about Temple procedure, and is more obviously folkloric than the canonical infancy narratives. All of this means that, in fact, we have no real knowledge that any or all of the infancy material came from a tradition for which there was a corroborating witness.[14]

3.2. The Problem of Conflicting Details

Since it is generally agreed among scholars that Matthew and Luke wrote independently of each other, without knowing the other's work, agreement between the two infancy narratives would suggest the existence of

[14] R. E. Brown, *The Birth of the Messiah* (New York: Doubleday Publishing Group, 1993), 34-35.

a common infancy tradition earlier than either evangelist's work - a tradition that would have a claim to greater antiquity and thus weigh on the plus side of the historical scale. The following eleven points are shared by the two infancy narratives:

a) The parents to be are Mary and Joseph who are legally engaged or married, but have not yet come to live together or have sexual relations (Matt 1:18; Lk 1:27,34).
b) Joseph is of Davidic descent (Matt 1:16,20; Lk 1:27,32; 2:4).
c) There is an angelic announcement of the forthcoming birth of the child (Matt 1:20-23; Lk 1:30-35).
d) The conception of the child by Mary is not through intercourse with her husband (Matt 1:20,23,25; Lk 1:34).
e) The conception is through the Holy Spirit (Matt 1:18,20; Lk 1:35).
f) There is a directive from the angel that the child is to be named Jesus (Matt 1:21; Lk 1:31).
g) An angel states that Jesus is to be Savior (Matt 1:21; Lk 2:11).
h) The birth of the child takes place after the parents have come to live together (Matt 1:24-25; Lk 2:5-6). The birth takes place at Bethlehem (Matt 2:1; Lk 2:4-6).
i) The birth is chronologically related to the reign of Herod the Great (Matt 2: 1; Lk 1:5).
j) The child is reared at Nazareth (Matt 2:23; Lk 2:39).

As we evaluate these common points, it is striking that all but the last are found in one section of the Matthean narrative (1:18-2:1), and the last is something that both evangelists could have known from the public ministry. Moreover, even in the restricted section of Matthew where the parallels occur, there is often a significant difference from Luke; for example, in (c), the angel speaks to Joseph in Matthew, while he speaks to Mary in Luke.

This underscores the intricate interplay between the Gospels, where similar events are depicted with variations that reflect the unique perspectives and emphases of each evangelist. Such divergences enrich our understanding of the infancy narratives and contribute to the broader tapestry of theological insights woven throughout the Gospels, highlighting the multifaceted nature of the Gospel message and its enduring relevance for readers across time and cultures.[15]

The rest of the Matthean infancy narrative diverges significantly from Luke's infancy narrative. The genealogy in Matt 1:1-17 differs notably from the genealogy placed outside the infancy story in Luke 3:23-38. In contrast to Luke, Matthew's account focuses on distinct events. These include the

[15] R. E. Brown, *The Birth of the Messiah*, 34-35.

star that guides the Magi, Herod's nefarious plot against Jesus, the tragic massacre of children in Bethlehem, and the subsequent flight into Egypt. These elements are absent from Luke's narrative, which, in turn, uniquely features the story of Elizabeth, Zechariah, and the birth of John the Baptist, the census leading Joseph to Bethlehem, the shepherds' adoration of Jesus, the presentation of Jesus in the Temple, and the poignant incident of Jesus being lost and found in the Temple at the age of twelve. Such differences underscore the diverse emphases and theological perspectives of the respective Gospel writers, enriching our understanding of the infancy narratives and their broader implications within the narrative frameworks of Matthew and Luke.

3.3. Historical Figures: The inclusion of historical figures such as Herod the Great and Quirinius, the governor of Syria, adds historical authenticity to Luke's infancy narratives. Herod the Great's reign and his reputation for cruelty are well-documented in historical records outside of the Bible. His role in the narrative as the ruler of Judea during Jesus' birth adds a political dimension to the story, showcasing the tensions and power dynamics of the time. Quirinius, as the governor of Syria, is associated with the census decree mentioned in Luke's Gospel, aligning with known historical events. These references to historical figures not only ground the narrative in a specific historical period but also demonstrate Luke's attention to detail and accuracy in his account.

3.4. Response to Historical Questions: The infancy narratives in Luke's Gospel address various historical questions that might arise regarding Jesus' birth and early life. For instance, the mention of the census decree issued by Caesar Augustus explains why Mary and Joseph traveled to Bethlehem, even though it was not their place of residence. This historical detail provides a rational explanation for Jesus' birth in Bethlehem, fulfilling the prophecy regarding the Messiah's birthplace. Similarly, the narrative explains the circumstances of Jesus' presentation in the Temple and the events surrounding his early years, offering a coherent account of how these events align with known historical and cultural practices of the time. By addressing these historical questions, the narratives provide a solid foundation for understanding the historical context and significance of Jesus' birth within the broader narrative of salvation history.[16]

These expanded explanations provide a more detailed exploration of each point, highlighting the historical, geographical, cultural, and theological dimensions of Luke's infancy narratives. Overall, these elements work together to create a historically grounded and culturally rich portrayal

---

[16] Jonathan Knight, *Luke's Gospel* (New York: Psychology Press, 1998), 21ff.

of Jesus' birth and early life in Luke's Gospel. They provide readers with a comprehensive understanding of the context, events, and significance of these foundational moments in Christian theology and history.

4. The Infancy Narratives as Vehicle of Theology

Biblical scholarship has entered a more fruitful stage of research as it delves into the value of the infancy stories as theology. This shift marks a departure from earlier focuses on the pre-Gospel history of narratives and sayings about Jesus, redirecting attention to the significance of these narratives and sayings within the finished Gospels. To diminish their value compared to other parts of the Gospels is to misunderstand the intentions of the evangelists, for whom the infancy narratives served as fitting vehicles for conveying a particular message. The infancy narratives stand out as uniquely succinct and imaginative expressions of theological concepts, presenting themes that are not as clearly articulated elsewhere in the Gospels.[17] This distinctiveness suggests a close theological relationship that transcends mere historical retelling. Consequently, the theory of pre-Lukan sources becomes a plausible explanation for the divergent nature of the infancy narrative between Matthew and Luke. Matthew and Luke, in crafting their infancy narratives, were not merely recounting historical events but were purposefully shaping theological narratives. Each evangelist employed distinctive themes, motifs, and literary techniques to convey their theological messages. Matthew emphasizes the fulfillment of Old Testament prophecies, the universal significance of Jesus as the Messiah, and the theme of divine protection amidst adversity. On the other hand, Luke highlights themes of social justice, inclusivity, and the role of marginalized figures such as Mary, the shepherds, and the poor.[18]

The infancy narratives serve as theological prologues to the Gospels, setting the stage for the larger narratives of Jesus' ministry, teachings, death, and resurrection. They provide insights into the evangelists' theological perspectives, their understanding of Jesus' identity, and the overarching themes they sought to communicate to their audiences. Moreover, the divergences between the Matthean and Lukan infancy narratives[19] do not diminish their theological significance but rather highlight the richness and complexity of early Christian theological reflection. These differences invite scholars and readers alike to explore the diverse theological emphases within the New Testament and to appreciate the multifaceted nature of the Gospel message.

[17] R. E. Brown, *The Birth of the Messiah*, 37-38.

[18] R. E. Brown, *The Birth of the Messiah*, 38.

[19] R. E. Brown, *The Birth of the Messiah*, 241.

5. The Literary Genre of the Lukan Narratives

In gospel studies, the infancy narratives, along with the passion and resurrection narratives, are commonly classified as a sub-form within the literary genre of the Gospel in Christian literature. This classification stems from the observation that these narratives lack a common structural form and do not neatly fit into the established categories of form criticism, which primarily focused on analyzing accounts of Jesus' public ministry. Despite this challenge, form critics have occasionally attempted to analyze the episodes in the Lukan infancy narratives and categorize them using popular forms such as "stories about Jesus" or "legends."[20] However, these attempts have been met with limitations due to the unique nature of the infancy narratives.

Brown has noted that the various episodes in the Lukan infancy narratives are intricately interconnected in a diptych-like fashion through the close parallelism of episodes about Jesus and John.[21] This observation suggests a cohesive unity within the infancy narratives, forming a self-contained unit within the larger Gospel narrative. Therefore, based on these arguments and observations, it can be concluded that the Lukan infancy narratives indeed constitute a continuous whole and represent a distinct sub-form within the literary genre of the Gospel in Christian literature. Their thematic coherence, narrative structure, and theological significance contribute to their classification as a cohesive and integral part of Gospel literature, despite their departure from traditional form-critical categories. If the Lukan infancy narratives can be categorized as a sub from in the literary genre of gospel in Christian literature, the task now is to discern and identify the kind of literary genre the narratives represent.

In gospel studies, it has been noted that the infancy narratives represent the latest part of the gospel tradition to take shape.[22] The late development is usually attributed to a widely accepted observation that gospels are out growth of the early Christian *kerygma*, fragments which are preserved in 1 Corinthians 15:3-4, Romans 1:3-4, 1 Thessalonians 1:9-10. The passion narratives are generally placed at the first stage development to which the accounts of Jesus' ministry were fixed. Then, at a still later stage, the resurrection narratives and the infancy narratives were added.[23]

---

[20] Vincent Taylor, *The Foundation of the Gospel Tradition* (London: Macmillan, 1935), 142.

[21] R. E. Brown, *The Birth of the Messiah*, 100-102.

[22] Rudolf Bultmann, *History of the Synoptic Tradition*, Trans by John Marsh, Revised Edition (New York: Harper and Row, 1963), 354.

[23] Joseph A. Fitzmyer, The *Gospel of Luke I-IX, AB 28* (New York: Doubleday, 1985), 305.

In the quest for the literary genre of the Lukan infancy narratives, one early proposition suggests that these narratives can be identified with Jewish *midrashim*[24] because of their heavily semitised language, as well as equally heavy dependence on Old Testament prototypes. Another proposition, which represents a number of similar but slightly different viewpoints, attempts to correlate and to structure the Lukan infancy narratives in relation to an extensive block of Old Testament materials. E. Burrows, for instance, applies the term "imitative historiography" to describe these narratives because he finds in them a strong resonance of the stories of 1Samuel 1-3.[25] M. D. Goulder observes that the narratives have a calendrical correlation with the temporal progression of Genesis 17-37. C. T. Ruddick notices that the structure of Genesis 27-43 has been followed in the Lukan infancy narratives. Though it cannot be denied that these correlations can be detected in some portions of the Lukan infancy narratives, the fact remain that they do not satisfactorily explain all of the Lukan infancy narratives.[26]

The third and final proposition locates the literary genre of the Lukan infancy narratives within the popular Greco-Roman biographical writings of Mediterranean antiquity.[27] Surprisingly, this proposition is not a new development but a revival of C. W. Votaw's attempt in 1915 to put the gospels on proper scholarly ancient Hellenistic biographies. However, with the rise of form criticism, this approach was suddenly abandoned without further discussions because, to form critics, the very word 'biography' was like a red rag to a bull and all attempts to look upon at the gospels as biographies were suspiciously looked upon as attempts to make Jesus into a "nice Victorian gentle man."[28] This simple and rather obvious technique was widely used even in sophisticated ancient biographical writing with its long literary tradition. Similar features can also be found in the gospels.[29] Therefore, the Lukan infancy narratives can be located within the genre of ancient Greco-Roman biography.

All these observation make it evident that the Lukan infancy narratives not only fit well within the popular literary genre of Greco-Roman biographical writings of Mediterranean antiquity but most probably they

---

[24] *Midrashim*-an ancient commentary on part of the Hebrew Scriptures, attached to the biblical text. The earliest Midrashim come from the 2nd century AD, although much of their content is older.

[25] Fitzmyer, The *Gospel of Luke I-IX,* 309.

[26] B. J. Syiemlieh, *God's Favourites*, 21.

[27] Charles H. Talbert, *What is a Gospel: The Genre of Canonical Gospels* (London: SPCK, 1978), 18.

[28] Graham N. Stanton, *The Gospels and Jesus*, The Oxford Bible Series (Oxford: Oxford University, 1992), 18.

[29] Graham N. Stanton, *The Gospels and Jesus*, 18-19.

belong to this genre, whose stand runs through the thought and expression of East as well. But more important for the present study is the literary function of these narratives would be immense as they would project and promote the future greatness of Jesus, which is made explicit in the later part of the Gospel.

6. The Lukan and the Matthean Infancy Narratives: A Comparison and Contrast

Among the four Gospels and within the broader New Testament, only Luke and Matthew delve into the stories surrounding the conception, birth, and childhood of Jesus. However, over time, and especially within certain segments of the lay and literalist communities, the narratives presented in these two Gospels have often been blended to the extent that distinguishing their individual elements has become challenging. Nevertheless, a thorough examination of these narratives reveals their distinctiveness. This section aims to undertake a comparative analysis of the infancy narratives found in Luke and Matthew, presenting a synopsis to explore whether any connection or relationship exists between the two accounts.

Both Luke and Matthew offer unique perspectives on the infancy of Jesus, with each Gospel highlighting different aspects and events. Lk's narrative emphasizes themes of social justice, humility, and inclusivity, showcasing the roles of Mary, the shepherds, and the marginalized in the story of Jesus' birth. On the other hand, Matthew's account focuses on themes of fulfillment of prophecy, divine guidance and protection, and the universal significance of Jesus as the Messiah, as seen through the perspectives of Joseph and the Magi.

The synoptic comparison will delve into key events such as the Annunciation, the Birth of Jesus in Bethlehem, the Visit of the Shepherds and the Magi, the Presentation in the Temple, the Flight to Egypt, and the Return to Nazareth. By juxtaposing these narratives side by side, we aim to discern any shared motifs, theological themes, or narrative parallels that may exist between Luke and Matthew's infancy narratives. Ultimately, this analysis seeks to shed light on the distinctiveness of each Gospel's portrayal of the infancy of Jesus while also exploring potential connections that contribute to the rich tapestry of the Gospel message.

When comparing the infancy narratives in the Gospels of Matthew and Lk, several key points of contact emerge. Both narratives coincide in occupying the initial two chapters of their respective Gospels (Matthew 1-2; Lk 1-2). They introduce Mary and Joseph as the parents of Jesus, initially described as engaged but not yet cohabiting or having a marital relationship (Matthew 1:18; Lk 1:27, 34), later coming to reside together after Jesus' birth (Matthew 1:24-25; Lk 2:5-6). Joseph is portrayed as of Davidic descent in both accounts (Matthew 1:16, 20; Lk 1:27, 32, 2:40), and angelic announcements precede and accompany the birth of Jesus (Matthew 1:20-23; Lk 1:30-35). Both narratives emphasize that Jesus is not conceived through human sexual intercourse but through the Holy Spirit (Matthew 1:18, 20, 23, 25; Lk 1:34, 35), with the name "Jesus" being instructed by an angel (Matthew 1:21; Lk 1:31), who also declares Jesus as the savior (Matthew 1:21; Lk 2:11). The narratives affirm Jesus' birth in Bethlehem (Matthew 2:1; Lk 2:4-6) and plot it chronologically during the reign of Herod the Great (Matthew 2:1; Lk 1:5), with Jesus growing up in Nazareth according to both accounts (Matthew 2:23; Lk 2:39).

However, a contrast emerges when examining the content and literary structure of the two narratives. The infancy narratives in Matthew and Luke exhibit significant differences from one another, showcasing unique emphases, events, and perspectives that contribute to their distinctiveness within the broader Gospel narratives.[30] In Matthew's portrayal of the infancy narrative, the atmosphere is notably gloomy, emphasizing themes of danger, escape, and persecution. This somber tone is particularly evident in events such as the star of Bethlehem, the arrival of the Magi, Herod's sinister plot to kill Jesus, the tragic massacre of children, and the subsequent flight to Egypt. These events and personalities dominate the major part of the Matthean narrative, creating a sense of urgency and danger surrounding Jesus' early life.

In contrast, Luke's infancy narrative is characterized by a joyful and euphoric ambiance, focusing on themes of hope, celebration, and divine favor. The story of Elizabeth, Zechariah, and the birth of John the Baptist sets a tone of anticipation and joy, followed by the census, the humble visit of the shepherds, and the prophetic encounters with Simeon and Anna at the temple. These elements contribute to a sense of awe and wonder surrounding the birth of Jesus in Luke's account.[31]

Furthermore, the prominence of characters differs between the two narratives. Joseph takes a central role in the Matthean infancy narratives, grappling with divine messages through dreams and acting as a protector and guide for the Holy Family. In contrast, Mary emerges as a central figure in Luke's narrative, embodying faith, humility, and obedience to God's will. Another notable contrast is the inclusion of a genealogy in the Matthean infancy narratives (Matthew 1:1-17), tracing Jesus' lineage back to David and Abraham. This genealogical emphasis is absent in Luke's account (Lk

---

[30] Chang-Wook Jung, *The Original Language of the Lukan Infancy Narrative* (London: A&C Black, 2004), 25ff.

[31] Stephen J. Binz, *The Infancy Narratives of Jesus* (Minnesota: Liturgical Press, 2020), 40ff.

3:23-38), which focuses more on the theological and spiritual aspects of Jesus' birth and early life.

Additionally, the Matthean infancy narratives abound in formula citations from the Old Testament, emphasizing fulfillment of prophecy and continuity with Jewish heritage. In contrast, the Lukan infancy narratives abound in psalms and hymns, highlighting themes of praise, thanksgiving, and divine intervention. While these points of contrast are mainly concentrated in one section of Matthew (1:18-2:1) and thinly dispersed over two sections in Lk (1:26-35; 2:4-6, 11, 39), contradictions in form and presentation are also evident. For instance, the two narratives disagree on the form of angelophanies, with Matthew depicting them through dreams and Luke through direct annunciations. These differences contribute to the distinctiveness and richness of the infancy narratives in each Gospel, reflecting the diverse theological emphases and narrative styles of the respective evangelists.

At the other end, the points of discord can be seen to occupy the bigger chunk of each of the narratives and they are widely disseminated throughout both the infancy narratives. But of utmost importance is the fact that the two narratives cannot be placed side-by-side in a synopsis because of high degree of variation. As such, it is most unlikely that any kind of relation exists between the two narratives in the sense that one is dependent on the other[32] or that both are dependent on a common source or tradition. Therefore, these two infancy narratives are completely independent of one another and, to put in the words and language of this work, the Lukan infancy narratives should be analyzed and interpreted on their own without any reference or allusion to their Matthean counterpart.[33]

7. The Relation of the Lukan Infancy Narratives to the Rest of Luke-Acts

In contemporary New Testament scholarship, the unity of Luke-Acts is often regarded as a foregone conclusion, with the two volumes seen as a seamless continuation and a "single literary enterprise."[34] However, Hans Conzelmann's influential essay on Lukan theology introduced a controversial perspective that diverged from this consensus. The controversy sparked by Conzelmann's work primarily revolves around the status of the Lukan infancy narratives within the narrative framework of Luke-Acts.

[32] Robert H. Gundry, *Luke, A Commentary on His Literary and Theological art* (Grand Rapids, Michigan: William B. Eerdmans, 1982), 20-21.

[33] B. J. Syiemlieh, *God's Favourites*, 28-29.

[34] Luke Timothy Johnson, *The Gospel of Luke,* Sacra Pagina (Collegeville, MN: The Liturgical Press, 1991), 1.

Conzelmann's essay raised serious doubts about the authenticity of the Lukan infancy narratives and, as a result, he chose to largely ignore and exclude them from his analysis of Luke's theological enterprise. His main contention for excluding these narratives is rooted in the belief that they are discordant with the broader themes and ideas presented in the rest of Luke-Acts. According to Conzelmann, the infancy narratives contain thoughts and concepts that are foreign to, and at times even contradictory to, the overarching theological message of Luke-Acts.

This controversy has led to ongoing debates and discussions among scholars regarding the role and significance of the Lukan infancy narratives within the context of Luke-Acts. While some scholars agree with Conzelmann's assessment and view the infancy narratives as potentially later additions or theological embellishments, others argue for their integral place within the narrative structure of Luke-Acts and their importance in understanding Luke's overall theological vision.[35]

Ultimately, the controversy surrounding the treatment of the Lukan infancy narratives underscores the complexity of interpreting and analyzing ancient texts, highlighting the diverse perspectives and methodologies within New Testament scholarship. Following Minear's lead, other critics also delved into the controversy sparked by Conzelmann's skepticism regarding the authenticity of the Lukan infancy narratives. Upon closer examination and re-evaluation of Conzelmann's claim, scholars discovered numerous significant commonalities between the Lukan infancy narratives and the broader narrative presented in Luke-Acts.[36]

These commonalities were so substantial and consistent that it became implausible, if not outright impossible, to dismiss the infancy narratives as inauthentic, disconnected, or incongruous with the rest of Luke-Acts. Instead, scholars found compelling evidence to suggest that the infancy narratives are integral to Luke's overall theological and narrative framework. The re-evaluation of Conzelmann's position brought to light the intricate thematic threads and theological motifs that tie the infancy narratives to the larger narrative of Luke-Acts. These include themes of divine intervention, fulfillment of prophecy, salvation history, and the overarching narrative of God's redemptive plan unfolding through Jesus Christ.

Furthermore, the infancy narratives serve as foundational elements that set the stage for the subsequent events and teachings presented in Luke-Acts. They provide essential background information about Jesus' birth, family background, and early life, which are crucial for understanding his identity

[35] Hans Conzelmann, *The Theology of St. Luke*, translated by Geoffery Buswell (London: Faber and Faber, 1961).

[36] B. J. Syiemlieh, *God's Favourites,* 27.

as the promised Messiah and the fulfillment of Old Testament prophecies. In light of these findings, scholars have shifted towards a more inclusive approach that recognizes the coherence and authenticity of the Lukan infancy narratives within the narrative framework of Luke-Acts. This re-examination underscores the dynamic nature of scholarly discourse and the ongoing quest for a deeper understanding of ancient texts and their theological significance.

Judith M. Ryan introduces the concept of "Lukan parallelism," emphasizing the literary correlation that links the Gospel of Luke with the Book of Acts. This parallelism serves as a structural and thematic connection between the infancy narratives and the subsequent events portrayed in Luke's narrative.[37] One example of this parallelism is seen in the forecasts of John the Baptist's role in preparing the way for Jesus, as depicted in Luke 1:76-77. These forecasts find concrete realization in the Gospel narrative, particularly in Luke 3:1-20, where John the Baptist's ministry is detailed.

Additionally, Ryan notes that the proclamation of Jesus' fulfillment of Israel's hope in Luke's narrative already foreshadows the beginning of Jesus' ministry. This is exemplified in Luke 4:18-26, which serves as a programmatic introduction to Jesus' ministry and recalls key biblical concerns that Luke incorporates into his narrative. Overall, these instances of "Lukan parallelism" underscore the continuity and coherence between the infancy narratives, the ministry of Jesus, and the early Christian community portrayed in Acts. They highlight Luke's intentional storytelling technique, where themes and prophecies introduced early in the narrative find fulfillment and significance in later events.

The infancy narratives in Luke's Gospel serve as a rich foundation that foreshadows and parallels significant themes and events throughout the rest of Luke-Acts. One prominent theme highlighted in the infancy narratives is the prophetic concern for the poor, oppressed, and disadvantaged. This concern is already evident in the roles assigned to women in these introductory chapters, reflecting Luke's emphasis on true discipleship characterized by hearing the Word of God and keeping it

Mary, as portrayed in Luke 1:38, exemplifies the ideal disciple who obediently follows God's word, while Anna in Luke 2:38 prefigures the disciples who will later proclaim the gospel of Jesus Christ. This emphasis on discipleship and prophetic ministry among the marginalized and oppressed sets the stage for the broader themes of social justice and inclusivity that permeate Luke's narrative. Moreover, the messianic joy depicted in the infancy narratives anticipates the joys experienced during Jesus' ministry and the early church. This joy serves as a foretaste of the transformative

[37] Judith M. Ryan, 'Luke's Infancy narrative', *The Bible Today 35* (1997): 342.

power of Jesus' message and the communal joy experienced by believers, as seen in passages such as Luke 10:17, 21; 24:52 and Acts 2:46-47.

Furthermore, the same Spirit of God that inspired and guided the prophetic figures of old, as depicted in Luke 1:41, 67; 2:25-27, continues to animate and direct the prophetic Spirit of the Church, as evidenced in Acts 1:8; 2:4, 33. This continuity of divine guidance underscores the interconnectedness between the infancy narratives and the broader narrative of Luke-Acts. Even the journey of the holy family to Jerusalem, as depicted in the infancy narratives, prefigures the travel narratives in Luke 9:51-19:27, ultimately leading to Jesus' final days in Jerusalem. This geographical and narrative progression symbolizes the expansion of the gospel message from Jerusalem to the ends of the earth, as articulated in Acts 1:8.

In summary, the strong correlation between the Lukan infancy narratives and the rest of Luke-Acts is evident through thematic continuity, prophetic ministry, discipleship motifs, and the overarching narrative trajectory that spans from Jesus' birth to the spread of the gospel worldwide. The discussion on the correlation between the Lukan infancy narratives and the rest of Luke-Acts would be incomplete without considering the perspective of narrative critics. Surprisingly, narrative critics align with the findings of historical critics in this regard. Jack Dean Kingsbury, for instance, posits that the infancy stories at the beginning of Luke's Gospel serve as an introduction to the overarching plot of the entire narrative of Luke-Acts.[38]

Narrative critics emphasize the strong literary correlation and narrative unity between the Lukan infancy stories and the subsequent events portrayed in Luke-Acts. They view these infancy narratives as integral components that set the stage for the broader themes, motifs, and character development seen throughout Luke's narrative. In light of these considerations, it becomes evident that Hans Conzelmann's claim regarding the inauthenticity or incongruity of the Lukan infancy narratives is invalid. Instead, these narratives are deemed integral and important for any comprehensive study of Luke-Acts. The consensus among historical and narrative critics underscores the necessity of including the infancy narratives as an integral part of the larger narrative framework of Luke-Acts. Their inclusion enriches our understanding of Luke's theological vision, narrative structure, and the interconnectedness of key themes and motifs throughout the Gospel and Acts.

8. The Purpose and Theology

In essence, Luke's Gospel presents a robust theological framework centered on salvation, highlighting God's redemptive plan through Jesus

---

[38] B. J. Syiemlieh, *God's Favourites*, 32.

Christ and inviting readers to participate in this life-transforming message. Absolutely, delving into the birth and childhood narratives of Jesus in Luke's Gospel offers a window into the social and historical context in which the Gospel unfolds. These early chapters not only set the stage for the story to come but also provide crucial insights into the world in which Jesus lived and ministered.

Luke 1:5-2:52 serves as a prelude to the larger narrative, introducing key characters, themes, and events that will shape the Gospel's message. The narrative beginnings in Luke invite the audience to engage fully with the story, encouraging them to explore the unfolding events and their implications.

One of the functions of these early chapters is to establish the historical and factual basis of the Christian faith, particularly for Gentile Christians. Luke, writing to a predominantly Gentile audience, seeks to ground their faith in firm historical realities. By detailing the birth of John the Baptist and Jesus, along with events such as the angelic announcements, the census, and the visitation to the temple, Luke presents a narrative that is rooted in historical events and eyewitness accounts.

Furthermore, Luke's emphasis on historical accuracy serves an apologetic purpose as well. By presenting a well-documented and historically sound account of Jesus' birth and early life, Luke addresses potential skepticism and reinforces the credibility of the Christian message. Additionally, Luke's narrative is not merely a historical recollection but also a theological proclamation. The events surrounding Jesus' birth and childhood are portrayed in a way that highlights his divine identity and mission. The inclusion of angelic announcements, prophecies, and divine interventions underscores the significance of Jesus as the promised Messiah and Savior. Overall, Luke's meticulous attention to historical detail in the infancy narrative serves multiple purposes: establishing the historical foundation of the Christian faith, addressing skepticism, inviting readers to engage with the narrative, and proclaiming the theological significance of Jesus' birth and early life.

9. Theological and Redactional Emphases in Luke 1-2

Indeed, the birth narratives in Luke's Gospel offer a unique perspective by focusing not only on Jesus but also on the individuals surrounding his birth and infancy. These characters and their interactions provide valuable insights into the author's theological emphases and narrative tendencies. One notable aspect of the Lukan birth narratives is the complexity and richness of the narrative material. Unlike some other Gospel accounts, Luke includes a significant amount of detail and introduces significant characters who play crucial roles in the story. This includes the emphasis on the human emotions and experiences associated with childbirth, such as joy and anxiety.

The portrayal of major figures in the birth narratives, particularly Elizabeth and Mary, is central to understanding Luke's theological and narrative priorities. Elizabeth, the mother of John the Baptist, and Mary, the mother of Jesus, are depicted as key figures who receive divine revelations and play instrumental roles in the unfolding of God's redemptive plan. The inclusion of two major hymns of praise, known as the Magnificat (1:46-55) and the Benedictus (1:67-79), along with the Nunc Dimittis (2:29-32), provides a structured framework for the narrative. These hymns of praise not only reflect the joy and gratitude of the characters but also convey profound theological truths about the Messiah and God's salvific work.

The absence of a genealogy in the birth or infancy narratives proper is also noteworthy. Unlike Matthew's Gospel, which includes a genealogy tracing Jesus' lineage back to Abraham, Luke's focus is more on the human drama and the individuals directly involved in Jesus' early life. Moreover, Luke's Gospel exhibits a notable emphasis on women throughout its narrative. In the birth narratives, it is Elizabeth and Mary who take center stage, receiving divine messages and offering praise and prophecy about the Christ child. This emphasis on women's voices and roles aligns with the broader theme of inclusivity and the importance of all individuals, regardless of social status or gender, in God's redemptive plan.

Overall, the Lukan birth narratives showcase a rich tapestry of characters, emotions, and theological reflections that highlight Luke's unique perspective and narrative style within the broader context of the Gospel story. The speeches and hymns in Luke's birth narratives play a significant role in conveying the major themes of the Gospel, including God's liberation for the oppressed and the inclusion of the Gentiles in salvation.

10. The Promise Fulfilled: Salvation and Liberation in Luke 1-2

The Magnificat, spoken by Mary in Luke 1:46-55, is a powerful expression of these themes. Mary's words echo the sentiments of liberation found in the Hebrew Scriptures, particularly in passages like the Song of Hannah (1 Samuel 2:1-10). Mary exalts God for remembering the lowly and lifting up the humble, highlighting God's concern for the poor and oppressed within Israel.[39]

Similarly, the Benedictus (Zechariah's song) in Luke 1:68-69 speaks of God's salvation and redemption for Israel, fulfilling the promises made to their ancestors. The imagery of light for the Gentiles in Luke 2:32 further

---

39 Raymond E. Brown et.al. (eds), *Mary in the New Testament* (New York/Mahwah, 1978), 8-16.

emphasizes the universal scope of God's salvation, extending beyond ethnic boundaries to include all peoples. The portrayal of key figures in Luke 1-2 aligns with these themes of liberation and salvation. Elizabeth, Mary, Simeon, and Anna are all depicted as devout individuals who eagerly anticipate the fulfillment of God's promises. They represent the faithful remnant within Israel, longing for the arrival of the Messiah and the redemption of their people.[40]

Mary, in particular, is portrayed as a figure of obedience and faithfulness. Her willingness to accept God's plan, despite the personal challenges and societal stigma she may face, reflects the obedience of the prophets in the Old Testament. Mary's role as God's servant underscores the theme of God's active involvement in the world, bringing about salvation and liberation for all who trust in Him. Overall, Luke's portrayal of these key figures and the themes expressed in their speeches and songs emphasize the universal nature of God's redemptive work. The birth narratives in Luke's Gospel serve as a proclamation of hope and liberation, extending God's grace to the poor, the oppressed, and the Gentiles, fulfilling the long-awaited promises of salvation.

11. Nature and Extent of Possible Sources

The discussion of multiple sources for the infancy narratives in Luke's Gospel is a common topic in biblical scholarship, and it reflects the complexity and richness of these passages. Scholars often propose various sources to account for different aspects of the narrative, including the canticles or hymns, specific units within Chapter 2, and the stories of John the Baptist and Jesus in Chapter 1.

11.1. Sources for the Canticles or Hymns: The Magnificat (Mary's song of praise), the Benedictus (Zechariah's song), the Gloria in Excelsis (the angelic hymn), and the Nunc Dimittis (Simeon's song) are often considered to have originated from a special source. These hymns are more poetic and distinct in style compared to the surrounding narrative. Some scholars argue that these hymns might have been part of an earlier liturgical or devotional tradition that Luke incorporated into his Gospel.

11.2. Sources for Units in Chapter 2: Chapter 2 of Luke's Gospel contains several distinct units, such as the account of Jesus' birth in Bethlehem, the presentation in the temple, and the episode of Jesus as a child in Jerusalem. Some scholars suggest that these units could have originated from separate sources and were later integrated into the Gospel narrative. The differences in style, focus, and details within these units support the idea of multiple sources.

[40] Graham H. Twelftree, *People of the Spirit* (Grand Rapids, 2009), 75.

11.3. Sources for John the Baptist and Jesus Stories in Chapter 1: The stories related to John the Baptist's birth and Jesus' conception and birth are also considered to have potentially originated from different sources. The detailed and intimate nature of these stories, including the involvement of family traditions, has led some scholars to propose the existence of specific sources for these narratives. For example, the thesis of a Marian source suggests that Mary's experiences were orally communicated and later incorporated into Luke's Gospel.

Overall, the consideration of multiple sources for the infancy narratives in Luke's Gospel reflects scholarly efforts to understand the diverse origins and compositional history of these passages. These discussions contribute to a deeper appreciation of the complexity and richness of the biblical text.[41]

12. Old Testament Influence on Luke's Infancy Narrative

The infancy narratives in the Gospel of Luke are rich with Old Testament influence, serving as crucial links between the history of Israel and the arrival of Jesus. These narratives are not merely historical accounts; they are intricately woven into a larger theological framework that emphasizes God's promises and actions on behalf of His people. By drawing on familiar themes, figures, and motifs from the Old Testament, Luke situates the birth of Jesus within the ongoing story of God's redemptive plan.

From the angelic announcements to the miraculous births, the infancy narratives echo the experiences of key Old Testament figures such as Samuel and Moses, highlighting God's faithfulness in fulfilling His promises. The use of prophetic language and imagery further reinforces the expectation of a Messiah who would restore Israel and fulfill the covenantal promises made to Abraham, David, and the prophets. Luke's emphasis on the Holy Spirit's role, as seen in the conception of Jesus and the prophetic utterances of figures like Zechariah and Simeon, reflects the active presence of God in guiding and empowering His people.

Moreover, the themes of joy, praise, and salvation prevalent in Luke's infancy narrative resonate with the Psalms and prophetic writings, illustrating the continuity of God's work throughout history. By framing the birth of Jesus within this rich Old Testament context, Luke not only affirms the significance of Jesus as the promised Messiah but also invites his readers to recognize the fulfillment of God's enduring commitment to His people. In this way, the infancy narratives serve as a profound reminder of the intersection of divine promise and human history, setting the stage for the transformative ministry of Jesus.

---

[41] Joel B. Green and Scot McKnight eds., 53.

12.1. Discursive Forces and Narrative Context: Luke's narrative is shaped by discursive forces, which refer to the underlying themes, promises, and acts of God found in Israel's Scriptures. These forces provide the narrative context within which events unfold. Rather than presenting a detached historical account, Luke's Gospel integrates these discursive forces to highlight the theological significance of Jesus' birth and childhood.

12.2. God's Promises and Acts: Throughout Luke's Gospel, there is a continuous thread of God's promises and actions in salvation history. The birth narratives of John the Baptist and Jesus are situated within this broader context of divine intervention and fulfillment of prophecy. The references to Old Testament prophecies and the inclusion of hymns and songs of praise further reinforce this theme of God's faithfulness to His promises.

12.3. Narrative Needs for Development and Resolution: Luke uses the infancy narratives not only to introduce Jesus but also to establish narrative needs that will be developed and resolved throughout Luke-Acts. These needs include the expectation of a Messiah, the fulfillment of divine promises, and the inclusion of Gentiles in God's redemptive plan. The infancy narratives set the stage for the larger narrative arc of salvation history unfolding in Luke's Gospel and its sequel, the Acts of the Apostles.

In essence, the force of Luke's narrative lies in its ability to connect the events of Jesus' birth and childhood to the broader theological framework of God's promises and actions. By doing so, Luke presents a cohesive and purposeful narrative that points towards the fulfillment of God's salvific plan for all humanity.[42] As Luke has already informed in his prologue, the events he will narrate are linked to the past history of God's salvific acts. Similarly, as Luke's employment of Israel's Scriptures in Luke 1:5-2:52 demonstrates, the proper "beginning" for his narrative is there, in the past, in God's redemptive purpose as set forth in the Scriptures. Luke is not introducing a new story but continuing an old one, whose real "beginning" is the LXX. He roots the coming of Jesus and the universal Christian movement in God's purpose, continue as one divine story.

Hence, Luke does not at this juncture think of augmenting salvation history into "stages" nor even simply of a hermeneutical pattern of fulfillment – prophecy. This is not to deny the important ways in which Luke 1:5-2:52 portray eschatological fulfillment or to suggest that Luke does not regard the OT as essentially forward-looking. Rather, it is to affirm that Luke self-consciously begin his narrative in the middle of the story, so to speak. The emphasis falls on salvation-historical unity: The God who has been working redemptive still is, now, and especially, in Jesus. Luke's use of the Abrahamic

[42] John Nolland, *Word Biblical Commentary,*. Volume 35a, Luke 1-9:20, 21.

material of Genesis 11-21 in the narration stories of John and Jesus. Luke's interest in Abraham is transparent at two points in the story, specifically in 1: 55, 73. There, God's merciful activity on behalf of Israel is related directly to his faithfulness to Abraham.

With respect to these points of contact between Genesis 11-21 and Luke 1:5-2:52, a number of observations may be made. These narratives share a common repertoire of elements where they interest with conventional forms found elsewhere in the biblical tradition. There is a surprising linguistic overlap between the LXX and the Greek text of Luke, including material unrelated to the literary convention of the relating of a birth announcement or such stock themes as barrenness. Luke's clear interest in directing Abrahamic material "our ancestor" "Abraham" "covenant" in Luke 1:55, 73.42 For Luke, the "beginning" can be located only in God's purpose, and his narrative beginning presupposes not only this divine aim, but also the articulation of that aim in the scriptures and a concern for that aim on the part of his audience.

12.4. Theological Significance: The narratives carry profound theological meaning. They emphasize that Jesus is the fulfillment of Old Testament prophecies and promises, such as the expectation of the Messiah coming from Bethlehem.[43] Mary's Magnificat and Zechariah's Benedictus contain theological reflections on God's mercy, salvation, and faithfulness.[44] The theological themes of redemption, salvation, and God's plan for humanity are woven into the story. Another significant purpose of the Lukan Infancy Narratives in the Gospel of Luke is to convey profound theological significance. These narratives contain theological themes and messages that contribute to the broader theological understanding of Jesus and His mission.[45]

12.5. Fulfillment of God's Promises: The Infancy Narratives in Luke's Gospel serve as a testament to the fulfillment of God's promises and prophecies made in the Old Testament. These narratives intricately weave together the historical context, geographical details, and cultural practices to underscore the divine orchestration behind Jesus' birth and early life. The genealogy of Jesus traced back to David fulfills the Messianic expectation of a descendant from David's line, as prophesied in scriptures like Isaiah 11:1. The inclusion of Bethlehem as the birthplace of Jesus aligns with the prophecy of Micah 5:2, further solidifying Jesus' role as the long-awaited Messiah.

---

[43] C. Kavin Rowe, *Early Narrative Christology: The Lord in the Gospel of Luke* (Berlin: Walter de Gruyter, 2012), 34.

[44] Stephen Farris, *The Hymns of Luke's Infancy Narratives: Their Origin, Meaning and Significance,* (London: Bloomsbury Publishing, 2015).

[45] Stephen J. Binz and Little Rock Scripture Study Staff, *The Infancy Narratives of Jesus* (Collegeville, MN: Liturgical Press, 2020), 66.

12.5.1. Messiahship: Central to Luke's Infancy Narratives is the affirmation of Jesus' identity as the Messiah. The angel Gabriel's announcement to Mary about her child being called the "Son of the Most High" (Lk 1:32) is a pivotal moment that establishes Jesus' Messianic identity. This theological theme resonates throughout the narratives, from the angelic pronouncements to the reactions of characters like Simeon and Anna in the Temple. The Messianic expectations of the Jewish people find fulfillment in Jesus' birth, marking the beginning of a new era of salvation and redemption.

12.5.2. Son of God: The concept of Jesus as the Son of God is prominently featured in Luke's Infancy Narratives. The angelic visitations, particularly Gabriel's message to Mary, emphasize the divine nature of Jesus' conception and birth. The declaration of Jesus as the "Son of the Most High" not only signifies His unique relationship with God but also points to His divine mission and authority. This theological concept lays the foundation for understanding Jesus' role in salvation history and His significance as the Savior of humanity.

12.5.3. Salvation: Mary's Magnificat and Zechariah's Benedictus contain profound theological reflections on God's mercy, salvation, and faithfulness. These hymns of praise highlight the redemptive aspect of Jesus' birth and His role as the Savior of humanity. The narratives emphasize that Jesus' coming brings salvation to all who believe in Him, fulfilling the promise of God's grace and forgiveness.

12.5.4. Inclusivity: One of the key theological themes in Luke's Infancy Narratives is the inclusivity of Jesus' mission. The angelic proclamation of "good news of great joy for all the people" (Lk 2:10) signifies that Jesus' message transcends boundaries of ethnicity, social status, or nationality. This inclusivity is further emphasized by the presence of characters like the shepherds, who represent the marginalized and the outcasts, receiving the first news of Jesus' birth. The narrative presents Jesus as the Savior for all humanity, extending God's love and salvation to everyone.[46]

12.5.5. Universal Scope: Simeon's declaration in the Temple that Jesus is "a light for revelation to the Gentiles, and for glory to your people Israel" (Lk 2:32) underscores the universal mission of Jesus. This theological theme highlights Jesus' role in the salvation of all nations, not limited to a specific ethnic group or geographical region. The narratives portray Jesus as the embodiment of God's love and redemption for the entire world, inviting people from every background to experience His transformative grace.

---

[46] Stephen Farris, *The Hymns of Luke's Infancy Narratives: Their Origin, Meaning and Significance,* 108.

12.5.6. Incarnation: The birth of Jesus represents the theological concept of the Incarnation, encapsulating the mystery of the eternal Son of God taking on human flesh. The narratives depict Jesus' humble birth in a manger, emphasizing His identification with humanity and His willingness to enter into the human experience. The Incarnation is a foundational aspect of Christian theology, signifying God's profound act of love and His desire to reconcile humanity to Himself through Jesus Christ.

12.5.7. Prophetic Fulfillment: The Infancy Narratives in Luke's Gospel intricately connect the events of Jesus' birth to the prophecies of the Old Testament, showcasing Jesus as the fulfillment of God's plan and the culmination of the prophetic tradition. The narratives reference numerous Old Testament prophecies, such as the virgin birth (Isaiah 7:14), the Messiah's lineage from David (Jeremiah 23:5), and the significance of Bethlehem (Micah 5:2), among others. These connections reinforce Jesus' Messianic identity and His role as the fulfillment of divine promises.[47]

12.5.8. Faith and Obedience: The characters in Luke's Infancy Narratives, including Mary, Joseph, Zechariah, Elizabeth, Simeon, and Anna, serve as models of faith and obedience to God's will. Their responses to divine messages and revelations demonstrate unwavering faith, trust, and obedience in God's plan. Mary's proclamation of "let it be to me according to your word" (Lk 1:38) exemplifies a profound sense of surrender and obedience. These examples of faith inspire believers to emulate their trust in God's providence and guidance.

12.5.9. Redemption and Hope: The narratives in Luke's Infancy Narratives bring a message of redemption and hope to humanity. The arrival of Jesus, announced as "good news of great joy," signifies a new era of hope and salvation for all who believe in Him. The narratives emphasize God's grace, mercy, and His desire to reconcile humanity to Himself through the redemptive work of Jesus Christ. The birth of Jesus symbolizes the beginning of God's plan of salvation, offering hope and eternal life to those who put their trust in Him.[48]

In summary, the Lukan Infancy Narratives serve to convey significant theological themes and messages that illuminate the identity and mission of Jesus Christ. They establish the theological foundation for understanding Jesus as the promised Messiah, the Son of God, and the universal Savior whose birth brings hope and redemption to all humanity.

---

[47] Julie Newberry, *Lukan Joy and the Life of Discipleship: A Narrative Analysis of the Conditions That Lead to Joy According to Luke* (Mohr Siebeck, 2023), 58.

[48] Richard J. Cassidy, *Jesus, Politics, and Society: A Study of Luke's Gospel* (Wipf and Stock Publishers, 2015), 30.

13. Universal Salvation

The Lukan Infancy Narratives stress the universal scope of Jesus' mission and the inclusivity of God's salvation plan. This is evident in the angelic announcement to the shepherds and Simeon's declaration that Jesus is a light for both Israel and the Gentiles. Luke's Gospel presents Jesus as the Savior not only of the Jewish people but of all humanity.[49]

13.1. Angel's Announcement to the Shepherds: The angelic proclamation to the shepherds in Luke 2:10 holds significant theological weight regarding universal salvation. The message of "good news of great joy that will be for all the people" signifies the inclusive nature of Jesus' birth. The shepherds, considered ordinary and marginalized in society, were chosen as recipients of this divine announcement, symbolizing that the message of salvation extends to all, regardless of social status or background. This announcement serves as a precursor to Jesus' ministry, where He reaches out to the outcasts and downtrodden, demonstrating God's inclusive love for humanity.[50]

13.2. Simeon's Proclamation: Simeon's prophetic words in Luke 2:32 affirm the universal scope of Jesus' mission. By referring to Jesus as "a light for revelation to the Gentiles, and for glory to your people Israel," Simeon acknowledges that Jesus' coming brings enlightenment and salvation not only to the Jewish community but also to the Gentiles. This declaration underscores the universal nature of God's redemptive plan, encompassing people from all nations and backgrounds. Simeon's recognition of Jesus as the Messiah with a global impact foreshadows the inclusive ministry of Jesus, who welcomes all who come to Him in faith, irrespective of their heritage or cultural identity.[51]

13.3. Anna's Testimony: Anna, the prophetess, provides additional affirmation of the universal significance of Jesus' birth in Luke 2:38. Her testimony to "all who were waiting for the redemption of Jerusalem" signifies that Jesus' arrival brings hope and redemption not only to a select few but to all who long for God's deliverance. Anna's words resonate with people from diverse backgrounds, emphasizing that Jesus' message of salvation is accessible to anyone who seeks it, regardless of their circumstances or past.

13.4. Inclusivity of Characters: The diverse cast of characters in the Infancy Narratives symbolizes the inclusivity of Jesus' message of salvation. Mary and Joseph represent humble obedience and faith, while the shepherds

---

[49] Mark Strauss, *The Davidic Messiah in Luke-Acts: The Promise and Its Fulfilment in Lukan Christology* (London: Bloomsbury Publishing, 1995), 92.

[50] Roger Stronstad, *Charismatic Theology of St. Luke, The* (Grand Rapids, MI: Baker Publishing Group, 1990), 30ff.

[51] Luke Timothy Johnson, *Sacra Pagina: The Gospel of Luke* (Liturgical Press, 2018).

exemplify the marginalized and overlooked members of society. Simeon and Anna, devout and righteous individuals, embody the yearning for God's redemption among different generations. Together, these characters showcase the universal appeal of Jesus' birth and ministry, welcoming people from every walk of life into the fold of God's love and grace.[52]

13.5. Continuity with Luke's Gospel: The theme of universal salvation introduced in the Infancy Narratives continues throughout the Gospel of Luke and into the Book of Acts. This continuity underscores the mission of the early Church to proclaim the gospel to all nations, as seen in the Great Commission (Lk 24:47; Acts 1:8). The inclusive nature of Jesus' ministry, highlighted in His interactions with diverse groups during His earthly life, serves as a model for the Church to embrace and share God's love with people from every background and culture.

In summary, the Lukan Infancy Narratives convey the theme of universal salvation by emphasizing that Jesus' birth is good news for all people, transcending cultural, social, and geographical boundaries. The inclusion of various characters and their responses underscores the message that Jesus is the Savior of the world, offering hope and redemption to everyone who believes in Him. This theme of universal salvation is a foundational element of Luke's Gospel and the broader Christian message.

Summary of Findings

This chapter has discussed some of the basic literary basic features of the Lukan infancy narratives, which may be of significance for the present study. First of all, the term "infancy" is found to be a misnomer since it does not adequately reflect the contents of the Lukan infancy narratives. However, as no other term is found that will give a more comprehensive description of these narratives, the popular term "infancy" is retained for use keeping in mind it's limited representation.

In the quest for the literary genre, it is found that the Lukan infancy narratives form a self-contained unit belonging to an intermix or fusion of the Greco-Roman biographical writings of Mediterranean antiquity and Old Testament literary traditions concerning the birth of some great and special person. Furthermore, this genre is common to the thought and expressions of the eastern world as well. However, the uniqueness of the genre of the Lukan infancy narratives stands out since it subverts the stereotype genre of the birth of a hero who normally hails from a rich and honorable family. Jesus is here characterized as a person hailing from a humble and low social

[52] Matthew A. Knight, *The Book of Luke: Physician and Historian* (Bloomington, IN: Xlibris Corporation, 2018), 46ff.

background. Besides, the conception of Jesus through divine agency is unparalleled in other traditions.

In the comparison between the Lukan infancy narratives and the Matthean, it is found that there are both similarities as well as dissimilarities between these two narratives. However, the overall findings suggest that even the similarities are engulfed in dissimilarities such that there is no way for the two narratives to be related to one another. Therefore, the Lukan and Matthean infancy narratives are independent of one another. With regard to the relation of the Lukan infancy narratives to the rest of the Luke-Acts the two are intrinsically related in that the former is part and parcel or integral to the latter.

2

The Ministry of John the Baptist in Luke and the Call to an Alternative Lifestyle

Introduction

The ministry of John the Baptist, a central figure in the Gospel of Luke, offers profound insights into the call to an alternative lifestyle that stands in stark contrast to the prevailing societal norms of his time. John's message, actions, and way of life challenge conventional beliefs and practices, serving as a powerful testament to radical devotion to God. He emerges not merely as a forerunner to Jesus but as a prophetic voice that calls for a transformative reorientation of life centered on repentance, justice, and humility.

In the context of first-century Judea, marked by political oppression and religious fragmentation, John's ministry becomes a beacon of hope and renewal. His call to repentance is not a mere invitation to regret past actions; it is a summons to embrace a new way of living — one that aligns with God's kingdom and prioritizes the well-being of others. Through his radical ascetic lifestyle, characterized by detachment from materialism and a focus on spiritual purity, John exemplifies the transformative power of faith.

This exploration delves into John's ministry as portrayed in the Gospel of Luke, highlighting key aspects of his call to an alternative lifestyle and examining their relevance for contemporary believers. By analyzing John's prophetic identity, ethical teachings, and interactions with various groups, we can glean insights into how his message continues to resonate today, challenging us to live with intentionality, integrity, and compassion in a world that often values the opposite.

1. Socio-Political Environment of First-Century Judea

The socio-political environment of first-century Judea was marked by a complex interplay of various cultural, religious, and political forces. Following the Roman conquest in 63 BCE, Judea became a client state under Roman authority, leading to significant tensions between the local population and their foreign rulers. The region was governed by a series of Roman prefects and procurators, including Pontius Pilate, whose heavy taxation and legal authority often incited resentment among the Jewish populace. This Roman rule was coupled with the presence of Herod Antipas, the Tetrarch of Galilee and Perea, whose local governance was often seen as oppressive and corrupt, further straining relations between the Jewish people and their rulers.

Religiously, Judea was a melting pot of beliefs and practices, with various sects such as the Pharisees, Sadducees, Essenes, and Zealots vying for influence and power. The Pharisees emphasized adherence to the Law and oral traditions, while the Sadducees, comprised mainly of the priestly class, focused on temple worship and political collaboration with the Romans. The Essenes, known for their ascetic lifestyle, withdrew from mainstream society, seeking to maintain purity in anticipation of God's intervention. In contrast, the Zealots advocated for armed resistance against Roman occupation, reflecting a growing desire among certain groups for national liberation.

Amid this tumultuous backdrop, the Jewish people were experiencing a profound longing for messianic deliverance. Many were looking for a savior who would restore their national identity and religious purity. It is within this socio-political context that John the Baptist emerged, calling for repentance and an alternative lifestyle that challenged both the moral decay of society and the oppressive political structures. His ministry, characterized by prophetic zeal, urged the people to prepare for the coming of the Lord, setting the stage for the transformative message of Jesus.

2. Religious Landscape During the Time of John the Baptist

The religious landscape of Judea during the time of John the Baptist was complex and multifaceted, reflecting a broad spectrum of beliefs and practices within Judaism. Central to this diversity were the Pharisees, Sadducees, Essenes, and Zealots, each representing distinct theological and ideological perspectives. The Pharisees were known for their emphasis on oral traditions and the interpretation of the Torah. They believed in the resurrection of the dead and held a relatively democratized view of religious practice, which made them popular among the common people. The Sadducees, on the other hand, were more conservative, rejecting oral traditions in favor of a strict adherence to the written Torah. They denied the resurrection and were closely associated with the Temple priesthood and the aristocracy, wielding considerable political influence.[1]

The Essenes, a more ascetic group, lived in isolated communities and practiced rigorous purity laws. They are often associated with the Dead Sea Scrolls and had a strong eschatological focus, believing they were living in the end times. The Zealots were a politically radical faction that advocated for the violent overthrow of Roman rule, seeing themselves as defenders of Jewish sovereignty and purity. This fragmented religious environment was marked by intense debates and tensions, as each group vied for influence and legitimacy within Jewish society. John's emergence as a prophetic figure must be understood against this backdrop of religious plurality and contention.[2]

John the Baptist did not shy away from critiquing the religious elite of his time, including the Pharisees and Sadducees. His criticism was emblematic of the prevailing sentiment among many Jews that the religious establishment had grown corrupt and hypocritical. John accused these leaders of being a "brood of vipers" and warned them that mere lineage to Abraham was not enough to escape divine judgment; genuine repentance and righteous deeds were necessary.

This confrontation with the religious leaders highlighted the broader religious and social tensions of the period. The Pharisees, known for their strict adherence to the law and oral traditions, and the Sadducees, who controlled the Temple and its practices, were seen by many as having strayed from the true spirit of the law. John's call for genuine repentance and his emphasis on moral and spiritual renewal were a direct challenge to their authority and practices.

John's critique also resonated with the common people, who often felt alienated by the rigid and hierarchical structures of the religious institutions. By advocating for a direct and personal relationship with God, marked by repentance and baptism, John democratized the religious experience and called for a faith that was accessible to all, not just the religious elite. His bold stance against the established order underscored his prophetic authority and aligned him with the tradition of the Hebrew prophets who called out the moral and spiritual failings of Israel's leaders.

The ministry of John the Baptist in the first century AD was situated within a complex historical and religious backdrop, particularly in the region of Judea. To fully comprehend John's role and message, it is imperative

[1] Joel Marcus, *John the Baptist in History and Theology* (Columbia, SC: University of South Carolina Press, 2018), 10ff.

[2] Thomas F. Marshall, *The New Testament: Its Background, Setting & Content* (Cincinnati, OH: Christian Publishing House, 2023), 115.

to explore the historical and religious milieu against which he operated. Historically, the land of Judea was under Roman rule during John's ministry. The Roman Empire, at the zenith of its power, had extended its dominion over vast territories, including the eastern Mediterranean. Governance in Judea was delegated to the Herodian dynasty, with figures like Herod the Great and later Herod Antipas serving as client kings under Roman authority. These rulers faced intricate political challenges, tasked with harmonizing Roman interests with local sensitivities and expectations.[3]

Within this historical framework, John's ministry took shape. To appreciate its significance fully, it is essential to examine the prevailing religious landscape and the expectations that characterized the period. John the Baptist's ministry was marked by confrontations with the religious leaders of his time, particularly the Pharisees and Sadducees. He boldly criticized their hypocrisy, calling them a "brood of vipers" and challenging their reliance on lineage and ritualistic observance without true repentance. This confrontation highlighted the religious tensions of the period, as John called for a genuine transformation of heart and spirit, in contrast to the outward piety emphasized by the religious elite.

John's denunciation of the religious leaders was a significant aspect of his prophetic role, echoing the tradition of earlier prophets who called out the moral and spiritual failings of Israel's leaders. His message resonated with the common people, who often felt alienated by the rigid and hierarchical religious structures. By advocating for a direct and personal relationship with God, marked by repentance and baptism, John democratized the religious experience, challenging the authority and influence of the established religious institutions.[4] This confrontation with the religious elite not only underscored the prophetic nature of John's ministry but also set the stage for the eventual conflict between Jesus and the religious authorities. John's fearless critique of the religious status quo paved the way for Jesus' more radical teachings and actions, which further challenged the existing religious and social order.[5]

In summary, John the Baptist's ministry in the Gospel of Luke occurred within a complex historical, political, and religious context. His role as a prophetic figure, the anticipation of the Messiah, the practice of baptism, and the political dynamics of Roman rule all played a crucial role in shaping

[3] Edward D. Andrews, *The Bible as History: A Historical Journey Through the Bible* (Cincinnati, OH: Christian Publishing House, 2023), 187.

[4] Anna Beresford, *Before You Were Born, I Anointed You: Uncovering Scripture's "Hidden" Female Prophets* (Eugene, OR: Wipf and Stock Publishers, 2022), 133.

[5] Jas' Elsner and Ian Rutherford, *Pilgrimage in Graeco-Roman and Early Christian Antiquity: Seeing the Gods* (Oxford: OUP Oxford, 2007), 448.

the narrative of his ministry. John's proclamation of the kingdom and his identification of Jesus as the Messiah were pivotal moments that set the stage for the ministry of Jesus and the unfolding of God's redemptive plan.[6]

3. Expectations of a Prophetic Figure in Jewish Tradition

Messianic expectations were deeply ingrained in Jewish thought during the Second Temple period, fueled by centuries of prophetic writings and the socio-political realities of Roman occupation. Many Jews anticipated a divinely anointed leader, the Messiah, who would liberate them from foreign rule and restore the Davidic kingdom. This hope was not monolithic; different sects had varied conceptions of what the Messiah would be like. The Pharisees often envisioned a Messiah who would be a great teacher and reformer of Jewish law, while the Essenes expected a priestly and kingly figure who would establish a community of the faithful in preparation for the final judgment. The Zealots likely saw the Messiah as a warrior-king who would lead a rebellion against Rome.[7]

John the Baptist's proclamation of the coming Messiah resonated powerfully within this context. His call for repentance and moral renewal was seen as a preparation for the imminent arrival of God's anointed. By positioning himself as a herald of the Messiah, John tapped into the widespread yearning for divine intervention and liberation. His message carried the implicit promise of a transformative leader who would fulfill the ancient prophecies and bring about a new era of righteousness and justice.

4. Historical and Cultural Context

The context of John the Baptist's ministry in the Gospel of Luke is integral to understanding his role as the forerunner of Jesus and the unique message he conveyed. To delve into the context of John's ministry as presented in the Gospel of Luke, it is important to consider various aspects that shaped his mission and message. Historical and Political Context: John the Baptist's ministry occurred during a period of Roman rule and political complexity. Judea was under the authority of the Roman Empire, and Herod Antipas governed the region as a client king. The presence of Roman forces and the political intricacies of the time created an environment of tension and uncertainty.[8]

---

[6] Giovanni Ruffini, *Life in an Egyptian Village in Late Antiquity: Aphrodito Before and After the Islamic Conquest* (Cambridge: Cambridge University Press, 2018), 112.

[7] Wil Rogan, *Purity in the Gospel of John: Early Jewish Tradition, Christology, and Ethics* (London: Bloomsbury Publishing, 2023), 62.

[8] Roberto Martinez, *The Question of John the Baptist and Jesus' Indictment of the Religious Leaders: A Critical Analysis of Luke 7:18-35* (Cambridge: James Clarke & Company Limited, 2012), 95.

5. The Prophetic Identity of John the Baptist

John the Baptist's ministry was deeply rooted in the prophetic tradition of Judaism. He was widely perceived as a prophet in the mold of Elijah, a comparison reinforced by his austere lifestyle, distinctive clothing, and fiery preaching. Like the prophets of old, John called for repentance and a return to God's ways, urging the people to prepare for a coming divine intervention. His choice to live in the wilderness, wearing camel's hair and eating locusts and wild honey, was a deliberate emulation of Elijah and other prophets who often retreated to the desert to receive and proclaim God's messages.[9]

John's prophetic role involved not just moral exhortation but also symbolic actions. His baptism in the Jordan River, for example, echoed the Israelites' crossing of the Jordan under Joshua, symbolizing a new beginning for the people of Israel. By situating his ministry in the wilderness, John also evoked the imagery of Israel's formative period, wandering in the desert and relying on God for sustenance and guidance. This setting underscored his message of renewal and purification, calling the people to prepare for a new exodus and a new covenant.[10]

Prophets frequently employed symbolic actions to convey their messages, serving as powerful visual metaphors to emphasize their words. These actions were often dramatic and intended to capture the attention of the people, illustrating the seriousness of their messages. For example, Isaiah's act of walking naked and barefoot for three years (Isaiah 20:2-4) was a sign against Egypt and Cush, symbolizing their future humiliation and captivity by the Assyrians.

Jeremiah's symbolic actions were particularly vivid. He wore a yoke around his neck to symbolize the coming bondage of Judah under Babylon (Jeremiah 27), and he purchased a field during the siege of Jerusalem to demonstrate his faith in God's promise of restoration (Jeremiah 32:6-15). These actions reinforced his verbal prophecies and provided a tangible illustration of his messages. Ezekiel's prophetic ministry was marked by numerous symbolic acts. He lay on his side for extended periods to symbolize the years of Israel and Judah's sin (Ezekiel 4:4-6), and he shaved his head and beard, dividing the hair to represent the fate of the people (Ezekiel 5:1-4). These symbolic actions were often shocking and perplexing but were designed to provoke thought, reflection, and ultimately repentance among the people.[11] The use of symbolic actions by prophets was a distinctive feature of

---

[9] Robert L. Webb, *John the Baptizer and Prophet: A Sociohistorical Study* (Eugene, OR: Wipf and Stock Publishers, 2006), 309.

[10] Robert L. Webb, *John the Baptizer and Prophet: A Sociohistorical Study,* 351.

[11] Sehyun Kim, *The Kingship of Jesus in the Gospel of John* (Eugene, OR: Wipf and Stock Publishers, 2018), 109.

their ministry, enhancing the impact of their messages and ensuring that their warnings and promises were vividly remembered. These actions underscored the seriousness of their divine calling and the urgent need for the people to heed their words.

5.1. John's Lineage and Birth Narrative (Lk 1:5-25, 57-80)

The birth narrative of John the Baptist in the Gospel of Luke vividly underscores his divine calling. This story begins with his parents, Elizabeth and Zechariah, a devout couple who were righteous in the sight of God but had no children because Elizabeth was barren and both were advanced in years (Lk 1:6-7). The angel Gabriel's appearance to Zechariah in the temple is a pivotal moment that echoes the divine callings of Old Testament figures. Gabriel announces that Elizabeth will bear a son, John, who will be great in the sight of the Lord and filled with the Holy Spirit even before his birth (Lk 1:13-15).[12]

Gabriel's prophecy places John within the grand narrative of salvation history, linking him to the prophetic tradition. Like Samuel, Samson, and other divinely appointed leaders of Israel, John's birth is marked by divine intervention, emphasizing his unique role in God's plan. The narrative highlights John's role as the forerunner of the Messiah, destined to "make ready a people prepared for the Lord" (Lk 1:17). This divine calling is further affirmed when Elizabeth, filled with the Holy Spirit, recognizes Mary as the mother of the Lord and the unborn John leaps in her womb (Lk 1:41-44), signaling his recognition of the Messiah even before birth.[13]

Zechariah's prophecy, the Benedictus, further elaborates John's mission. Zechariah speaks of John as the prophet of the Most High, who will go before the Lord to prepare his ways, giving knowledge of salvation to his people by the forgiveness of their sins (Lk 1:76-77). This prophetic declaration sets the stage for John's ministry and underscores the divine orchestration behind his life and mission.[14]

5.2. Parallels with Old Testament Prophets (Elijah, Isaiah)

John the Baptist's ministry was deeply embedded in the prophetic tradition within Judaism. Prophets in the Hebrew Bible, such as Isaiah, Jeremiah, and Elijah, often called the people of Israel to repentance and

---

[12] Judith N. Ryan, 'Luke's Infancy Nairative:' 342.

[13] James Keith Elliott, *A Synopsis of the Apocryphal Nativity and Infancy Narratives: Second Edition, Revised and Expanded* (Leiden: Brill, 2016), 52.

[14] Noah Knowles Davis, *The Story of the Nazarene in Annotated Paraphrase* (Grand Rapids, MI: Revell, 1903), 417. Cf. Darrell L. Bock et al., *The Luke Commentary Collection: An All-In-One Commentary Collection for Studying the Book of Luke* (Grand Rapids, MI: Zondervan Academic, 2016).

moral renewal, warning of divine judgment while also offering hope for redemption. These prophets served as intermediaries between God and the people, delivering messages intended to realign the community with God's covenant.

John's ministry mirrored this prophetic tradition in several ways. His message was one of urgent repentance and preparation for an impending divine intervention. He warned of the consequences of failing to repent, using vivid imagery such as the axe laid to the root of the trees and the winnowing fork separating the wheat from the chaff. This language was reminiscent of the warnings given by earlier prophets about the coming day of the Lord.[15]

John's ascetic lifestyle further aligned him with the prophetic tradition. Like Elijah, who lived in the wilderness and wore simple garments, John adopted an austere mode of living, dressing in camel's hair and subsisting on locusts and wild honey. This lifestyle underscored his message of repentance and moral purity, emphasizing the need to turn away from worldly distractions and focus on spiritual preparation. Through his actions and teachings, John positioned himself as a contemporary prophet, calling the people of Israel to prepare for the fulfillment of God's promises. His ministry was a bridge between the prophetic voices of the Hebrew Bible and the new covenant that would be established through Jesus.[16]

A significant belief among Jews during this period was the anticipation of the return of the prophet Elijah before the arrival of the Messiah. This expectation was based on the prophecy in Malachi 4:5-6, which foretold that Elijah would come to prepare the way for the great and dreadful day of the Lord. Elijah, known for his zealous advocacy for God's covenant and his dramatic ascension to heaven in a chariot of fire, was a powerful symbol of prophetic authority and divine intervention. John the Baptist's ministry, attire, and message led many to regard him as the fulfillment of this expectation. His clothing of camel's hair and leather belt mirrored the description of Elijah in 2 Kings 1:8. Additionally, his choice to conduct his ministry in the wilderness and his call for repentance were reminiscent of Elijah's own prophetic activities. These parallels were not lost on the people of his time, and many saw John as the promised Elijah who would prepare the way for the Messiah.[17]

---

[15] Ralph P. Martin and Carl N. Toney, *New Testament Foundations: An Introduction for Students* (Eugene, OR: Wipf and Stock Publishers, 2018), 273.

[16] Jonathan Griffiths, *Preaching in the New Testament: An Exegetical And Biblical-Theological Study* (London: SPCK, 2017), 13.

[17] B. A. Sarma, *Hermeneutics of Mission in Matthew: Israel and the Nations in the Interpretative Framework of Matthew's Gospel* (Eugene, OR: Langham Monographs, 2015), 108.

The identification of John with Elijah was significant in the context of Messianic expectations. It lent credibility to his message and underscored the urgency of his call for repentance. By embodying the role of Elijah, John was not only continuing the prophetic tradition but also signaling that the long-awaited Messianic age was imminent. This identification provided a clear and compelling link between the prophecies of the Hebrew Bible and the emerging narrative of Jesus as the Messiah. John's lifestyle drew direct parallels to the Old Testament prophet Elijah, reinforcing his role within the prophetic tradition. Elijah, known for his own ascetic lifestyle, also lived in the wilderness and relied on simple sustenance provided by God (1 Kings 17:2-6). By emulating Elijah, John positioned himself as a successor to the prophetic legacy, embodying the qualities of earlier prophets who had called the people back to faithfulness and repentance.[18]

Both Elijah and John used their wilderness abodes and simple diets to symbolize their separation from the corrupting influences of society and their complete dependence on God. This connection to Elijah was not only symbolic but also prophetic, as Jesus later identified John as the "Elijah who was to come" (Matthew 11:14), fulfilling the prophecy of Malachi 4:5-6.

5.3. Symbolic Meaning of Ascetic Lifestyle: Detachment from Materialism and Call

John's ascetic lifestyle extended beyond his dietary choices to encompass his entire way of living. He practiced severe self-discipline and abstained from the pleasures and comforts of ordinary life, choosing instead a path of rigorous devotion to God. This asceticism was not an end in itself but a means to achieve a deeper spiritual focus and purity. Living in the wilderness, John was isolated from the distractions of society, allowing him to concentrate fully on his spiritual mission. His life of simplicity and austerity was a powerful testament to his commitment to God and his prophetic calling. It emphasized the need for personal sacrifice and discipline in the pursuit of spiritual goals, serving as a model for those who sought to follow his teachings.[19]

John the Baptist's diet, consisting of locusts and wild honey, was a striking contrast to the luxurious and indulgent eating habits of the elite in his society. This simple and austere diet was a deliberate choice that underscored John's commitment to a life of humility and self-denial. Locusts and wild honey were not only readily available in the wilderness but also inexpensive,

[18] C. H. Dodd, *Historical Tradition in the Fourth Gospel* (Cambridge: Cambridge University Press, 1976), 261.

[19] Gary Yamasaki, *John the Baptist in Life and Death: Audience-Oriented Criticism of Matthew's Narrative* (London: A&C Black, 1998), 123.

making them food for the common people rather than the wealthy. By subsisting on such a humble diet, John distanced himself from the opulence and excesses that characterized the lifestyles of the rich and powerful. His choice of food symbolized a rejection of materialism and indulgence, aligning with his broader message of repentance and spiritual renewal. It also resonated with the people who were marginalized and impoverished, as it demonstrated that true spiritual authority did not require wealth or luxury.

John's diet and ascetic lifestyle had profound symbolic meaning. His detachment from material possessions and worldly comforts was a direct critique of the societal values that prioritized wealth and luxury over spiritual integrity. In a society marked by significant economic disparities, John's lifestyle was a radical call to focus on what truly mattered: one's relationship with God and inner moral state.[20] John's ascetic practices were a call to the people to repent and renew their spiritual lives. His message emphasized that true repentance required more than superficial changes; it necessitated a profound inner transformation and a genuine commitment to living according to God's will. By living an ascetic life, John embodied this message, demonstrating through his own actions what it meant to lead a life dedicated to spiritual renewal and purity.

John's asceticism was characterized by self-denial and rigorous discipline, teaching the value of self-control and the importance of mastering one's desires for the sake of a deeper spiritual connection. His lifestyle involved significant personal sacrifice, as he chose to live in the harsh conditions of the wilderness, away from the comforts and conveniences of urban life. This self-denial was not just a physical act but a spiritual discipline that reflected his total commitment to God. Through his ascetic practices, John demonstrated the importance of prioritizing spiritual growth over physical comfort. His disciplined lifestyle served as a model for his followers, illustrating how self-control and mastery over one's desires could lead to a closer relationship with God. John's emphasis on self-denial challenged people to examine their own lives, encouraging them to forsake worldly pleasures and focus on their spiritual journey.

John's rigorous discipline also underscored the seriousness of his prophetic mission. His unwavering dedication to his ascetic lifestyle was a testament to his authenticity and the depth of his commitment to God's calling. This discipline reinforced his message that true repentance and spiritual renewal required more than superficial changes; it demanded a fundamental transformation of heart and mind, achieved through continuous self-discipline and devotion. John the Baptist's ascetic lifestyle, including

[20] Georg Strecker, *Theology of the New Testament: German Edition Edited and Completed* (Berlin: Walter de Gruyter, 2012), 222.

his simple diet and clothing, emphasized his commitment to simplicity and self-discipline. He wore a garment made of camel's hair and a leather belt, a deliberate departure from conventional attire, symbolizing his identification with the prophetic lineage and his role as a messenger of God (Matthew 3:4). His diet, consisting of locusts and wild honey, was equally austere and reflected his rejection of materialism and indulgence.

This ascetic lifestyle paralleled the practices of the Qumran community, who also embraced simplicity and self-discipline. The Essenes of Qumran practiced communal living, held property in common, and followed strict dietary regulations. Their commitment to an ascetic lifestyle and communal living mirrored John's emphasis on austerity and his call for a return to simplicity and spiritual purity. In summary, John's countercultural message, identification with the marginalized, and emphasis on spiritual discipline were integral aspects of his ministry. By rejecting worldly excess, he challenged societal values and demonstrated that true spirituality was independent of material wealth. His relatability to the poor emphasized his solidarity with the marginalized, while his ascetic practices taught the importance of self-denial and discipline in pursuing a deeper connection with God. Through these elements, John the Baptist embodied a powerful call to repentance, simplicity, and spiritual renewal.[21]

In summary, John the Baptist's diet and asceticism were not only personal choices but also integral components of his prophetic message and alternative lifestyle. These practices symbolized his detachment from materialism, his emphasis on spiritual renewal, and his countercultural challenge to the prevailing excesses of his society. John's asceticism made him relatable to the marginalized and served as a call to self-discipline and inner transformation in preparation for the coming of the Messiah.

5.4. John's Role as the Forerunner to Jesus (Lk 1:76, 3:4-6)

John's withdrawal to the wilderness was motivated by a desire for solitude, contemplation, and communion with God. The wilderness, a place of solitude and desolation, was where he began his ministry, preaching a baptism of repentance for the forgiveness of sins (Lk 3:2-3). This setting was not just a backdrop for his preaching but a crucial part of his prophetic identity. For John, the wilderness represented a space of spiritual significance. It was where the prophet Elijah had found refuge and encountered God (1 Kings 19), and John's choice of location echoed this prophetic tradition. By following in the footsteps of Elijah, John positioned himself within the

[21] Roberto Martinez, *The Question of John the Baptist and Jesus' Indictment of the Religious Leaders: A Critical Analysis of Luke 7:18–35* (Eugene, OR: Wipf and Stock Publishers, 2011), 50.

prophetic tradition, embodying the qualities of the prophets who had come before him.

The Qumran community also viewed the desert as a place of spiritual retreat and contemplation. They believed that their separation from the impurities of the world was essential for maintaining ritual purity and cultivating a righteous community. The desert location offered an ideal setting for their contemplative and ascetic practices. John the Baptist's primary role, as described in the Gospels, is to prepare the way for the coming of the Messiah. This mission aligns him with the prophets of old, who were chosen by God to deliver His messages to the people of Israel. John's message was one of repentance and the imminent arrival of the kingdom of God, urging people to prepare for the Messiah's coming.

John's ministry took place in the wilderness, a setting that evokes the prophetic tradition and symbolizes a return to purity and renewal. In Luke 3:2-3, the word of God comes to John in the wilderness, and he begins proclaiming a baptism of repentance for the forgiveness of sins. His message is a direct call from God, as he boldly proclaims, "Prepare the way of the Lord, make his paths straight" (Lk 3:4). This declaration fulfills the prophecy of Isaiah, indicating that John is the herald who will announce the arrival of the Lord. John's proclamation of repentance is crucial for preparing the hearts of the people. He challenges the crowds, calling them a "brood of vipers" and warning them to produce fruits worthy of repentance (Lk 3:7-8). This echoes the confrontational style of the Old Testament prophets, who often rebuked the Israelites for their unfaithfulness and called them back to God.

Moreover, John's role as a messenger of God is validated by Jesus himself. In Matthew 11:9-10, Jesus describes John as more than a prophet and identifies him as the one about whom it is written, "I will send my messenger ahead of you, who will prepare your way before you." This recognition by Jesus not only underscores John's importance but also affirms his divine commission to prepare the people for the Messiah.[22] According to the Gospel of Luke, John the Baptist's mission was to prepare the way for Jesus, the long-awaited Messiah. This role as a forerunner underscored John's significance in the unfolding narrative of salvation. His identification of Jesus as the Messiah and his act of baptizing Jesus were pivotal moments that marked the beginning of Jesus' public ministry. John's ministry set the

---

[22] Dorothy Kelley Patterson, Rhonda Kelley, and Rhonda Harrington Kelley, *Women's Evangelical Commentary: New Testament* (Nashville, TN: B&H Publishing Group, 2011), 86.

stage for Jesus' message and mission, aligning with the prophetic tradition of preparing the people for a new covenant with God.[23]

John's proclamation that Jesus was the "Lamb of God who takes away the sin of the world" highlighted his recognition of Jesus' redemptive role. This identification was a profound declaration that connected Jesus' ministry to the sacrificial system of the Temple and the broader narrative of salvation in Jewish theology. By baptizing Jesus, John affirmed the validity and importance of Jesus' mission, and his own ministry was seen as the necessary precursor to the advent of the Messiah.

6. The Message of John the Baptist

The message of John the Baptist, as depicted in the Gospel of Luke, serves as a clarion call for transformation and renewal in a world that desperately needed it. His ministry is characterized by a passionate plea for repentance, ethical living, and an urgent proclamation of the coming Kingdom of God. John's call to repentance (Lk 3:3) is not merely an invitation to feel remorse for sins but a comprehensive demand for a radical change of heart and behavior, signaling a new beginning for individuals and the community.

Moreover, John's ethical teachings and exhortations (Lk 3:10-14) provide practical guidance for those seeking to align their lives with God's will. By addressing the moral dilemmas faced by various groups, including the crowds, tax collectors, and soldiers, he highlights the importance of justice, compassion, and integrity in everyday life. This emphasis on ethical conduct is a crucial aspect of John's ministry, reflecting his deep concern for social righteousness and the well-being of the marginalized.

Finally, John's proclamation of the coming Kingdom (Lk 3:15-17) encapsulates the essence of his message, heralding a time when God's reign would be fully realized. He prepares the way for Jesus, underscoring the imminent arrival of the Messiah who would bring hope, salvation, and the promise of a transformed world. Together, these elements of John's message not only frame his ministry but also resonate with the core themes of the Gospel, calling believers to embrace a life of repentance, ethical responsibility, and anticipation of God's Kingdom.

6.1. Call to Repentance (Lk 3:3)

In Judaism, prophets were regarded as individuals who received a divine calling directly from God. This calling was often experienced through visions, dreams, or a profound sense of God's presence and message. These divine encounters were pivotal moments that marked the beginning of their prophetic mission. For instance, Isaiah's vision of God in the temple,

[23] W. Barnes Tatum, *John the Baptist and Jesus: A Report of the Jesus Seminar* (Santa Rosa, CA: Polebridge Press, 1994), 80.

described in Isaiah 6, where he sees the Lord sitting on a throne, high and lifted up, is a classic example of a prophetic call. Similarly, the call of Jeremiah in Jeremiah 1:4-10 depicts God directly speaking to Jeremiah, appointing him as a prophet before he was born.

These divine callings were not merely personal experiences but were understood as authoritative commissions from God. The prophets felt compelled to deliver God's messages to the people, often despite personal reluctance or fear. Moses, for example, initially resisted his calling, expressing doubt about his ability to speak effectively. Yet, his encounter with God at the burning bush (Exodus 3-4) was a transformative moment that solidified his role as a prophet and leader of Israel.[24] The divine calling of prophets underscored their role as intermediaries between God and humanity. They were entrusted with communicating God's will and purposes, often in times of crisis or moral decline. This divine mandate gave their words weight and authority, demanding attention and response from their audiences.

6.2. Ethical Teachings and Exhortations (Lk 3:10-14)

Prophets were often known for their uncompromising commitment to moral and ethical values. They spoke out against social injustices, corruption, and moral decay within society, challenging the status quo and calling for a return to righteous living. The prophet Amos, for example, vehemently condemned the exploitation of the poor and the perversion of justice (Amos 2:6-7). He denounced the wealthy who amassed riches at the expense of the needy and called for justice to "roll on like a river, righteousness like a never-failing stream" (Amos 5:24).

Prophets like Micah also highlighted ethical behavior as integral to true worship of God. Micah 6:8 succinctly summarizes this prophetic ethic: "He has shown you, O mortal, what is good. And what does the Lord require of you? To act justly and to love mercy and to walk humbly with your God." This call to justice, mercy, and humility was a recurring theme in prophetic literature and underscored the belief that true piety was demonstrated through ethical conduct and social responsibility.[25] The commitment of prophets to moral and ethical values often put them at odds with the ruling elites and societal norms. Their fearless critique of injustice and corruption made them both revered and reviled figures. Yet, their unwavering dedication to these

---

[24] Daniel S. Dapaah, *The Relationship Between John the Baptist and Jesus of Nazareth: A Critical Study* (University Press of America, 2005), 77.

[25] Roberto Martinez, *The Question of John the Baptist and Jesus' Indictment of the Religious Leaders: A Critical Analysis of Luke 7:18-35* (Cambridge: James Clarke & Company Limited, 2012), 176.

principles reinforced their credibility and authority as true spokespeople for God.[26]

John the Baptist's lifestyle was a stark rejection of the prevailing culture of excess and extravagance. By choosing to abstain from luxurious foods and a comfortable lifestyle, he presented a powerful countercultural message that genuine spirituality and righteousness did not depend on material wealth or indulgence. In a society where the elite indulged in opulence and excess, John's simple diet of locusts and wild honey (Matthew 3:4) was a deliberate contrast. This rejection of luxury was a direct critique of the societal values that equated wealth with divine favor and moral superiority. John's lifestyle challenged these assumptions, demonstrating that true spiritual authority and righteousness were found in humility, simplicity, and devotion to God. His ascetic practices underscored the idea that spiritual wealth was far more valuable than material wealth, and that one's worth was not determined by external possessions but by internal virtue and faithfulness to God.

Prophets in Judaism were primarily seen as messengers of God, conveying His words and will to the people. Their messages varied but commonly included calls to repentance, warnings of impending judgment, and promises of future blessings. The content of their messages was directly linked to the current spiritual and moral state of the community. When the people strayed from God's commandments, prophets like Amos and Hosea issued stern warnings about the consequences of their disobedience, emphasizing the need for repentance and a return to covenantal faithfulness. This role as messengers placed prophets in a unique and often challenging position within society. They were tasked with delivering difficult and sometimes unwelcome truths. For instance, the prophet Nathan confronted King David about his sin with Bathsheba and the murder of Uriah (2 Samuel 12). This act required immense courage, as prophets risked their lives and reputations to deliver God's messages.[27]

Furthermore, prophets were not merely passive conduits of divine messages; they were deeply invested in the spiritual well-being of the people. They often interceded on behalf of the people, pleading with God for mercy and forgiveness. This dual role of messenger and intercessor highlighted their deep commitment to their divine mission and their compassion for their community.

---

[26] Brian C. Dennert, *John the Baptist and the Jewish Setting of Matthew* (Mohr Siebeck, 2015), 49.

[27] Amy-Jill Levine, Dale C. Allison Jr, and John Dominic Crossan, *The Historical Jesus in Context* (Princeton, NJ: Princeton University Press, 2009), 56.

6.3. The Proclamation of the Coming Kingdom (Lk 3:15-17)

John the Baptist's central message was the announcement that the "kingdom of God" or the "kingdom of heaven" was at hand. This proclamation was charged with eschatological urgency, urging people to prepare for the imminent arrival of God's rule. The concept of the kingdom of God was deeply embedded in Jewish eschatological expectations, often associated with the restoration of Israel, the establishment of justice, and the renewal of creation. John's proclamation of the "kingdom of God" or the "kingdom of heaven" presented an alternative vision of sovereignty that stood in stark contrast to Roman imperial authority. This message implied that God's kingdom was superior to any earthly empire, including the Roman Empire. In this alternative vision, true justice, peace, and righteousness would be established under God's rule, challenging the legitimacy and moral authority of the Roman rulers.

John's message called for immediate action: repentance and righteous living. He depicted the coming kingdom as a decisive intervention by God in human history, which required a moral and spiritual reformation from those who wished to be part of it. This call to repentance was not merely a personal moral exhortation but a communal call to reorient the entire society towards God's will. The imagery John used—such as the axe laid to the root of the trees and the winnowing fork separating the wheat from the chaff—emphasized the urgency and inevitability of the coming judgment.

7. Baptism and the Symbolism of Water

John's practice of baptism in the Jordan River was a central element of his ministry, carrying profound symbolic meaning within the Jewish tradition of ritual purification. In Judaism, immersion in water was a common practice for achieving ritual purity, especially in preparation for religious activities and festivals. However, John's baptism went beyond the traditional purification rites. It was an outward sign of an inward transformation, a call to repentance and a symbolic cleansing of sin in anticipation of the coming Messiah.[28]

The act of baptism signified a break from the past and a readiness to embrace a new way of life. By calling people to be baptized, John emphasized the necessity of moral and spiritual renewal as a prerequisite for participating in the forthcoming kingdom of God. The Jordan River, with its historical associations with the entry into the Promised Land, added a layer of significance to the ritual. It represented a crossing over into a new phase of spiritual existence, mirroring the Israelites' journey from slavery in Egypt

[28] Unknown Hebrew, *Symbolic Meaning of Water Baptism* (Unknown Hebrew, 2019). Cf. also Mark A. Kramer, *A Stir in the Waters* (Maitland, FL: Xulon Press, 2011), 228.

to freedom in the Promised Land. For John's followers, baptism in the Jordan was a powerful act of faith and commitment to the impending divine order.

John's call for repentance and baptism represented a significant break with established religious practices. Traditionally, ritual purity in Judaism was largely attained through Temple rituals and the observance of purity laws, including the use of mikvehs. However, John's baptism was a radical departure from these norms. It emphasized personal repentance and a transformative encounter with God over ritualistic observance. By advocating for baptism in the Jordan River, John highlighted the necessity of a personal commitment to spiritual renewal. This act of baptism was a public declaration of repentance and a symbolic cleansing from sin, signifying a new beginning and readiness to participate in the coming kingdom of God. It challenged the notion that purity could be achieved solely through traditional Temple practices and instead underscored the importance of an inner, spiritual transformation.

John's emphasis on baptism as a means of preparing for the coming Messiah also reflected a broader eschatological theme. It was a call to break with the past and embrace a new era of divine intervention and renewal. This message resonated deeply with those who felt disenfranchised by the existing religious structures and were yearning for a more direct and personal experience of God's grace and forgiveness. Through his call for baptism, John redefined the concept of purity and repentance, making it more accessible and immediate. His message was a powerful invitation to all who sought to align themselves with God's impending kingdom, emphasizing that true purity and readiness for the Messiah required an inward change of heart and mind.[29]

In summary, John the Baptist's ministry emerged within a historical and religious context characterized by Roman dominion, a mosaic of Jewish sects, Messianic expectations, and a complex interplay of religious traditions. His message of repentance, baptism, and preparation for the imminent kingdom resonated profoundly with the prophetic tradition and the hopes and anxieties of his era. John's pivotal role as a precursor to Jesus and his influence on early Christianity make his ministry a momentous chapter in the annals of religion and spirituality. John the Baptist's use of baptism as a ritual of cleansing and preparation stands as a powerful symbolic action within the prophetic tradition. Baptism, as practiced by John, was a public demonstration of an inner transformation and a preparatory act for the coming Messiah.[30]

---

[29] Robin Jensen, *Living Water: Images, Symbols, and Settings of Early Christian Baptism* (Leiden: Brill, 2010), 82.

[30] Clare K. Rothschild, *Baptist Traditions and Q* (Tübingen: Mohr Siebeck, 2005).

The act of baptism carried deep symbolic meaning. In Jewish tradition, water rites were associated with purification and the removal of ritual impurities. John's baptism, however, went beyond ritual purity, signifying a profound moral and spiritual cleansing. By immersing themselves in the waters of the Jordan River, individuals were not only seeking forgiveness for their sins but also publicly committing to a life of repentance and ethical renewal. John's choice of the Jordan River as the site for baptism is also symbolically significant. The Jordan River held historical and spiritual importance for the Israelites, being the river that Joshua and the Israelites crossed to enter the Promised Land. By conducting baptisms in the Jordan, John evoked the memory of a new beginning and a divine transition, symbolizing the entry into a renewed relationship with God.[31]

This symbolic act of baptism was closely tied to the prophetic tradition. Prophets often used symbolic actions to convey their messages. For instance, Jeremiah's wearing of a yoke symbolized the coming Babylonian captivity (Jeremiah 27:2), and Ezekiel's act of lying on his side for an extended period symbolized the siege of Jerusalem (Ezekiel 4:4-8). Similarly, John's baptism visually represented the inner transformation and purification necessary for receiving the Messiah. Moreover, baptism as practiced by John prefigured the Christian sacrament of baptism. Jesus himself was baptized by John, an event that marked the beginning of his public ministry and affirmed the significance of John's symbolic act. In Christian tradition, baptism became a sacrament that signifies entry into the faith, purification from sin, and the reception of the Holy Spirit, carrying forward the symbolic richness of John's prophetic baptism.

In summary, John the Baptist's ministry can be viewed as a continuation of the prophetic tradition within Judaism. He embodied the characteristics of a prophet, from his divine calling to his role as a messenger of God, champion of moral values, advocate for repentance, and his use of symbolic actions. John's ministry was rooted in the rich heritage of Jewish prophecy, and his message paved the way for the arrival of Jesus, whom he identified as the long-awaited Messiah. Through his prophetic ministry, John played a significant role in shaping the religious landscape of his time.

8. The Call to an Alternative Lifestyle

Repentance was a central theme in the messages of the prophets. They called on the people to turn away from sinful behaviors, seek forgiveness, and return to a faithful relationship with God. This call to repentance was not just about individual moral failings but addressed communal and systemic

[31] Stephen Kuhrt and Gordon Kuhrt, *Believing in Baptism: Understanding and Living God's Covenant Sign* (London: Bloomsbury Publishing, 2020), 141.

sin. Prophets like Joel called for a communal response to sin, urging the people to rend their hearts and not their garments and return to the Lord with fasting, weeping, and mourning (Joel 2:12-13). The prophetic call to repentance often involved a stark warning of the consequences of continued disobedience. Jeremiah, for example, warned the people of Judah about the impending destruction of Jerusalem and their exile to Babylon if they did not repent and turn back to God (Jeremiah 25:1-11). These warnings were meant to provoke a sense of urgency and the necessity of immediate action to avert disaster.[32]

However, the prophets also offered hope and the promise of restoration upon repentance. Isaiah spoke of a future where the people would be redeemed and restored to their land (Isaiah 40:1-5). This message of hope was integral to the prophetic call to repentance, providing assurance that God's mercy and forgiveness were available to those who sincerely turned back to Him.[33] At the heart of John the Baptist's ministry was a call to repentance, a central theme that underscored his message and mission. Repentance, in the biblical context, involves a profound transformation of heart and mind, turning away from sin and towards God. John's baptism of repentance for the forgiveness of sins was a tangible expression of this call (Lk 3:3).

John's message was urgent and compelling, as he proclaimed, "Repent, for the kingdom of heaven is at hand!" (Matthew 3:2). This proclamation highlights the immediacy of his message, urging people to prepare themselves for the coming of the Messiah. John's baptism was not just a symbolic act but a radical call for individuals to reorient their lives and embrace a new way of living in anticipation of the Messiah's arrival. The act of baptism itself was a powerful symbol of repentance and purification. In Jewish tradition, ritual washing symbolized cleansing from impurity, and John's use of baptism built on this practice, infusing it with a new meaning. By immersing themselves in the waters of baptism, individuals publicly demonstrated their commitment to repent and seek forgiveness. John's baptism was a preparatory rite, emphasizing the need for spiritual readiness and moral renewal.[34]

John's call to repentance was inclusive and far-reaching, addressing various groups within society. He admonished the crowds to bear fruits worthy of repentance, warning them not to rely on their Abrahamic lineage for salvation (Lk 3:8). This challenge emphasized that true repentance required

---

[32] Robert A. Stein, *Luke: An Exegetical and Theological Exposition of Holy Scripture* (Nashville, TN: B&H Publishing Group, 1993), 132.

[33] Telford Work, *Living and Active: Scripture in the Economy of Salvation* (Grand Rapids, MI: Wm. B. Eerdmans Publishing, 2004), 98, 118.

[34] Kevin W. Irwin, *Sunday Worship, a Planning Guide to Celebration* (Boulder, CO: Pueblo Publishing Company, 1983), 340.

genuine transformation, not just external compliance or ancestral heritage.[35] Furthermore, John's call to repentance paved the way for Jesus' ministry. Jesus began his public ministry by echoing John's message, "Repent, for the kingdom of heaven is near" (Matthew 4:17). This continuity highlights the foundational role of John's ministry in preparing the people for Jesus' message and mission.

8.1. John's Critique of Societal Norms and Religious Practices

John the Baptist stood as a champion of moral values in a society riddled with corruption and moral decay. His fearless confrontation of sin, regardless of the social status of the offenders, highlights his commitment to upholding divine standards of righteousness and justice. One of the most notable instances of John's moral courage is his denunciation of King Herod's marriage to Herodias, his brother's wife. This union was not only unlawful according to Jewish law but also morally reprehensible. John's public rebuke of Herod's actions (Lk 3:19) exemplifies his role as a prophet who does not shy away from condemning sin, even when it involves powerful figures. His courage in calling out Herod's immorality eventually led to his imprisonment and martyrdom, underscoring the high cost of his commitment to truth and righteousness.

John's critique extended beyond the powerful elite to ordinary people, including tax collectors and soldiers, who were often seen as corrupt and abusive. In Lk 3:12-14, tax collectors and soldiers come to John asking what they should do to align with his call for repentance. John's responses are practical and ethical: he tells tax collectors to collect no more than what is owed and soldiers to refrain from extortion and be content with their wages. These instructions reflect a deep concern for social justice and fairness, advocating for a moral society where individuals act justly and honorably in their everyday lives.

John's call for moral integrity resonates with the prophetic tradition, where prophets like Amos, Isaiah, and Micah vehemently opposed social injustice and called for a return to righteous living. By addressing the ethical failings of his contemporaries, John positioned himself as a moral arbiter, urging society to align with God's standards.

8.2. The Ethical Demands of John's Teachings

John the Baptist's emphasis on ritual immersion or baptism can be best understood within the context of Jewish purity laws. In Judaism, achieving ritual purity was essential for maintaining a proper relationship with God, particularly before participating in religious rites and Temple worship.

---

[35] Robert H. Stein, *Luke* (Nashville, TN: B&H Publishing Group, 1992), 132.

The practice of immersion in a mikveh, a ritual bath, was a key element of these purity laws, symbolizing cleansing from impurity and sin. Baptism, as practiced by John, was an adaptation of this traditional Jewish practice. It involved immersion in the Jordan River and signified a public declaration of repentance and a commitment to a renewed way of life. This act of baptism was a profound ritual symbolizing spiritual cleansing and preparation for the coming kingdom of God. Unlike the regular purifications required by Jewish law, John's baptism was a one-time event marking a decisive break with the past and a readiness to embrace the new era heralded by the Messiah.

John's call for baptism challenged the conventional reliance on the Temple rituals for achieving purity. It emphasized the necessity of personal repentance and moral transformation as prerequisites for participating in the anticipated Messianic age. By promoting baptism as a means of preparing for the coming kingdom, John was calling the people to a deeper, more personal engagement with their faith and a sincere commitment to live in accordance with God's will.[36] John's choice of clothing and lifestyle resonated with the poor and marginalized segments of society. His attire and practices were devoid of ostentation, making him relatable to those who felt marginalized by the religious and political elites of his time. By wearing simple, humble clothing and living an ascetic lifestyle, John demonstrated a solidarity with those who were often overlooked and oppressed. His message of repentance and renewal was inclusive, addressing the spiritual needs of all people, regardless of their social status.[37]

John's clothing and appearance communicated a powerful message of detachment from worldly concerns. By adopting a minimalist lifestyle, he demonstrated the value of detachment from material possessions and the pursuit of a deeper, more meaningful connection with God. This message of detachment was not just about rejecting material wealth but about prioritizing spiritual values over earthly concerns. John's lifestyle was a living testimony to the importance of focusing on one's relationship with God and preparing for the coming of the Messiah.

8.3. The Radical Nature of the Alternative Lifestyle Proposed by John

John the Baptist's decision to live in the wilderness was a direct rejection of the excesses and materialism associated with urban life. This choice exemplified his countercultural message that true spirituality and righteousness did not depend on wealth or luxury. In the context of a society

[36] James F. McGrath, *John of History, Baptist of Faith: The Quest for the Historical Baptizer* (Grand Rapids, MI: Wm. B. Eerdmans Publishing, 2024) and J. Ian H. McDonald, *The Crucible of Christian Morality* (New York: Routledge, 2016), 87.

[37] J. Ramsey Michaels, *Servant and Son: Jesus in Parable and Gospel* (Eugene, OR: Wipf and Stock Publishers, 2017), 12.

where the elite flaunted their wealth and indulged in opulence, John's austere lifestyle in the wilderness served as a powerful critique of these values.[38] By adopting a simple and ascetic way of life, John demonstrated that spiritual integrity and closeness to God were not tied to material possessions or social status.[39] His lifestyle was a stark reminder that genuine spirituality required humility, simplicity, and a focus on inner moral values rather than outward displays of wealth. This countercultural stance resonated deeply with the common people, who often found themselves marginalized by the societal structures that favored the rich and powerful.

9. John's Interaction with Various Groups

John the Baptist was a pivotal figure in the New Testament, known for his role as the forerunner of Jesus Christ. His message of repentance and preparation for the coming Messiah drew large crowds from all walks of life. In Luke 3, John's interactions with various groups—ranging from the common people to tax collectors, soldiers, religious leaders, and even Herod—highlight his boldness in calling for moral transformation.[40] Through these encounters, John challenged individuals to live out genuine repentance, addressing both personal and systemic injustices while preparing the way for the coming Kingdom of God.

9.1. The Response of the Crowds (Lk 3:7-9)

John's message to the crowds was direct and confrontational. He did not shy away from addressing their sinful condition and calling them to repentance. **Harsh Address**: John calls the people a "brood of vipers" (v. 7), warning them about their hypocrisy and complacency. The imagery of vipers evokes danger and deceit, implying that the people were in spiritual danger and needed genuine transformation.[41] **Warning Against Superficial Repentance**: John challenges the crowd not to rely on their lineage as children of Abraham (v. 8). He emphasizes that true repentance is shown through a change in behavior, not just through ancestry or religious affiliation. He tells them to "bear fruits in keeping with repentance," calling for visible moral transformation in their lives.[42] **Urgent Call for Repentance**: John speaks of

---

[38] Robert L. Webb, *John the Baptizer and Prophet: A Sociohistorical Study* (Eugene, OR: Wipf and Stock Publishers, 2006), 358.

[39] David P. Gushee, *The Moral Teachings of Jesus: Radical Instruction in the Will of God* (Eugene, OR: Wipf and Stock Publishers, 2024), 4.

[40] Brian C. Dennert, *John the Baptist and the Jewish Setting of Matthew* (Tübingen: Mohr Siebeck, 2015).

[41] Matthias Wenk, *Community-Forming Power*, 177.

[42] John F. Walvoord and Roy B. Zuck, *The Bible Knowledge Commentary Gospels* (Colorado Springs, CO: David C Cook, 2018), 48.

judgment using the metaphor of an ax already at the root of the trees (v. 9). This imagery conveys the immediacy of the coming judgment. If the people do not repent, they will face the same fate as trees that do not produce good fruit – they will be cut down and thrown into the fire, symbolizing divine judgment.[43]

A. Interaction with Tax Collectors and Soldiers (Lk 3:12-14)

John's interactions with specific groups within the crowd, like tax collectors and soldiers, provide insight into his practical guidance on what repentance looks like. **Tax Collectors**: Tax collectors were notorious for their corruption, often collecting more than what was required and profiting from the surplus. When they ask, "Teacher, what shall we do?" (v. 12), John's response is straightforward: "Collect no more than what you are authorized to do" (v. 13). His instruction directly addresses the injustice associated with their profession. John's call to honesty and fairness reflects his broader message of moral integrity.

Soldiers: Similarly, soldiers, who likely served as enforcers of the Roman occupation, ask John what they should do. His response is: "Do not extort money from anyone by threats or by false accusation, and be content with your wages" (v. 14). This addresses their potential misuse of power, warning them against using intimidation for personal gain. John's guidance here calls for contentment and ethical behavior, even in positions of authority and influence. **Repentance as Practical Action**: In both cases, John's response moves beyond spiritual platitudes and into the realm of practical ethics. Repentance, for John, involves real-world changes in behavior that reflect justice, fairness, and humility.

9.2. Confrontation with Religious Leaders and Herod (Lk 3:19-20)

John's prophetic ministry inevitably brought him into conflict with both religious leaders and political authorities. **Critique of Religious Leaders**: While not detailed in Luke 3, John's confrontational attitude towards religious leaders (like the Pharisees and Sadducees) is more fully documented in other Gospel accounts (e.g., Matthew 3:7). He rebukes them for their external piety and lack of internal transformation. This critique echoes his call for genuine repentance and his rejection of those who rely solely on religious status. **Confrontation with Herod**: Luke mentions John's rebuke of **Herod the tetrarch** (v. 19-20). John publicly denounces Herod's immoral behavior, particularly his marriage to Herodias, his brother's wife. This act of calling out a ruler's personal sins was bold and dangerous, but it highlights John's role as a prophet who speaks truth to power, regardless

[43] Tucker S. Ferda, *Jesus, the Gospels, and the Galilean Crisis* (London: Bloomsbury Publishing, 2018), 170.

of the consequences. **Imprisonment and Its Aftermath**: Herod's response to John's bold proclamation was to have him imprisoned (v. 20). This marks the beginning of John's eventual martyrdom, but also signifies the cost of being a prophetic voice in a world resistant to moral correction. John's unwavering commitment to truth, even at great personal risk, serves as a model of prophetic courage.[44]

In Luke 3, we see John the Baptist engaging with different groups—crowds, tax collectors, soldiers, religious leaders, and rulers—challenging each to genuine repentance in ways that address their specific contexts. **His message was consistent:** repentance must result in ethical transformation and righteous living, and no one was exempt from this call. John's interactions reveal his role as a prophet who not only announced the coming of the Messiah but also called the people to prepare their hearts by living out God's justice and mercy.

10. The Impact of John's Ministry

John's choice to live an ascetic life in the wilderness can also be interpreted as a form of resistance against the Roman colonial powers. By rejecting the material comforts and luxuries associated with urban life under Roman influence, John distanced himself from the values and practices imposed by the colonial rulers. His ascetic lifestyle was a statement of independence and defiance, embodying a commitment to spiritual and moral principles over conformity to the dominant culture.[45] John's asceticism underscored his message of repentance and the coming kingdom of God. It highlighted the need for personal and collective transformation, emphasizing that true liberation and justice could only be achieved through a return to spiritual purity and a rejection of worldly corruption. This message of inner renewal and divine sovereignty was a powerful counter-narrative to the Roman Empire's claims of power and legitimacy.[46] John's message of the coming kingdom of God was inherently subversive. It suggested that the existing political and social order, dominated by Roman power, was temporary and would ultimately be replaced by a divine order. This vision offered hope to the oppressed and marginalized, promising a future where God's justice would prevail over human corruption and tyranny.[47]

---

[44] Allison A. Trites and William J. Larkin, *Luke, Acts* (Carol Stream, IL: Tyndale House, 2016), 66.

[45] Michael R. Licona, *Why Are There Differences in the Gospels?: What We Can Learn from Ancient Biography* (Oxford: Oxford University Press, 2016), 123.

[46] Kent L. Yinger, *The Pharisees: Their History, Character, and New Testament Portrait* (Eugene, OR: Wipf and Stock Publishers, 2022), 125.

[47] Thomas R. Schreiner, Shawn Wright, and E. Ray Clendenen, *Believer's Baptism: Sign of the New Covenant in Christ* (Nashville, TN: B&H Publishing Group, 2007), 27.

John the Baptist's message of repentance and his ascetic lifestyle can be viewed through an anti-colonial lens in the context of Roman rule in Judea. While the Gospels do not explicitly frame John's message as anti-colonial, his emphasis on repentance, justice, and the coming kingdom of God carried implicit challenges to the oppressive colonial powers of his time.[48] John's call to repentance was not merely a call for personal moral renewal but also carried an element of resistance against the Roman imperial presence. By urging people to turn away from sinful ways, John indirectly critiqued the moral decay associated with the Roman occupation. The Roman authorities were often seen as corrupt and unjust, exploiting the local population for their gain. John's message of repentance, therefore, also implied a call to reject the corrupt practices and injustices perpetuated by the colonial rulers.

Summary of Findings

In summary, John the Baptist's choice to live in the wilderness and his ascetic lifestyle were a direct rejection of the excesses and materialism of urban life. His countercultural message and emphasis on repentance, justice, and the coming kingdom of God carried implicit challenges to the oppressive Roman colonial powers. John's call to repentance can be seen as a form of resistance against the moral decay associated with the Roman occupation, while his proclamation of the kingdom of God presented an alternative vision of sovereignty that subverted Roman imperial authority. Through his life and message, John the Baptist embodied a powerful critique of the existing political and social order, calling for a return to spiritual integrity and divine justice.

The ministry of John the Baptist, as presented in the Gospel of Luke, serves as a pivotal moment in the narrative of salvation history, bridging the Old and New Testaments. His prophetic call for repentance and the establishment of an alternative lifestyle resonate deeply with the socio-political and religious dynamics of first-century Judea. As a figure who emerges amidst a turbulent backdrop marked by Roman oppression and religious fragmentation, John embodies the long-awaited prophetic voice that the Jewish people had been yearning for. His role as the forerunner to Jesus not only highlights the continuity of God's redemptive plan but also emphasizes the transformative nature of the message he proclaimed.

John's emphasis on repentance reflects a profound understanding of the human condition, calling individuals to a radical reorientation of their lives toward God. His ethical teachings, urging acts of compassion, honesty, and contentment, challenge societal norms and religious complacency. By

[48] Mike Licona, *Why Are There Differences in the Gospels?: What We Can Learn from Ancient Biography* (Oxford: Oxford University Press, 2017).

critiquing the moral decay prevalent among both the populace and religious leaders, John sets the stage for a radical shift in understanding what it means to live a life aligned with God's will. His message demands not merely an external adherence to religious rituals but a deep, inner transformation that manifests in tangible acts of justice and mercy.

Moreover, John's use of baptism as a symbolic act of purification underscores the urgency of his call for a renewed relationship with God. The imagery of water in his baptism signifies not only cleansing from sin but also the promise of new life—a theme that finds its fulfillment in the ministry of Jesus. Through his interactions with various groups, including the crowds, tax collectors, soldiers, and religious leaders, John demonstrates the inclusivity of his message while also confronting the injustices embedded in the structures of society.

The impact of John's ministry extends beyond his lifetime, laying a crucial foundation for the work of Jesus and the early Christian movement. His call to an alternative lifestyle, characterized by a commitment to justice, community, and authentic faith, continues to resonate with contemporary audiences. In an age where societal values often prioritize individualism and materialism, John's message remains a clarion call to embrace a life rooted in humility, service, and radical love. Ultimately, the ministry of John the Baptist serves as a powerful reminder of the transformative potential inherent in repentance and the ongoing relevance of prophetic voices in the pursuit of justice and truth in our world today.

3

Recent Studies on Luke's Gospel An Overview and Critique[1]

Introduction

The Gospel of Luke is an interesting area of study in the New Testament for the various issues in it and the profound literature, which are published in this area of study. Over the years, scholars have analyzed the Gospel of Luke from various precincts of studies such as the thematic study, methodological analysis and other issues like Luke the historian/ theologian and so on. The growing interest to study the Gospel of Luke is its unity with Acts and its theology and the social world of Luke-Acts that highlights the social dimensions of the first century Mediterranean world. This paper tries to survey the theological works on the Gospel of Luke that appeared 1950-2008. The starting point is 1950s, for this, it represents a turning point in the study of the Gospel of Luke. In 1961, C. K. Barrett said that 'recent years have witnessed a revolution in the Lukan studies.'[2] After five years, W. C. van Unnik, called Luke-Acts as 'a storm center in contemporary scholarship,' and interpretation, continued to present substantial complexities

---

1 cf. Jayasree Jerald, "Recent Studies on Luke's Gospel: An Overview and Critique" SATHRI Journal, 2013.

2 C. K. Barrett, *Luke the Historian in Recent Study* (London: The Epworth Press, 1961), 50.

for interpretation.[3] His observation holds until today and the studies on Lk-Acts have grown much more in depth and wide. It can be seen in François Bovon's, *Luke the Theologian: Fifty-Five Years of Research* (1950–2005), second edition[4] which provides the recent definitive and near-exhaustive critical discussion of scholarship on Lk-Acts from 1950-2005 and covers some seven hundred pages of summaries and assessments on Lk.

Hans Conzelmann's *Die Mitte der Zeit* (1953) which was translated into English under the title *The Theology of St. Lk*[5] (1960) would be marked as the turning point in the recent Lukan Scholarship. According to Joseph A. Fitzmyer, four German scholars, Martin Dibelius, Hans Conzelmann, Ernst Haenchen and Philipp Vielhauer have contributed most to the recent radical critical approach to Luke-Acts. All their works on Luke-Acts appeared in the 1950s. If these scholars were considered as the pioneers of recent scholarship in Luke-Acts then it would be plausible to say the recent scholarship in Lukan studies started in the 1950s. This paper tries to overview some of the scholarship, which takes the Gospel of Luke into consideration. The primary focus of the studies in 1950s was the theology of Gospel of Luke, later it shifted from Luke the historian to the point of view of Luke the theologian. The studies have been done from feminist perspective and from the sociological perspective analyzing the role of various elements in the Gospel of Luke. It is also important to note in the beginning of this paper itself that it is not possible to swim through all the works on the Gospel of Luke. This paper gives an overview of the literature and at the end of each of the works, a critique is added. The whole paper is divided into five sections as (1). 1950-1969, (2). 1970-1979, (3). 1980-1989, (4). 1990-1999 and (5). 2000-2008 and discusses the works published within those years. The concluding remarks give a survey of some more works that were not included in the detailed overview of the literature on the Gospel of Luke.

1. 1950-1969

1.1. Hans Conzelmann (1953)

No one who makes a serious study of Luke can ignore the work of Hans Conzelmann. His work was the turning point in the study of Luke's Gospel. In 1953, Hans Conzelmann published *Die Mitte der Zeit, which*

[3] W. C. van Unnik, "Lk-Acts, a Storm Center in Contemporary Scholarship," *Studies in Lk-Acts,* edited by Leander E. Keck and J. Louis Martyn (London: SPCK, 1966), 18.

[4] François Bovon, *Luke the Theologian: Fifty-Five Years of Research (1950–2005),* 2nd edition (Waco: Baylor University Press, 2006).

[5] Hans Conzelmann, *The Theology of St. Luke,* tr. by Geoffrey Buswell (London: Faber and Faber, 1961).

was translated into English under the title *The Theology of St. Luke*[6] (1960). This was divided into five major parts. *Part one*-Geographical Elements in Composition of Luke's Gospel, which is divided into two parts, the prologue of John the Baptist and the course of Jesus' ministry in Galilee and the journey to Jerusalem. In *part two* Luke's Eschatology is discussed with the problem, Luke and *eschaton* with summary. *Part three*-God and Redemptive History, discusses the situation of the church in the world, the rule of God in redemptive history in determining, planning and electing the people of God and the Past, Israel, scripture and world history. In *part four*, the center of History which Jesus Christ, his relation to God, history and life of Jesus is studied. *Part five*-Man and Salvation: the Church, discusses the growth of the church and its message and man as the recipient of salvation.

Conzelmann argues that Luke divides the time between creation and *parousia* into three epochs (p.16); first, the period of Israel, that is the Law and the prophets which is concluded with John the Baptist (p.101). Second, the period of Jesus' ministry, this is characterized by the absence of Satan. "When Jesus was alive, was the time of salvation; Satan was far away, it is a time without temptation (cf. Luke 4:13 with 22:3)" (p.101); third, is the period of the church, that is "The period since the Ascension, on earth the period of the *ecclesia pressa*, during which the virtue of patience is required, and it is possible, by virtue of looking back to the period of Jesus, also to looking forward to the parousia" (p.16f). The period of Jesus and the period of the Church are represented as two distinct, but systematically interrelated epochs" (p.14). According to Conzelmann, "Luke is confronted by the situation in which the Church finds herself by the delay of Parousia and her existence in secular history" (p.14).

Conzelmann's study on Luke brought out a fresh understanding on Luke's theology. According to him, Luke was no more a historian but a theologian. Conzelmann had theologized the history. This is one of the serious flaws of his study. History is always written from some perspectives. Thus, one can be both a historian and a theologian at the same time. If Luke was the first Christian writer who has understood the delay of *Parousia* and the continuation of the church in the world, as Conzelmann argues, then Luke would be a first-rate historian, hence, he wrote history from a theological perspective. Socio-scientific criticism has shown how meticulously Luke recorded the social milieu of the first century Mediterranean world. Conzelmann underplays the individual spirituality. Conzelmann's approach shows how theological message can be brought out from the Gospel of Luke. This seminal work is a guide for theological studies in Luke.

---

[6] Hans Conzelmann, *The Theology of St. Luke,* tr. by Geoffrey Buswell (London: Faber and Faber, 1961).

1.2. C. K. Barrett (1961)

C. K. Barrett's, *Luke the Historian in Recent Study*[7] is the lecture which is an answer to a major question 'who is Luke, the historian?' and few supplementary questions, What made Luke a historian to write the story of Christianity from the birth of Jesus to Paul's mission to Rome? How is his work affected by the example of older historians? What was his attitude to the theological problems of his day? What did he set out to achieve in his two volumes? What are the lessons the 20th century church can learn from his work? This book is an examination of Luke's claim to write history. Originally, it was the lecture of Barrett on A. S. Peake Memorial Lecture at Methodist Conference of 1961. The author himself acknowledges its limitation because it is just the publication of the lecture and not a detailed monograph.

1.3. Leander E. Keck and J. Louis Martyn (1966)

Leander E. Keck and J. Louis Martyn's edited work *Studies in Luke-Acts*[8] appeared in 1966 with essays presented in honor of Paul Schubert Buckingham Professor of New Testament Criticism and Interpretation at Yale University. This edited work is divided into mainly three parts with the articles of scholars. Part 1 includes "Luke-Acts, a Storm Center in Contemporary Scholarship" by W. C. Van Unnik, "On the "Paulinism" of Acts by Philipp Vielhauer, "The Perspective of Acts" by Erwin R. Goodenough and "Interpreting Luke-Acts in a Period of Existentialist Theology" by Ulrich Wilckens.

In the second part, Henry J. Cadbury, "Four Features of Lucan Style", A. F. J. Klijn, "In search of the Original Text of Acts", Paul S. Minear, "Luke's Use of the Birth Stories", William C. Robertson, "On Preaching the Word of God (Lk 8:4-21)", Nils A. Dahl, "The Story of Abraham in Luke-Acts", C. F. D. Moule, "The Christology of Acts", Eduard Schweizer, "The Concept of the Davidic "Son of God" in Acts and Its Old Testament Background" and "Concerning the Speeches in Acts", Günther Bornkamm, "The Missionary Stance of Paul in 1 Corinthians 9 and in Acts" and Hans Conzelmann's "The Address of Paul on the Areopagus." Part three includes the following articles, "Jewish Christianity in Acts in the Light of the Qumran Scrolls" by Joseph A. Fitzmyer, "The Book of Acts as Source Material for the History of Early Christianity" by Ernst Haenchen, "Acts and the Pauline Letter Corpus" by John Knox, "Ephesians and Acts" by Ernst Kasemann and "Luke's Place in the Development of Early Christianity"

---

[7] C. K. Barrett, *Luke the Historian in Recent Study* (London: The Epworth Press, 1961).

[8] Leander E. Keck and J. Louis Martyn (ed), *Studies in Luke-Acts* (London: SPCK, 1966).

by Hans Conzelmann. Each of the articles is unique in itself. Important new understandings of the early church have been brought to light by comprehensive studies Luke-Acts. It opens up a range of stimulating approaches to the study of Luke-Acts.

1.4. Helmut Flender (1967)

Helmut Flender in *St. Luke: Theologian of Redemptive History*[9] maintains that Luke's theology is guided by "a certain dogmatic understanding" (p. 1). He holds the view that "the received tradition is built into a dogmatic framework with a resultant modification of its original meaning (p. 1)." Hence, he argues that P. Vielhauer, R. Bultmann, E. Käsemann and H. Conzelmann treated Luke "as one who has fallen from the heights of Pauline theology (p. 4)." He divided the work into three major sections. 1. The Dialectical Structure of Luke-Acts which includes the complementary parallelism in Luke-Acts, climatic parallelism and antithetical comparison. 2. The Christian Message in the world; it includes the Christological presuppositions, responsible witness in the Gospel of Luke, the Christian message and the secular order 3. Jesus Christ and History; this section includes the exaltation of Christ: The Consummation of Salvation in Heaven, Israel and the Church and the Presence of Salvation in the Community.

According to Helmut Flender, the structure of Luke-Acts is a dialectical one and Luke arranged his material in complementary, climatic and antithetical parallelism. He treats Luke as a 'Historian' but he disagrees with the school of Bultmann, which talks about "Luke's 'historization' of the Gospel message (p. 36)." According to Helmut Flender, Luke's Christology is in conformity with an early Christological tradition, which is both pre-Pauline and post-Pauline (p. 37ff). Luke's Christological framework is provided by Hellenistic pattern of the earthly and the heavenly modes of Christ's experience (p. 56). Luke begins and ends the Gospel in the Temple (Lk. 1:5-9; 24:53). Flender observes, "Jerusalem is the scene where redemptive history is fulfilled. The divine salvation is planted firmly in a definite place in history, which prevents it from evaporating into a timeless idea and preserves the humanity of the divine revelation (p. 107)."

Flender differs from Conzelmann in the identity of the Church as true Israel. There is no discontinuity between the people of God (Israel) and the church. According to Flender, the Church is continuous with 'the law and the prophets', but it also transcends them through the preaching of the kingdom of God. It is the new act of God in Christ (p. 124). In *St. Luke: Theologian of Redemptive History*, Flender takes the stand that Luke has built his theology

[9] Helmut Flender, *St. Luke: Theologian of Redemptive History*, tr. by Reginald H. and Ilse Fuller (London: SPCK, 1967).

upon the "dogmatic framework" of the early church in other words, Luke is not a creative theologian. Flender treats Luke as a historian and a theologian of the post-apostolic age. His reason to put Luke into the post-apostolic age is not convincing. Flender rejects unilinear salvation history in Luke-Acts.

1.5. Jerome Kodell (1969)

The investigation on Luke's use of the *Laos*, people/crowds is an interesting area of study. Jerome Kodell wrote the scholarly article particularly referring to the Jerusalem narrative[10] in the article titled "Luke's use of Laos, People, especially in the Jerusalem Narrative (Lk. 19:28-24:53)". The author discusses the trends of Laos-usage in Luke-Acts, the *Laos* and the leader, discordant usage of *Laos*, the use of *Laos* in Matthew, the *Laos* in the redemptive history of Luke, the Church and Israel, and Israel in the Gospel and Acts. One of the ways Luke expresses the continuity between the people of Israel and Christians is his use of *Laos* in the Jerusalem narrative of the Gospel. He does not deny the fact that the Jewish nation was guilty in the death of Jesus, but he presents the guilt as softened by ignorance and does not in the least consider the Jewish people cursed or rejected. By using *Laos* consistently means the distinction between the people and their leaders during the account of the Passion, Luke preserves the traditional biblical word and the concept behind it for further use in his narrative. It may still designate the people of God, but the people as it is now, the NT Church of Jew and Gentile. Kodell analyzed the text thoroughly and brought out the study in detail. It is a good article for any student who studies the concept of *Laos* in the Gospel of Luke.

2. 1970-1979

2.1. I. Howard Marshall (1970, 1978)

I. Howard Marshall's *Commentary on Luke: New International Greek Testament Commentary*[11] was published in 1970. According to Marshall, the Gospel of Luke was written as an historical account of the ministry of Jesus. It claims place for Christianity in history. Christ's ministry is a realized prophecy. In Luke's Gospel, Christ's message of salvation is directed to the weak, poor and needy with an emphasis on the importance of self-denial and of whole-hearted discipleship. According to Marshall, while Luke is the most conscious historian of the Gospel writers, his history is a vehicle of theological interpretation in which the significance of Jesus is expressed. In

---

[10] Jerome Kodell, 'Luke's use of Laos, People, Especially in the Jerusalem Narrative (Lk. 19:28-24: 53)', *CBQ* 31/3 (July, 1969): 327-343.

[11] I. Howard Marshall, *The Gospel of Luke: A Commentary on the Greek Text,* New International Greek Testament Commentary (Michigan: W. B. Eerdmans and Exeter: The Paternoster Press, 1978).

this book, the author calls attention to the theological message of Luke, the evangelist. It is detailed verse-by-verse exegetical study on the Greek text of the Gospel of Luke.

The introduction to the commentary is another book, which is written by Marshall, *Luke: Historian and Theologian*[12] has been divided into nine chapters. 1. The Modern Approach to Luke-Acts 2. History or Theology? 3. Luke as a Historian 4. The Theology of Salvation 5. God my Savior 6. To save the Lost 7. the Word of the Salvation 8. What must I do to be saved? 9. Luke the Evangelist. Marshall includes a discussion of the nature of history and a review of Luke's qualities as an historian. This is a critique of H. Conzelmann's *The Theology of St. Luke*. Marshall makes it clear that "our exposition of the main theme of Luke's theology constitutes a corrective of the thesis associated with Conzelmann (p.19)." He maintains that Luke is both historian and theologian and that the best term to describe him is 'evangelist', a term which can include both of the other. Marshall Emphasized that Luke's theology is grounded in his tradition. Marshall argues that Luke's purpose was evangelistic and therefore his concern was not much in line with 'salvation history' rather witness to the salvation revealed in Jesus Christ and proclaimed by the early church. According to Marshall, Luke is the theologian of 'salvation-history heeds some correction of emphasis (p. 19).

Marshall is of the view that Luke did not re-frame the Christian message into salvation history. Luke's purpose, as Marshall observes, is to present the Gospel of salvation to his reader in order to lead them to faith or to confirm their faith. For him, the idea of salvation is the key to the theology of Luke not the theme salvation-history, instead he says Luke does operate with a principle that may be termed salvation-history (p. 84). Marshall finds that Luke, the evangelist, is a faithful expositor of the tradition. Luke is not a reproducer of tradition, but he has given his own interpretation as a theologian as well as historian. In 1978, I. H. Marshall published *The Gospel of Luke: A Commentary on the Greek Text.* He used both tradition criticism and redaction criticism to elucidate the Gospel of Luke. It was called as a theological commentary (p. 32). Both the book and the commentary of Marshall are a critique of Conzelmann's *Theology of St. Luke.* Marshall takes pain to establish the historicity of Luke-Acts, thereby showing Luke as an outstanding historian. Marshall oversimplifies the purpose of Luke as 'evangelistic'. For him, the main message of Luke is the 'salvation' yet Marshall does not tell whether that salvation is spiritual or physical. Both the works of Marshall contribute to the historical study of Luke.

---

[12] I. Howard Marshall, *Luke: Historian and Theologian* (Exeter: The Paternoster Press, 1970).

2.2. Jacob Jervell (1972)

Luke and the People of God[13] by Jacob Jervell have a significant place in the study of the Gospel of Luke. He is a perceptive commentator whose insights deserve consideration. Jervell discusses the problem of 'the restoration of Israel and salvation for the Gentiles', where he argues that Luke knows only one Israel, i.e. the Jewish people, so that the Gentile mission forms a difficult problem for him. He thinks, Luke argues that the apostles have already completed the mission to Jews: 'the conversion of Gentiles is itself a fulfillment of the promises to Israel so that the apostolic mission to Jews turns out indirectly to be Gentile mission' (p. 68). The most interesting part of Jervell's book is the chapter entitled: 'The Twelve on Israel's Thrones: Luke's understanding of the apostolate' (75-112); here he argues for a link between the Twelve and Israel. In this context, Jervell presents the church as the restored Israel. It can be taken for the connection between the Old and New Testament and Christians as the new people of God. This book is a contribution to the study of the connection between the people of God, old and new.

2.3. Donald Juel (1973)

Donald Juel in the work, *Luke-Acts: The Promise of History*[14] interprets Luke and Acts together, demonstrating their thematic unity. This monograph is divided into six chapters. The introduction of the book also gives an introduction to the Gospel of Luke. The first chapter discusses the infancy narrative. The second chapter deals with the ministry of Jesus. The third chapter deals with the Acts of the Apostles. The fourth chapter *the life of faith* includes the virtues of Christians found in Luke-Acts. The fifth chapter *the People of God* deals with the inclusion of the Gentiles into Christianity and the major themes in Luke-Acts, which are related to it. The last chapter discusses the establishment of Christianity as a fulfillment of promise, which has witnessed sweeping changes and social upheavals.

3. 1980-1989

3.1. Joseph A. Fitzmyer (1981/1989)

Joseph A. Fitzmyer's two-volume commentary, *The Gospel According to Luke*[15] gives an introduction, which deals with issues such as authorship, source, theology and so on. The theology section covers Luke's themes such as Luke's Kerygma, structure of Luke, Luke's geography, Luke's history,

---

[13] Jacob Jervell, *Luke and the People of God* (Minneapolis: Augsburg, 1972).

[14] Donald Juel, *Luke-Acts: The Promise of History* (Atlanta: John Knox Press, 1973).

[15] Joseph A. Fitzmyer, *The Gospel According to Luke,* 2 vols, Anchor Bible (Garden City: Doubleday, 1981, 1985).

Christology, the Spirit, eschatology, discipleship and Luke's portrait of Jesus and so on. Joseph A. Fitzmyer's intention is not to limit his work on the historical-critical exegesis; but to combine it with the theological interest and purpose of Luke. According to Fitzmyer, Luke's historical concern is subordinated to his theology, for Luke's historical concern serves a theological end (p. 16). Fitzmyer agrees with F. Bovon that salvation history "is not an identification of history of salvation, but rather the entrance of salvation into the history (p. 179)." According to Fitzmyer, salvation in history did not replace Israel with the Church, because the people of Israel continue to be the Jewish people whereas the church is made up of Jews and Gentiles (p. 191). In 1989, Joseph A. Fitzmyer published a collection of his articles on Luke-Acts, entitled *Luke the Theologian: Aspects of his Teaching.*[16] This book is an introduction to the various Lukan themes. It deals with eight theological themes such as the authorship of Luke-Acts, infancy narrative, Mary, John the Baptist, discipleship, Satan and demons, Jewish people and Mosaic Law and the paradise. It functions as a companion to his commentary on Luke.

This, as its title implies, considers some of the theological motifs that one encounters in the Gospel. Much of the material is covered in other books, although arguably rather less well. His book is easy to read and serves as an admirable introduction to Luke's theology. This is not, however, in any sense a 'literary' reading of Luke. According to Joseph A. Fitzmyer, in both the commentary and the monograph, Luke has little concern for history but his main concern is theology. If Luke's intention is theology then why does Luke fix the life of Jesus in the timeline of world history (Lk 1:5; 2:1-2; 3:1-2)? Why does Luke, unlike other evangelists, give more information about the social milieu of first century Greco-Roman world? These show that Luke is equally interested both in history and in theology. Fitzmyer makes a clear distinction between Israel and the church, which is reasonable. His work is an added flavor to the study of New Testament particularly the Gospel of Luke.

3.2. Robert Maddox (1982)

One of the useful books for the study of the Gospel is Robert Maddox's *The Purpose of Luke-Acts.*[17] This book deals with many issues of Luke's interpretation, including questions of Luke's eschatology and setting, in a helpful and illuminating way. The book summarizes scholarly literature in its different chapters on the period before the early 1980s. Maddox's view of

[16] Joseph A. Fitzmyer, *Luke the Theologian: Aspects of His Teaching* (London: Geoffrey Chapman, 1989).

[17] Robert Maddox, *The Purpose of Luke-Acts* (Edinburgh: T&T Clark, 1982).

Luke's eschatology is that Luke's emphasis lies in the reality of the present fulfillment of eschatological hopes (p. 145). He thinks that Luke was written to reassure the Christian community about the significance of the tradition of faith in which it stood: 'Luke encourages his readers not only to look forward with hope to the consummation of all things at the End, but also to appreciate that "salvation," the grace and power of God in action is *present reality* in which they already stand' (p. 187). This book analyses Luke-Acts together as one volume and brings out various issues related to both the works to find the purpose of Luke-Acts.

3.3. Richard J. Cassidy and Philip J. Scharper (1983)

Richard J. Cassidy and Philip J. Scharper edited *Political Issues in Luke-Acts*[18] with ten articles by different scholars. Robert F. O'Toole, "Luke's Position on Politics and Society in Luke-Acts", Willard M. Swartley, "Politics and Peace in Luke's Gospel", J. Duncan M. Derrett, "Luke's perspective on Tribute to Caesar", Frederick W. Danker, "Reciprocity in the Ancient World and in Acts 15:23-29", Quentin Quesnell, "The Women at Luke's Supper", J. Massyngbaerde Ford, "Reconciliation and Forgiveness in Luke's Gospel", Charles H. Talbert, "Maryrdom in Luke-Acts and the Lukan Social Ethics", Daryl Schmidt, Luke's "Innocent" Jesus: A Scriptural Apologetic", E. Jane Via, "According to Luke, Who Put Jesus to Death" and Richard J. Cassidy, "Luke's Audience, the Chief Priests and the Motive for Jesus' Death". Each article stands independently and discusses various elements related to Jesus, politics and society in Luke-Acts. The above scholars have covered profound literature for writing the articles. Their contributions to political issues in Luke-Acts are to be appreciated.

3.4. Eduard Schweizer (1984)

Eduard Schweizer's *The Good News According to Luke*[19] (1984) brought out theological insights from the Gospel of Luke. He did his studies in the sources of the Gospel of Luke. According to him, the Gospel of Luke and the Acts of Apostles were written separately. In the view of Schweizer, the Gospel of Luke does not provide a clear Christology and equally unclear of the grounding of salvation. Jesus used parables to speak of God and the kingdom, sin and forgiveness, death and the life to come. According to Schweizer, Luke makes no direct statements about who Jesus is and how human salvation comes through him. Who Jesus is and what he means for faith-can be stated only in the full wealth of the tradition. Luke

---

[18] Richard J. Cassidy and Philip J. Scharper (eds.), *Political Issues in Luke-Acts* (NewYork: Orbis Books, 1983).

[19] Eduard Schweizer, *The Good News According to Luke,* tr. by David E. Green (Atlanta: John Knox Press, 1984, c.1913).

presents an ideal community in Luke-Acts. Luke always points clearly to Jesus of Nazareth, who lived, died and rose again at a particular time in a particular place. The miracle God performed with Jesus reflects the act of God. Eduard Schweizer's commentary gives practical theological insights. The theological insights that he presents in the commentary are helpful to understand the purpose of Luke.

3.5. Jerome Neyrey (1985)

Jerome Neyrey's *The Passion According to Luke: A Redaction Study of Luke's Soteriology*[20] (1985) is a fresh look at Luke's Passion narrative. Neyrey, as the title of the book suggests, taken a redaction critical approach to investigate the Luke's Passion Narrative. He was pursuing a redaction-critical approach with vigor, fresh light that can shed on the text and its rich and distinctive theology made available for lovers of the third Gospel. He picks up five episodes from Luke's passion narrative and analyses them. They are 1. Jesus' farewell speech (Lk. 22:14-38), 2. Jesus in the Garden (Lk 22:39-46), 3. the trials of Jesus in Luke-Acts , 4. Jesus' address to the women of Jerusalem (Lk. 23:27-31) and 5. the crucifixion scene. In the last chapter, he discusses the salvific significance of Jesus' death, which serves as the climactic moment when the pattern of obedience and faith reaches its completion and the true character of Jesus as the new Adam is definitively achieved. The book breaks a new ground in suggesting a distinctive soteriology of the cross and a corresponding Christology. Study of the faith of the dying Jesus becomes a major clue for seeing Jesus as the New Adam in Luke-Acts. Although rich in detail, this book continually offers a unified view of the text; readers are constantly offered overviews, summaries of the data and interpretation of it.

Jerome Neyrey brings a remarkably enlightened approach to the Passion Narrative, and to Luke's particular version of it. The book begins where previous studies have left off, for it goes beyond traditional questions of source and historicity and treats the Lukan Passion Narrative from the standpoint of redaction criticism. Neyrey offers a fresh literary analysis of the text, along with significant thematic and theological insights into Luke's version of Jesus' passion. In this monograph, Neyrey concentrates on the soteriological significance of Luke's Passion Narrative. Some New Testament scholars have concluded that Luke's Passion Narrative does not have any theological significance. Neyrey's work refutes their claims. Neyrey argues that Jesus as the new Adam. The 'New Adam' concept is very much of Pauline. Neyrey's study on Luke's passion narrative has unfolded

[20] Jerome Neyrey, *The Passion According to Luke: A Redaction Study of Luke's Soteriology* (New York: Paulist Press, 1985).

the theological motivation of Luke. However, the arrangement and unity of the book is at times confusing still this book goes beyond traditional questions of source and historicity and treats Luke's passion narrative from the standpoint of redaction criticism. Neyrey offers a fresh literary analysis of the text, along with significant thematic and theological insights into Luke's version of Jesus' passion.

3.6. Robert J. Karris (1985)

Robert J. Karris, in his *Luke: Artist and Theologian: Luke's Passion Account as Literature,*[21] argues that Luke brings out his theology through his artistry. He states, that Luke's artistry is a vehicle for his theology. He delves into Luke's artistry through a study of Luke's themes such as faithful God, and Justice and food. He also focuses on the Christology and soteriology in the Gospel of Luke. According to Karris, Jesus' righteous life and his concern for justice and the poor led him to the cross. He analyses Luke 23 thematically and concludes that Luke does not view Jesus' death as expiation for sin. In Luke-Acts Jesus' death is not an isolated event, but us a part of Jesus' entire life of revealing a faithful God. Karris approaches Luke's passion narrative as a piece of literature. He applies the reader response theory to analyze Luke's passion narrative. This leads to various subjective interpretations, thus it fails to bring out the original meaning of the text. Instead, it is a story which has no theological significance. This interpretation is a subjective reading of the text, and it is defective.

3.7. Robert C. Tannehill (1986)

Robert C. Tannehill published a two-volume work on Luke-Acts entitled *The Narrative Unity of Luke-Acts: A Literary Interpretation.*[22] According to Tannehill, the controlling theme of Luke-Acts unifies both the works, because the chief human characters such as John the Baptist, Jesus, the apostles and Paul share in a mission, which expresses a single controlling purpose that is the purpose of God. The purpose of God is universal salvation and at the end of Acts this purpose of God is only partially fulfilled and that means the purpose of God is continuing in the human history to save the last person. In the literary analysis of Luke-Acts, Tannehill takes the position on the borderline between character and plot. He views Luke-Acts as a unified narrative, because there are internal connections among different parts of the narrative. Themes are developed, dropped then presented again. Characters and actions may echo characters and actions in another part of the story. The

---

[21] Robert J. Karris, *Luke: Artist and Theologian: Luke's Passion Account as Literature* (NewYork: Paulist Press, 1985).

[22] Robert C. Tannehill, *The Narrative Unity of Luke-Acts: A Literary Interpretation,* vol.1. The Gospel of Luke (Philadelphia: Fortress Press, 1986).

work is divided into eight chapters, including the infancy narrative, ministry of John and Jesus, Jesus and the people, Jesus and the authorities, Jesus and the disciples and the risen Lord's revelation to His followers.

Tannehill's literary analysis of Luke-Acts showed the narrative unity of Luke-Acts. According to him, the characters and the purpose of Luke-Acts make Luke-Acts as a unified narrative. It is a commendable effort to show Luke-Acts as a literary whole. However, the structure of the Book is not quite impressive; the author is successful in bringing out the theology of the Gospel of Luke with the help of narrative criticism and its components. The book is an evidence of his great scholarship. It is an added contribution to the study of the Gospel of Luke.

3.8. Philip F. Esler (1987)

Philip F. Esler's *Community and Gospel in Luke-Acts: The Social and Political Motivations of Lucan Theology*[23] applies both social sciences and redaction criticism to study the interrelationships between Luke's theology and the social and political pressures upon his community. Esler sees Luke-Acts as written for Christian community in a Hellenistic city of the Roman East, which was experiencing difficulties from within and opposition from without, which threatened its continued existence and unity. Esler thinks that this predicament originated largely in the very mixed nature of the individuals comprised of its membership. According to Esler, Luke shaped the Gospel tradition at his disposal in response to social and political pressures experienced by his community. Esler highlights that historical methods such as form criticism and redaction criticism had initially referred to the social context of the Gospel tradition, but the evangelists failed to utilize the methods for investigating the social context of the world.

Esler argues that Luke responded to the first of these problems by re-writing early Christian history to present the phenomenon of table-fellowship between Jews and Christians as inaugurated by Peter with divine permission. Luke responds to the second by intensifying the preference for the poor, which he found in Mark and [illegible] the scheme of salvation inaugurated by Jesus. On the political level, Luke's message for the Romans in his community is that there is no clash between Christianity and Rome. To this extent Luke's theology is molded by the social and political forces that operated upon his community.

According to Esler, the table-fellowship, concern for the poor and critique of the rich in Luke-Acts are intra-community affairs. These make up Esler's main thesis that Luke wrote the Gospel to a particular community. In

[23] Philip F. Esler, *Community and Gospel in Luke-Acts: The Social and Political Motivations of Lucan Theology* (Cambridge: Cambridge University Press, 1987).

the first place, there is no indication in the Gospel of Luke that it is written to a particular community. In the second place, Jesus' table-fellowship with the socially outcast and his concern for the poor expose the injustice that was done against the powerless by the powerful in the society; hence Jesus' attitude towards the socially outcast and the poor expresses Jesus' concern for social justice. Thus, fixing the recipients of Luke's writings to a community and labeling them as sectarian, perhaps, undermine Luke's purpose. The socio-economic and political concerns in Luke highlight that Luke had a wider world in his mind. This book gives a fresh approach to understand Luke's community.

3.9. David P. Moessner (1988)

David P. Moessner's article "The Leaven of the Pharisees' and 'this Generation': Israel's Rejection of Jesus According to Luke"[24] gives a survey of *laos* in the Gospel of Luke as an introduction. Variety of explanations, both theological and source traditional, studied by various scholars are viewed in this article. Within the interaction of characters and events of the plot development, Luke has not provided his readers with an adequate or at least consistent explanation of the demand of the *laos* for the death of Jesus. Moessner also gives the survey of the use of the term 'Pharisees' in the Gospel of Luke. The major thrust of the article is to find the problem of Luke's consistency in laying the responsibility for the death of Jesus at the feet of both the leaders and the people posed actually at the beginning of Jesus' ministry. The nation as a whole, the people and their leaders are guilty of rejecting God's messenger of repentance sent to them. Even the disciples are placed with a theological interpretation. According to Moessner, Luke has presented a theological interpretation of the inescapable enigma that Israel as a whole had rejected its messianic fulfiller of salvation. The analysis of the Gospel of Luke shows the blame upon the Jews for the death of Jesus than the Romans. This article brings to light that Luke was not blaming the Pharisees in particular, instead it is a common reference to the *people* in the passion narrative who rejected Jesus. According to Moessner, it is the Pharisees who are the link between the people and the leaders who are blamed for the death of Jesus. Those who make their studies on the passion narrative and the role of Pharisees in Luke's Gospel can find this article helpful.

---

[24] David P. Moessner, 'The Leaven of the Pharisees' and 'this Generation': Israel's Rejection of Jesus According to Luke,' *JSNT* 34 (Oct, 1988): 21-46.

3.10. Frederick W. Danker (1988)

The revised and expanded edition of Frederick W. Danker's commentary on Luke appeared in 1988[25] with the title *Jesus and the New Age: A Commentary on St. Luke's Gospel*. He finds that the writer of the Third Gospel possessed more of the spirit of Hellenistic culture. According to Danker, Luke's linguistic versatility, compositional technique and dramatic skills show that 'he does not take second rank among Hellenistic writers (p.2). Danker treats the Gospel of Luke as a coherent literary work. He pays close attention to the Greco-Roman cultural environment as it is represented in many ancient historical writings and documents. He focuses on Luke's linguistic style, compositional technique and dramatic skills. Moreover he discloses how Luke is the matter of a medium that would communicate with both Jewish and gentile religious-cultural experience, customs and ideals. He accomplishes it with his portrayal of Jesus as the great benefactor. Danker's commentary gives an important cultural information of Luke's social world. He discloses the literary merit of Luke's Gospel. Danker does this by comparing the Gospel of Luke with the works of the Greco-Roman writers of antiquity. If Danker is correct in his assessment that the Gospel of Luke was written in a literary style that attracted all sections of first century Greco-Roman world then Luke wrote his Gospel for a wider world. If Luke wrote the Gospel for a wider world then what was his purpose? Why did Luke highlights the social injustice and economic inequality of the first century Greco-Roman world? These issues are not adequately analyzed in this commentary. This commentary is a useful source for the study of Luke's Gospel.

3.11. Halvor Moxnes (1988)

Halvor Moxnes describes the purpose of his work, *the Economy of the Kingdom: Social Conflict and Economic Relation in Luke's Gospel,*[26] is to offer a picture of Palestinian society at the time of Jesus as it is portrayed in Luke's Gospel. His point of entry into the world of Luke is 16.14 where Jesus calls the Pharisees as 'lovers of money'. This book has ten chapters; in the first two chapters Moxnes concentrates on the background and role of the Pharisees in the Gospel of Luke. In chapter three, he explains the method he applied to study the social interaction and ancient economy. He uses both social anthropology and ancient economics. Chapter four discusses the economic interaction in Luke's Palestine. Chapter five analyzes Luke's

[25] Frederick W. Danker, *Jesus and the New Age: A Commentary on St. Luke's Gospel* (Philadelphia: Fortress Press, 1988).

[26] Halvor Moxnes, *The Economy of the Kingdom: Social Conflict and Economic Relation in Luke's Gospel* (Philadelphia: Fortress Press, 1988).

perspective: the Moral Economy of the peasant. Chapter six deals with the Rules of Purity and Social order: The role of the Pharisees. Chapter seven and eight discusses Purity and Almsgiving: A New Social Structure and Hospitality and a New Community. Chapter nine is a significant one because it discusses the major thrust of the book, which analyzes what it meant to be Lovers of Money-Slaves of Mammon: The Cosmological Implications of the Love of Money. The final chapter is a great challenge with the title, the economy of the kingdom and present-day challenges such as, Luke's Alternative: an economy of the Kingdom, which is found in the Gospel of Luke and Acts. The challenge is to see the world 'from the viewpoint of the poor'.

In this book, Moxnes gives an overview of economic interaction in Luke's Palestine. He sees the first century Palestine divided into various segments of social groups based on economy. This aspect is overlooked by some social science critics of New Testament, but Moxnes has brought it into the central stage of studies on Luke's Gospel. He gives valuable information about the village economy of antiquity (Chs. 3-5). It is a commendable work. Moxnes maintains that Luke has identified the Pharisees with the exploitative system. Moxnes makes a vital observation here that Jesus criticized them because they had joined hands with the exploitative system, which have plundered the economy of the Palestine peasants. According to Luke, the ruling classes have found that Jesus is a threat to their monopoly over economy. That led Jesus to the cross. Hence, to have a holistic view of the economic system of the first century Palestine one needs to analyze the role of the high priest family and the Jerusalem aristocracy along with Pharisees. This book, therefore, studies only the Pharisee's role in the economy of the first century Palestine. The social-scientific study of the Luke's text in its original context proves an embracing framework for appreciating both the initial and the contemporary significance of its radical social message and Moxnes has succeeded in it.

3.12. Joseph B. Tyson (1988)

Tyson's *Luke-Acts and the Jewish People*[27] includes eight scholarly articles which try to trace the treatment of Jewish people and institutions in Luke-Acts: Jacob Jervell's "The Church of Jews and God fearers", David L. Tiede's[28] "'Glory to Thy People of Israel": Luke-Acts and the Jews",

---

[27] Joseph B. Tyson (ed), *Luke-Acts and the Jewish People: Eight Critical Perspectives* (Minneapolis: Augsburg Publishing House, 1988).

[28] He is the author of *Prophecy and History in Luke Acts* (Philadelphia: Fortress press, 1980) and of *Augsburg Commentary on the New Testament: Luke* (Augsburg, 1988).

David P. Moessner's[29] "The Ironic Fulfillment of Israel's Glory", Jack T. Sanders'[30] "The Jewish People in Luke-Acts", Marilyn Salmon's[31] "Insider or Outsider? Luke's Relationship with Judaism", Robert C. Tannehill's[32] "Rejection by Jews and Turning to Gentiles: The Pattern of Paul's Mission in Acts", Michael J. Cook's "The Mission to the Jews in Acts: Unrevealing Luke's "Myth of the 'Myriads'" and Joseph B. Tyson's[33] "The Problem of Jewish Rejection in Acts." In this article, he gives the conclusion that 'for Luke the mission to the Jewish people has failed and it has been terminated'. Luke-Acts has become the center on the interpretation of the author's understanding of Jews and Judaism. This controversial question involves a variety of issues such as the nature of the Christian mission to the Jews as pictured in Acts; Luke's intended audience, the God fearers and the relation of Christians to other components of early Judaism. The eight perspectives discussed in this book serve not only to display the range of interpretation of the issues but also draw the reader into intense discussion.

3.13. David P. Moessner (1989)

David P. Moessner's *Lord of the Banquet: The Literary and Theological Significance of Lukan Travel Narrative*[34] is the thesis that Luke has used Deuteronomy in shaping his Gospel and it brings out the subtle relationship between the Two Testaments. This book is divided into five parts. 1. The problem expanded: Dissonance of Form from Content, it gives the survey of the critical approaches to the form and content of the Central Section in Luke's Gospel 2. The Preview of the Journey of the Prophet like Moses of Deuteronomy, it gives a fourfold Exodus typology based on the calling and fate of Moses in Deuteronomy as a heuristic principle for the plotted story in 9:51-19:44. 3. The Deuteronomistic view of Israel's prophetic History and the central section of Luke, it is the main chapter of this work with evidence classified for Jesus as a prophet in 9:51-19: 44. The author provides an extrinsic literary-critical check, that is, a Deuteronomic-Exodus typology, the popular Deuteronomistic notion of the role and fate of Israel's

[29] His major work in Luke named *Lord of the Banquet: The Literary and Theological Significance of the Lukan Travel Narrative*. This has been overviewed in the following part of this paper.

[30] One of his major works is *The Jews in Luke-Acts* (Fortress, 1987).

[31] His Ph.D. dissertation was titled as 'Hypotheses about First-Century Judaism and the Study of Luke-Acts.'

[32] His work on Luke-Acts is *The Narrative Unity of Luke-Acts: A Literary Interpretation.*

[33] He is editor of this book as well as the writer of *The Death of Jesus in Luke-Acts* (University of South Carolina Press, 1986).

[34] David P. Moessner, *Lord of the Banquet: The Literary and Theological Significance of Lukan Travel Narrative* (Minneapolis: Fortress, 1989).

prophets in her history as it is expressed in Palestinian Jewish literature of the intertestamental period is brought to bear on the text. 4. Jesus the Deuteronomistic rejected prophet as the Prophet like Moses of Deuteronomy; it applies the extrinsic literary comparison of Moses of Deuteronomy to the Jesus of the Central section and 5. Conclusions: The Significance of the Travel Narrative in Luke-Acts.

This work gives some conclusions, explores the theological implications of the Luke's studies and suggests some further lines for research. The content of the central section of the Gospel of Luke is Jesus' journey from Galilee to Jerusalem (Lk. 9:51-19; 44) and it has been studied in this book. Moessner finds that Jesus' speech parallels Moses' speech and his journey recapitulates and fulfills Israel's journey as it is summarized and anticipated in Deuteronomy. The eating and drinking of Jesus, the anointed prophet like Moses and Lord of the Kingdom's Banquet, leads to Jesus' rejection, which is the consummation of the history of Moses and all the prophets. It is this overlooked intertextuality of Jesus' journey with Israel's dynamic exodus story that unlocks the mystery of Luke's portrait of Jesus. This book analyzes one of the difficult sections in the Gospel of Luke. He clarifies various questions such as what was in Luke's mind to convey the particulars of the journey. Moessner seems to have solved the riddle of Luke's travel narrative.

3.14. Charles H. Talbert (1989)

Charles H. Talbert's *Reading Luke*[35] is written with an aim to read Gospel of Luke's literary characteristics and theological significance. The study has been done with the help of redaction criticism, narrative and genre criticism. It is a verse-by-verse commentary on the Gospel of Luke. Without much introduction or background study, the author jumps into the text and interprets the Gospel of Luke. There are no major conclusions or findings within the commentary. Talbert has written or edited several books on Luke but for our purpose, the most significant is his *Reading Luke.* It is interesting that Talbert spends very little time on the introductory preamble. There is, for instance, no initial attempt to explain the mechanics of the plot. Talbert is already reading Luke 1 on p. 7. This is not quite a sequential reading. Talbert arranges the Luke's material according to themes. Thus, he places together all the material that deals with 'John, prototype of the Christian Evangelist.' Nor does it read the whole Gospel. Talbert's reading of Luke works from the belief that it belongs to the genre of ancient biography.

---

[35] Charles H. Talbert, *Reading Luke: A Literary and Theological Commentary on the Third Gospel* (NewYork: Crossroad, 1989).

3.15. Mark Allan Powell (1989)

Mark Allan Powell's *What are they saying about Luke*?[36] has six chapters, 1. Luke: Historian, Theologian, Artist 2. The Composition of Luke's Gospel 3. The Concerns of Luke's Community 4. Christ and Salvation in the Gospel of Luke 5. Political and social Issues in Luke's Gospel and 6. Spiritual and Pastoral Concerns in the Gospel of Luke. Powell tries to identify trends in Luke's scholarship rather than to simply review or recommend particular books. The first chapter considers various methodological approaches to Luke that have been used by scholars who approach the Gospel with different goals in mind. Chapter two presents the dominant theories concerning Luke's use of sources in the composition of his Gospel. The third chapter addresses the question, why Luke wrote this Gospel in the first place? what were the needs of his own community that prompted such an undertaking? Chapter four is devoted to what have unquestionably been the major theological issues in the study of the Gospel of Luke: Christology, eschatology and salvation history. The fifth chapter focuses on less traditional matters that are nevertheless receiving a great deal of attention, namely the political and social implications of this Gospel. Finally, chapter six considers questions related to Luke's concept of discipleship and the Christian life. The focus of this book is on Luke's Gospel, although it is sometimes necessary to consider insights based on previous studies. This book helps the readers to read the Gospel of Luke with new interest, new insight and new appreciation.

3.16. D. B. Gowler (1989)

D. B. Gowler's "Characterization in Luke: A Socio-Narratological Approach"[37] is an introductory article for the Ph.D. dissertation, "A Socio-Narratological Character Analysis of the Pharisees in Luke-Acts." This article tries to analyze the persons portrayed in the NT narratives have seldom been analyzed in a detailed and systematic fashion. Literary criticism offers a way to sift the evidence critically and to evaluate these characters carefully. Additional skills are used to analyze the characters. Thus, the study of the characterization in the NT needs to be integrated to the social and narrative context and the Gospel of Luke is used for the analysis. The author makes an analysis of characters as the first step, direct definition and indirect presentation, cultural scripts in direct definition follow that. It is true that a study of characterization in Luke needs to be supplemented by knowledge of cultural scripts assumed by the text. The recognition of the various cultural

[36] Mark Allan Powell, *What are They Saying About Luke?* (Mahwah: Paulist Press, 1989).

[37] D. B. Gowler, 'Characterization in Luke: A Socio-Narratological Approach,' *BTB* 19 (1989): 54-62.

codes inherent in the text of Luke opens new vistas for the NT scholars. The narrative is examined through the eyes of literary criticism and is informed by appropriate cultural scripts, the natures of the characters and the implications of their actions will become clearer and clearer. Thus, literary criticism and cultural analysis need not be seen as competing or conflicting approaches to the text. Instead, the use of cultural scripts should be seen as complementary to literary analysis, where both methodologies offer reciprocal control and correction. It is right that merging of disciplines must be made in order for the text to be heard more clearly and this article is an example for it.

4. 1990-1999

4.1. Mark Allan Powell (1990)

Mark Allan Powell's, "the Religious Leaders in Luke: A Literary-Critical study"[38] focuses on the religious leaders in the Gospel of Luke, the people who were with Jesus and remained with him through his trials (Lk. 22: 28). The task in understanding the religious leaders as characters in Luke's narrative is to discern the character traits and point of view he attributes to them. Powell's study on the religious leaders takes the following things into consideration, (i) the character trait which characterizes the Pharisees, (ii) the point of view which is one of the elements in the literary criticism as the religious leaders in Luke are characters who seek to justify themselves before people (16:15). Their point of view is aligned with that of humans rather than with that of God. Luke's reader realizes that what is an abomination to God is of great value to them. (iii) The line of opposition which speaks of the religious leaders in the Gospel of Luke are characters who 'reject the purpose of God' (7:30). The basic line of opposition between them and Jesus may be understood from the perspective of salvation history. Jesus is presented as the initiator of a new age; the leaders view themselves as custodians of the old age, which they seek to preserve. (iv) The story line of the religious leaders in Luke's Gospel is secondary to that of Jesus. It is the story of Jesus that gives shape and continuity to the work as a whole.

It is possible to trace a story line for the leaders that develops throughout the Gospel. The introductory episodes: Zechariah (1:5-23; 57-79), first stage: The leaders respond to the life and mission of Jesus (2:41-19:44), stage two: the leaders plot to kill Jesus (19:45-23:49) and concluding episode: Joseph of Arimathea, excursus: a brief comparison with Matthew (9:4, 12:34 etc) and the literary effect of Luke's treatment. The author investigates their relationship with other characters in the narrative, especially Jesus, who is the protagonist of Luke's story. The author claims that not many studies are

[38] Mark Allan Powell, 'The Religious Leaders in Luke: A Literary-Critical study,' *JBL* 109/1 (1990): 93-110.

done on the literary-critical analysis of the religious leaders in the Gospel of Luke, but there are some scholarly works in the same area of study which the author refers to it in the footnote (p. 93). Powell finds that the leaders in Luke are able to serve as negative examples of discipleship. They exhibit the qualities that the implied author wants his readers to avoid. Luke's portrayal of the religious leaders provides the background for his presentation of Jesus as one who not only preaches love for enemies (6:27-31) but practiced it. Luke's portrayal of the conflict between Jesus and the religious leaders affects the reader's perception of what God has done in Christ. Powell finds that the religious leaders in Luke's Gospel function as a component of the narrative. They serve as elements in the story he tells and may be understood as such apart from any identification with historical figures outside the story world.

4.2. Jack D. Kingsbury (1991)

Jack D. Kingsbury's *Conflict in Luke: Jesus, Authorities, Disciples*[39] brings out the various levels of conflicts in the Gospel of Luke. He argues that this Gospel story is intertwined with three primary story lines and one secondary story line. The Gospel story of Luke is rich in characters. The primary story lines and the main characters are Jesus, religious authorities and disciples. The secondary story line is the crowd. The minor characters are John the Baptist, Pilate, Herod Antipas, God, angels, Satan and demons. The introduction of the book gives a narrative frame work for the study and it introduces the world of Luke's Gospel to the reader and elements that fills it with life and drama, such as settings, characters and plots. In the second chapter the story of Jesus is studied. Chapter three deals the story of the authorities and the final chapter discusses the story of the disciples. Chapters two to four trace and interpret the three chief story lines in Luke's Gospel, that of Jesus, of the religious authorities and of the disciples. Kingsbury argues that the Luke's story of Jesus is arranged in a defined plot, it begins with 1.5-2.52 where John and Jesus are presented to the readers. The middle part with three phases, 3:1-9:50 [illegible] Israel from Galilee; 9:51-19:46, Jesus journeys to Jerusalem; 19:47-21:38, Jesus discharges his ministry and the end in Luke 22-23, Jesus suffers, dies, is raised and ascends to heaven. The conflicts in Luke are not the creation of the author but they are the reflection of the society. This conflict is mainly between Jesus and the religious authorities. God accomplishes his plan of universal salvation through Jesus' ministry, suffering and death.

[39] Jack D. Kingsbury, *Conflict in Luke: Jesus, Authorities, Disciples* (Minneapolis: Fortress Press, 1991).

Kingsbury shows that Luke's story of Jesus is constructed in conflict plot. For Kingsbury, the conflicts in Luke are the reflection of real world. He treats the literary text as a historical product. The text reflects the historical context. It is the conflict between Jesus and the religious leaders that led Jesus to the cross. The way he has presented and proved the thesis, the conflict in Luke, is not without basis. The resources that he has used and argued with and against show the scholarship of this work. If he had added a conclusion for the whole book, it would have been much more interesting to the reader. This book is a useful resource for the studies in the Gospel of Luke.

4.3. Luke T. Johnson (1991)

Luke T. Johnson states in his *The Gospel of Luke*[40] that Luke-Acts fits very well into the conventional literary form of Hellenistic historiography of antiquity (p. 5-10). According to Johnson, Luke is an apologetic historian who tells how events happened 'in order', Luke shows how God fulfilled his promises first to Israel and only then extended these blessings to the Gentiles. The saving of Israel was necessary for the security of Gentile faith. Johnson reads Luke-Acts from the perspective of prophecy and fulfillment formula, he suggests that Luke-Acts has a definite prophetic structure. He argues that Luke presents Jesus as the prophet (prophet-like-Moses) for the people of God. According to him, Luke-Acts is a historiography of antiquity. For him, Luke is an apologetic historian who narrates the historical events 'in order' which means the sequence of the fulfillment of God's promise, first to the Jews and then to the non-Jews. This commentary is showcased in aesthetic style and it is an exemplary literary work.

4.4. Jerome H. Neyrey (1991)

Jerome H. Neyrey has edited a valuable collection of essays in *The Social World of Luke-Acts: The Models for Interpretation,*[41] which is the outcome of the 'Context Group' seminar in 1986. It is a study of the social world in which the different documents came to birth and it is an increasingly important aspect of New Testament research. The contributors of this volume are Jerome H. Neyrey, Bruce J. Malina, Richard L. Rohrbaugh, Douglas E. Oakman, John J. Pilch, John H. Elliott, Halvor Moxnes, Vernon K. Robbins and Mark McVann. This volume has thirteen articles, which are arranged in three parts. 1. Social psychology 2. Social institutions and 3. Social dynamics. Of particular interest are the essays by Malina and Neyrey on 'Honor and shame in Luke-Acts: Pivotal values of the Mediterranean world' (pp. 25-65); by Rohrbaugh on 'The Pre-industrial city in Luke-Acts: Urban

---

[40] Luke T. Johnson, *The Gospel of Luke* (Minnesota: Liturgical Press, 1991).

[41] Jerome H. Neyrey (ed), *The Social World of Luke-Acts: The Models for Interpretation* (Peabody: Hendrickson, 1991).

Social Relations' (pp. 125-49); and by Robbins on 'The Social Location of the Implied Author of Luke-Acts' (pp. 305-32). The nature of this volume means that it ought to be required reading for those who want to gain a contemporary understanding of the Gospel. Neyrey in the preface makes it clear that the handbook is not aimed at historical reconstruction or social description. He avows the intention is to bring out this handbook in the following words: the authors aim to discover the meaning that implicit in Luke-Acts through attention to the values, social structures and conventions of Luke's society which determines and convey those meanings. Every topic in this book begins with a social science theory or model and as the essay develops that theory or model is applied in the text of Luke-Acts. This book appraises the usefulness of social sciences in the New Testament. The contributors of this volume have disclosed their methodologies. These methodologies provide insights and tips to the new researches to develop their own social sciences methodology. This volume also provides guidelines how to apply social sciences theory and method to a given text. This is a very useful resource book for social-scientific methodologies.

4.5. Gerald F. Downing (1992)

Gerald F. Downing in the article titled "The Ambiguity of "The Pharisee and the Toll-Collector" (Lk 18:9-14) in the Greco-Roman World of Late Antiquity"[42] discusses the presentation of the Pharisees and tax-collectors in the Gospel of Luke particularly in the parable found in Lk. 18:9-14. The author brings out the source for the text as the Wider Greco-Roman World, the Diaspora Hellenistic Judaism and Palestinian (still Hellenistic) Judaism (including early Christianity). In the next part, the author brings out Luke 18:10-13 in the Tradition of the Teaching of Jesus. The conclusion is that the parable is free from apparent Lukan additions one finds in a narrative whose internal integrity Luke seems to respect. It presents two figures, both of whom are ambiguous, subtly effective parodies. If one chooses to reject the words and actions of the second figure as well as those of the first, one finds himself/herself affirming the kind of approach of God that Jesus in the tradition elsewhere teaches. By the criterion of coherence, it seems to have as good a claim as any other to be Jesus' own. On one side, the article is almost like raising problem to a familiar text, which was not problematic up to then. The author is aware of the same and it says that for most commentators Lk. 18:9-14 is quite unproblematic (p. 80). The author tries to argue from various sources to prove the point. The conclusion is not adequate. But, on

[42] Gerald F. Downing, 'The Ambiguity of 'The Pharisee and the Toll-Collector' (Lk 18:9-14) in the Greco Roman World of Late Antiquity,' *CBQ* 54/1 (January 1992): 80-99.

the other side the author is raising a genuine question for a scholarly thinking for the source and context of Lk. 18:9-14.

4.6. Eric Franklin (1994)

Another book to be considered is Eric Franklin's *Luke: Interpreter of Paul, Critic of Matthew.*[43] According to Franklin Luke has a clear understanding of Paul's position on the Law. This is that the Law no longer has a part in defining the boundaries of the people of God. Luke has a continuing concern with the Jewish people. According to Franklin, Luke's primary purpose was nothing less than a presentation of the truth of the Gospel as he understood it (p.135). Luke sees Christianity as the fulfillment of Judaism in such a way as to make him detect an over-riding continuity between the two religions. The final part of Franklin's book presents a survey of Luke's use of Matthew. Luke is consistently less hostile to the Jewish people than is Matthew.

4.7. Interpretation 48 (1994)

In 1994, the *Interpretation*[44] journal has published an issue on Luke. The articles in this issue are written from narrative critical and social-scientific perspectives. Mark A. Powell, Robert C. Tannehill and Jack D. Kingsbury have employed narrative criticism and Mary A. Beavis and Halvor Moxnes have used social-scientific criticism to understand the Gospel of Luke. Powell, in his article "Toward a Narrative-Critical Understanding of Luke," shows how historical criticism and narrative criticism ascertain the theology of Luke. He explains how Luke's Infancy Narrative (Lk. 1-2) is viewed by historical criticism and narrative criticism. According to him, the infancy narrative functions as the introduction to the main plot.

Jack D. Kingsbury, in his article "The Plot of Luke's Story of Jesus," maintains that the Gospel of Luke has a plot with a recognizable beginning, middle and end. According to him, the plot of Luke revolves around conflict. Kingsbury observes that at the human level conflict is between Jesus and the Jewish religious authority. Mary A. Beavis' "'Expecting Nothing in Return': Luke's Picture of the Marginalized', notices that Luke's writing is a 'fertile theological ground for deriving a message of hope for the politically oppressed and economically dispossessed, a warning to the privileged elites and an important source of ethical and social teaching. Beavis makes use of the social history to interpret Luke-Acts. Social history unfolds the social interactions and economic relations of a society. Halvor Moxnes, in his article, "the Social Context of Luke's Community," attempts to study the *Sitz*

---

[43] Eric Franklin, *Luke: Interpreter of Paul, Critic of Matthew,* Issue 92, JSNT Supplement Series (Michigan: JSOT Press, 1994).

[44] Interpretation 48 (1994).

im Leben of Luke's community. Moxnes locates the first readers of Luke-Acts in an urban setting in the eastern parts of the Mediterranean.

Narrative criticism treats the Gospel of Luke as a pure literature. The articles of Powell, Tannehill and Kingsbury exhibit the way in which narrative criticism can be used in interpreting the Gospel of Luke. Powell and Tannehill have underplayed the historicity of the Gospel of Luke. If the Gospel accounts were not historical then how would it answer the human plights that s/he faces in his/her historical context? Hence, their interrelations are not very clear. Kingsbury, on the other hand, demonstrates how the Luke's story of Jesus can be read as a plot without interruption from the beginning to the end. Both the articles of Beavis and Moxnes have exposed the economic inequalities and social injustice of the Greco-Roman antiquity. According to them, Luke is not a mere spectator but rather a social critic who stands in the line of the Old Testament prophets. They have showed that the social world that Luke lived and preached is not different from today and thus his message is very much relevant to this time. Their articles also reveal that other social sciences tools are applied to study Luke's Gospel that will throw new light in Luke's social world. These articles are valuable tools in discovering the social world of Luke.

4.8. Turid Karlsen Seim (1994)

In *The Double Message: Patterns of Gender in Luke-Acts*[45] Seim present a sophisticated and carefully argues thesis that the author of Luke-Acts preserves strong traditions about women, giving them positive functions for the Christian community, while concurrently betraying a masculine preference which limits women's roles, particularly in the public missionary activity of the church in Acts. Luke's program thus does not deny dignity to the women in his narrative, in that women are presented as fully qualified for even apostolic or prophetic roles; but they are not accepted as appropriate witnesses to the public proclamation of Jesus' resurrection. This "double message" of Luke-Acts thus preserves the qualifications of the women as witnesses, in spite of Luke's masculinization of these traditions and his promotion of male dominance in early Christian leadership. Luke's preferential treatment of men, however, leads to the limitation of women's roles in early Christian missionary activity as described in Acts.

Seim begins her discussion with an overview of recent scholarship on the role of women in Luke-Acts in which she rejects as simplistic the tendency of scholars to argue that Luke's writings are either friendly or hostile to women's concerns. Chapter 2 provides a nicely nuanced discussion

[45] Turid Karlsen Seim, *The Double Message: Patterns of Gender in Luke-Acts* (Edinburgh: T&T Clark, 1994).

of Luke's supposed tendency towards "complementarity" of traditions concerning men and women. Chapter 3 discusses the implications of Luke 8:1-3 for understanding the role of women in the Christian community in terms of patronage and service. Chapter 4 discusses both the "Mary and Martha" pericope (Lk 10) and the resurrection stories featuring women (Lk 24). Chapter 5 outlines the role of women's prophetic speech in Luke's theme of the outpouring of the Holy Spirit as a fulfillment of Joel 2:28-29: in the age of the spirit both women and men shall prophesy. The conclusions drawn from her analysis in large part coincide with other recent treatments of the topic. This book is a solid, sophisticated, and nicely nuanced contribution to the current discussion of the function of gender in Luke-Acts and the role of women in early Christian groups.

4.9. Joel B. Green (1995/1997)

In *The Theology of the Gospel of Luke,*[46] Joel B. Green offers a concise but remarkably thorough description of the theological witness of Luke's Gospel. Green does not attempt to resolve questions concerning authorship or date and he proceeds with scant reference to source theories. He views the third Gospel as a literary whole and endeavors to read it "on its own terms, albeit against the backdrop of what we otherwise know about the first-century world it purports to portray" (p. 6). Socio-anthropological studies become a primary tool for analysis as he seeks to relate the literary world of Luke's narrative to the political and social world in which it was produced. The focus of the study is clearly on Luke's first volume, though Green recognizes an essential narrative and theological unity between the Gospel and Acts. Green's understanding of Luke's theology is laid out in chapters 2-5. Luke's Gospel relates the life and work of Jesus to a larger notion of "the purpose of God," which is articulated in Scripture and has been affirmed through miracles, angels, and the Holy Spirit. Without giving way to strict determinism, Luke is certain that God's aim will be accomplished in spite of opposition. In essence, the divine purpose is "to bring salvation in all its fullness to all persons" (p. 24).

By using literary criticism, Green constructs the theology of the Gospel of Luke. According to Green, Luke's narrative presents a theological program deeply embedded in the cultural currents of the first-century Mediterranean world. He displays his knowledge of Mediterranean sociology but his approach sacrifices sociology for the sake of literary criticism. He charges redaction criticism for failing to read Luke's narrative as a whole as

---

[46] Joel B. Green, *The Theology of the Gospel of Luke,* New Testament Theology (Cambridge: Cambridge University Press, 1995).

theological document. Green attempts to explore the 'narrative theology' of the Gospel of Luke with the help of literary criticism.

Green analyses the theology of the Gospel of Luke under six topics 1. the world of Luke 2. the purpose of God 3. Jesus, John and the Jewish people 4. mission and salvation 5. discipleship and 6. Luke's Gospel in the church. He argues that Luke related the life and ministry of Jesus to the larger theme of 'the purpose of God,' which is articulated in Scripture and has been affirmed through miracles, angels and the Holy Spirit. The theme 'the purpose of God' unifies the narrative. The purpose of God is 'to bring salvation in all of its fullness to all persons.' According to Green it includes various elements. Salvation is pre-eminently status reversal and the people of Israel as a people promised liberation from the oppressive hand of Rome. Salvation is also the coming of the Kingdom of God and it entails membership in the new community God is drawing together around Jesus to participate in the blessings of the kingdom as well as to share in its service. Green argues that for Luke the salvation is the present reality. But salvation in the present does not destroy the eschatological hope, because the Kingdom of God in Luke is both present (Lk. 18:7-8; 21:31-32) and future (Lk. 12:45; 19:11).

In 1997, Green Published his commentary on Luke entitled *The Gospel of Luke*. This commentary is a natural development of his monograph *The Theology of the Gospel of Luke*. Green adheres firmly to literary criticism and he does not compare the Luke's text with other Gospels. A text is compared only with the co-text in Gospel of Luke. He describes the method which he applies as 'discourse analysis', which correlated the 'cultural-critical and narratological concerns. According to him, the narrative text is a cultural product. He treats the Gospel of Luke as a pure literature and literary tools are used to understand the meaning of the text. This is a typical literary critical commentary. It is a strict and complete example of a recent trend to abandon the methods of tradition history, form criticism, and redaction criticism. Green does not even make comparisons of Luke's material with other Gospels. He does not assume, however, that a literary work can be understood apart from a cultural context. This commentary, however, is not a technical work of narrative criticism. Much of Green's theoretical framework remains in the background. The commentary follows this pattern: sections of Luke are presented in the NRSV translation (which is occasionally modified), followed by several pages of general commentary and then by comments on two to four verses at a time.

The comments on verses are written in full paragraphs rather than short notes. This procedure results in more extensive comment on fewer issues than the alternative approach. Even though this is a large commentary, it overlooks some issues of detailed interpretation that could affect the way a passage is understood. But it gives full and helpful discussion of other issues. Little space is given to the argument with opposing views, although some critique is found in the text and some in the footnotes. Comments on the Greek are confined to the footnotes. Green's overall perspective on Luke is convincing. Green's interpretation of Luke is presented clearly, in full detail, and in a format that will be useful not only to the specialist but to a broader public.

In both his monograph and commentary, Green introduces 'narrative theology'. His methodology blends narrative criticism and social science. He avows that Luke's narrative deeply embedded in the cultural currents of first century Mediterranean world, but his narrative theology takes a historical approach. According to Green, the 'narrative world' of Luke is not the 'real world'. If the 'narrative world' of Luke is different from the 'real world' then how would his account be historically reliable? The gulf that Green has created between the 'narrative world' and the 'real world' is unbridgeable. For Green, salvation is not simply spiritual but it 'embraces the totality of embodied life, including its social, economic and political concerns. He shows how this Liberative aspect is unfolded in the Gospel.

4.10. Mark L. Strauss (1995)

Mark L. Strauss' *The Davidic Messiah in Luke-Acts: The Promise and Its Fulfillment in Lukan Christology*[47] is in many respects a traditional study of NT Christology, with attention to issues ranging from form, redactional and historical matters to some of the more recent literary emphases. The study is a good indicator of how difficult it has become to hold the whole scholarly tradition together, addressing such a broad spectrum of concerns while trying to make a coherent argument. The thesis demonstrates convincingly that messianic tradition-by which Strauss means traditions about the anointed king from the line of David-is a major component in Luke's Christology. The real burden of his thesis is to investigate how Luke can draw on Jewish messianic tradition, with attention to biblical texts and sophisticated exegetical method, and at the same time sketch a picture of so unconventional a Messiah. His arguments are difficult to assess. They accord a greater role to the exegesis on the texts by OT scholars than to the way they were read in post-biblical Judaism, as reconstructed by scholars in that field. The argument is not simply that there are inter-textual relations between Luke and Isaiah. There is plenty in Strauss' work for everyone, including students of Luke-Acts, of the use of Israel's scriptures in the NT, and of NT Christology. One can be particularly grateful for Strauss has called our attention to a basic feature of the Christian tradition that can apparently be

[47] Mark L. Strauss, *The Davidic Messiah in Luke-Acts: The Promise and Its Fulfillment in Lukan Christology*, JSNT Sup 110 (Sheffield: Sheffield Academic Press, 1995).

overlooked: the confession of Jesus as the Christ. This is one of the scholarly works on Luke and every student of the Gospel of Luke may take this work into consideration.

4.11. Willi Braun (1995)

In *Feasting and Social Rhetoric in Luke 14*[48] Braun aims his readers toward a milieu analysis combined with the rhetoric of persuasion-a socio-rhetorical analysis. This includes situating Luke- Acts in the milieu of popular literature that employs an episodic style for moral edification and transformation. Luke 14:1-24 is one such episode. The book undertakes two primary ventures. One is to study the individual units of the episode using form criticism, source criticism, and milieu analysis. This analysis comprises on the healing of the dropsical man, Jesus' advice on table places and dinner invitations, the story of the banquet, and the transformation of the host in the story of the banquet. The second venture is to evaluate the rhetoric of persuasion. Conspicuous in range, depth and competence, the book is innovative not only in methodology but also in advancing options for interpretation. One notable proposal is that the dropsical man stands metaphorically for craving desire.

Genuinely provocative, this book raises some questions. Methodologically, Braun performs source analysis and traditional redaction criticism. However, of heuristic value, recovery of an antecedent version is superfluous for interpreting the final form, especially given Braun's emphasis on the milieu. What is at stake is the revision of norms. Nevertheless, this means revision of the unwritten cultural repertoire rather than the revision of written sources. Further, adherence to the method restricts the story of the banquet from fulfilling its parabolic capacity. Based on context, including the programmatic statement in Luke 4:43, is not the story theocentric? More than an example illustrating a 'truth' about inclusive social relationships, does the story not provoke readers to envision the way things are when God rules? Braun succeeds in exposing the social dynamics in Luke 14. This book is innovative, finely nuanced, and one of the most satisfactory investigations of Luke 14.

4.12. H. Douglas Buckwalter (1996)

In *The Character and Purpose of Luke's Christology,*[49] Buckwalter devotes most of his first chapter to a summary and assessment of various

---

[48] Willi Braun, *Feasting and Social Rhetoric in Luke 14*, Society for New Testament Studies Monograph Series 85 (Cambridge: Cambridge University Press, 1995).

[49] H. Douglas Buckwalter, *The Character and Purpose of Luke's Christology,* Society for New Testament Studies Monograph Series 89 (Cambridge: Cambridge University Press, 1996).

presentations of Luke's Christology. Buckwalter's method to address this deficiency is to offer four studies that provide the outline of the rest of the book. First, Buckwalter will examine "Luke's Christology and the purpose of Luke-Acts" (Part One, chaps. 2-3); second, "Luke's Christology and Mark's Gospel" (Part Two, chaps. 4-7); third, "Luke's Christology and Jesus' Lordship" (Part Three, chaps. 8-10); fourth, "Luke's Christology and Jesus' humiliation-exaltation" (Part Four, chap. 11). Chapter 12 presents Buckwalter's summary and conclusions. Before proceeding with this study, Buckwalter offers a set of criteria to assess whether a Christology adequately represents the unifying and overall Christological point of view. Such a proposed Christology should (1) coincide with Luke's purpose in writing, (2) plausibly explain his redactional motives and the unique literary features of Luke-Acts, (3) resolve the stated ostensible Christological tension between the Luke's expressions of Jesus' Lordship and subordination, and, above all (4) explain the character and purpose of his diverse Christologies (p. 31).

Buckwalter returns to these criteria in his conclusion and shows how his presentation of Luke's Christology does address the criteria. In such a long book, he would have helped readers by reviewing the criteria more explicitly and discussing, perhaps at the end of each part, how his presentation was progressing in addressing these criteria. Luke's explicit expansion of Mark's more subtle presentation of these issues leads Buckwalter to explore in greater detail three Christological issues in Part Three. He first examines Jesus' relationship with the Father (ch. 8), arguing against both adoptionism and subordinationism and concluding that "Luke and his readers . . . most likely . . . firmly believed that Jesus was by nature as much God as the Father was" (p. 192). Chapter. 9 explores Jesus' relationship with the Spirit. Exploiting the similarities between the ways Luke describes this relationship and the way the Jewish Scriptures describe the relationship between Yahweh and the Spirit, Buckwalter concludes that Jesus continues to be present among his people. This fact heightens the significance of Luke's Christology. Finally, chapter. 10 studies the relationship between Jesus and the end of history, arguing that Jesus stands at the center both of salvation history and of history's consummation, again heightening the significance of Luke's Christology. In fact, "the center of Luke's theology is not eschatology or salvation history but Christology" (p. 226). The book is well documented and written in conversation with many interpreters. This book can be received by readers with its implied Christological apology.

4.13. Peter Doble (1996)

In *The Paradox of Salvation: Luke's Theology of the Cross*[50] by means of a close examination of the crucifixion scene in Luke 23 against the horizon of the wider Luke's corpus, he argues that Luke does indeed have a clear, coherent understanding of Jesus' death within God's salvific plan. Working from the assumption that Luke-Acts was addressed to a Christian, readership in order to provide scriptural confirmation that they were the genuine heirs of God's promises, Doble attempts to show how Luke has drawn on words and patterns from the Wisdom of Solomon to demonstrate that Jesus' execution, far from constituting a shameful rejection, brought to expression the divine plan evident in "the paradox of salvation." Paradoxically, from one point of view, his was a shameful death, from another it was notable; from one point of view he suffered an *exodos,* from another, an *exodos* to standing at God's right hand in the presence of those who persecuted him. Luke's *theologia crucis* is built on this paradox of salvation (pp. 224-25). Along similar lines, one is left wondering how Luke's manifest interest in the portrayal of Jesus as the Davidic Messiah might be correlated with Doble's concern with the emphasis on patterns from Wisdom in Luke's construal of the cross. At the same time, by working exegetically with several components of Luke's Jerusalem narrative and theologically with "Wisdom's *dikaios* model," Doble is able to set his more general thesis on firm soil. *The Paradox of Salvation* would have been stronger, then, had it attempted to argue a more limited thesis. Even with this caveat, however, Doble's study is a welcome contribution to the growing appreciation of a distinctively Luke's way of construing the significance of the cross.

4.14. Barbara E. Reid (1996)

In *Choosing the Better Part?: Women in the Gospel of Luke*[51] Reid's first three chapters are preludes to her detailed and valuable commentary on the individual pericopes that Luke's Gospel devotes to women. Chapter 4 concerns Elizabeth and Mary and is the only chapter to have a section on "Contemporary Quandaries". Anna, the prophetic widow, is the subject of Chapter 5. The remainder of Reid's chapters are gold mines of feminist interpretations and bibliography as she shows her readers how to "choose the better part" of reinterpreting Luke against his patriarchal intentions. Her chapter headings often provide a summary of the gist of her interpretation: "Simon's Mother-in-Law: Healed for Service"; "The Widow of Nain:

[50] Peter Doble, *The Paradox of Salvation. Luke's Theology of the Cross* Society for New Testament Studies Monograph Series 87 (Cambridge: Cambridge University Press, 1996).

[51] Barbara E. Reid, *Choosing the Better Part?: Women in the Gospel of Luke* (Collegeville: Liturgical Press, 1996).

Voiceless Protester Against Death"; "The Woman Who Showed Great Love"; "Mary Magdalene, Joanna, and Susanna: Ministering Galilean Women"; "Jairus' Daughter and a Woman with a Hemorrhage: Resuscitation and Bold Faith"; "Pitting Mary Against Martha"; "Bent No More and Glorifying God!"; "A Woman Mixing Dough"; "A Woman Searching for a Lost Coin"; "A Persistent Widow"; "A Widow Who Gives All"; "The Galilean Women: Disbelieved Witnesses."

The book ends with a clear written summary of its major points, a Bibliography, and Indexes of Scripture Quotations and Authors. The chapter on discipleship needs to be more deeply integrated into the commentary section. In her treatment of Luke 10:38-42 Reid considers some provocatively positive medieval interpretations of Martha, thus fulfilling one of her goals of bringing "tradition" to bear on the process of reinterpretation (p. 13). The studies in the Gospel of Luke particularly from the feminist perspective are always motivating. Reid's work is one of the scholarly work which discuss the role of women in the Gospel of Luke in detail. All those who undertake the study on the Gospel of Luke must have a reading of this monograph.

4.15. Scott Cunningham (1997)

"Through Many Tribulations?": The Theology of Persecution in Luke-Acts[52] is revision of the Cunningham's Ph.D. thesis which offers itself as the first full-length treatment of the theme of persecution in both Luke and Acts. It argues that the Luke's theme of persecution makes six related assertions: (1) persecution is part of the plan of God; (2) persecution is the rejection of God's agents by those who are supposedly God's people; (3) the persecuted people of God stand in continuity with God's prophets in the past; (4) persecution is an integral consequence of following Jesus; (5) persecution is the occasion of the Christian's perseverance; (6) persecution is the occasion of divine triumph. Cunningham's methodology is eclectic but mostly conventional, employing elements of redaction criticism and of the brand of literary criticism exemplified by R. Tannehill. Throughout the work is grounded in traditional historical-critical exegesis. Cunningham reads Luke and Acts together, assuming that they articulate a coherent point of view.

The book argues a clear thesis with proficiency and thoroughness. The discussion shows a competent command of the relevant secondary literature and of widely accepted exegetical practices. The result is a case that offers little by way of new insights or surprises but little with which to disagree. Cunningham's conclusions mostly confirm the results of several well-

---

[52] Scott Cunningham, *'Through Many Tribulations?': The Theology of Persecution in Luke-Acts,* JSNT Sup 142 (Sheffield: Sheffield Academic Press, 1997).

established studies on closely related themes in the Gospel of Luke. Jesus and his followers experience what Israel's prophets experienced, God's plan is at work in Jesus and the church. Many of these conclusions place the book with a growing body of scholarship that sees Luke-Acts as telling the story of Jesus and the church to defend the Christian claim to the religious heritage of Israel. The larger picture into which conclusions are integrated is also unsurprising. Like many in the wake of redaction criticism, Cunningham makes a quasi-allegorical connection between elements of Luke's narrative and the situation of their audience. Thus, Luke wrote for a persecuted church. The very fact that this work is so conventional and unsurprising is its great strength. It employs time-honored exegetical methods to reach coherent, plausible conclusions. Having pursued a topic for its relevance to human experience instead of its scholarly currency, Cunningham does not define an agenda for future controversy in Luke's studies, but elucidates findings that should prove difficult to refute in the community of scholars and worthy to contemplate in the persecuted community of faith.

4.16. Jonathan Knight (1998)

Jonathan Knight's *Luke's Gospel*[53] is a significant contribution to the study of the Gospel of Luke. It is in a series entitled New Testament Readings, which reads each of the individual books of the NT with a fresh and stimulating approach. In the preface, the author says that this book draws on a fusion of methodologies to present what is called as a balanced reading of Luke. The book is divided into six chapters 1. An Introduction to the text, which deals with the authorship, date, sources of the Gospel and a synopsis of Luke. 2. Luke as a Narrative, which deals with narrative criticism and the components of narrative criticism 3. A Reading of Luke, which gives a chapter by chapter-summary reading of the Gospel of Luke 4. Alternative Readings of Luke, it gives a deconstructive reading and a feminist reading of the Gospel of Luke 5. The Themes of Luke's Gospel, such as seeing is believing, Luke's eschatology, the kingdom of God, Jews and Gentiles in Luke, [illegible] in the history of salvation, Luke's ethics and the [illegible] 6. A Reading of Readings, which examines some of the substantial secondary literature on Luke. This book makes use of narrative criticism in its exegesis. This is one of the scholarly works by Knight.

4.17. Kyoung-Jin Kim (1998)

Kyoung-Jin Kim's *Stewardship and Almsgiving in Luke's Theology,*[54] discusses Luke's interest in the theme of poverty and wealth is obvious and

[53] Jonathan Knight, *Luke's Gospel* (New York: Routledge, 1998).

[54] Kyoung-Jin Kim, *Stewardship and Almsgiving in Luke's Theology,* JSNT Sup 155 (Sheffield: Sheffield Academic Press, 1998).

many have taken in hand to discuss various aspects of his approach to the subject. But questions concerning Luke's specific focus, especially relating to the topic of discipleship, led Kyoung-Jin Kim to submit a dissertation on the subject to the University of Glasgow (1993). The present work is a slightly revised version. To shore up this proposal, Kim first of all probes the theme of discipleship in Mark (written 64-70 CE in Rome) in order to compare it with Luke's treatment and thus shed light on the latter's views of stewardship. The members of Luke's community are viewed principally as Gentiles, with rich and poor among them representing the extremes of contemporary society. Therefore, Kim concludes his study with a chapter on the practice of benefaction in Greco-Roman society. Against a political background of relatively little interest in the needs of the poor, the teaching of Jesus and practices of the early Christian community takes on special significance in Luke-Acts.

The kinds of questions that Kim addresses to Luke's work unearth aspects of Luke's literary art and theological acumen that have at times been smothered under contentious exegetical debris. But occasionally Kim inadvertently weakens his argumentative structure through questionable interpretations and dubious subordinate conclusions. So stimulating is Kim's very interesting study that one is tempted to go beyond the restrictions of a brief review and enter other avenues of inquiry and critique. But readers of his enterprising work will take up the challenge and are certain to be enriched by taking account of what needs to be modified, corrected, or simply pursued because it needs the doing. The task of future study of Luke-Acts is here considerably lightened through an excellent bibliography and indexes of biblical and Greco-Roman works. This monograph is an added wealth to the study on the Gospel of Luke from an economic perspective.

4.18. David A. Holgate (1999)

Holgate's *Prodigality, Liberality and Meanness in the Parable of the Prodigal Son: A Greco- Roman Perspective on Luke 15:11-32*[55] was published in 1999. Part I of Holgate's monograph focuses on the parable itself. He begins by surveying the analyses of the prodigal son that employed a reading informed by Greco-Roman perspectives, and he notes a number of parallels between this parable and elements of Greco-Roman literature and thought. Of special significance to Holgate are the parallels between the parable and the moral teachings of the Greco-Roman philosophers. After

[55] David A. Holgate, *Prodigality, Liberality and Meanness in the Parable of the Prodigal Son: A Greco-Roman Perspective on Luke 15:11-32,* JSNT Sup 187 (Sheffield: Sheffield Academic Press, 1999).

this survey he examines the composition and message of Luke 15:11-32, establishing the text and its structure.

The result of this examination is Holgate's contention that the father plays the central role in this parable, a role Luke designed to teach his readers about the virtue of compassionate liberality. The final chapter of this section searches for a milieu-what Holgate terms "co-texts" - for the parable. Unhappy with the interpretative strictures posed by limiting the parable to its immediate context of Luke 15 (the "lost and found" parables), Holgate argues that the "L parables" - those found only in Luke's Gospel-offer a better context for understanding the meaning(s) of the prodigal son. In particular, these co-texts emphasize the proper use of money and possessions; the parable's teachings about liberality in the use of money fits far better, he argues, with Luke 16 than with the rest of Luke 15.

Part II of the book examines other Greco-Roman moral texts for their use of the *Topos* on Covetousness. This chapter offers to the reader a very good tour through this particular arena of classical literature, explaining the use of *topoi*, examining the moral teachings about money and possessions across a wide range of texts, and describing the characteristic features of the *Topos* on Covetousness. Having argued that the parable of the prodigal is better read in light of Luke's message(s) about possessions, and having surveyed the ancient moral literature about the proper use of possessions, Holgate moves to Part III of his monograph: an analysis of the parable in light of ancient moral instruction concerning the proper use of possessions. In order to make his argument, however, Holgate makes some interesting interpretative assumptions. Often these are made in his attempt to free the parable from its connection with the preceding parables of the lost sheep and the lost coin.

Holgate's argument that the Luke's parables constitute the proper co(n)-text for the prodigal son is an interesting one, but he seems to want to give Luke credit for composing them and placing them within the travel narrative without also giving Luke credit for the narrative introductory tags that move this narrative forward. Holgate's argument that Luke's primary intention in including this parable is to teach the virtue of liberality ignores the narrative context too quickly. The parable is not just about the proper attitude toward possessions; it is also about the accepting nature of the reign of God and the complex social and religious relationship between Christianity and Judaism. Holgate's monograph is a worthy addition to the JSNT Supplement Series. The book offers a thoughtful contribution to the interpretation of the prodigal son as well as Luke's Gospel. Holgate's interaction with such a wide range of primary and secondary literature will also be helpful to any serious student of the New Testament.

5. 2000-2010

5.1. Mark A. Matson (2001)

In his work, *In Dialogue with Another Gospel? The Influence of the Fourth Gospel on the Passion Narrative of the Gospel of Luke,*[56] argues that Luke had used the Gospel of John in his composition of passion narrative (Lk 22-24). He deals with issues such as relationship between John and Synoptics and similarities between Luke and John. It is because of the literary dependence of Luke on John. His work has nine chapters: in the first chapter, he deals with John's relationship with the synoptic Gospels and Luke's method of writing; second chapter is a review of literatures; and the next chapter analyses the similarities between Luke and John; chapter four focuses on the text-critical analysis of the Western non-interpolations. Matson's main purpose is to analyze the composition of Luke's passion narrative (Lk. 22-14). His main hypothesis is that Luke is the last Gospel written. If Luke is the last Gospel written, then it belongs to the second century. In the beginning verses of the Gospel one finds that the account is from the 'eye witness' and to place the Gospel in the second century stands on a shaky ground. Most of the scholars agree that Luke was written between A.D. 80 and A.D. 90 and John was written between A.D. 90 and A.D 99. If these dates are probable then the literary relationship will be the other way round. Thus, Matson's analysis of Luke's passion narrative failed to do Justice in setting the date for Luke's Gospel. But Luke might have had access to the same sources which were used by John. It is a new way of looking at the sources of passion narrative. Any studies in the passion narrative may take this work for consideration, because it gives a wide range of material for the sources of passion narrative.

5.2. Barbara Shellard (2002)

In *New Light on Luke: Its Purpose, Sources and Literary Context,*[57] Barbara Shellard gives a comprehensive redaction-critical analysis of Luke. She argues that this Gospel shows literary dependence upon the other three that would come to accompany it in the canon, thereby manifesting the Evangelist's attempt to reconcile Markan, Matthean and Johannine theological perspectives within a single "corrective" Gospel. Her thesis overturns several tables (if one may employ such a distinctly non-Luke's image) in the courts of contemporary Gospel studies, contending that Luke (writing ca. 100 C.E.)

---

[56] Mark A. Matson, *In Dialogue with Another Gospel? The Influence of the Fourth Gospel on the Passion Narrative of the Gospel of Luke* (Atlanta: Society of Biblical Literature, 2001).

[57] Barbara Shellard, *New Light on Luke: Its Purpose, Sources and Literary Context,* JSNT Supp. Series 215 (London: Sheffield Academic Press, 2002).

relied heavily upon the Markan narrative frame, creatively wove in elements of Matthean teaching discourse, and supplemented the story with approved material from the Gospel of John (which Shellard dates in the early 90s). The author lays out her position in two main movements, first demonstrating Luke's dependence upon Matthew and then showing that affinities between Luke and John, best explained by Johannine priority.

The second major section of the book contends that thematic and verbal similarities shared by Luke and John indicate, not simply shared access to related traditions, but a direct literary relationship between these Gospels. The book's conclusion comprises Shellard's explanations of the impulses behind Luke's treatment and reconciliation of Mark, Matthew, and John. She reviews similarities and differences between the theological outlooks of Luke and each of the others (several of her generalizations about the tendencies of a given Evangelist ring the bells of hotly debated topics), determining that Luke's purpose was essentially pastoral.

This volume pursues its goals in an enterprising manner. Its author recognizes that, to be persuasive, Shellard's argument about Luke's use of sources must make its case cumulatively, so the author articulates her connections clearly and attends consistently to the theological perspectives that might have prompted the redactional activity Shellard finds in the Gospel of Luke. Author treats other scholarship graciously and evenhandedly, especially when addressing the Synoptic Problem and the question of Luke's and Johannine similarities. Shellard's thesis is controversial and therefore a stimulus to consider aspects of Luke that pose challenges to more conventional hypotheses about Gospel relationships and theological currents within the early church.

5.3. Guy D. Nave (2002)

In *The Role and Function of Repentance in Luke-Acts,*[58] Nave carefully examines the meaning of *metanoio* and *metanoia* in a wide range of classical and Hellenistic literature culminating in Luke's two-volume narrative. These terms for "repentance" appear twenty-five times in Luke-Acts representing almost half of all New Testament usage. A major portion of the book (over one hundred pages) charts the occurrences of "repentance" language in pagan, Jewish, and Christian Greek writings outside of Luke- Acts, focusing on the works of Plutarch, Josephus, and Philo, the LXX, the rest of the New Testament, and *1 Clement*. *Repentance* means a change in thinking that usually leads to a change in behavior and or way of life (p.145).

[58] Guy D. Nave, *The Role and Function of Repentance in Luke-Acts* (Atlanta: Society of Biblical Literature/Leiden: Brill, 2002).

In his analysis of Luke-Acts, Nave employs a blend of redaction criticism, assuming the traditional two-source (Mark and Q) hypothesis without argument, and narrative criticism, discerning the role of repentance within the developing plot of God's overarching plan of salvation for Israel and the world. In terms of structure, the intertwined themes of "fruits/deeds worthy of repentance" and "the salvation of God" frame the entire narrative at strategic points (Lk 3:6, 8; Acts 26:20; 28:28) and unfold successively in the preaching of John the Baptist, Jesus, and his disciples. This book represents a superb foundational study of an important Lukan theme. Nave surprisingly provides little investigation of this "sermon." Also, the use of Cornelius in Acts as a model of Gentile repentance "associated with a change of religion" (p. 214) needs to be elaborated, since he was already a devout worshiper of Israel's God and faithful supporter of the poor. However, wanting Nave to go further on these matters is a tribute to what he has already achieved.

5.4. Amy-Jill, Levine and Marianne Blickenstaff (eds.) (2002)

The Gospel of Luke has been at the center of intense feminist scholarly and theological debate for the past decade. The basic question comes down to this: Does Luke evince a positive attitude toward women past and present or a negative one? *A Feminist Companion to Luke,*[59] ably edited by Amy-Jill Levine with Marianne Blickenstaff, includes essays by leading scholars, all of whom address an aspect of this debate. Luke is an especially promising text for feminist interpretation, not only because it contains numerous references to women, but also because it lends itself to such diverse, mutually exclusive feminist readings. Perhaps the most decisive critique of Luke is offered by Mary Rose D. Angelos, 'The *ANHR* Question in Luke-Acts: Imperial Masculinity and the Deployment of Women in the Early Second Century' (pp. 44-69). This essay points out that, in spite of Luke's numerous references to women, these references are paired with stories about men and are often shorter and the women in them are rarely allowed to speak. This virtually erases a female point of identification.

Most of the other essays in the volume, however, avoid an outright critique of Luke. Thus, for example, Turid Karlsen Seim's 'The Virgin Mother: Mary and the Ascetic Discipleship in Luke' (89-105) avoids an explicit critique, though it points to the irreconcilable polarization of, on the one hand, the ascetic ideal of virginity, and, on the other, motherhood. Pointing to ambiguity and contradiction as evidence of textual complexity is Brigitte Kahl's Reading Luke against Luke: Non-uniformity of Text,

[59] Amy-Jill, Levine and Marianne Blickenstaff (eds), *A Feminist Companion to Luke: Feminist Companion to the New Testament and Early Christian Writings* (Sheffield: Sheffield Academic Press, 2002).

Hermeneutics of Conspiracy and the 'Scriptural Principle' in Luke 1 (pp. 70-88), which juxtaposes father's time and mother's time, arguing for a position that refuses any uniform or decisive reading of Luke. Kahl argues that the Magnificat in Luke 1 establishes Mary as the founder of Christian theology and feminist readings. In 'The Woman Is a Sinner/The Sinner Is a Woman' (pp. 121-33), Teresa J. Honsby questions interpretations that constructed the anointing woman in Luke 7:36-50 as a prostitute. According to her liberationist reading, these interpretations are not suggested by the text itself. In 'The Lukan Mary Magdalene and the Other Women Following Jesus' (pp. 140-60), Esther A. de Boer argues that Luke emphasizes Jesus' women followers more than do Mark and Matthew. Loveday C. Alexander exonerates Martha in her essay 'Sisters in Adversity: Retelling Martha's Story' (pp. 197-213).

In 'Women and Discipleship in Luke 10:38-42 and Acts 6:1-7, The Literary Context of Luke-Acts' (pp. 161-96) argues that various readings by Elizabeth Schüssler Fiorenza, Adele Reinhartz, Turid Karlsen Seim, and others have attempted to establish Luke's authorial intention. Carol Schersten LaHurd's 'Reviewing Luke 15 with Arab Christian Women' (pp. 246-68) focuses on the positive reception of Luke 15 by women in Northern Yemen. LaHurd concludes her essay with a call for a 'hermeneutics of suspicion' toward Western feminist interpretations rather than toward the biblical text. Most of the fourteen essays in this volume seek to establish Luke as a text that has the ability to appeal to and even empower contemporary women. Whether they use sociological, anthropological, historical, or literary approaches, for the most part they focus on positive elements in the text or in readers' responses to the text.

On the other hand, the feminist critiques that target specific androcentric expressions in Luke continue to constitute a formidable challenge, a fundamental questioning that cannot be ignored. Thus, the debate to which Amy-Jill Levine refers in her Introduction continues to simmer right beneath the surface of so many essays. Whether the positive, optimistic, or affirmative reading of the New Testament will become the norm is not clear at this point. The debate the volume captures so well may continue for some time to come, generating deeper and even more exciting insights into texts and readers alike.

5.5. François Bovon (2002)

François Bovon's *Luke 1: A Commentary on the Gospel of Luke 1:1-9:50*[60] is the translation of his German work, which was published in 1989.

---

[60] François Bovon, *Luke 1: A Commentary on the Gospel of Luke 1:1-9:50*, Hermeneia, tr. by Christine M. Thomas (Minneapolis: Fortress Press, 2002).

Bovon is of the opinion that in spite of Luke's interest in history, he remains as a theologian of God's word. He argues that Luke had adopted the biblical narrative technique to emphasize continuity between the Septuagint and his work. Bovon observes that even through Luke made use of Hellenistic historiographic techniques in his work, it is reminiscent Jewish historiography (p. 5). According to Bovon, Luke wishes to set forth how God, through his agency of his son, accomplished the decisive act of deliverance and how news of this event spread everywhere through its witnesses, with the help of the holy spirit (p. 5). Luke's purpose is to show how this salvation is proclaimed in the concrete historical context. This commentary gives a comprehensive interpretation of the Gospel of Luke. This commentary has dealt with the infancy narrative and the Galilean ministry of Jesus; it is part of the three volume of Hermeneia Series. The commentary especially its introductory section -'the work of Luke'- is an interesting one.

5.6. Takatemjen (2003)

Takatemjen in his work, *The Banquet is Ready: Rich and Poor in the Parables of Luke,*[61] focuses on the issue of rich and poor in Luke's parables. He applies both redaction criticism and sociology (socio-history) to study eight parables of Luke (Lk. 7:41-43; 10:30-36; 12:16-21 14:16-24; 16:1-13, 19-31; 18:25; 19:12-27) that deal with rich and poor. He has divided the work into five chapters. They are 1. the social setting of Jesus and Luke 2. Parables with explicit mention of rich and poor 3. parables without explicit mention of rich and poor 4. rich and poor in non-parabolic passages and 5. Luke's theology of rich and poor in the parables.

He follows the idea that the Luke's community which was an urban community, which combined both rich and poor. Luke turns the parables of Jesus into example stories following the wisdom tradition of the Old Testament to refer primarily to the richer members of his community. Luke warns the rich about the dangers of riches and exhorts them to use their wealth for the sake of the poor in providing meals giving alms and doing good works. According to Takatemjen, salvation of the rich members depends in what they do with their riches and what they do to the poor. He relates his study to the present Indian context by which he makes the Gospel of Luke relevant to the present day context. In this book, Takatemjen argues that Luke's community was comprised of rich and poor, and the parables reflect the tension that existed among them. For him, Luke wrote the Gospel aiming to solve the problem of the rich and the poor in his community. Wealth and poverty was one of the major problems of first century Mediterranean world.

---

[61] Takatemjen, *The Banquet is Ready: Rich and Poor in the Parables of Luke* (Delhi: ISPCK, 2003).

Takatemjen assumes that the parables of Jesus are metaphors and example stories after the wisdom tradition. This work is an added treasure for the study of parables in the Gospel of Luke.

5.7. Thomas E. Phillips (2003)

Thomas E. Phillips, in his article "Reading Recent Reading of Issues of Wealth and Poverty in Luke-Acts"[62] gives a review of important works on wealth and poverty in Luke-Acts from mid 1960s to 2001. He divides the variety of works to various critical perspectives, such as redaction, social-scientific, literary and reader response. Phillips divides their work under fourteen sub-headings. These headings capture the main argument of each author. He observes that in the history of Luke's interpretation, time and again attempts are made to incorporate social and economic factors to understand the Luke's text, but in the 19th and 20th centuries several scholars began to suggest that social and economic factors played a decisive role in the message of Jesus and the early church. He notices that the recent scholarship had dominated by two dominant reading strategies, which are redaction and literary criticism. The redaction critics hold the view that the first century readers created a consistent reading of the texts based on their first-century extra-textual knowledge or experience. This study emphasizes that the texts' consistent symbolic level, that is, the text's presentation of economic issues serves one consistent symbolic function throughout the text. The article encapsulates the current debate on wealth and poverty in Luke-Acts. Phillips coherently presents the diverse views of scholars. The fourteen different reading strategies show the cardinal importance of wealth and poverty in Luke-Acts. This article is a handy survey of recent studies on wealth and poverty in Luke-Acts.

5.8. Todd Klutz (2004)

Todd Klutz in *The Exorcism Stories in Luke-Acts: A Sociostylistic Reading*[63] has made a welcome contribution in his study of the key exorcism [illegible] a wide range of ancient Near Eastern, Jewish, Greek, Roman and Christian sources on demonology for comparative study while integrating literary criticism. This study integrates a detailed literary critique of Luke's exorcism studies with a wide-ranging investigation of ancient sources on demonology, spirit affliction and exorcistic healing. Klutz finds that lexical semantics

---

[62] Thomas E. Phillips, "Reading Recent Reading of Issues of Wealth and Poverty in Luke-Acts," *Currents in Biblical Research* 1 (2003): 231-269.

[63] Todd Klutz, *The Exorcism Stories in Luke-Acts: A Sociostylistic Reading,* Society for New Testament Studies Monograph Series 129 (Cambridge: Cambridge University Press, 2004).

have made such contributions to biblical studies in the last forty years that explanation of concepts can be kept to a minimum. The four chapters cover Luke 4:33-37 (Sociostylistics and the Exorcism); 8:26-39 (Purity and the Exorcism); 9:37-43a (Discipleship and the Exorcism); and Acts 16:16-18 (Paul, Jewish Identity and the Exorcism).

Klutz's conclusions often compel one to see the text in a new and challenging way. Thus, on Luke 4:33 against the background of the antecedent repetition of synagogue in 4:15, 16, 20, 28, where Jesus' impolite interpretation of Scripture almost gets him killed by people from the synagogue . One can only admire the way Klutz tackles a scene such as the Synoptic tradition of the Gerasene demoniac, which many interpreters have underestimated at their peril. He notes the imposition of multiple personality disorder, a modern medical category; the interpretation of Legion as a refutation of the Roman military garrison; and the request for the demonic power's name as less Christian than magical, a problem that dissolves as soon as the distinction between magic and Christianity (or Religion) is recognized as less substantive than perspectival.

5.9. Joseph Grassi (2004)

Grassi's *Peace on Earth: Roots and Practices from Luke's Gospel*[64] deals with an admirable review of Luke's writings from the perspective of nonviolence. For Grassi, Luke seems to be writing against *pax Romana* and suggesting that *pax Christi* promotes a different power over the earth and among people. Grassi suggests that the conflict is between Jesus, who brings the internal power of peace, and the emperor of Rome, who uses external power for peace. Grassi also writes that the passion and suffering of the cross are God's method of bringing about peace for those suffering under a violent government. The agents of this nonviolent peace are repentance, forgiveness, and the witness of Christ to the world. Grassi points out that *repentance, peace, the poor, today, heart, grace/forgiveness, the way, power,* and *redemption* are words that occur more frequently in Luke-Acts than in the other Gospels combined. These terms according to Grassi, are the method of bringing peace to the people of God without violence, war, and oppression. The simple style of writing and easy explanations can give students a different overview of the Gospel as well as of the early Christian community. Grassi's emphasis on words and themes unique to Luke also provides a resource for students.

---

[64] Joseph Grassi, *Peace on Earth: Roots and Practices from Luke's Gospel* (Collegeville: Liturgical Press, 2004).

5.10. B. J. Syiemlieh (2005)

B. J. Syiemlieh in his book, *God's Favorites: A Socio-Narrative Analysis of the Characters in the Lukan Infancy Narratives (Lk 1:5-2:52),*[65] argues that God reverses the fortunes of people who live in the low social status. The explanation unfolds how, of all the characters within the narratives, one group of characters stand out as unique in that they are initially portrayed to be of low standing in the social scale whereas the final portrait vindicates them as recipients of God's favor. There are seven chapters including the theoretical principles of characterization in narrative criticism. Syiemlieh employs narrative criticism and social sciences to analyze the characterization of people in the Luke's infancy narrative. He argues that the theme 'salvation-as-reversal' in Luke 1-2 is Luke's theology programme in which the lowly and humble are exalted by God but the arrogant are humbled. His analysis is Luke's infancy narratives show that the marginalized and people of low social status are God's favorites.

This book exhibits how Luke's theme 'salvation-as-reversal' exemplifies in Luke's infancy narrative. The poor and the powerless in Luke 1-2 have found, God's favor but on the other hand the rich and the powerful are rejected by God. Syiemlieh brings out this theme in the best possible way. The methodology that he has employed (Narrative-social-scientific criticism) has assisted him to bring out the social setting of the characters and the unity of the text. The methodology employed for the study can be very well taken, the socio-narrative analysis. The social-scientific criticism has helped Syiemlieh to overcome the historical tendency of narrative criticism. Much of the scholarly work on the Gospel of Luke in general and infancy narrative in particular has been used for discussion. It gives a biblical foundation to strengthen the theological standpoint that God is on the side of the socially low and marginalized or that such people are God's favorites.

5.11. Kenneth Duncan Litwak (2005)

In *Echoes of Scripture in Luke-Acts: Telling the History of God's People Intertextually,*[66] from the beginning it is clear that Litwak presents his study as different. He stresses that other scholars often reduce Luke's use of the Scriptures of Israel to a relatively small number of isolated phenomena but that he will show that these Scriptures pervade Luke-Acts from its beginning to its end: Scriptures play a hermeneutical role in shaping Luke-Acts. In the

---

[65] This book is originally a doctoral dissertation submitted to the Senate of Serampore College in 2003. B. J. Syiemlieh, *God's Favorites: A Socio-Narrative Analysis of the Characters in the Lukan Infancy Narratives (Lk 1:5-2:52)* (Delhi: ISPCK, 2005).

[66] Kenneth Duncan Litwak, *Echoes of Scripture in Luke-Acts: Telling the History of God's People Inter-textually,* JSNT Supp. Series 282 (London: T&T Clark, 2005).

first chapter he defines basic terminology, reviews previous research, and presents the aim of his study. Litwak chooses to focus on the Scriptures of Israel because, he argues, although Luke and his audience may have known other Jewish or non-Jewish texts, he quotes explicitly only passages from the Scriptures of Israel (with the exception of Acts 17:28). After this he reviews literature in recent scholarship on Scripture in Luke-Acts, focusing only on hermeneutical issues, without giving too much attention to what he means by hermeneutical (p. 8).

Litwak sees three different groups: authors who argue that Luke uses the promise-fulfillment, or proof-from-prophecy schema; those who stress the imitation or continuity theme; and those who argue that typology is Luke's model. In the final section, Litwak deals with intertextual studies. Litwak argues that these studies mostly focus on the Christological function of the quotations and stresses the fact that the majority opinion of Luke's use of Scripture is some derivation of a promise-fulfillment/proof-from prophecy schema (p. 30). In a second chapter Litwak explains his assumptions, for example, that Luke-Acts is a unity of genre, authorship, and narrative. He wants to examine the full range of intertextual connections between Luke-Acts and the Scriptures of Israel, the quotations, common traditions, echoes or allusions. After sketching these important preliminaries, Litwak looks for intertextual relations that frame the discourse in Luke's beginning. Chapter 3 he focuses on the echoes in Luke 1 of biblical annunciations, of the Abrahamic covenant, and of deliverers, prophets and commissioned individuals among Israel. In chapter 4 he argues that Peter uses the quotation from Joel to show that those who called on the name of the Lord formed a new community. In his last chapter Litwak stresses that the end of a narrative is crucial and that Luke presents to us Paul, who as prophet uses the Scriptures of Israel to show that this new community, the followers of the Way, are the true remnant of Israel. One of the main points under attack in Litwak's book is the statement that Luke uses a proof-from-prophecy model. Instead of this model, Litwak repeatedly stresses that the function of Luke's use of Scriptures is continuity. There are sometimes weird and small mistakes. One example: although Litwak seems to know that, according to Luke, Jesus reads Isaiah in Nazareth (Lk 4:16.30), he twice argues that it happened in the synagogue of Capernaum (p.111 and 186).

5.12. Michael F. Patella (2005)

The Gospel according to Luke,[67] The New Collegeville Bible Commentary series aims to make the Bible comprehensive and

[67] Michael F. Patella, *The Gospel according to Luke* New Collegeville Bible Commentary (Collegeville: Liturgical Press, 2005).

understandable to preachers, teachers, Bible study groups and other readers, bringing recent scholarship to bear on issues of background and context. After the introductions, Patella moves into a section-by-section commentary. Surfacing at key points of interest are notes derivative of the author's background in the geography and archeology of the Holy Land, such as his discussion of homes built for extended families (Lk. 2:1–7), materials used in roof construction (Lk. 5:17–26), the sort of boat in which Jesus and his disciples would have crossed (Lk. 8:22–25), and his identification of Luke's Emmaus account and the theological issues in the Gospel of Luke, Patella notes several emphases, including the significance of dining, anticipation of the Gentile mission and Jesus' battle with evil. On the whole, Patella takes a dim view of Luke's historical and geographical accuracy, leaves little of no room for predictive prophecy, and remains cautiously agnostic on the question of whether various miracles actually happened. Nevertheless, it is easy to congratulate Patella on his having written a general commentary that should serve well the aims of the New Collegeville Bible Commentary.

5.13. Bart J. Koet (2006)

Dreams and Scripture in Luke-Acts: Collected Essays,[68] includes nine essays, grouped in three sections. The four essays in section 1. "Studies in Luke-Acts", deals with "themes related to interpretation of Scripture in Luke Acts in general", contributing "insights into the way in which the author designed Luke Acts as a unity." Koet first documents the extensive use of dream-visions in Acts and compares these divine communications with contemporary Jewish sources where scriptural accounts are formative. In the dreams, Luke scores the same point as in the scriptural interpretations: "in all of these visions, *the same message* is revealed: the Gentile mission is a divine command (p. 16). In the Gospel, Luke's emphasis on Jesus' prayers and his role as a Mosaic prophet mean that, like Moses, Jesus does not need dreams because he speaks face to face with God. 2. "Trustworthy Dreams? About Dreams and References to Scripture in 2 Maccabees 14–15, Josephus' *Antiquitates Judaicae* 11, 302–347 and in the New Testament." It is the thesis of this article that in Jewish circles of the Second Temple Period, dreams could also be used as propaganda, but especially those dreams were trustworthy which were related in one way or another to Scripture (p. 25). 3. "Isaiah in Luke-Acts." This essay is a many-faceted gem, illuminating sequentially all explicit quotations from Isaiah and allusions to Isaiah texts, which are quoted elsewhere in Acts (p. 54). 4. "Purity and Impurity of the Body in Luke-Acts."

---

[68] Bart J. Koet, *Dreams and Scripture in Luke-Acts: Collected Essays,* Contributions to Biblical Exegesis and Theology 42 (Leuven: Peeters, 2006).

Koet observes that much New Testament scholarship is ignorant of the importance and complexity of purity regulations in Second Temple Jewish sources, including the New Testament. Responding with both appreciation and criticism to the work of Jerome Neyrey, Koet argues, "Luke depicts Jesus and other important figures of Luke-Acts as law-abiding and conscious of purity regulations (p. 86). Two essays in section 2, "Studies in Luke 2", are focused on Luke's use of biblical passages in the prophetic portrayals of Simeon and Anna. Section 3, "Acts 16 and Acts 18", includes three essays on the interpretation of dreams and scripture in these two chapters of Acts. This text gives new lights to the study of Luke-Acts.

5.14. François Bovon (2006)

Bovon's *Luke the Theologian: Fifty-Five Years of Research,*[69] gives a wide summary of fifty-five years of studies on Luke's theology, and is a noteworthy work of research and review. The book is organized thematically in ten chapters. The first seven correspond to the first edition of this book (1976) and survey Lukan research from 1950 to 1975. They are divided thematically: (1) "The Plan of God, Salvation History and Eschatology"; (2) "The Interpretations of the Scriptures in Israel"; (3) "Christology"; (4) "The Holy Spirit"; (5) "Salvation"; (6) "The Reception of Salvation"; and (7) "The Church". Each chapter contains a thematic bibliography, an introduction by Bovon where he summarizes the theological issue being studied, then an introduction to the development of the theological debate reviewing the books of the main scholars who wrote on the subject. In the review of the publications, Bovon expresses some comments, his ideas on the subject are to be looked for in the short conclusions of each chapter, where he shows to the reader, after having contributed to the scholarly debate, what was Luke's theological thinking. In these sections, Bovon is very good in outlining the development of the scholarly research, the issues at stake and why and how the scholars defend their theses. Bovon's book can be a good help in choosing the right reference books, in order to avoid stuffing a book with hundreds of titles; a bibliography should be a guide to the books with which an author has seriously confronted himself or herself. Bovon's tome is a guide for it.

5.15. Paul Borgman (2006)

In The *Way According to Luke: Hearing the Whole Story of Luke-Acts*[70] the approach followed is narrative criticism the author approaches the text as a "story, not sermon-of narrative art, not theological treatise" (p. 5). The

---

[69] François Bovon, *Luke the Theologian: Fifty-Five Years of Research (1950–2005),* 2nd edition (Waco: Baylor University Press, 2006).

[70] Paul Borgman, *The Way According to Luke: Hearing the Whole Story of Luke-Acts* (Grand Rapids: Eerdmans, 2006).

author merely retells the story of Luke's "Way"-group in his own words, highlighting certain lines of thought, motifs and "signal words." The book is divided into four parts. Part 1 deals with "The Way: Narrative Preparations (Lk 1:1–9:50)" and consists of four chapters. Part 2 deals with "The Way: Principles Taught (Lk 9:51–19:44)," with nine chapters. Part 3 looks at "The Way Demonstrated (Lk 19:45–24:53)" and has two chapters. Part 4, comprising eight chapters, looks at how "The Way Spreads" and focuses mainly on Acts. The question of whether Luke 1-2 and Acts 17 are truly Luke's compositions, and all the inter-textual connections with Mark and Q, in fact the whole issue of the Synoptic problem, simply cannot be ignored after many years of scholarship. True to an exclusively narrative approach to the text, however, these historical matters become irrelevant for the author.

5.16. Mikeal Parsons (2007)

Parsons' *Luke: Storyteller, Interpreter, Evangelist*[71] is not another overview of Luke-Acts but a series of more limited studies in six chapters arranged under the three headings of "Luke the Storyteller," "Luke the Interpreter" and "Luke the Evangelist". Parsons' "series of forays into the Lukan terrain" (p. xi) does not add up to a full interpretation of Luke's writings, but the reader will benefit from suggestive approaches to selected issues that deserve further exploration. Past scholarship has pointed to some significant differences between the Paul of the letters and the Paul of Acts. Parsons should have given more attention to these differences, showing either that they do not really exist or that they would not have troubled the original audience of Acts. Apart from that discussion, Parsons' section on Paul is unconvincing because it is incomplete. As Parsons no doubt recognizes, many of his claims in this book are suggestive rather than definitive. They need further investigation to test whether they apply broadly to Luke's writings rather than to isolated texts.

5.17. Rick Strelan (2008)

The purpose of Rick Strelan's *Luke the Priest: The authority of the author of the Third Gospel*[72] is to give a contribution to the debate of the authority of Luke, the author of third Gospel, to a new direction and stimulate further discussion and study. It is a search for an answer to how authority and control of stories might have worked among the first Christians, particularly, what authority someone like Luke had to teach, to interpret and to transmit the tradition as he did. The aim of the book is to construct the

[71] Mikeal Parsons, *Luke: Storyteller, Interpreter, Evangelist* (Peabody: Hendrickson, 2007).

[72] Rick Strelan, *Luke the Priest: The Authority of the Author of the Third Gospel* (London: Ashgate Publishing Company, 2008).

writer of the third Gospel, 'The Gospel According Luke' as it has become known. Basic questions of the author are: who, or what gave this 'author' the authority to write the Gospel and Acts? What authority did he have to interpret the traditions of Israel including its scriptures? By what authority did he interpret the traditions about Jesus and about some of the apostles, especially Paul? Why did he write a Gospel at all, especially since he was aware of other attempts? (p. 1). Rick Strelan suggests in this book that the author, whom tradition has called 'Luke', might well have been a Jewish priest who, of course, had come to believe that Jesus is God's Lord and Christ, the fulfillment of Israel's Scriptures. It was the author's status as priest that gave him the authority to interpret the various traditions he deals with and to write his interpretations as authoritative texts for his audiences.

He could have clubbed some of the chapters and make ch. 9 more scholarly by analyzing up to date state of Lukan scholarship on the authorship of Luke and make his addition to that. The Church has inherited a Gospel that interprets and re-interprets, not only God's revelation to humanity in Israel, but also the received traditions of the early Church itself. Amongst other storylines, Peter and Paul are depicted in Luke–Acts as mutually supportive leaders. This book provokes considerable discussion on identity and occupation of Luke and Theophilus.

6. Bibliography from 2009-2024

6.1. 2009-2020

MacArthur, John. *Luke 1-5 MacArthur New Testament Commentary*. Moody Publishers, 2009.

Card, Michael. *Luke: The Gospel of Amazement*. InterVarsity Press, 2010.

Farley, Lawrence R. *The Gospel of Luke: Good News for the Poor*. Ancient Faith Publishing, 2010.

Green, Joel B. *Methods for Luke*. Cambridge University Press, 2010.

Morgan, G. Campbell. *The Gospel According to Luke*. Wipf and Stock Publishers, 2010.

W. Mark Tew, *Luke: Gospel to the Nameless and Faceless* (Wipf and Stock Publishers, 2011).

Dario Andres Lopez Rodriguez, *The Liberating Mission of Jesus: The Message of the Gospel of Luke* (Wipf and Stock Publishers, 2012).

chultz, *The Gospel of Luke* (Lulu.com, 2013).

Dinger, Dennis. *A Study of the Gospel of Luke*. Lulu.com, 2014.

Patrick Whitworth, *Gospel for the Outsider: The Gospel in Luke & Acts* (Sacristy Press, 2014).

Bock, Darrell L. *A Theology of Luke and Acts: God's Promised Program, Realized for All Nations*. Zondervan Academic, 2015.

Byrne, Brendan. *The Hospitality of God: A Reading of Luke's Gospel*. Liturgical Press, 2015.

Edwards, James R. *The Gospel According to Luke*. Wm. B. Eerdmans Publishing, 2015.

Woodward, James, Mark Pryce, and Paula Gooder. *Journeying with Luke: Reflections on the Gospel*. Presbyterian Publishing Corp, 2015.

Ponessa, Fr Joseph L., and Laurie Watson Manhardt. *Come and See: The Gospel of Luke*. Emmaus Road Publishing, 2015.

Ponessa, Fr Joseph, and Laurie Watson Manhardt. *Come and See: The Gospel of Luke*. Emmaus Road Publishing, 2015.

Bartholomew, Craig G. *Revealing the Heart of Prayer: The Gospel of Luke*. Lexham Press, 2016.

Strauss, Mark L. *Luke*. Zondervan Academic, 2016.

Wolter, Michael. *The Gospel According to Luke*. Baylor University Press, 2016.

LLC, Alabaster Co. *Gospel of Luke*. Alabaster Company LLC, 2017.

Moore, Thomas. *Gospel--The Book of Luke*. Turner Publishing Company, 2017.

Thomas, Keith. *The Book of Luke: A Walk Through the Life of Jesus*. Lulu Press, Incorporated, 2017.

Pawson, David. *A Commentary on the Gospel of LUKE*. Anchor, 2017.

Gadenz, Pablo T. *The Gospel of Luke (Catholic Commentary on Sacred Scripture)*. Baker Academic, 2018.

Johnson, Luke Timothy. *Sacra Pagina: The Gospel of Luke*. Liturgical Press, 2018.

Knight, Matthew A. *The Book of Luke: Physician and Historian*. Xlibris Corporation, 2018.

Levine, Amy-Jill, and Ben Witherington III. *The Gospel of Luke*. Cambridge University Press, 2018.

Lukather, Steve. *The Gospel According to Luke*. Post Hill Press, 2018

Roberson, Carroll. *Luke the Lord'S Gospel*. WestBow Press, 2018.

Reeder, Caryn A. *Gendering War and Peace in the Gospel of Luke*. Cambridge University Press, 2018.

Patella, Michael F., and Little Rock Scripture Study. *The Gospel According to Luke, Part Two*. Liturgical Press, 2018

Osborne, Grant R. *Luke Verse by Verse*. Lexham Press, 2018.

Nethercott, Mary. *Introduction to the Gospel of Luke and Themes in the Synoptic Gospels for CCEA A Level*. Colourpoint Books, 2018.

Allen, Amy Lindeman. *For Theirs Is the Kingdom: Inclusion and Participation of Children in the Gospel According to Luke*. Rowman & Littlefield, 2019.

Baltrip, Ryan. *The Gospel of Luke*. Two Worlds Publishing, 2020.

Darby, John Nelson. *Notes on the Gospel of Luke*. BoD – Books on Demand, 2020.

Edwards, James R. *The Gospel According to Luke*. Inter-Varsity Press, 2020.

Wilson, Ralph F. *Discipleship Training in Luke's Gospel*. JesusWalk Publications, 2020.

Peters, George N. H. *The Testimony of Luke: 1907 Biblical Study Notes on the Gospel of Luke*. BookLocker.com, Inc., 2020.

Nickle, Keith F. *Preaching the Gospel of Luke: Proclaiming God's Royal Rule*. Westminster John Knox Press, 2000.

6.2. 2021-2024

Caird, G. B. (George Bradford). *The Gospel of Saint Luke*. HASSELL STREET Press, 2021.

Francis, Pope. *The Gospel of Luke: A Spiritual and Pastoral Reading*. Orbis Books, 2021.

Strong, Justin David. *The Fables of Jesus in the Gospel of Luke: A New Foundation for the Study of Parables*. Brill, Ferdinand Schöningh, 2021.

Shines, Roberto. *Luke's Gospel: The Gospel Of The Savior For Lost People Everywhere: Unique Features Of Luke'S Gospel*. Independently Published, 2021.

Gallagher, Edmon L. *The Gospel of Luke*. Heritage Christian University, 2022.

Hamilton, Adam. *Luke: Jesus and the Outsiders, Outcasts, and Outlaws*. Abingdon Press, 2022.

Knight, Matthew a. *The Book of Luke*. BookTrail Publishing, 2022.

France, R. T. *Luke (Teach the Text Commentary Series)*. Baker Books, 2013.

Wright, Nicholas Thomas, and Michael L. Kirkindoll. *Luke for Everyone*. Westminster John Knox Press, 2023.

James, King. *The Gospel According to ST. LUKE*. National Book Network, 2024.

Concluding Remarks

This paper is inadequate to give a detailed overview and critique of the commentaries such as William Hendriksen's *Luke*[73] which has a good outline for each section, literal translation of the Greek New Testament and detailed exegesis and proper footnoting; G. B. Caird's *Saint Luke*[74] which gives chapter divisions with outline, translation of the original text and exposition of the text; E. Earle Ellis's *The Gospel of Luke*[75] gives exegesis; Michael Fallon, *The Gospel According to Saint Luke*[76] gives translation and exposition to the Gospel of Luke; Eugene LaVerdiere, *Luke*[77] gives a detailed theological commentary on the Gospel of Luke; R. C. H. Lenski[78] gives an exegetical study on the Gospel of Luke; James Massey[79] gives a running commentary on the Gospel of Luke with some contextual reflection; David Gooding[80] gives an exposition to Luke's Gospel; G. W. H. Lame[81] gives a good commentary on the Gospel of Luke; Craig A. Evans, *Luke*;[82] Bruce Malina's[83] and Jane Schaberg's[84] works are the sources for the study of the Gospel of Luke particularly from the feminist perspective. No student of the Gospel of Luke can neglect the scholarly article in the *New Jerome*

---

[73] William Hendriksen, *Luke: New Testament Commentary, Exposition of the Gospel According to Luke* (Michigan: Baker Book House, 1978).

[74] G. B. Caird, *Saint Luke: The Pelican New Testament Commentaries* (England: Penguin Books, 1963).

[75] E. Earle Ellis, *The Gospel of Luke:* New Century Bible Commentary (Michigan: W. B. Eerdmans, 1980).

[76] Michael Fallon, *The Gospel According to Saint Luke: An Introductory Commentary* (Bangalore: ATC, 1997).

[77] Eugene LaVerdiere, *Luke: New Testament Message; Biblical-Theological Commentary,* vol. 5, edited by Wilfrid Harrington and Donald Senior (Wilmington, Delaware: Michael Glazier, 1980).

[78] R. C. H. Lenski, *The Interpretation of St. Luke's Gospel: Commentary on the New Testament* (Peabody: Hendrickson, 1946 c. 2001).

[79] James Massey, *The Gospel of Luke,* Dalit Bible Commentary-NT, vol. 3 (New Delhi: CDS, 2007).

[80] David Gooding, *According to Luke: A New Exposition of the Third Gospel* (Michigan: W. B. Eerdmans, 1987).

[81] G. W. H. Lame, 'Luke,' *Peake's Commentary on the Bible*, edited by Matthew Black (Nairobi, Kenya: Thomas Nelson, 1977).

[82] Craig A. Evans, *Luke: New International Biblical Commentary* (Peabody: Hendrickson, 1990).

[83] Bruce Malina and Richard L. Rohrbaugh, *Social Science Commentary on the Synoptic Gospels* (Minneapolis: Fortress Press, 1992).

[84] Jane Schaberg, 'Luke,' *The Women's Bible Commentary,* edited by Carol A. Newsom and Sharon H. Ringe (London: SPCK, 1992).

Biblical Commentary[85] which gives an introduction to the Gospel of Luke, a detailed outline and commentary of the Gospel of Luke and Interpreter's[86] commentary which gives a small introduction and exegetical study of Luke.

William Manson's *The Gospel of Luke*[87] is one of the old commentaries. There are three sections, introduction, commentary and appendices. In the introduction, the general character of the Gospel narrative, sources of the Gospel of Luke, historical and religious value of the work and the author of the Gospel. The second part gives a detailed commentary on the Gospel of Luke and in the appendices three short essays are included, was Luke the author of Acts and of the third Gospel?, The birth narratives in Luke's Gospel and the resurrection narratives in the Gospels. Michael Goulder is an able and significant figure in British New Testament scholarship. His *Luke-A New Paradigm* (1989) falls within the province of redaction criticism. Those who are prepared to work through two detailed volumes will find a journey that is magisterially conducted with a conclusion powerfully argued. Its section-by-section analysis makes it much easier to read. Stephen Moore's *Mark and Luke*[88] came in 1992 which is more of undoubted flair with word and it militates to some extent against the impact of the book. In this book, Stephen D. Moore offers a dazzling new reading of the Gospels of Mark and Luke, applying the poststructuralist techniques of Derrida and Foucault to illuminate these texts in a way that no one has done before. Writing with wit and a great sensitivity to words and to wordplay, Moore approaches the Gospels of Mark and Luke as if they were pictograms or dream work to decipher and interpret, writing a response that is no less visceral and immediate than the biblical texts themselves.

E. J. Tinsley's *The Gospel According to Luke*[89] gives a background introduction to the Gospel of Luke in the first part and in the second part Tinsley gives the commentary for the Gospel of Luke with different titles such as the Coming of the Messiah, In Galilee: Success and Opposition, Journeys and Encounters, Challenge to Jerusalem and The Final Conflict.

---

[85] Robert J. Karris, 'The Gospel According to Luke,' *The New Jerome Biblical Commentary,* edited by Raymond E. Brown, Joseph A. Fitzmyer and Roland E. Murphy (Bangalore: TPI, 2004).

[86] William Baird, 'The Gospel According to Luke,' *The Interpreter's One Volume Commentary on the Bible*, edited by Charles M. Laymon (Nashville: Abingdon, 1971), 672-706.

[87] William Manson, *The Gospel of Luke: The Moffatt New Testament Commentary* (London: Hodder and Stoughton, 1930).

[88] Stephen D. Moore, *Mark and Luke in Poststructuralist Perspectives: Jesus Begins to Write* (London: Yale University Press, 1992).

[89] E. J. Tinsley, *The Gospel According to Luke* (Cambridge: Cambridge University Press, 1969).

This book can be taken for the exegetical study of the Gospel of Luke. John Nolland's three-volume commentary on Luke[90] takes the reader to various possible interpretation of Luke. He observes that the evangelists were engaged in proclamations and not just reporting; their concern was so to tell the story of the historical Jesus that their readers might encounter the living Christ. Stephen G. Wilson's *The Gentiles and the Gentile Mission in Luke-Acts*[91] gives the picture of the role of the gentiles in Luke-Acts. Wilson justifies the Gentile mission in Luke by showing that it is 'rooted in the words of Jesus, as a promise in his earthly ministry and as commands after resurrection' (p. 243). Jack Sander's *The Jews in Luke-Acts*[92] sees Luke as roundly condemning the Jews for their rejection of Jesus. Sanders sees Luke as supplying further evidence for the development of an anti-Jewish perspective in the literature of primitive Christianity.

This paper has not given overview of the significant monographs in the Gospel of Luke such as Matthew Black's *The Gentiles and Gentile Mission in Luke-Acts,*[93] Charles H. Talbert, *Perspectives on Luke-Acts,*[94] Christopher M. Tuckett, *Luke,*[95] Stevan M. Sheeley, *Narrative Asides in Luke-Acts,*[96] Philip P. Esler, "The Socio-Redaction Criticism of Luke-Acts;"[97] Richard N. Longenecker, "Taking Up the Cross Daily: Discipleship in Luke-Acts;"[98] Daniel Manika Raj, *The Inheritors of the* Βασιλεια Του Θεου;[99] R. J. Raja, "'Rich Towards God': Bhakti in the Gospel of Luke;"[100] L. R. Arul Sam,

---

90 John Nolland, *Luke*, Word Biblical Commentary, 3 vols. (vo.1 – 1989; vol. 2 - 1993; vol. 3 - 1993) (Dallas: word Books, 1993).

91 Stephen G. Wilson, *The Gentiles and the Gentile Mission in Luke-Acts* (Cambridge: Cambridge University Press, 1973).

92 Jack Sander, *The Jews in Luke-Acts* (Philadelphia: Fortress Press, 1989).

93 Matthew Black, *The Gentiles and Gentile Mission in Luke-Acts* (Cambridge: Cambridge University Press, 1973).

94 Charles H. Talbert, *Perspectives on Luke-Acts* (Edinburgh: T&T Clark, 1978)

95 Christopher M. Tuckett, *Luke* (Sheffield: Sheffield Academic Press, 1996)

96 Stevan M. Sheeley, *Narrative Asides in Luke-Acts* (Sheffield: Sheffield Academic Press, 1992).

97 Philip P. Esler, "The Socio-Redaction Criticism of Luke-Acts," *Social Scientific Approaches to New Testament Interpretation*, edited by David G. Horrell (Edinburgh: T&T Clark, 1999).

98 Richard N. Longenecker, 'Taking Up the Cross Daily: Discipleship in Luke-Acts,' *Patterns of Discipleship in the New Testament,* edited by Richard N. Longenecker (Michigan: W. B. Eerdmans, 1996).

99 Daniel Monika Raj, *The Inheritors of the* Βασιλεια Του Θεου: *According to Lucan Perspective* (Delhi: ISPCK, 2008).

100 R. J. Raja, "'Rich towards God': Bhakti in the Gospel of Luke," *The Gospels with an Indian Face* (Madrass, CLS, 1996).

The Love Commandments of Jesus;[101] Israel Selvanayagam, "The Parable of the Prodigal Son: A Contextual Reflection;"[102] B. Varghese, *Women in the Gospel of Luke*;[103] John Gillmann, *Possessions and the Life of Faith: A Reading of Luke-Acts*;[104] Sharon H. Ringe, *Luke*;[105] Talbert's "Promise and Fulfillment in Lucan Theology"[106] which has two fold purpose, to briefly describe the paradigm shift in the study of the Gospel of Luke-Luke the historian-Luke the theologian. Another book on Luke is from Talbert is *Literary Patterns*;[107] and Jack T. Sanders, "The Salvation of the Jews in Luke Acts;"[108] Kenneth Ewing Bailey, *Poet and Peasant*[109] and J. Stanly Glean, *The Parables of Conflict in Luke.*[110] When one overview the literature on the Gospel of Luke rarely forgets R. H. Fuller's *Luke's Witness to Jesus Christ,*[111] there are five chapters in this book. 1. the Prelude 2. the Galilean Ministry 3. the Journey to Jerusalem 4. the Jerusalem Ministry and 5. the Passion and Resurrection of Jesus. The book is partially a commentary but with a scholarly introduction.

[101] L. R. Arul Sam, *The Love Commandments of Jesus in the Gospel of Luke and its Implication in the Indian Context* (Delhi: ISPCK, 2008).

[102] Israel Selvanayagam, "The Parable of the Prodigal Son: A Contextual Reflection," *Light on Our Dusty Path: Essays for a Bible Lover*, edited by Israel Selvanayagam (Bangalore: BTESSC/SATHRI, 2008).

[103] B. Varghese, *Women's in the Gospel of Luke*: *The Role of Woman in the Portrayal of Salvation in the Gospel of Luke* (Delhi: ISPCK, 2005).

[104] John Gillmann, *Possessions and the Life of Faith: A Reading of Luke-Acts,* Zachaeus Studies: NT (Collegeville: The Liturgical Press, 1991).

[105] Sharon H. Ringe, *Luke*, Westminster Bible Companion (Louisville: John Knox Press, 1995).

[106] Charles H. Talbert, 'Promise and Fulfillment in Lucan Theology,' *Luke-Acts*- New Perspectives From the Society of Biblical Literature Seminar (NewYork: Cross Road, 1984).

[107] Charles H. Talbert, *Literary Patterns, Theological Themes and Genre of Luke-Acts* (Montana: SBL and Scholars Press, 1974).

[108] Jack T. Sanders, 'The Salvation of the Jews in Luke Acts,' Luke-Acts- New Perspectives from the Society of Biblical Literature Seminar (NewYork: Cross Road, 1984).

[109] Kenneth Ewing Bailey, *Poet and Peasant: A Literary Cultural Approaches to the Parables in Luke* (Michigan: W. B. Eerdmans Publishing company, 1976).

[110] J. Stanly Glean, *The Parables of Conflict in Luke* (Philadelphia: The Westminster Press, 1952).

[111] R. H. Fuller, *Luke's Witness to Jesus Christ* (London: Lutterworth Press, 1963).

The author do not wish to ignore some of the recent works on *the Gospel of Luke*, Michael Card, *Luke: the Gospel of the Amazement*[112] gives a detailed commentary for each chapter of the Gospel of Luke with the major thrust as what leads Luke to focus on the marginalized and the unlikely. Donald L. Griggs and Paul W. Walaskay, *Luke's Gospel from Scratch: The New Testament for Beginners.*[113] It is a simple text book in the form of a commentary. Raj Nadella, *Dialogue Not Dogma: Many voice in the Gospel of Luke*,[114] is a scholarly work by examining the strands of the narratives in the Gospel of Luke highlighting the 'many voices' in the Gospel and this thrust is elaborated as a unique feature of Luke's writing. This work is a contribution to the study of Luke's Gospel emphasizing the ethical implications of a dialogic reading of Luke.

Geir Otto Holmås', *Prayer and Vindication in Luke-Acts: The Theme of Prayer within the Context of the Legitimating and Edifying Objective of the Lukan Narrative*[115] is a comprehensive study of the literary function of the theme prayer in Luke-Acts, employing narrative critical methodology. Luke Timothy Johnson's, *Prophetic Jesus, Prophetic Church: The Challenge of Luke Acts to the Contemporary Christians*[116] with the eclectic approach, reads the Gospel of Luke with the theme 'prophetic vision' and highlights that the voice and vision of Luke-Acts has a prophetic function for the church today. Robert H. Gundry's, *Commentary on Luke,*[117] gives detailed commentary on the gospel of Luke.

It is motivating to study the divergent arguments and perspectives of various scholars regarding the Gospel of Luke. Ever since Conzelmann published his seminal work, theology of the Gospel of Luke, rigorous efforts were made to study the Gospel of Luke. Recent researches on the Gospel of Luke have brought out the theological and social motifs of Luke into limelight. Historical critical studies pay more emphasis on the theology and historicity of Luke; literary critical studies focus more on the literary plot/structure and theology of Luke, social scientific criticism pays much

[112] Michael Card, *Luke: the Gospel of the Amazement* (Downers' Grove: IVP, 2011).

[113] Donald L. Griggs and Paul W. Walaskay, *Luke's Gospel from Scratch: The New Testament for Beginners* (Louisville: Westminster John Knox Press, 2011).

[114] Raj Nadella, *Dialogue Not Dogma: Many Voices in the Gospel of Luke* (London: T&T Clark international, 2011).

[115] Geir Otto Holmås, *Prayer and Vindication in Luke-Acts: The Theme of Prayer within the Context of the Legitimating and Edifying Objective of the Lukan Narrative* (London: T&T Clark, 2011)

[116] Luke Timothy Johnson, *Prophetic Jesus, Prophetic Church: The Challenge of Luke-Acts to the Contemporary Christians* (Cambridge: W.B. Eerdmans, 2011).

[117] Robert H. Gundry, *Commentary on Luke* (Michigan: Baker Academic, 2010, e-book 2011).

attention on the social aspects of Luke. The different critical approaches that are applied in the studies of Luke's Gospel helped to unravel different theological and social motifs of Luke. The eclectic approaches, which some scholars have employed, have brought good results. Nevertheless, the diverse and eclectic critical approaches have not fully divulged the theological richness of Luke's Gospel. However, the above survey of the literature in the area of the Gospel of Luke indicates that most of the areas are still open and are being discussed by various scholars in this area of study and calls for new approaches and further researches in the Gospel of Luke.

4

The Beatitudes and Woes in Luke
A Critique of Wealth and Poverty

The attitude of Jesus as described in the beatitudes draws the reader's attention. He meets people who are weary and burdened who can bear no further injustice imposed on them by political repression, by socio-economic, religious-cultural or ethical exploitation. This devastated condition of the crowds forced Jesus to act and to create a space for them to speak. The Beatitudes and Woes found in the Gospel of Luke, often referred to as the "Blessings and Woes," provide a profound critique of wealth and poverty, challenging societal norms and emphasizing the values of God's kingdom. The Beatitudes describes the divinely approved lifestyle of those who have repented at the arrival of His Kingdom in Jesus' words and works. It contains the high ethical standards and practices, which are not contrary to the Christian living. The social life setting of the society is under various contests and struggles. These passages, found in Luke 6:20-26, offer a distinctive perspective on wealth and poverty compared to the more well-known Beatitudes in Matthew's Gospel. In this critique, we will explore how Luke's Beatitudes and Woes address issues of wealth, poverty, and social justice.

1. Etymology of "Beatitude"

A literary formula, generally beginning with the expression "blessed is" or "happy is."[1] In Hebrew אשׁר (*asher*) and Greek μακάριος (*makarios*), which

[1] James Strong, 'Beatitude,' *A Concise Dictionary of the Words in the Greek Testament: With their Rendering in the Authorized English Version* (New Jersey: Madison, 1890), 571.

pronounces a blessing upon or declares praise of an exemplary individual.[2] A description of a believer's inner condition.[3] "Macarisms" are essentially commendations, congratulations, statements to the effect that a person is in a good situation,[4] sometimes even expressions of envy. In content beatitudes, which are common in both poetry and prose throughout the centuries, reflect the sorrows and affliction, the aspirations and is deals, of the Greeks.

To make a review of some areas of Beatitudes look into Bensi P. George, Socio-Ethical Significance of Matthean Beatitudes and Its Implication to the Indian Pentecostal Churches In Pathanamthitta District, Thesis Unpublised, ETS, Ayur, 2020.

Praise is naturally accorded to those who have found the great happiness of love, even more to those who have a good understanding or who are free from tribulations. The beatitudes[5] are a Joyous chord. Beatitudes occur in both pagan and Judeo-Christian literature. The Greek adjective μακάριος (happy) has spawned the verb μακάρισω (*makarizo*) (to call happy) and the derivative noun μακάρισμος (*makarismos*) a (calling happy), a beatitude. Such "macarisms" are normally single statements, and there is no close parallel to Matthew's carefully structured set of eight beatitudes.[6] The Greek term for blessed (by God) is *eulogetos*, not *makarios*.

2. Matthean Beatitudes Compared with Lukan

While both discourses begin with beatitudes, the two sets are very different. Firstly, Luke has four beatitudes against Matthew's eight, corresponding roughly to Matthew's first, fourth, and eighth. Secondly, Luke has four balancing "woes" to which Matthew has no parallel. Thirdly, Luke's are cast in the second person, while Matthew uses the third person. Fourthly, the "tone" is quite different. In Matthew the qualities commended are essentially spiritual and ethical, particularly in contrast with the security and satisfaction which the rest of society seeks.

---

2 Allen C. Myers, 'Beatitude,' *The Eerdmans Bible Dictionary* (Grand Rapids: William B Eerdmans Publishing Company, 1987), 131.

3 Homer A. Kent, 'Matthew,' *The New Testament and the Wycliffe Bible Commentary* (New York: The Iverseb-Norman Associates, 1980), 15.

4 T. France, 'The Gospel of Matthew,' *The New International Commentary on the New Testament* (Grand Rapids: William B. Eerdmans Publishing Company, 2007), 160.

5 Servais Pinckaers, *The Pursuit of Happiness-God's Way*, translated by Mary Thomas Noble (Oregon: Wipf and Stock Publishers, 1998), 23.

6 The Hebrew equivalent of μακάριος is אָשֵׁר (*asher*) rather than the more theologically loaded בָּרוּךְ (barukh), 'blessed (by God),' the traditional English rendering 'blessed' thus also has too theological a connotation in modern usage.

Lukan beatitudes and woes directly to the disciples of their own material and social disadvantages as a result of their following Jesus.[7] Fifthly, the cumulative effect of these observations is to cast serious doubt on the common assumption that there was a single original set of beatitudes which either Matthew has 'spiritualized' or Luke has 'radicalized.' Jesus may well have used the familiar beatitude form on various occasions in the course of his teachings and for various purposes as indeed the substantial number of other beatitudes scattered singly through these two gospels indicates.

3. Influence of Non/Biblical World into Beatitudes of Jesus

The "blessings" pronounced by Jesus upon those worthies of admission to the kingdom of God. The general theme is "Happy are the righteous."[8] The word Beatitude comes from the Latin 'Beatitudo,' meaning Blessedness[9] referring specifically to the eight blessings (Matt 5:3-12).[10]

3.1. Beatitudes In the Old Testament and Judaism

The usage of the beatitudes, Μακάριος or μακάριζειν is often used in the LXX for other words than רשֶׁאָ (*asher*) with the same or similar radicals.[11] In the LXX only רשֶׁאָ (*asher*) is translated as μακάριος and דּוּרבָ (*baruk*) translated as εὐλογητός (*eulogetos*), "to speak well of."[12] Therefore, there is a minimal significance of the (*barukh*) דּוּרבָ formulas for understanding the background of the beatitudes in Matthew (5:3-12) and Luke (6:20-22). Thus, in sharp contrast to the Hellenistic usage it always refers to a person.

It also never refers to a thing or state.[13] The characteristic beatitudes of the Old Testament and Judaism mainly refer "to the one who trusts in God,

---

[7] T. France, 'The Gospel of Matthew,' *The New International Commentary on the New Testament*, 163.

[8] Frederick C. Grant, 'Beatitudes,' *The Encyclopedia America*, vol. 3 (Danbury: Grolier Incorporated, 1983): 430.

[9] [illegible], 'Beatitude,' *The World Book Encyclopedia*, vol. 2 (Chicago: World Book Child craft International, Inc., 1982): 144.

[10] Kendrick Grobel, 'Beatitudes,' *Encyclopedia Britannica*, vol. 3 (Chicago: William Benton Publisher, 1971): 335.

[11] Beatitudes or blessings are also found in the Old Testament and Judaism where the key words are אָשֵׁר (*asher*) or בָּרוּךְ (barukh). The word אָשֵׁר (*asher*) is not applied to God in the Old Testament and is less sacred and solemn than בָּרוּךְ (baruk).

[12] W. E. Vine, 'εὐλογητός,' *An Expository Dictionary of New Testament Words*, 133

[13] Blessedness is understood in terms of fullness if the life in the Old Testament and Judaism, and God is the giver of all blessedness. Blessedness first relates to earthly blessings. Wisdom and piety are understood as the presupposition of all blessedness in the Old Testament and Judaism.

who hopes and waits for him, who fears and loves Him."[14] The eschatological woe, the counterpart of the eschatological blessings, forms another notable development in the history of makarism in the bible/Judaism. Beatitudes in the second person are rare on the Old Testament, but are found in the later Jewish literature.

The Old Testament sense of beatitude is maintained in Rabbinic Judaism. There are five beatitudes found in Qumran texts. They are from 50 BC to 50 AD. Both form and content of beatitudes echoes familiar Old Testament passages and themes. Isaiah 61:1-3 tells of good news to the poor (cf. 5:3 and note that in Matthew "good news" has already been defined in terms of the kingdom of heaven" in 4:23) and of comforting those who mourn (cf. Matt 5: 4).

Verse 5 reproduces the LXX wording of Psalms 37:11. Verse 8 reflects the "pure in heart" who "seek the face of God" in Psalms 24: 3-6. "Meek" and "poor" are used interchangeably who features largely in the Psalms and elsewhere as the true people of God whom he will ultimately vindicate against the "proud" and "wicked" who appears them. In other beatitudes, the teaching reflects that of the Old Testament, especially the Psalms, for those who hunger and thirst for righteousness (cf. Ps 42:1-2; Isa 55:1-2); for reciprocal principle of mercy to the merciful (cf. Ps 18:25-26); for the peacemakers (cf. Ps 34:14).

This usage is a common "Old Testament literary form called Beatitudes." Here the blessings are the promises of the kingdom for those who live the repentant life. The future kingdom was sometimes defined by the images from the creation narratives or from Israel's exodus from Egypt, which the Jewish people regarded as their original redemption. Μακάριος or Μακάριζειν is repeatedly used in the LXX for other words than אֶשֶׁר (*asher*) with the equal or comparable revolutionaries.[15] Of the 45 occurrences of אֶשֶׁר (*asher*) in the Hebrew Bible,[16] most of which are found in wisdom literature, 26 are found in the Psalter, 8 in Proverbs, and the other 11 are scattered throughout the rest of the canonical books.

3.2. Beatitudes in the New Testament

The special feature of the group Μακάριος, Μακάριζειν, Μακάρισμός in the New Testament is that it refers overwhelmingly to the distinctive

---

[14] Vanlalchhawna Khiangte, *Matthean Beatitudes in Socio-Historical Context: Their Implications for Contemporary Christian Discipleship* (New Delhi: Christian world imprints, 2016), 125.

[15] Raymond F. Collins, 'Beatitudes,' *The Anchor Bible Dictionary*, vol. 1, edited by David Noel Freedman (New York: Doubleday, 1992), 629-631.

[16] Jonathan T. Pennington, *The Sermon on the Mount and Human Flourishing: A Theological Commentary* (Grand Rapids: Baker Academic, 2018), 43.

religious joy which accrues to man from his share in the salvation of the kingdom of God.[17] The New Testament[18] contains 37 beatitudes. The Matthean beatitudes (5:3-12), and the Lukan beatitude (6:20-23) are not the only beatitude found in the New Testament, for in fact, beatitudes are found also in other places of the New Testament.

In the New Testament the word Μακάριος occurs fifty times: thirteen in Matthew, fifteen in Luke, two in John, two in Acts, seven on Pauline corpus. Thus, there are 44 beatitudes are there in the New Testament refers to persons, things (eyes, ears in Matt 13:16; Womb, Breasts in Lk.11:27). These usages are influenced by the Jewish modes of thought, regards members of the body as bearing independent life.

The New Testament makarisms exhibit diverse form and function, and display all of the features heretofore noted in Jewish literature. There are also isolated beatitudes (Jn 13:17; 20: 29; Rom 14:22, Jas 1:12) as well as beatitudes in series (Matt 5:3-12; Lk 6: 20-22; 11: 27- 28). Though there are many individual and isolated beatitudes. And even among the beatitudes in series, Matthean beatitude (5:3-12) and Lukan beatitudes (6.20-23) are prominent ones, and they stand out distinctively with distinctive teachings. Pauline beatitude has a specific gnomic form.[19]

3.3. Beatitudes in the Greek Literature

First found in Pindar, μακάριος, is a Poetic word, also found later in common speech.[20] The latter is referred predominantly, at first, to gods. It denotes the transcendent happiness of a life beyond care, labour and death. Μάκαρ is then used of men to denote the state of godlike blessedness hereafter in the isles of the blessed. In keeping with its relation to μάκαρ, μακάριος describes first the happy state of the gods above earthly sufferings and labours. It is then used for the dead who have attained to the supraterrestrial life of the gods.

The Greek word blessed is used in pagan literature to denote the highest stage of happiness and well-being.[21] It is used to describe the social stratum of the wealthy who in virtue of their riches are above the normal cares and worries of lesser folk. Μακάριος[22] In the beatitudes the Lord indicates not

[17] Hauck, 'μακάριος,' *Theological Dictionary of the New Testament*, 367.

[18] Raymond F. Collins, 'Beatitudes,' *The Anchor Bible Dictionary*, 629-631.

[19] Hauck, 'μακάριος,' *Theological Dictionary of the New Testament*, 369.

[20] Hauck, 'Μακάριος,' *Theological Dictionary of the New Testament*, 362.

[21] George Arthur Buttrick, "Matthew," *The Interpreter's Bible*, vol. VII (New York: Abingdon Press, 1951), 280.

[22] W. E. Vine, 'εὐλογητός,' *An Expository Dictionary of New Testament Words with their Precise Meanings for English Readers* (New Jersey: Fleming H. Revell Company, 1966), 133.

only the characters that are blessed, but the nature of that which is the highest good.

4. The Blessings (Beatitudes) in Luke 6:20-23

4.1. Blessed are the Poor

Luke's version begins with "Blessed are you who are poor" (Lk 6:20), highlighting the special favor God bestows on those in poverty. This blessing challenges the conventional wisdom that equated material wealth with divine favor and highlights God's concern for the economically disadvantaged.

The passage from Luke 6:20-23, commonly known as the Beatitudes, presents a series of blessings pronounced by Jesus to a crowd of his disciples. Each blessing is followed by an explanation and a commentary:

4.2. Blessedness of the Marginal

Happiness is the dream of those who experience extreme struggles/ marginalized in their life. To have the exact understanding of the "blessedness" we need to go through the etymological meaning, biblical meaning, Christian concept and must know the life that the people had undergone, especially the Jesus' Community.

No greater thing could come to our land to-day than the revival of the spirit of religion that would sweep through the homes of the nation and strengthen the hearts of men and women of all faiths to a reassertion of a belief in God, and their dedication to His will for themselves and for the world. I doubt if there is any problem, social, political, or economic, that would not melt away, before the force of such a spiritual awakening.

The word μακάριος (*makarios*) used with a religious connotation, The word μακάριοι (*makarioi*) used fifty five times in the New Testament, and it is important to understand its history, which is interesting because this is one of those numerous words, which exhibit the influence of Christian community and usage in enlarging and dignifying their meaning.[23] The happiness of or hail to those, someone who receives divine favour,[24] congratulations to,[25] etc. Its root word μακάρ (*makar*) meaning supposed to be 'great' and its earlier meaning appears to be limited to 'outward' prosperity, so that it used at times as synonymous with 'rich.'[26] A beatitude or 'blessedness' consists of

---

[23] William F. Arndt and F. Wilbur Gingrich, *A Greek-English Lexicon of the New Testament and other Early Literature* (Chicago: The University of Chicago Press, 1957), 487.

[24] William D. Mounce, *The Analytical Lexicon to the Greek New Testament* (Grand Rapids: Zondervan Publishing House, 1993), 307.

[25] Robert H. Gundry, *A Survey of the New Testament*, 139.

[26] Marvin R. Vincent, *Word Studies in the New Testament* (Massachusetts: Hendrickson Publishers, 2009), 27.

a pronouncement concerning who are blessed, often followed by a promise as to why they are blessed (here introduced by ὅτι (*hoti*) for, since, because).

4.3. The Blessings Contrasted

In comparison to the Grecian gods, the gods were 'blessed' because of their power and dignity, not because of their holiness. This word also applied to the 'dead', indicating the despair of earthly happiness underlying the thought of even the cheerful and the merciful Greek. So the word used as synonymous with dead. Only the dead could be called blessed. The biblical usage of the word μακάρ (*makar*) lifted in spiritual realm, as distinguished from the merely intellectual and besides, interested alone the task of representing this higher conception.

In the Old Testament, the meaning involves more of outward prosperity than the New Testament, yet it emphasises a sense of God's approval founded in righteousness, which rests υλτιματελψ on love to God. Thus, the word μακάρ (*makar*) passed up into the higher region of Christian thought with all the rich significance of gospel blessedness. The Christian word 'blessed' is full of light of heaven. It throws away all human troubles, and emphasises something, which thrives on trial and persecution, which glories in tribulation, which not only endures but also conquers the world, and expects its crown in heaven.

A beatitude or 'blessedness'[27] consists of a pronouncement concerning who are blessed, often followed by a promise as to why they are blessed (here introduced by ὅτι (*hoti*) for, since, because). To be blessed is to be the happy recipient of divine favour or approval. The focus is not on the subjective feelings of the blessed person but on the objective reality of the inauguration of the rule of God in Jesus. The opposite of "blessed" is not "unhappy" but "cursed."

The beatitude unveils the key hallmark that God approves in his people.[28] God approves those who relate to him by admitting their spiritual poverty and mourning over sin and oppression, humbly seeking spiritual fullness. God accepts those who relate to others mercifully and purely as peacemakers, even though they may be persecuted for their righteous behaviour. Jesus' teachings establish the values that guides to true bliss and ultimate comfort for his followers. To be blessed is to be the happy recipient of divine favour or approval. The focus is not on the subjective feelings of the blessed person but on the objective reality of the inauguration of the rule

---

[27] 'Beatitudes,' *The Universal Standard Encyclopedia*, vol. 2, edited by Joseph Laffan Morse (New York: Unicorn Publishers, 1955), 740.

[28] David L. Turner, *Baker Exegetical Commentary on the New Testament: Matthew* (Grand Rapids: Baker Academic, 2008), 146.

of God in Jesus. The opposite of "blessed" is not "unhappy" but "cursed." The beatitude unveils the key hallmark that God approves in his people. Jesus' teachings establish the values that guides to true bliss and ultimate comfort for his followers.

The verse clearly says about the real picture of the social life of the first century. In relation to the degrees of poverty and wealth, rich and the poor are relative terms and their exact meaning depends on the relation of one's possession to the total wealth of the nation. Extreme poverty prevailed throughout Palestine in Jesus Christ's time, partly because the laws of Moses for the prevention and alleviation of property were a dead letter.

Rich man is he who has more than the standard of living in his country requires; a man is poor if he falls below that standard and a pauper is a person who is permanently dependent on others.[29] Jesus knew the struggle of the poor. Here will have a look on the various facts that created the socio-ethical struggle for the identity within the society.

4.4. Social Constrains of the Poor

The social life of the people of the Antioch measured by our modern standards, it was a small city, the density of the people were high. They lived in petite cubicles in multi-storied tenements, which occasionally collapsed and became susceptible to infectious diseases.[30] Living in such crowded life setting, most of the inhabitants had to suffer various problems, such as sanitation, garbage clearance and water supply. In Antioch, the existed sewage facility was so poor for the crisis of sanitation and garbage disposal.[31] The main source of the water supply to Antioch remained the springs on the side of Mount Silpius.[32]

Many farmers were dispossessed of their land after lengthy service abroad and they drifted into the city of Rome, becoming part of the urban mob. Homeless and footless, they wander about with their wives and children.[33] Roman conquests provided a massive influx of prisoners of

---

[29] Philip Vollmer, *New Testament Sociology*, 244.

[30] Rodney Stark, *The Rise of Christianity: A Sociologist Reconsiders History* (New Jersey: Princeton University Press, 1996), 147-150.

[31] Laurence Culas, *Good News Amidst Crises Antioch and the Gospel of Matthew* (New Delhi: ISPCK, 2010), 25.

[32] Majority of the people generally collected water in jugs and preserved it in unhealthy situations, guiding to its contamination. The limited sewage facility and infected water caused to poor health, recurrent epidemics and infectious diseases. Existence of these transmittable diseases caused high mortality in infancy and childhood causing death almost half of the children at birth.

[33] Edwin Yamauchi, *Harper's World of the New Testament* (Philadelphia: Harper & Raw Publishers, 1981), 90.

war who provided cheap labour for the wealthy. Small farmers, who could not strive, sold their lands to the wealthy.[34] Only minority of free citizens were able to earn their own living. Free citizens who were not members the senatorial or the equestrian classes comprised the so-called 'third estate.' Most of them formed a lower class rather than the middle class.

Most of the poor people lived in overcrowded blocks of flats without plumbing or adequate heating. In fact, the slaves of wealthy men were far better off than most free. Poor Roman citizens 'Sons of freeborn men give way to rich man's slave.'[35] Those who are rich in their own eyes do not ask in faith, and receive the blessings of God. Thus, social environment were looking for a blessed socio-ethical status within them.[36]

4.5. Socio-Ethical Environment of Poor

Religious life within the socio-ethical environment faced deep struggles and conflicts. They are humble and lowly as opposed to the Pharisees[37] with their self-esteem and religious accomplishments. There were many temples were dedicated to various gods with their statues and inscriptions. Since a rich cultural mix existed in Antioch, there had sanctuaries of different kinds, enclosed areas with statues and divinities, worshipped in public or private. Zeus, Apollo, Hera, Dionysus, Athena, and Aphrodite, were the prominent gods.

Gods became the guarantors of law and order in society and personifications of the virtues of the citizens.[38] The Romans constructed temples, dedicated to all their gods. Jupiter, Pantheon being the head of all gods. In some instances, rulers forced the people to worship him as God, especially Gaius, Caligula. Apart from the official public religious cults, private or foreign cults vastly expanded in Antioch, due to the cultural mix, from Egypt, goddess Isis was the popular goddesses.

The introduction of private cults required the approval of the authority, the emperor. The private or foreign cult organizations became *collegia* in form. All inhabitants of the city participated in the official or public cult. This means that in addition to the participation in the official worship, religious

---

[34] Cynthia Long Westfall and Bryan R. Dyer, *The Bible and Social Justice: Old Testament and New Testament Foundations for the Church's Urgent Call* (Eugene: Wipf and Stock Publishers, 2015), 113.

[35] Edwin Yamauchi, *Harper's World of the New Testament*, 91.

[36] Ellen Gould White, *Thoughts from the Mount of Blessing* (Germany: Jazzybee Verlag, 2014), 7.

[37] W. P. Deboer, 'Beatitudes,' *The International Standard Bible Encyclopedia*, edited by Geoffrey W. Bromiley (Michigan: William B. Eerdmans Publishing Company, 1979), 443-444.

[38] Laurence Culas, Good *News Amidst Crises Antioch and the Gospel of Matthew*, 27.

permanence of the *collegia* became one expression of city religion. Generally, a member of a certain *collegium* did not ignore his or her responsibility to take part in the public worship, sacrifices, and festivals.

All participated in the official religious cult because non-participation could have resulted in exile or even death.[39] The one considered lucky and fortunate by the world are not the real winners when it comes to salvation and spiritual reward.[40] Religiously there was a need for the upliftment from this marginalization.

4.6. Political Insecurity of Poor

There were struggles between the elite and the marginalized or the rulers and the ruled within the political life.[41] The population of Antioch included a great verity of races. There were Macedonians and Greeks, native Syrians and Phoenicians, Jews and Romans, besides a contingent from further Asia. The Jewish presence in Antioch, able to oppose the anti-Jewish measures of their rulers. The Jews also were hired for service in the army under Seleucus I. Macedonians, Greeks resided in a quarter protected by city walls, and the native population existed in another quarter, probably outside the wall. The Jews resided in the South eastern area of the city, outside Seleucus I Nicator's wall, but inside the walls of Tiberius and later those of Justinian.

Thus, Jews had been among the original settlers when the city was founded. Jews belonged to all social and economic classes, from the educated Greek elite through Greek-Speaking or bilingual (Greek/Aramaic) artisans and farmers and down to the very poor. The anti-Jewish measures Antiochus IV Epiphanes brought hardship for the Jews. He desired unified religious practice, and promoted his Hellenistic, universalistic model. Therefore, he urged the people to give up their customs.

However, many Jews kept themselves away from the changed religious activities. The Jewish non-participation in the cultic activities caused conflicts in Judea, Antiochus dedicated the Jerusalem temple to Olympian Zeus and devastated Jerusalem. But he was met with resistance, Maccabean revolt, marked the beginning of an uprising. The Gentile majority accepted the command of the king. During the period of Demetrius II Nicator (145-139 BC), Jonathan the Hasmonean ruler supplied 3000 Judean-Jewish soldiers to subdue the revolt.[42]

---

[39] Laurence Culas, *Good News Amidst Crises Antioch and the Gospel of Matthew*, 29.

[40] Dario Lisiero, *Faith and Science: Christian Insanity* (Morrisville: Lulu Press, 2012), 23.

[41] W. P. Deboer, 'Beatitudes,' *The International Standard Bible Encyclopedia*, 443-444.

[42] M. Gwyn Morgan, 'Hellenism and Persecution: Antiochus IV and the Jews,' *Hellenistic History and Culture*, edited by Peter Green (London: University of California Press, 1993), 234-263.

As a result, the Jewish-joining in the killing of the innocents and stealing of their possessions had direct consequences on the Jewish community in Antioch. During the time of Roman rule Gaius Cassius Longinus seized property from the Jews from Judea and Syria, to fund his military plan. Caligula Temple edict (39-40 BC) Gaius tried to set up an image of himself within the Jerusalem temple. This increased tension in Antioch between outraged Jews and Gentile citizens, loyal to Rome. As a result, the Gentile mobs attacked the Antiochene Jews, killing many Jews and burning their Synagogues, and it culminated in war. Thus, Political struggles also was a reason to the poverty in their socio-ethical life.

4.7. Economic Disparity among the Common People

The economic factor is the major one relates to the life of the society. Because it deals with the question, of what shall we eat? What shall we drink? Wherewith shall we clothed? In addition, where shall we live? Everybody including animals are interested in asking these questions. The historical situation reveals an unfair distribution of wealth was found in all sections of the Roman Empire. Wealth in the hands of a few, resulted in coarse luxury and immorality too horrible for description, while the mass of the people were known as the 'proletariat,' because they could call nothing their own except children.[43]

From time-to-time agrarian revolutions were broke out. To get rid from such conflicts wealthy people and the government distributed corn and tickets for amusements,[44] while the Cynic and Stoic philosophers exhorted the poor to endure hardship and fortitude. In Palestine extreme poverty reigned, because the humane Old Testament laws for the relief of poverty were not enforced. Jesus showed much interest in earthly possessions, because his family and friends belonged to the dependent class and felt pressure of the unfair economic system in vogue.

The acquirement of wealth is the all-absorbing wish of most men because under our system of private ownership and of production for profit, [illegible], the possession of some property is necessary to self protection of the family. Wealth[45] is power and opens the way to honours and

[43] Philip Vollmer, *New Testament Sociology* (New York: Fleming H. Revell Company, 1923), 213.

[44] Philip Vollmer, *New Testament Sociology*, 213.

[45] Albino Barrera, *Biblical Economic Ethics: Sacred Scripture's teachings on Economic Life* (New York: Lexington Books, 2013), 199.

distinction.[46] Thus poor in the economy also caused for the degradation of the socio-ethical life, which gave the expectation of blessedness.[47]

4.8. Cultural Conflict of the Poor

The more menacing cultural conflict was that between the Christianity and Pagan Society. The ordinary pagan thought of the Christian as essentially anti-social, and on this basis, their relations must have been very strained. The races of Antioch was a mixture of Macedonians and Greeks, native Syrians and Phoenicians, Jews and Romans,[48] besides a contingent from further Asia. The Roman society was divided into social classes. All freeborn were separate from slaves who originally had no legal rights or even personality.

Many were treated like brute-beasts. Already Jewish slaves were unpopular as they insisted on the observance of the seventh day and refused to eat pagan food. Similar trends might well have developed with Christian slaves. Slavery degraded marriage, for it introduced concubines into family life.[49] As the migration of the peoples intensified with the expansion of the empire, mystic cults of the east-of Osiris, Mithras, and numerous lesser superstitious were introduced. As a result, many immoral rites were associated with the eastern cults. Such marginalized poor cultural living also expected to have a blessed life.

4.9. Ethical Milieu the Poor

In relation with the ethical milieu, the state of affairs, no woman need blush to break her off her marriage since the most illustrious ladies have adopted the practice of reckoning the year not by the names of the counsels but by those of their husbands. They divorce in order to remarry. They marry in order to divorce.[50] Children tended to be spoilt. Infanticide was common, an unwanted baby being 'exposed', often left on the rubbish heap to die of hunger, cold or be devoured by the dogs.

---

[46] The method employed in gathering wealth either promotes or destroys the happiness of individuals, social groups and nations.

[47] Liz Theoharis, *Always with us? What Jesus Really Said about Poor* (Michigan: William B. Eerdmans Publishing Company, 2017), 101.

[48] R. T. France, *Luke* (Grand Rapids: Baker Books, 2013), 105.

[49] J. M. Houston, 'An Environmental Background to the New Testament,' *The Layman's Bible Commentary*, vol. 1, edited by G. C. D. Howley, F. F. Bruce and H. L. Ellison (Grand Rapids: Zondervan Publishing House, 1979), 1094.

[50] J. M. Houston, 'An Environmental Background to the New Testament,' *The Layman's Bible Commentary*, 1094.

The boredom and leisure of the populace could be dangerous to the state. It was in the political interest,[51] therefore, that the chariot races of the circus diverted the passions of the masses with their thrills and gambling. In the theatre, slices of pagan life were served up, hot and spicy, nearing the limit of even Roman conventions. The amphitheatre with its gladiatorial spectacle of human slaughter was foul and debased. The baths where the citizens took their daily afternoon wash were the most innocent of daily pleasures, but even here, the social life and the opportunities for promiscuity made them feared by the Christians. The one meal of the day, in the evening, was the occasion of much drunkenness and gluttony. Clubs were an important feature of Roman life where further licence was found. Faced by all these features of daily life, the Christians had to reject a great deal. Thus, the painful socio-ethical atmosphere among the people waits for a good life.

4.10. Blessedness of the Poor

Gospel of Matthew brings out the blessings for those who struggle for the identity; theirs is the Kingdom of Heaven. Jesus did not mean it is good to be poor without any spiritual riches or spiritual virtues. He meant that I dealing with God it is a blessed thing to have the humility of the poor, humble,[52] the broken heart of the poor. One who is under struggle feels his need, his poverty; so that he can pray as a poor and needy creature begging for help, then blessed is that man, for he will be heard. God loves particularly those who are in struggle, oppressed, marginalized, for their identity in crisis. Jesus preached the Gospel especially to the poor.

The poor in spirit is happy because he has the kingdom of God. Matthew refers[53] those who, regardless of their economic or social status, manifest the humble dependence of God's grace. This beatitude promises those who remember their need for God and call upon God, that God will make them contributors to the divine reign on earth.

For you shall be satisfied: The explanation affirms that those who hunger for righteousness will be satisfied. This satisfaction comes from aligning one's life with God's values and experiencing God's presence and provision.

[51] Daniel J. Harrington and James F. Keenan, *Jesus and virtue Ethics: Building Bridges Between New Testament studies and Moral Theology* (United states of America: Rowman & Littlefield Publishers, 2002), 63.

[52] Warren W. Wiersbe, *Be Loyal: Discover the Excitement of Knowing and Serving the king of Glory* (England: Victor Books, 1987), 33.

[53] He creates a condition within the man, which enables him to find happiness everywhere. He does not create happiness by new surroundings. He creates new surroundings by happiness.

Those who hunger for righteousness will find their fulfillment in God. This promise underscores the idea that true contentment and satisfaction are found in living according to God's ways and pursuing justice and righteousness.

Blessed are you who weep now: The third blessing speaks to those who are currently experiencing sorrow and weeping, likely due to the hardships and trials of life.

Weeping in this context represents the struggles and challenges that people face in life. Jesus acknowledges their pain and suffering, and He offers comfort by promising future joy and laughter. This suggests that God is present even in times of sorrow and will ultimately bring joy and redemption.

Expectation of blessedness from a mourning socio-ethical society is depicted here. The second beatitude is ascribed to the dominical saying, which was preserved in Q. It has its basis in Isaiah 61:2, which talks about the comfort for all those who mourn. Probably Matthean version represents the original Q form. In Greek *penthein* or *penthos* means, "to mourn, to grieve, to bewail". Denotes sorrow of heart, which is outwardly expressed in some way.[54] The words are used especially for mourning for the dead, though also for other sufferings.

In the New Testament, denotes the sorrow expressed in lamentation and tears. Matthew uses the mourning in general.[55] Matthew's Gospel is the gospel of sorrow.[56] The sorrow for our sins in true contrition should not be excluded from this mourning, mourners.[57] The mourning is a constant cry to God in their distress.[58] This was particularly applicable to Lord Jesus[59] (Heb 5:7). The blessing of the *penthountes*- mourners is to be taken eschatologically, the expectation of the downtrodden and poor, those who suffer. It takes up the prophetic promises, so the mourning to which the promise refers is that of men who suffer under the present aeon, which is an aeon of suffering. It is evident that not all who mourn are called blessed.

---

[54] Bultmann, 'πενθεῖν/πενθος,' *Theological Dictionary of the New Testament*, vol. VI, edited by Gerhard Friedrich (Grand Rapids: William B. Eerdmans Publishing Company, 2006), 40-43.

[55] W. E. Vine, 'Mourn,' *Vine's Expository Dictionary of Old and New Testament Words* (Lowa: World Bible Publishers, 1981, 1149.

[56] Augustus H. Strong, *Popular Lectures on the Books of the New Testament* (Chicago: The Judson Press, 1914), 60.

[57] Arther Robertson, *Matthew* (Chicago: Moody Press, 1983), 37.

[58] R. C. H. Lensky, *The Interpretation of St. Matthew's Gospel* (Minneapolis: Augsburg Publish-ing House, 1964), 187.

[59] J. Vernon McGee, *Moving Thru Matthew* (California: Thru the Bible Books, 2006), 16.

The reference is plainly to those who see this suffering aeon as it is and who are not led astray by its charms like the laughing in (Luke 6:25).[60] The "mourn" of these men is a sign of their demarcation from this aeon and of their expectation of the Kingdom of Heaven.[61] The grief finds expression in various customs associated with mourning, wearing of cloths of a particular colour, self-inflicted torture or pain, the cutting of hair, the tearing of cloths, lamentation, and eulogy of the deceased, fasting, various religious proscriptions etc. Here we go to analyse the socio-ethical reasons of first century community in Palestine who mourn and need deliverance from the pains to the happy life.

4.11. Social Grief of those Mourn

The troubled life of the Palestinian society caused them to a mourned life. Mourning[62] is a form of outward expression of grief over a death or on any kind of public or national disaster. They mourn not only because of the loss of their loved ones; rather they mourn the loss of their innocence, their righteousness, their self-respect. Because of his perfect humanity, Jesus has been touched with our infirmities and feels with us. Thus, the gospel is designed to comfort the afflicted. Matthew records mothers in Bethlehem mourning their innocent children who had been killed in a brutal and ruthless massacre by Herod (Matt 2:16). Most of Jesus' followers of Jesus were poor and downtrodden people.

They were afflicted with the concomitant problems such as illness and death, the mourning in this beatitude in its original context of Jesus' teaching could largely refer to grief because of bereavement, affliction with acute illness and lack of proper treatment, heavy burdens because of heavy debts amidst their acute poverty and other hardships caused by imperial powers.

People who mourn are fill with deep regret for their own waywardness and for the evil so prevalent in the world. Those who mourn are not simply those who have gone through difficult times but those who understand that all the suffering in the world stems from the sinful and self destructive human tendency to act as if God did not exit. It is the expectation of the downtrodden and poor, those who suffer to have a blessed socio ethic life.

Religious conflicts within the community also caused deep cry within them. The Rabbis referred to the Messiah as the 'Comforter' because of his mission in the messianic age. The Sanhedrin, the appointed authorities of

[60] Bultmann, 'πενθέω/πένθος,' *Theological Dictionary of the New Testament*, 43.

[61] W. E. Vine, *Vine's Expository Dictionary of New Testament Words*, 769.

[62] Catherine Judaison, 'Mourn,' *A Dictionary of Believers and Nonbelievers* (Moscow: Progress Publishers, 1985), 366.

the Jews, rejected Christ.[63] People grieved because of the national apostasy. It includes not only the broken heart, but also the contrite of spirit. They are those whose spiritual misery and their ability to alleviate it is such that they must look to their king to make things right.[64]

The socio-ethical life degraded through the political harshness towards the people. Those who mourn do so because of the seeming slowness of God's justice. But they are now to rejoice, even in their troubled circumstances, because their salvation has found its beginning. Roman conquered Palestine in 63 BC, their harshness led to constant quarrels with the Jews. Probably the focus is more on those who mourn over afflictions and persecutions that arise because of their allegiance to the kingdom. During this troubled time of Roman oppression,[65] and cries Jesus began teaching a new religion and philosophy of life. People grieved as they are by injustice. The reason for all kinds of mourning was, they were in the hands of adversaries. The Matthean audience were not strangers to mourning. They too fell victim to daily injustice and violence perpetrated by brutal colonial powers. Thus, the expectation of Justice lived.

We find the normal combination of "mourning" for the dead and "comfort" in this beatitude. The mourning envisioned here most probably involves the loss of family and kin. Someone lacks parents, family, and kin, with the entire economic and social loss attendant upon this. People mourned and longed for justice and righteousness, because they had been denied justice and they lived under the pressure of debts, taxes and landlessness. In short, they constantly lived under the shadow of death. Thus, economic reasons also was a cause for the socio-ethical degradation within the society.

Its message is of the restoration of oppressed Israel, for who, as God's people, find their current situation intolerable and incomprehensible,[66] there are better times ahead. The act of marginalization has seemed a necessary response to the severity of the national conflict, the harsh violence of the Israeli occupation, and the enduring struggle for Palestinian national liberation. Popular culture's frequent appearance in commodity form has made the labour of marginalization seem more necessary.[67] The emergence

---

[63] Augustus H. Strong, *Popular Lectures on the Books of the New Testament*, 60.

[64] Neil J. McEleney, 'The Beatitudes of the Sermon on the Mount/Plain,' *The Catholic Biblical Quarterly* vol. 43/1 (January 1981): 1-13.

[65] Yehuda Harry Levin and Winfred E. Garrison, 'Palestine,' *The World Book Encyclopedia*, vol. 14 (Chicago: Field Enterprises Educational Corporation, 1962): 86.

[66] R. T. France, *New International Commentary of New Testament: The Gospel of Matthew, 165.*

[67] Rebecca L. Stein and Ted Swedenburg, *Palestine Israel and the Politics of Popular Culture* (London: Duke University Press, 2005), 1.

of great religious and imperial figures mark the great cultural shifts in their life.[68]

The loss of the death is also the reason for a man to have lost his family. The cultural point is that, people without family or kin truly lack, it marks the identity and value that derive from ascribed honour or birth into a family. Those who mourn have suffered a blow to their social standing, that is, their honour and worth. Thus, this cultural elements too made a reason for the grieves and expectation of the goodness in the socio-ethical life.

People grieved of their personal sin. They desired to see right prevail and to do what is right. The problems caused are the sin of violence, the sin of sexual immorality, the sin of mental dishonesty[69] etc. It is not the sorrow of bereavement to which Christ refers, but the sorrow of repentance. Jesus wept over the sins of others, over their bitter consequences in judgement and death, and over the impenitent city, which would not receive him.

We need to see other materials in Matthew, which deal with fractured families to appreciate more fully that "mourning" probably refers to loss of family through banning. The Roman regime used excessive force to discourage any attempt at opposition to its interests, ironically called the "peace of Rome." Therefore, there is a need and expectation of the regenerated socio-ethical life in the people.

The promise implies the special comfort, which the mourner needs; 'comforted' he shall be with the sense of pardon and peace, of restored purity and freedom. The comfort is Messianic. The blessing promised in Jesus' preaching was not evident in earthly reality.[70] In the context of the Matthean Community, this beatitude would function as a promise of a ultimate comfort from God, from all kinds of sufferings which include their suffering under the oppressive Roman administration, under the persecution from both Jews and Gentiles, and because of all the poverty-related illness and death, as well as the natural calamities, etc. That means, they will experience God's comfort in its fullness, in the eschatological kingdom of God as against all their mourning at present.

The explanation following the blessing assures that those who weep will experience joy and laughter in the future. This promise conveys the idea that God will ultimately bring about a reversal of fortunes. Sorrow and suffering will not have the final word. Instead, God's work in the lives of

[68] John Riches, *The World of Jesus First-Century Judaism in Crisis* (Cambridge: Cambridge University Press, 2001), 4.

[69] Myron S. Augsburger, *The Expanded Life* (New York: Abingdon Press, 1972), 36-48.

[70] Patience and perseverance under persecution were more necessary than ever as the Christian Community settled down to await the Lord's return. In these changed, yet unchanged, circumstances Matthew handed on and adapted the beatitudes transmitted to them.

believers will lead to joy and celebration.[71]The fourth blessing addresses those who face hatred, exclusion, and revilement from others because of their association with Jesus.

Jesus acknowledges that following Him may lead to persecution and opposition from those who reject His message. However, this opposition is not a reason for despair but rather a sign of being on the path of righteousness.

The explanation highlights the mistreatment that followers of Jesus may endure, including exclusion and revilement. This mistreatment is not a reflection of the disciples' failure but rather a consequence of their commitment to Christ. It aligns with the prophetic tradition of the Old Testament, where God's messengers often faced rejection and persecution. The commentary concludes by specifying that the mistreatment and opposition arise because of the disciples' association with the Son of Man, a title used by Jesus to refer to Himself. The opposition faced by the disciples is linked directly to their allegiance to Jesus and His mission. The Son of Man represents Jesus' authority and divinely appointed role, and those who reject Him will also oppose His followers.[72]

Despite the mistreatment and opposition, the disciples are encouraged to rejoice and leap for joy because of the great reward awaiting them in heaven. This statement underscores the idea that the disciples' ultimate reward is not in earthly recognition or comfort but in the heavenly realm. It encourages them to maintain their faith and commitment in the face of adversity, knowing that God's reward is of immeasurable value. In summary, Luke 6:20-23 presents a series of blessings (Beatitudes) followed by explanations and commentary. These blessings emphasize the spiritual qualities and values that God values, such as humility, hunger for righteousness, and perseverance in the face of opposition. They offer hope and encouragement to those who follow Jesus, reminding them of the ultimate reward in God's kingdom.[73]

5. The Kingdom of God

The kingdom of God lay at the heart of Jesus' teaching. As proclaimed by Jesus the kingdom of God had continuity with the OT promise as well as with Jewish apocalyptic thinking, but differed from them in important respects. For example, it denoted God's eternal rule rather than an earthly kingdom, its scope was universal rather than limited to the Jewish nation, and it was imminent and potentially present in him rather than a vague future

[71] Megan McKenna, *Blessings and Woes: The Beatitudes and the Sermon on the Plain in the Gospel of Luke* (Maryknoll, NY: Orbis Books, 1999) 123.

[72] Mark Harding and Alanna Nobbs, *The Content and the Setting of the Gospel Tradition* (Grand Rapids, MI: Wm. B. Eerdmans Publishing, 2010), 382.

[73] Geoffrey William Bromiley, *The International Standard Bible Encyclopedia* (Grand Rapids, MI: Wm. B. Eerdmans Publishing, 1979), 416.

hope, being inextricably connected with his own person and mission. The phrase 'Kingdom of God' sums up the mission and message of our Lord Jesus Christ. The announcement of the kingdom was nothing less than the purpose for which Jesus came into the world. All the work which he had done was for the Kingdom. The parables were the parables of the kingdom and the miracles were the miracles of the Kingdom. The phrase 'Kingdom of God' is a translation of the Greek expression 'he basileia tou theou' (ἡ Βασίλειω των Θεου). In Greek it can mean kingship, royal rule, sovereignty as well as kingdom in the sense of the territory rule by a king.

The Kingdom of God is the central theme of the proclamation of Jesus.[74] Teachings of Jesus deal with the kingdom of God[75] and they speak of the coming of the kingdom, characteristics the kingdom and values related to the kingdom. Teachings of Jesus are related to its nature, its coming, its value, its growth, the sacrifices it calls for and so on.[76] They indirectly give the guideline to enter into it. Teachings of Jesus aim at a line of conduct to which Jesus wants to impel His listeners or against which he wants to warn them. The teachings of Jesus have concern for the behavior of the listener, not direct but theological and it requires the qualities which are to be found in them on the basis of their changed behavior. It must be part of life of its audience.[77]

The central motif of the life and ministry of Jesus was the 'Kingdom of God'. This is adopted from the notion of God's coming rule and its impact upon the people of God in the Old Testament.[78] His concept was universalistic in designation and implication.[79] The Kingdom of God represents a set of universal values such as freedom, fellowship and justice as the basis for a new society.[80] They are the parameters of Kingdom's thrust towards the total liberation of humans. 'Kingdom' is translated from the Greek, *basileia. Basileia* in the Gospels implies 'a sphere or rule', to which one can enter.

---

[74] Eugene S. Wehrill, *Exploring the Parables: Let Him Hear* (Philadelphia: Boston, 1963), 111.

[75] John Ermiakulathil, "Kingdom of God in the Teaching of Jesus," *Bible Bhashyam* 23/2 (June, 1997). 90-101 gives a study on the same topic including the background of the theme, nature and meaning, and its various dimensions.

[76] R.V.G. Tasker and I. Howard Marshall, "Parable," *New Bible Dictionary*, 869.

[77] Herman Hendrickx, *The Parables of Jesus: Studies in the Synoptic Gospels*, 0

[78] Cf. Donald S. K. Palmer, *The Kingdom of God* (Welwyn: Evangelical Press, 1986), 17ff.

[79] George W. Peters, *A Biblical Theology of Missions* (Chicago: Moody Press, 1972), 42.

[80] George M. Soares-Prabhu, 'The Kingdom of God: Jesus' Vision of a New Society,' *Theology of Liberation: An Indian Biblical Perspective, collected writings of George M. Soares-Prabhu,* vol. 4, edited by F. X. D'Sa (Pune: Deepa Vidyapeett Theological, 2001), 239.

But the dominant meaning of the word is the act of God in His Kingly power, exercising His Sovereignty. This is eternal and therefore beyond time, it has already begun but has also an eschatological significance.[81] The concept of Kingdom of God has a past, present and future implication. C. H. Dodd calls it as 'realized eschatology.'[82]

Luke's Beatitudes emphasize the promise of the "kingdom of God" (Luke 6:20), emphasizing the ultimate fulfillment of God's reign and justice. This spiritual kingdom transcends material wealth and represents a counter-cultural vision of a just and equitable society. In Luke 6:20-23, Jesus pronounces blessings, commonly known as the Beatitudes, to a crowd of his disciples. The blessings are followed by explanations and commentary. In this section, we will focus on the concept of "The Kingdom of God" as it appears in these verses:

The term "The Kingdom of God" is central to Jesus' teachings throughout the Gospels. It refers to the reign or rule of God in the hearts and lives of believers and the broader cosmic order. Jesus often used parables and teachings to illustrate the nature and significance of the Kingdom of God.[83] When Jesus pronounces blessings on the poor and those who hunger for righteousness, he connects these blessings with the Kingdom of God. This linkage underscores the idea that the Kingdom of God is not merely a future, heavenly realm but a present reality. Those who recognize their spiritual poverty and hunger for righteousness are participants in the Kingdom of God.

The Kingdom of God represents God's rule, justice, and values. It is characterized by love, mercy, and the transformation of individuals and communities. In this context, Jesus is inviting his disciples to embrace the values and principles of the Kingdom, emphasizing that those who do so will experience its blessings. The Kingdom of God also implies a reversal of worldly values and expectations. The poor, the hungry, and those who weep—often marginalized in society—are elevated and blessed in God's Kingdom. It challenges societal norms and offers hope to those who may be oppressed or suffering.

The Beatitudes in Luke 6:20-23 underscore that the Kingdom of God is not limited to a future eschatological event but is a present and transformative reality. Believers are invited to participate in this Kingdom by embodying its values and principles in their lives. The promise of a great reward in heaven for those who endure opposition and mistreatment (verse 23) further

---

[81] A.M. Hunter, *The Work and Words of Jesus* (Delhi: ISPCK, 1969), 76ff.

[82] C. H. Dodd, *The Parables of the Kingdom* (London: Nisbet, 1961).

[83] Judith M. Lieu, *The Gospel of Luke: Epworth Commentaries* (Eugene, OR: Wipf and Stock Publishers, 2012), 50.

emphasizes the eschatological aspect of the Kingdom of God. It assures believers that their ultimate reward transcends earthly circumstances and is secured in the heavenly realm.[84]

In summary, the concept of "The Kingdom of God" in Luke 6:20-23 represents the central theme of Jesus' teachings. It is both a present reality and a future hope, characterized by God's rule and transformative power. The Beatitudes connect the experience of God's Kingdom with qualities such as humility, hunger for righteousness, and perseverance in the face of opposition, offering hope and encouragement to those who follow Jesus.

6. Hungry and Mourning

The blessings also extend to those who hunger and those who mourn (Luke 6:21), emphasizing God's compassion for those who suffer. These blessings challenge societal attitudes that often stigmatize or marginalize those in need. In Luke 6:20-23, specifically focusing on the blessings related to the hungry and those who mourn, Jesus offers profound spiritual insights that provide comfort, hope, and guidance to His disciples.[85] Here, we'll explore the significance and meaning of these blessings:

When Jesus says, "Blessed are you who are hungry now," He is addressing not only physical hunger but also a deep spiritual hunger for righteousness, justice, and the fulfillment of God's promises. Hunger in this context symbolizes a strong desire for righteousness and justice. It's the inner longing for things to be made right in a world often marked by injustice and inequality. It reflects a recognition of the brokenness in the world and a yearning for God's transformative work. By pronouncing a blessing on those who hunger, Jesus acknowledges the legitimacy of this spiritual longing. He encourages His disciples to seek after righteousness and to be passionate about justice, knowing that such hunger is a sign of a heart aligned with God's values. Importantly, Jesus promises that those who hunger for righteousness "shall be satisfied." This statement assures believers that their longing for righteousness will not go unanswered. God will bring about justice and righteousness, both in the world and in their lives.[86]

---

[84] Hans Dieter Betz, *The Sermon on the Mount: A Commentary on the Sermon on the Mount, Including the Sermon on the Plain (Matthew 5:3-7:27 and Luke 6:20-49)* (Minneapolis, MN: Fortress Press, 1995), 574.

[85] Ndekha Louis, *Identity and Socio-Economic Relations in Luke's Gospel: The Sermon on the Plain (Lk 6:20-49) and Greco Roman Panegyrics* (Bamberg: University of Bamberg Press, 2023), 67.

[86] Adrian Hastings, Alistair Mason, and Hugh S. Pyper, *The Oxford Companion to Christian Thought* (Oxford: Oxford University Press, USA, 2000), 655.

Jesus continues with, "Blessed are you who weep now." This speaks to those who are currently experiencing sorrow and grief. Weeping in this context represents the pain, suffering, and grief that people encounter in life. It acknowledges the reality of human suffering, loss, and hardship. Jesus is compassionate toward those who are in the midst of sorrow. The blessing here conveys the idea that God is present even in times of sorrow. By pronouncing a blessing, Jesus offers comfort and hope to those who mourn. It reassures them that their present suffering is not the end of the story. When Jesus promises, "For you shall laugh," He points to a future transformation of sorrow into joy. This promise echoes the prophetic tradition of the Old Testament, where God's redemptive work brings about joy and restoration.[87]

Overall, the blessing on those who mourn emphasizes the redemptive nature of God's Kingdom. It suggests that even in the midst of suffering, there is a deeper joy that comes from knowing God's presence and experiencing His transformative power. In summary, the blessings related to the hungry and those who mourn in Luke 6:20-23 address both spiritual and emotional aspects of the human experience.[88] They highlight the significance of hungering for righteousness and justice and offer comfort to those who are currently in a state of mourning. These blessings convey the hope that God's Kingdom brings fulfillment to our deepest longings and transforms our sorrows into joy.

7. The Woes in Luke 6:24-26

7.1. Woe to the Rich

In contrast to the blessings, Luke presents a series of woes, including "Woe to you who are rich" (Luke 6:24). This warning reflects Jesus' critique of the wealthy who may prioritize material gain over spiritual values and social responsibility. In Luke 6:24-26, Jesus pronounces woes, contrasting the blessings (Beatitudes) from the previous verses. Here, we'll focus on the specific woe pronounced upon the rich: In this passage, Jesus issues a warning or "woe" to those who are rich. He addresses those who have accumulated wealth and material possessions. The term "rich" here refers not only to those who possess material wealth but also to those who may place their trust, security, and identity in their riches. It's a warning against the pursuit of wealth at the expense of spiritual priorities.

---

[87] Cynthia A. Jarvis and E. Elizabeth Johnson, *Feasting on the Gospels--Luke, Volume 1: A Feasting on the Word Commentary* (Louisville, KY: Presbyterian Publishing Corp, 2014), 158.

[88] Sung Min Hong, *Those Who Weep Shall Laugh: Reversal of Weeping in the Gospel of Luke* (Eugene, OR: Wipf and Stock Publishers, 2018); James W. Thompson and Richard A. Wright, *Ethics in Contexts: Essays in Honor of Wendell Lee Willis* (Eugene, OR: Wipf and Stock Publishers, 2019), 104.

Jesus' warning serves as a cautionary reminder that wealth can become a stumbling block, leading to self-sufficiency and a lack of dependence on God. It is not inherently wrong to have wealth, but it carries a responsibility to use it wisely and generously. The "woe" pronounced on the rich suggests that their present condition, characterized by abundance and self-reliance, may hinder their recognition of their need for God's grace and provision.[89]

The contrast between the blessings and woes in this passage highlights a spiritual truth: those who may be materially well-off but lack a hunger for righteousness and a recognition of their spiritual poverty face the risk of spiritual complacency. Jesus' warning is a reminder that wealth can be a deceptive source of security. It underscores the importance of humility, dependence on God, and a commitment to justice and righteousness even when one has material abundance. Ultimately, this woe challenges individuals to examine the role of wealth in their lives and to ensure that their pursuit of God's Kingdom and His righteousness takes precedence over the accumulation of material possessions.[90]

In summary, the woe to the rich in Luke 6:24 serves as a cautionary message from Jesus, reminding individuals of the potential dangers associated with wealth and material abundance. It calls for a balanced perspective on wealth, emphasizing the importance of prioritizing spiritual values and justice over the pursuit of material gain.

7.2. Full and Laughing

The woes also extend to those who are "full" and those who "laugh now" (Luke 6:25), highlighting the danger of complacency and hedonism. This critique challenges the pursuit of pleasure and luxury at the expense of others' well-being. In Luke 6:24-26, Jesus pronounces woes, contrasting the blessings (Beatitudes) from the previous verses. Here, we'll focus on the specific woe pronounced upon those who are "full" and "laughing."

Woe to the Full and Laughing: In this passage, Jesus issues a warning or "woe" to those who are described as "full" and "laughing." These terms suggest a state of self-satisfaction and complacency, where individuals may be content with their current circumstances and worldly pleasures. The term "full" implies a sense of satisfaction and contentment, often associated with material well being and a life of comfort. It can also indicate a lack of hunger or longing, both physically and spiritually. "Laughing" conveys a sense of joy and mirth, but in this context, it is used to describe a disposition of

89 Ndekha Louis, *Identity and Socio-Economic Relations in Luke's Gospel: The Sermon on the Plain (Lk 6:20-49) and Greco-Roman Panegyrics*, 108.

90 Dale C. Allison, *Constructing Jesus: Memory, Imagination, and History* (Grand Rapids, MI: Baker Academic, 2010), 339.

carefree and worldly pleasure, potentially at the expense of deeper spiritual concerns.[91]

Jesus' warning serves as a reminder that a life marked by self-indulgence, complacency, and a focus on temporary pleasures can lead to spiritual neglect. It suggests that those who are "full" and "laughing" may be at risk of overlooking their spiritual hunger and the need for God's grace. The contrast between the blessings and woes highlights the spiritual danger of becoming too comfortable and satisfied with worldly success and pleasures. It underscores the importance of maintaining a hunger for righteousness, justice, and God's Kingdom.[92]

This woe challenges individuals to reflect on their priorities and the source of their joy. It calls for a balance between enjoying the good things of life and recognizing the deeper spiritual needs that only God can satisfy. Ultimately, Jesus' warning is a call to humility and a reminder that true fulfillment and lasting joy come not from earthly abundance alone but from a relationship with God and a commitment to His values.[93] In summary, the woe to those who are "full" and "laughing" in Luke 6:25 serves as a cautionary message from Jesus, warning against complacency and self-indulgence. It emphasizes the importance of maintaining spiritual hunger and a commitment to God's Kingdom amid the comforts and pleasures of life.

7.3. False Prophets

The final woe is directed at those who are spoken well of by others, including false prophets (Luke 6:26). This warning underscores the contrast between societal acclaim and God's assessment, emphasizing the importance of discernment. In Luke 6:24-26, Jesus pronounces woes, contrasting the blessings (Beatitudes) from the previous verses. Here, we'll focus on the specific woe pronounced upon false prophets:

In this passage, Jesus issues a warning or "woe" to false prophets. False prophets are individuals who claim to speak on behalf of God but deliver messages that are not in line with God's truth and will. False prophets were a significant concern in the religious context of Jesus' time, as they could lead people astray and promote teachings that deviated from the true message of God.

---

[91] Eduard Schweizer, *The Good News According to Luke* (Louisville, KY: Westminster John Knox Press, 1984), 118.

[92] Stanley Hauerwas et al., *The Wisdom of the Cross: Essays in Honor of John Howard Yoder* (Eugene, OR: Wipf and Stock Publishers, 2005), 152.

[93] Cynthia A. Jarvis and E. Elizabeth Johnson, *Feasting on the Gospels--Luke, Volume 1: A Feasting on the Word Commentary*, 160.

Jesus' warning is a cautionary message about the dangers of false spiritual leaders who manipulate and deceive others for personal gain or misguided purposes. The term "woe" signifies a serious and lamentable state of those who engage in false prophecy. It is a declaration of judgment and divine disapproval. The contrast between the blessings and woes highlights the contrast between true spiritual values and those who distort or misrepresent them for their own benefit. Jesus' warning underscores the importance of discernment and the need for individuals to test the authenticity of those who claim to be spiritual leaders or prophets. The broader message is a call to seek genuine spiritual guidance and to be cautious of those who may lead others astray with false teachings or motivations.[94]

In summary, the woe to false prophets in Luke 6:26 serves as a stern warning from Jesus about the dangers of misleading or deceptive spiritual leaders. It emphasizes the importance of discernment and a commitment to seeking genuine spiritual truth and guidance.

8. Critique of Wealth and Poverty

The Gospel of Luke, one of the synoptic Gospels in the New Testament, presents a profound and challenging critique of wealth and poverty. This critique is deeply rooted in Luke's theological perspective and ethical concerns. Throughout the Gospel, Jesus' teachings and actions consistently challenge societal norms and values related to wealth, materialism, and the treatment of the poor and marginalized.[95] In this exploration, we will delve into the critique of wealth and poverty as presented in the Gospel of Luke, examining the key themes, parables, and ethical implications.

8.1. Prophetic Challenge

Luke's Beatitudes and Woes align with the prophetic tradition of challenging societal injustices and calling for repentance. They challenge the common assumption that material prosperity equals divine blessing and righteousness. In the Gospel of Luke, particularly in its portrayal of Jesus' teachings and actions, there is a pronounced critique of wealth and poverty. This critique is rooted in the prophetic tradition of the Old Testament and represents a significant aspect of Luke's theological and ethical perspective[96]. Here, we'll explore the prophetic challenge regarding wealth and poverty in the Gospel of Luke:

---

[94] William Barclay, *The Gospel of Luke* (Philadelphia, PA: Westminster Press, 1956), 73.

[95] Walter Pilgrim, *Good News to the Poor: Wealth and Poverty in Luke-Acts* (Eugene, OR: Wipf and Stock Publishers, 2011), 39ff.

[96] Ndekha Louis, *Identity and Socio-Economic Relations in Luke's Gospel: The Sermon on the Plain (Lk 6:20-49) and Greco-Roman Panegyrics*, 62.

The prophetic challenge in the Gospel of Luke is a call to address issues of wealth and poverty in light of God's justice and righteousness. It draws on the prophetic tradition of the Old Testament, where prophets like Amos and Isaiah denounced social injustice and called for the restoration of righteousness in society.[97]

Throughout the Gospel of Luke, Jesus' teachings and actions consistently challenge the prevailing social and economic norms of His time. He confronts a society marked by economic disparities, exploitation, and neglect of the poor. One of the central themes in Luke is the reversal of fortunes, where the poor and marginalized are elevated, and the rich and powerful are challenged to repent and change their ways. Jesus' parables, such as the Parable of the Rich Man and Lazarus (Luke 16:19-31) and the Parable of the Rich Fool (Luke 12:13-21), illustrate the dangers of greed and the consequences of prioritizing wealth over God's kingdom.

The Gospel of Luke also highlights Jesus' interactions with marginalized individuals, including tax collectors, prostitutes, and lepers, demonstrating His concern for those on the margins of society.

In the Magnificat (Luke 1:46-55), Mary's song of praise, there is a prophetic declaration of God's preferential treatment of the lowly and the hungry, while the rich and powerful are brought down from their thrones. The encounter with Zacchaeus (Luke 19:1-10) showcases a transformation in a wealthy tax collector's life, emphasizing the possibility of repentance and justice for those who have accumulated wealth through unjust means.[98]

Jesus' call to discipleship includes an invitation to sell one's possessions and give to the poor (Luke 12:33) and to use wealth for acts of mercy and compassion (Luke 10:30-37). The overall message of the prophetic challenge in Luke is a call to prioritize justice, compassion, and care for the marginalized over the pursuit of personal wealth and status. It reflects a vision of God's kingdom where societal inequalities are addressed and righteousness prevails. Importantly, this prophetic challenge is not solely concerned with individual actions but also calls for systemic change and a transformation of society's values and structures.

In summary, the prophetic challenge regarding wealth and poverty in the Gospel of Luke draws deeply from the Old Testament prophetic tradition. It calls for a reevaluation of societal values, a commitment to justice and

---

[97] Philip Francis Esler, *Community and Gospel in Luke-Acts: The Social and Political Motivations of Lucan Theology* (Cambridge: Cambridge University Press, 1989), 171.

[98] Rachel L. Coleman, *The Lukan Lens on Wealth and Possessions: A Perspective Shaped by the Themes of Reversal and Right Response* (Leiden: Brill, 2019), 64.

compassion, and a recognition of the transformative power of God's kingdom in addressing issues of wealth and poverty.[99]

8.2. Reversal of Values

The blessings and woes represent a radical reversal of societal values, highlighting the importance of humility, compassion, and justice. They underscore the ethical and spiritual dimensions of wealth and poverty. In the Gospel of Luke, a prominent theme is the reversal of values, particularly as it pertains to issues of wealth and poverty. This theme reflects Luke's theological perspective and is closely linked to the prophetic challenge discussed earlier. Here, we'll explore the concept of the reversal of values in the context of wealth and poverty in the Gospel of Luke:

The reversal of values in Luke's Gospel refers to a fundamental shift in how society's norms and priorities are understood and evaluated. It challenges the conventional wisdom and societal hierarchies, particularly in relation to wealth and poverty. Jesus' teachings and actions in the Gospel of Luke consistently challenge the prevailing values of His time.[100] He overturns societal expectations and calls for a radical reevaluation of priorities. The Beatitudes (Luke 6:20-23) exemplify this theme by pronouncing blessings on the poor, the hungry, and those who weep, while issuing woes to the rich, the full, and those who laugh. This reversal of blessings and woes challenges the conventional understanding of success and happiness.

In the Parable of the Rich Man and Lazarus (Luke 16:19-31), Jesus illustrates the dramatic reversal of fortunes between a wealthy man who ends up in torment and a poor beggar named Lazarus who finds comfort in the afterlife. This parable underscores the ultimate futility of wealth without compassion. The Magnificat (Luke 1:46-55) contains a song of praise by Mary that celebrates God's reversal of values. She declares that God has brought down the mighty from their thrones and exalted the humble and hungry.

Jesus' encounters with marginalized individuals, such as Zacchaeus the tax collector (Luke 19:1-10) and the sinful woman who anoints His feet (Luke 7:36-50), highlight the transformative power of grace and the willingness of those on the margins to repent and embrace God's values. The call to discipleship in Luke includes radical demands, such as selling possessions and giving to the poor (Luke 12:33) and taking up one's cross

---

[99] Christopher M. Hays, *Luke's Wealth Ethics: A Study in Their Coherence and Character* (Tübingen: Mohr Siebeck, 2010), 9.

[100] Ndekha Louis, *Identity and Socio-Economic Relations in Luke's Gospel: The Sermon on the Plain (Lk 6:20-49) and Greco-Roman Panegyrics*, 85.

(Luke 9:23). These demands challenge the pursuit of personal wealth and comfort in favor of a commitment to God's kingdom and justice.[101]

The reversal of values extends beyond individual actions to societal structures. The story of the Good Samaritan (Luke 10:30-37) challenges ethnic and social biases by highlighting the compassion of a despised Samaritan towards a wounded traveler. The overall message of the reversal of values is that God's kingdom upends the world's priorities. It calls for a shift from self-centeredness and accumulation of wealth to a focus on justice, mercy, and the well-being of others. Ultimately, the Gospel of Luke presents a vision of a transformed world where the marginalized are lifted up, the proud are humbled, and the values of God's kingdom prevail.[102]

In summary, the concept of the reversal of values in the Gospel of Luke challenges societal norms, particularly regarding wealth and poverty. It calls for a radical reevaluation of priorities, emphasizing God's kingdom values of justice, compassion, and humility. This theme underscores the transformative power of God's grace in individual lives and society as a whole.

One of the central themes in the Gospel of Luke is the reversal of fortunes. This theme is introduced early in the Gospel through the Beatitudes and corresponding woes in Luke 6:20-26. In these verses, Jesus pronounces blessings on the poor, hungry, and those who weep, while issuing woes to the rich, full, and those who laugh. This reversal challenges conventional notions of success and happiness. It emphasizes that God's values differ significantly from worldly standards.[103]

The Beatitudes highlight God's concern for the marginalized and the disadvantaged. They underscore that those who are often overlooked and oppressed are recipients of God's special favor. Conversely, the woes serve as warnings about the dangers of wealth and complacency. They caution against the pursuit of material comforts at the expense of spiritual well-being.

8.3. Social Justice and Compassion

These passages emphasize the importance of social justice and compassion for the marginalized and suffering. They call believers to actively engage in addressing economic disparities and advocating for the vulnerable. In the Gospel of Luke, the themes of social justice and compassion are prominently featured as integral components of Jesus' teachings and actions. These themes reflect Luke's emphasis on the ethical dimension of following

---

[101] G. R. Evans, *A History of Pastoral Care* (London: A&C Black, 2000), 37.

[102] Raj Nadella, *Dialogue Not Dogma: Many Voices in the Gospel of Luke* (London: Bloomsbury Publishing, 2011), 99.

[103] Thomas E. Phillips, *Reading Issues of Wealth and Poverty in Luke-Acts* (Lewiston, NY: Edwin Mellen Press, 2001), 23.

Christ and serve as a call to embody God's love and care for others. Here, we'll explore the concepts of social justice and compassion in the context of Luke's Gospel:

Social justice in the Gospel of Luke involves the pursuit of equity, fairness, and the establishment of a just and righteous society. Compassion, on the other hand, entails a deep sense of empathy and a willingness to alleviate the suffering of others. Jesus' teachings and actions consistently demonstrate a concern for social justice and compassion. He challenges oppressive systems and calls for the inclusion of marginalized individuals in society.[104]

In summary, social justice and compassion are central themes in the Gospel of Luke. They reflect Jesus' commitment to addressing societal inequalities, extending compassion to the marginalized, and calling His followers to emulate His example. These themes emphasize the ethical dimension of discipleship and underscore the transformative power of God's love in creating a more just and compassionate society

8.4. The Parables of Jesus

In the Parable of the Good Samaritan (Luke 10:30-37), Jesus illustrates the concept of compassion by highlighting the care shown by a despised Samaritan towards a wounded man. This parable underscores the importance of loving one's neighbor and practicing compassion across social boundaries. Jesus' interactions with tax collectors, prostitutes, and sinners (Luke 5:27-32, Luke 7:36-50) demonstrate His willingness to extend compassion and forgiveness to those society had marginalized. The story of Zacchaeus (Luke 19:1-10) illustrates the transformative power of social justice. Zacchaeus, a wealthy tax collector, repents of his unjust practices and commits to making amends by restoring what he had wrongfully taken from others. This narrative emphasizes the potential for repentance and restitution.[105] The Magnificat (Luke 1:46-55), Mary's song of praise, celebrates God's preference for the humble and hungry and His commitment to social justice. It reflects a vision of societal transformation where the lowly are lifted up.

In the Parable of the Rich Man and Lazarus (Luke 16:19-31), Jesus addresses the issue of economic disparities and neglect of the poor. The rich man's lack of compassion and indifference to Lazarus' suffering result in severe consequences. Jesus' call to discipleship includes commands to sell possessions and give to the poor (Luke 12:33) and to use wealth acts

[104] Leon Morris, *New Testament Theology* (Grand Rapids, MI: Zondervan Academic, 2011), 178.

[105] Daniel Monikaraj, *The Inheritors of the [Basileia Tou Theou]: According to Lucan Perspective* (Delhi: ISPCK, 2008), 84.

of mercy and compassion (Luke 10:30-37). The overall message of social justice and compassion in Luke's Gospel is a call to emulate Jesus' example by caring for the marginalized, advocating for the oppressed, and working towards a just and equitable society. These themes align with the prophetic tradition of the Old Testament, where justice and mercy are central concerns. They also resonate with Jesus' summary of the greatest commandments: to love God and to love one's neighbor as oneself (Luke 10:27).[106]

Throughout the Gospel of Luke, Jesus uses parables to illustrate and reinforce his critique of wealth and poverty. Several parables focus on the dangers of materialism and the ethical implications of one's economic status: **The Parable of the Rich Fool (Luke 12:13-21):** In this parable, a rich man plans to store up his abundant harvest for himself, only to have his life required of him that very night. Jesus warns against the folly of hoarding wealth for personal gain while ignoring one's eternal destiny[107]. The parable underscores the emptiness of material accumulation when it is not aligned with spiritual priorities. **The Parable of the Rich Man and Lazarus (Luke 16:19-31):** This powerful parable contrasts the starkly different destinies of a wealthy man and a poor beggar named Lazarus. The rich man, who lived in luxury and ignored Lazarus's suffering, ends up in torment, while Lazarus finds comfort in the afterlife. This parable serves as a poignant reminder of the consequences of neglecting the needs of the poor.

8.5. Zacchaeus' Transformation

The story of Zacchaeus (Luke 19:1-10) is a remarkable example of how encountering Jesus can lead to a transformation in one's attitude towards wealth and poverty. Zacchaeus, a wealthy tax collector known for his exploitation of others, climbs a tree to see Jesus. When Jesus invites himself to Zacchaeus's home, it results in a radical transformation. Zacchaeus repents of his unjust practices and commits to making amends by restoring what he had wrongfully taken from others.[108] This narrative demonstrates the possibility of redemption and social responsibility, even for those who have amassed wealth through unethical means.

---

[106] Cynthia A. Jarvis and E. Elizabeth Johnson, *Feasting on the Gospels--Luke, Volume 2: A Feasting on the Word Commentary* (Louisville, KY: Presbyterian Publishing Corp, 2014), 106.

[107] Susan R. Holman, *Wealth and Poverty in Early Church and Society* (Grand Rapids, MI: Baker Academic, 2008), 17ff.

[108] Fernando Mendez-Moratalla, *The Paradigm of Conversion in Luke* (London: A&C Black, 2004), 156.

8.6. The Magnificat: A Song of Social Justice

Mary's song of praise, known as the Magnificat (Luke 1:46-55), celebrates God's preference for the humble and hungry while challenging the proud and rich. It is a profound declaration of God's commitment to social justice. In the Magnificat, Mary proclaims that God has "brought down the mighty from their thrones and exalted those of humble estate." This song envisions a world where societal inequalities are overturned, and God's justice prevails. It reflects the prophetic tradition of the Old Testament, where justice and righteousness were central concerns.

8.7. Call to Discipleship

Jesus' call to discipleship in the Gospel of Luke includes radical demands that have significant implications for one's relationship with wealth and possessions. For example: **Selling Possessions and Giving to the Poor (Luke 12:33):** Jesus instructs his followers to sell their possessions and give to the poor. This command challenges the notion that personal wealth should be accumulated for its own sake and underscores the importance of caring for those in need. **Taking Up One's Cross (Luke 9:23):** Jesus calls disciples to take up their crosses, symbolizing a willingness to endure suffering and self-sacrifice for the sake of the kingdom. This call challenges the pursuit of comfort and self-indulgence.[109]

These demands of discipleship in Luke's Gospel emphasize the need for a reevaluation of priorities and a commitment to God's kingdom, which includes justice, compassion, and a concern for the well-being of others.

8.8. Social Engagement and Inclusivity

Throughout the Gospel of Luke, Jesus engages with marginalized individuals, including tax collectors, sinners, and those considered social outcasts. His willingness to associate with and care for those excluded by society challenges societal norms and underscores the importance of inclusivity and social engagement. It sends a clear message that God's love extends to all, regardless of their economic status or social standing.[110]

8.9. Prophetic Challenge

The critique of wealth and poverty in the Gospel of Luke draws deeply from the prophetic tradition of the Old Testament. Prophets like Amos and Isaiah denounced social injustice, economic exploitation, and the neglect of the poor. In a similar vein, Luke's Gospel issues a prophetic challenge to the

---

[109] Sarah Harris, *The Davidic Shepherd King in the Lukan Narrative* (London: Bloomsbury Publishing, 2016), 129.

[110] Pyung-Soo Seo, *Luke's Jesus in the Roman Empire and the Emperor in the Gospel of Luke* (Cambridge: James Clarke & Company Limited, 2015), 89.

prevailing economic and social norms of the time. It calls for righteousness, compassion, and a commitment to God's justice.

8.10. Ethical Implications

The critique of wealth and poverty in Luke's Gospel carries profound ethical implications for individuals and communities. It challenges the pursuit of material wealth at the expense of ethical considerations. It calls for a commitment to justice, compassion, and care for the poor and vulnerable.[111] It also underscores the need for a collective responsibility to address societal inequalities and advocate for systemic change.

9. Contemporary Relevance

Luke's critique of wealth and poverty remains relevant in contemporary discussions of income inequality and economic disparities. It challenges societies to address systemic injustices and prioritize the well-being of all citizens. The issue of income inequality remains a pressing concern in contemporary society, and it is a topic that resonates with the themes of wealth and poverty found in the Gospel of Luke. Here, we'll explore the contemporary relevance of income inequality in light of Luke's teachings and actions: Income inequality refers to the unequal distribution of income and wealth among individuals and groups within a society. It often results in disparities in living standards, access to resources, and opportunities.[112]

9.1. Income Inequality

Income inequality is a global issue that affects nations at various levels of economic development. It has become a topic of increasing concern due to its far-reaching social, economic, and political implications. The Gospel of Luke's critique of wealth and its emphasis on the reversal of values have contemporary relevance in addressing income inequality. The following points illustrate this connection:

Luke's emphasis on social justice and compassion aligns with contemporary efforts to address income inequality. Advocacy for policies and practices that promote equitable access to education, healthcare, and economic opportunities reflects a commitment to social justice. Luke's concern for the poor and marginalized resonates with contemporary poverty alleviation initiatives. These efforts include social welfare programs, charitable organizations, and community-based projects aimed at reducing

[111] David J. Bosch, *Transforming Mission: Paradigm Shifts in Theology of Mission* (Maryknoll, NY: Orbis Books, 2011), 99.

[112] Megan McKenna, *Blessings and Woes: The Beatitudes and the Sermon on the Plain in the Gospel of Luke*, .

poverty and improving the well-being of disadvantaged individuals and families.

Luke's call to sell possessions and give to the poor (Luke 12:33) resonates with contemporary discussions about wealth redistribution. Tax policies, social safety nets, and debates about progressive taxation are examples of mechanisms designed to address income inequality.[113] In the business world, the concept of corporate social responsibility (CSR) reflects a growing awareness of the need for ethical business practices. Companies are increasingly expected to consider their impact on society and address income inequality through fair wages, equitable employment practices, and community engagement. Luke's focus on caring for the marginalized finds contemporary relevance in advocacy for vulnerable populations, including refugees, immigrants, and those facing discrimination or exclusion. Addressing income inequality often involves advocating for the rights and well-being of these groups.

Many faith-based organizations and communities draw inspiration from the Gospel of Luke to engage in social justice initiatives. These initiatives may include food banks, shelters, educational programs, and advocacy efforts aimed at reducing income inequality. In summary, the teachings and actions of Jesus in the Gospel of Luke offer a lens through which contemporary society can address the issue of income inequality. The themes of social justice, compassion, poverty alleviation, and wealth redistribution provide a framework for ethical and practical responses to the challenges posed by income inequality in the modern world.[114]

9.2. Consumerism and Hedonism

The warnings against pursuing wealth and pleasure at the expense of others resonate with critiques of modern consumerism and hedonism. They call individuals to consider the ethical implications of their choices and lifestyles. Consumerism and hedonism are contemporary phenomena that resonate with the themes of wealth, values, and priorities found in the Gospel of Luke. Here, we'll explore the contemporary relevance of consumerism and hedonism in light of Luke's teachings and actions:

Consumerism is a societal mindset characterized by the excessive pursuit and acquisition of material goods and possessions. Hedonism, on the other hand, is a philosophy or lifestyle that prioritizes pleasure and self-indulgence, often at the expense of deeper values and ethical considerations.

---

[113] Bart B. Bruehler, *A Public and Political Christ: The Social-Spatial Characteristics of Luke 18:35–19:43 and the Gospel as a Whole in Its Ancient Context* (Eugene, OR: Wipf and Stock Publishers, 2011), 3.

[114] Delbert Burkett, *An Introduction to the New Testament and the Origins of Christianity* (Cambridge : Cambridge University Press, 2019), 198.

Both consumerism and hedonism have become dominant cultural forces in many parts of the world, influencing individual behavior, economic systems, and societal values. The Gospel of Luke's critique of wealth and its emphasis on the reversal of values offer relevant insights into addressing these contemporary challenges:

Luke's teachings challenge the materialistic mindset associated with consumerism. The emphasis on prioritizing God's kingdom and righteousness (Luke 12:31) over the accumulation of possessions encourages individuals to reconsider their priorities and the role of material wealth in their lives.[115] Consumerism often promises fulfillment through the acquisition of goods, but Luke's message highlights the limitations of such pursuits. The Parable of the Rich Fool (Luke 12:13-21) serves as a cautionary tale about the emptiness of amassing wealth without regard for one's soul. Hedonism's focus on personal pleasure contrasts with Luke's call to compassion and caring for the marginalized. The Parable of the Good Samaritan (Luke 10:30-37) challenges self-centeredness and underscores the importance of empathy and assistance to those in need. Luke's emphasis on selling possessions and giving to the poor (Luke 12:33) encourages a spirit of generosity and sharing, countering the excessive accumulation of goods associated with consumerism. It promotes a sense of responsibility for the well-being of others.

Consumerism often raises ethical concerns related to production practices, environmental impact, and labor conditions. Luke's teachings align with contemporary movements advocating for ethical consumption, fair trade, and sustainability. The Gospel of Luke's vision of societal transformation, where the marginalized are lifted up and the proud are humbled, offers an alternative to the individualistic values promoted by consumerism and hedonism. It encourages the pursuit of justice, compassion, and community well-being.[116] Faith communities and organizations draw inspiration from Luke's teachings to engage in initiatives that counteract consumerism and hedonism. These efforts may include voluntary simplicity, ethical consumer choices, and promoting values aligned with the Gospel. In summary, the themes in the Gospel of Luke provide a relevant framework for addressing contemporary challenges related to consumerism and hedonism. They encourage a reevaluation of priorities, a shift away from self-indulgence, and a commitment to values such as compassion, generosity, and justice.

---

[115] James A. Metzger, *Consumption and Wealth in Luke's Travel Narrative* (Leiden: Brill, 2007), 125.

[116] Rachel L. Coleman, *The Lukan Lens on Wealth and Possessions: A Perspective Shaped by the Themes of Reversal and Right Response*, 164.

Luke's message offers an ethical and spiritual perspective on navigating the complexities of a consumer-driven and pleasure-seeking culture.[117]

9.3. Social Responsibility

Luke's emphasis on social responsibility and compassion underscores the importance of advocacy for the poor and vulnerable in today's world. It encourages believers to actively engage in efforts to alleviate poverty and promote justice. Social responsibility is a crucial contemporary concept that aligns with the ethical and moral teachings found in the Gospel of Luke. Luke's emphasis on caring for the marginalized, practicing compassion, and addressing issues of wealth and poverty carries significant relevance in discussions of social responsibility today. Here, we'll explore the contemporary relevance of social responsibility in light of Luke's teachings and actions: Social responsibility refers to the ethical obligation and commitment of individuals, organizations, and societies to act in ways that promote the well-being and welfare of others, particularly those who are vulnerable or marginalized[118]. The teachings and actions of Jesus in the Gospel of Luke provide a moral and ethical foundation for understanding and practicing social responsibility in contemporary society. The following points illustrate the connections:

Luke's Gospel consistently portrays Jesus as reaching out to and caring for marginalized individuals, including tax collectors, prostitutes, and those considered social outcasts. This narrative emphasizes the importance of inclusion, empathy, and assistance to vulnerable populations in today's society. Luke's emphasis on compassion aligns with the core principle of social responsibility: recognizing the suffering and needs of others and responding with empathy and practical support. Contemporary social responsibility efforts often focus on addressing issues such as poverty, hunger, homelessness, and healthcare disparities.[119] Luke's critique of wealth and his call to sell possessions and give to the poor (Luke 12:33) resonate with contemporary efforts to alleviate poverty. Social responsibility includes initiatives such as charitable giving, community development, and support for economic opportunities in disadvantaged areas.

Luke's focus on justice and the reversal of values parallels contemporary calls for social justice and advocacy. Social responsibility extends to advocating for systemic change, policies that promote equity, and addressing issues such

[117] Larry Hollar, *Hunger for the Word: Lectionary Reflections on Food and Justice* (Collegeville, MN: Liturgical Press, 2004), 207.

[118] Michael S. Moore, *WealthWise: A Study of Socioeconomic Conflict in Hebrew Wisdom* (Eugene, OR: Wipf and Stock Publishers, 2021), 166.

[119] Ron Clark, *Jesus Unleashed: Luke's Gospel for Emerging Christians* (Eugene, OR: Wipf and Stock Publishers, 2014), 82.

as racial discrimination, gender inequality, and environmental justice. In the business world, the concept of corporate social responsibility (CSR) aligns with Luke's teachings on ethical conduct and fair treatment of others. CSR encourages businesses to consider their impact on society and engage in ethical practices, including fair labor conditions, environmental sustainability, and philanthropy. Luke's emphasis on community and collective responsibility finds resonance in contemporary community engagement initiatives. Social responsibility involves individuals and organizations actively participating in their communities, supporting local causes, and fostering a sense of belonging and solidarity. Many faith-based organizations and communities draw inspiration from Luke's teachings to engage in social responsibility efforts. These initiatives often include providing food, shelter, healthcare, and educational opportunities to those in need, both locally and globally.[120]

Summary of Findings

The Gospel of Luke offers a profound ethical and moral framework for understanding and practicing social responsibility in contemporary society. Luke's emphasis on caring for the marginalized, practicing compassion, advocating for justice, and addressing issues of wealth and poverty provides guidance and inspiration for individuals and organizations committed to promoting the well-being and welfare of all members of society. Social responsibility, rooted in these principles, seeks to create a more just, compassionate, and equitable world.

The Beatitudes and Woes in the Gospel of Luke provide a powerful critique of wealth and poverty, challenging societal norms and highlighting the values of God's kingdom. They call for a radical reevaluation of priorities, emphasizing humility, compassion, and social justice. These passages continue to inspire reflection and action in contemporary discussions of economic disparities and ethical living. The critique of wealth and poverty in the Gospel of Luke is a central and enduring theme that challenges societal norms, values, and priorities. It offers a radical reevaluation of wealth and materialism while emphasizing justice, compassion, and inclusivity. The teachings and actions of Jesus in Luke's Gospel provide a moral and ethical framework for addressing contemporary issues related to wealth disparities, materialism, and the treatment of the poor. It inspires individuals and communities to strive for a more just, compassionate, and equitable society, aligning their values with the priorities of God's kingdom.

---

[120] Stanley E. Porter, *Hearing the Old Testament in the New Testament* (Grand Rapids, MI: Wm. B. Eerdmans Publishing, 2006), 200.

5

Characteristics of Lukan Parables

Introduction

Lukan parables represent economic sketches of life's ambiguities and contradictions of the first century Mediterranean world. The L parables retain the diffuse particulars of their worlds, but these particulars are re-framed theologically within the Gospel narrative. The ethical, rhetorical and theological directions attributed by Lukan parables belong to their Gospel narrative framing and resolution. Lukan parables are frequently used to illustrate the values of the kingdom of God. However, without their frames, these stories can be interpreted in any direction. This chapter discusses the characteristics; such as the function, purpose, context and meaning of parables, features of Lukan parables, and analyzes literary types of the narrative parables.

1. Jesus and His Parables

Large portion of the teaching of Jesus recorded in the Gospels are in parables.[1] The parables of Jesus were situational, and highlighting human life and manners.[2] They have come through the channel of the early Christian

[1] W. T. Dayton, 'Teaching of Jesus,' *The Zondervan Pictorial Encyclopedia of the Bible,* vol. 5, edited by Merrill C. Tenny (Michigan: Zondervan Publishing House, 1975): 609.

[2] Reginald H. Fuller, 'Jesus Christ,' *Oxford Companion to the Bible,* edited by Bruce M. Metzger and Michael D. Coogan (New York: Oxford University Press, 1993), 357.

tradition.[3] The teaching of Jesus was characterized by memorable stories and sayings.[4] According to James D. G. Dunn, the parables of Jesus are "characterized by the skill of a brilliant story teller."[5] Parables of Jesus have provoking power. Many of the parables begin with question, it is asked through the characters in the parable to the listeners. The listeners already had an answer with them which they thought to be right, but the parables directed them to a higher level of understanding at times it reversed their expectation.

Jesus taught on faith, prayer, discipleship, wealth and poverty, how to face coming adversities and so on through the parables. Sometimes parables were response to questions and controversies. Still other times he delivered scathing indictments of his opponents by the parable.[6] Jesus used parable to speak about the kingdom.[7] The parables of Jesus give particular types of contrasting attitudes in the parables, the surprising points that Jesus made is also a challenge that involved in the parables.[8] Luke develops the story through telling and retelling or reflecting the genius of a unique teller of tales, and parables which Jesus certainly was.[9]

2. The Function of Parables

Jesus did not use parables to illustrate general truth but to force the people to determine their attitude towards Him and His message of the Kingdom of God.[10] This is reflected in the fact that parables often break the grounds of realism and conventional expectation. For example, no Jewish father would lovingly greet and accept a wayward son[11] (as in the prodigal son). Interpreting a parable in some times destroys what the parable is because

---

[3] Herman Hendrickx, *The Parables of Jesus: Studies in the Synoptic Gospels* (London: Geoffrey Chapman, 1983), 1.

[4] John Drane, *Introducing the New Testament,* revised edition (Oxford: Lion Publishing, 1999), 122.

[5] James D. G. Dunn, *The Evidence for Jesus* (Kentucky: The Westminster Press, 1985), 33.

[6] Donald Juel, *Luke-Acts* (London: SCM Press, 1984), 32.

[7] Günther Bornkamm, *Jesus of Nazareth*, tr. by Irene Fraser Mc Luskey and James M. Robinson (London: Harper and Row Publishers, 1975), 69.

[8] Paddy Meagher, *Paddy Fields and a Grain of Rice,* edited by Francil Gonsalves (Delhi: VIEWS/ISPCK, 2006), 160.

[9] Loretta Dornisch, *A Women Reads the Gospel of Luke* (Minnesota: The Liturgical Press, 1996), 132.

[10] R. V. G. Tasker, 'Parable,' *The New Bible Dictionary,* edited by J. D. Douglas (London: IVP, 1962), 933f.

[11] W. M. Klein, C. L. Blomberg & R. L. Hubbard, *Introduction to Biblical Interpretation* (Dallas: Word Publishing, 1993), 337.

it is like interpreting a joke. The immediacy of the parable is what makes it so effective in provoking people. Explaining the points of comparison of a parable is like explaining a joke and the impact is lost. The parables of Jesus include: aphoristic[12] parables, extended parables, and narrative parables.[13] Jesus' parables capture the listener's attention, bringing them face to face with his message, which would have been much less effective if stated normally.[14]

Parables do not illustrate Jesus' teaching with 'picture words' and they were not told to serve as vehicles for revealing spiritual truth although they most certainly end up doing this. Parables were told to provoke a response to address the audience, capture their attention, show them up and cause them to decide and act.[15] The unusual twist in the story is what gives the parable its impact and biting force. Parables jolt people into seeing things in a new way, bringing them to a point of decision and action.

The parables of Jesus invite one to follow to a certain direction: it begins with one way of looking at things and s/he finds that there is another, a better way. In this juncture, the view of the narrator is seen as opposed to the view of the audience. They are led from their initial position which was considered solid in the beginning is now led to a point where they can see that the opposite view is more solid. They are challenged to reconsider their point of view and follow the new way.[16]

3. Purpose of Parables

The parables of Jesus are not merely illustrations of Jesus' preaching. The parables are to engage and instruct, but it is not fair to say that the

---

[12] There are aphoristic metaphors in the Jesus tradition and these may be present with or without the explicit term "parable" being present (Cf. Mk 2:21–22; Mt 9:16–17). Aphoristic parables also appear in single, double, triple, or even multiple units, and these may either expand or contract as the transmission progresses. They could be formed either synonymously, with twin positives or twin negatives, or else antithetically, with a balanced positive and negative, in whichever order. All the preceding doublets were in synonymous parallelism. Examples in antithetical parallelism appear in the next section. Cf. John Dominic Crossan, 'Parables,' *ABD*, vol. V, edited by David Noel Freedman (New York: Doubleday, 1992), 148.

[13] The most famous parables in the Jesus tradition are not the extended but the narrative parables. They give the language for the images of the prodigal son and the Good Samaritan. It must be remembered, however, that Jesus was an oral teacher and that those stories, may well be no more than plot summaries of stories which might have taken hours to tell.

[14] David Wenham, *The Parables of Jesus* (London: Hodder & Stoughton, 1989), 13.

[15] G. D. Fee and Stuart D, *How to Read the Bible for All its Worth* (Michigan: Zondervan, 1993), 138.

[16] Herman Hendrickx, *The Parables of Jesus: Studies in the Synoptic Gospels,* 7.

parables are themselves the preaching.[17] They are highly complex literary forms.[18] The parables demand interpretation and they point to something else and they are not merely stories to enjoy. They hold up one reality to serve as a mirror of another, the kingdom of God. Jesus told parables to confront people with the character of God's kingdom and to invite them to participate in it and to live in accordance with it.[19]

The parables constitute an art-form whose interpretation is not entirely dependent on reconstruction of their original content and form; as parables, the stories told by Jesus are capable of showing fresh facets of meaning. It is clear, however, that exposition of the parables for today must be with a careful understanding of what Jesus meant by the parables as is possible; otherwise one may fall back into the error of regarding them as illustrations of general truths.[20]

The parables were meant to help people to *decide* their attitude towards Jesus and his message and thus to bring them into a new relationship with him. Through the parables the kingly rule of God comes to human with its promises, judgments, demands and gifts. The study of the parables is done by the help of the insights from modern linguistics and semantics have shown that they are not simply ways of conveying information in some attractive form. Instead, they have a variety of logical forms and functions. Often their aim is to jolt the audience into seeing things from a new point of view and to be the actual means of bringing them into a new situation.[21]

4. Setting of the Parables

In contrast to the liberal tendency to generalize the lessons of the parables, the interpreter of the parables may try to find out the setting of a parable in the situation contemplated by the Gospels and hence the application which would support itself to one who stood in that situation.[22] In the historical development of Jesus' ministry, the timing of the parable is not accidental. He spoke a number of parables in response to the religious leaders' rejection of Him, and so those parables were weapons of controversy in exposing the

---

[17] K. R. Snodgrass, 'Parable,' *Dictionary of Jesus and the Gospels*, edited by Joel B. Green, Scot McKnight and I. Howard Marshall (Downer's Grove: IVP, 1998), 596.

[18] Mike Graves, 'Preaching Lukan Parables: A Socio-Rhetorical Approach,' *SWJT* 40/1 (Fall 1997): 21.

[19] K. R. Snodgrass, 'Parable,' *Dictionary of Jesus and the Gospels*, 596.

[20] K. R. Snodgrass, 'Parable,' *Dictionary of Jesus and the Gospels*, 597.

[21] R. V. G. Tasker, 'Parable,' *The New Bible Dictionary,* 934.

[22] R. H. Stein, *An Introduction to the Parables of Jesus* (Philadelphia: Westminster Press, 1981), 59.

self-righteousness of the opposition and in extolling the kingdom of God.[23] "Jesus' parables are survivors of a long history of capricious and whimsical hermeneutical treatments that have often distorted their message."[24]

According to Doerksen, "the modern critical method is to remove the parable from the setting."[25] Whether allegorized or taken with a totally aesthetic bias, the historical settings of the parables have been overlooked in favor of seeking to find existential implications for the present. According to Hunter, there may be a double historical setting: "The parables, in the earliest context, had two settings–their original setting in the life of Jesus, and their secondary one in the life of the early church."[26]

But today one could also say that there are four levels of tradition for parables. First, the context of parable as it was pronounced by Jesus; second, the context and form of the parable in the oral transmission by the early church; third, the context and content of the parable as it is found in the Gospels and fourth, the context in which the parables are to be interpreted today.[27]

Jesus taught the model of right and wrong behavior through the parables.[28] The interpreter must also be aware of any Old Testament allusions in parables (e.g., Mk 12:1-12 and Isa 5). The difficulty to interpret parables in modern society because it is, at times, different in time and culture from the original audience.[29] The historical distance is not only chronological

---

[23] Peter R. Jones, *The Teaching of the Parables* (Nashville: Broadman, 1982), 37; cf. A. T. Cadoux, *The Parables of Jesus: Their Art and Use* (London: Clarke, 1930), 11-13. Apparently Cadoux coined the idea of the parables as 'weapons of controversy'.

[24] Brad H. Young, *Jesus and His Jewish Parables: Rediscovering the Roots of Jesus' Teaching* (New York: Paulist Press, 1989), 21.

[25] Vernon D. Doerksen, 'The Interpretation of the Parables,' *Grace Journal* 11 (Spring, 1970): 11. Various methodologies are used to read and re-read the parables. Dalit reading of the parables, reading various themes in the parable and feminist reading of selected parable are also coming up. Cf. Susan Durber, 'The Female Reader of the Parables of the Lost,' *JSNT* 45 (Mar, 1992), 59-78. For a literary reading of parable see B. B. Scott, "Lost Junk, Found Treasure," *BT* 26/1 (Jan, 1988): 31-34.

[26] Archibald Hunter, *Interpreting the Parables* (Philadelphia: Westminster, 1960), 70.

[27] Three level tradition of the parable (context of Jesus, early church and present Gospel traditions are put forward by Herman Hendrickx, *The Parables of Jesus: Studies in the Synoptic Gospels*, 12. John Topel finds three levels of transmission in "On being Parabled," *BT* (Dec. 1976): 1010-1017.

[28] John Dominic Crossan, 'Parable and Example in the Teaching of Jesus,' A Structuralist Approach to the Parable, edited by Robert W. Funk, *Semeia* I (1974): 63ff.

[29] G. D. Fee and Stuart D, *How to Read the Bible for All its Worth*, 137.

but social, political and religious. Parables always occur as part of a larger context.[30]

Therefore, they need to be interpreted within this larger literary context and with respect to other parables and other sayings and events. This is particularly true of the parables of Jesus, which must be interpreted in relation to his proclamation of the Kingdom of God. The context[31] in which the parable told is a significant element for the interpretation[32] of the parable.

5. The Meaning of Parables

Historically, the parables are interpreted as allegories but the modern scholarship has rejected this practice, because it ignores the realism, clarity and simplicity of parables. Allegorical interpretations were an important method in the history of the interpretation of the parable. According to John Dominic Crossan, "Allegory and Parable agree in that both operate on two levels: they disagree in that allegory is reducible and parable is not."[33] Although parables do have some allegorical elements, these are the exceptions not the general rule.[34] These allegorical elements are called as the points of reference or points of comparison.[35]

Some parables go very close to allegorical interpretation because most of the details in the story are intended to represent something or someone else (ie. they have many points of comparison). However, these parables are not allegories[36] because of the function they perform. The interpreter must also

---

[30] W. M. Klein, C. L. Blomberg & R. L. Hubbard, *Introduction to Biblical Interpretation*, 272.

[31] Gowler examines how stories in the Old Testament, rabbinic commentaries, and Hellenistic culture can help us interpret them. He concludes in the contexts of Jesus' Parables, one can respond more fully to the message of Jesus who spoke these parables with one ear already listening for our responses. Cf. David B. Gowler, *What Are They Saying About the Parables?* (New Jersey: Paulist Press, 2000). Cf. also Robert B. Kruschwitz, "Introduction," *Parables: Christian Reflection,* A Series in Faith and Ethics, edited by Robert B. Kruschwitz (Waco: Baylor University, 2006), 8.

[32] The interpretation of the parable would some time difficult. Cf. Edwyn Hoskyns Bart, and F. Noel Davey, *The Riddle of the New Testament* (London: Faber and Faber, 1947), 126ff.

[33] John Dominic Crossan, 'Parable and Example in the Teaching of Jesus,' 87.

[34] Craig L. Blomberg, *Interpreting the Parables* (Downers Grove: Intervarsity, 1990), 17, 32.

[35] W. M. Klein, C. L. Blomberg & R. L. Hubbard, *Introduction to Biblical Interpretation,* 337.

[36] Cf. G. D. Fee and Stuart D, *How to Read the Bible for All its Worth*, 140. The parable in Luke 7:40-42 is not allegorical although it appears that way. The purpose of the story is not found in the points of comparison but in the intended response (of Simon and the woman). The details of a parable must be interpreted with strict reference to the points of comparison so the focus remains on the central meaning of the parable. Sometimes none of the details are

be sensitive to the shape and form of parable. The assumption of one single point per parable is not always true. Some parables are simple and some are complex. Simple parables have one central message but complex ones may have a central message and several related messages.[37] A parable may also have multiple shades of meaning depending on the perspective of the hearer.[38]

6. Kingdom of God and the Parables

The Kingdom of God is the central theme of the proclamation of Jesus.[39] Parables of Jesus deal with the kingdom of God[40] and they speak of the coming of the kingdom, characteristics the kingdom and values related to the kingdom of God. Parables are related to its nature, its coming, its value, its growth, the sacrifices it calls for and so on.[41] They indirectly give the guideline to enter into it.

Parables of Jesus aim at a line of conduct to which Jesus wants to impel His listeners or against which he wants to warn them. Four narrative parables are examples for it. The parable of the Good Samaritan (10:25-37); the parable of the Rich fool (12:16-21); the parable of the Rich man and Lazarus (16:19-31); and the parable of the Pharisee and Publican (18:9-14). The parables of Jesus have concern for the behavior of the listener, not direct

---

important and do not need interpretation (eg. The Good Samaritan). Sometimes a few of the details are significant (eg. Parable of the Tenants) and sometimes all the details are important (eg. Parable of the Weeds). W. M. Klein, C. L. Blomberg & R. L. Hubbard *Introduction to Biblical Interpretation,* 95-96.

[37] David Wenham, *The Parables of Jesus,* 17. For example, the parable of the Prodigal Son teaches that God accepts repentant sinners and also that God wants faithful people to accept repentant sinners. David P. Kuske, Biblical *Interpretation: The Only Right Way* (Milwaukee, Wisconsin: Northwestern Publishing House, 1995), 97. In fact the majority of parables make exactly 3 points. Cf. W. M. Klein, C. L. Blomberg & R. L. Hubbard, *Introduction to Biblical Interpretation,* 21.

[38] When Jesus told the parable in Luke 7.40-48, the messages received by Simon and the woman would have been very different. W. M. Klein, C. L. Blomberg & R. L. Hubbard, *Introduction to Biblical Interpretation,* 338. Simon received a message of rebuke but the woman, a message of acceptance and forgiveness. Also, Jesus told some parables (with modifications) on different occasions to different audiences in order to provoke a different response (Eg. Parable of 10 minas - Luke 19.10-26 and Parable of 10 talents - Matthew 25:14-28). David P. Kuske, Biblical *Interpretation: The Only Right Way,* 98.

[39] Eugene S. Wehrill, *Exploring the Parables: Let Him Hear* (Philadelphia: Boston, 1963), 111.

[40] John Erniakulathil, 'Kingdom of God in the Teaching of Jesus,' *Bible Bhashyam* 23/2 (June, 1997): 90-101 gives a study on the same topic including the background of the theme, nature and meaning, and its various dimensions.

[41] R. V. G. Tasker and I. Howard Marshall, "Parable," *New Bible Dictionary*, 869.

but theological and it requires the qualities which are to be found in them on the basis of their changed behavior. It must be part of life of its audience.[42]

The central motif of the life and ministry of Jesus was the 'Kingdom of God'. This is adopted from the notion of God's coming rule and its impact upon the people of God in the Old Testament.[43] His concept was universalistic in designation and implication.[44] The Kingdom of God represents a set of universal values such as freedom, fellowship and justice as the basis for a new society.[45]

They are the parameters of Kingdom's thrust towards the total liberation of humans. 'Kingdom' is translated from the Greek, basileia. Basileia in the Gospels implies 'a sphere or rule', to which one can enter. But the dominant meaning of the word is the act of God in His Kingly power, exercising His Sovereignty. This is eternal and therefore beyond time, it has already begun but has also an eschatological significance.[46] The concept of Kingdom of God has a past, present and future implication. C. H. Dodd calls it as 'realized eschatology.'[47] There is a close connection between Jesus and His proclamation of the Kingdom. Because, the purpose of Jesus' life is the announcement of the Kingdom. Parables give the moral ideals of the kingdom. Those moral ideals can be called as the kingdom values. Therefore, becoming the disciple of Jesus can mean, entering into this kingdom.

Those who follow Jesus are expected to have such values for their life. It includes all: the world, the human person and society; the totality of reality is to be transformed by God.[48] According to J. D. Crossan, the parables of Jesus, as interactive education, are ethically appropriate genre for His claims about the kingdom of God. That kingdom as God's will for this earth can be entered here and now through a transformed life style of horizontal sharing of possessions by the haves to the bottom of society and upwards.[49] Parables

---

[42] Herman Hendrickx, *The Parables of Jesus: Studies in the Synoptic Gospels*, 9.

[43] Cf. Donald S. K. Palmer, *The Kingdom of God* (Welwyn: Evangelical Press, 1986), 17ff.

[44] George W. Peters, *A Biblical Theology of Missions* (Chicago: Moody Press, 1972), 42.

[45] George M. Soares-Prabhu, 'The Kingdom of God: Jesus' Vision of a New Society, *Theology of Liberation: An Indian Biblical Perspective, Collected writings of George M. Soares-Prabhu,* vol. 4, edited by F. X. D'Sa (Pune: Deepa Vidyapeett Theological, 2001), 239.

[46] A. M. Hunter, *The Work and Words of Jesus* (Delhi: ISPCK, 1969), 76ff.

[47] C. H. Dodd, *The Parables of the Kingdom* (London: Nisbet, 1961).

[48] Donald Senior and Caroll Stuhlmueller, *The Biblical Foundations for Mission* (New York: Orbis books, 1983), 151.

[49] John Dominic Crossan, 'The Parables of Jesus,' *Interpretation* 56/3 (July, 2002): 258.

peculiar to Luke[50] have the quality of presenting the values of the kingdom in the context of conflict. The poor in the Gospel of Luke, are the recipients of God's special blessings, because they are poor and needy.[51] Kingdom values[52] are in conflict with the normal/popular expectation of its audience.

7. Parables in Luke's Gospel

The central section of the Gospel of Luke is known as the travel narrative, because it gives a journey narrative, towards Jerusalem. Parables used in this section are with the primary intention of teaching. In this section, there are some of the parables which have no parallel passages in other Gospels. Therefore, these parables are called as special Lukan parables. One of the achievements of the Gospel of Luke is its treasure of parables. "As stories within the story they take stock of its movement along the line of time by reflecting, from the moment between which they occupy on the past which has been told, and the future, which has yet to be told."[53]

7.1. Luke and the L Parables

L parables are understood to be the parables collected by Luke[54] and he has transmitted those traditions through the Gospel. Luke seems to be conservative about making deletions from Mark and Q.[55] Luke is free in

---

[50] Parables in the Gospel Luke are interesting to note. One of the significant things in the parables of Luke is its presentation of various kingdom values. The parables of the Good Samaritan (10:25ff), the parable of the rich fool (12:13-21), like the anecdotes of the Unrighteous steward (16:1-9) and the rich man and Lazarus (16:19-31)shows the futility of serving mammon, i.e., wealth or property; and the stories summon the hearer-reader to use what he has for the poor while there is still time, a theme common both to parables that refer explicitly to the kingdom. Cf. Richard H. Hiers, *The Kingdom of God in the Synoptic Tradition* (Gaineville: University of Florida Press, 1970).

[51] Philip van Linden, *The Gospel of Luke and Acts* (Wilmington: Michael Glazier, 1970), 81.

[52] Jesus taught about His Kingdom (ultimately God's Kingdom); the parables were the parables of the Kingdom. In the parables one could find the qualities one must possess to enter into the kingdom. Those qualities are commonly called as Kingdom values.

[53] John Drury, *The Literary Guide to the Bible,* edited by Robert Alter and Frank Kermode (London: Fortress Press, 1989), 428.

[54] Source analysis of the narratives has began in 1924 by B. H. Streeter, *The Four Gospels,* making elevations and conclusions on Q, special Mark, Matthew and Luke, priority of Mark and proto-Luke hypothesis. For criticism tried to discover the literary forms of the narratives and sayings of the individual scenes which make up the records. Cf. Ralph P. Martin, *New Testament Foundations: A Guide for Christian Students,* vol.1, revised edition (Michigan: W. B. Eerdmans, 1985), 30.

[55] Howard C. Kee, finds the Q document is characterized with the eschatological message in *Jesus in History: An Approach to the study of the Gospels*, second edition (New York: Harcourt Brace Jovanovich publishers, 1977), 76ff. Harry T. Fleddermann, analyzes

using his own words in transmitting the individual units and he seems to have no scruples about introducing 'modernizing' modifications[56] (eg. Lk 21:20-24). L parables consist of various themes such as, salvation, commitment and faithfulness, daily life issues and humility.[57]

In the Gospel of Luke all national barriers are down. This characteristic is reflected in the parables too.[58] Lukan parables are known for direct morality, narrative beauty and absence of allegorical mystification, usually attributed to Jesus Himself.[59] Lukan parables are highly valued for its ancient quality of *philanthropia,*[60] it is a kind of mirror image to friendship. One of the characteristics of Lukan parables is its presentation of rich and poor. It is to be relevant to the *Sitz-im-Leben* of Luke's Gospel.[61] L parables, specially narrative parables, are the examples of Luke's literary masterpieces. They are both like story parable presenting significant characters.[62] Following in

---

the mid-level techniques in Luke's redaction of Q in 'Mid-Level Techniques in Luke's Redaction of Q,' *ETL* (*Ephemerides Theologicae Lovanienses*) LXXIX/1 (April 2003): 53-71. Cf. also Edward P. Meadors, "The "Messianic" Implications of the Q Material," *JBL* 118/2 (Summer, 1999): 253-277 and Vincent Taylor, *The Formation of the Gospel Tradition* (London: Mac Millan and co., 1933), 93.

[56] Douglas M. Parrott, 'The Dishonest Steward (Luke 16:1-8a) and Luke's Special Parable Collection,' *NTS* 37/4 (1991): 506.

[57] For more details see, Mikeal C. Parsons, "Land Marks Along the Way: The Function of the "L" Parables in the Lukan Travel Narrative," *SWJT* 40/1 (Fall, 1997): 34f.

[58] Leslie B. Flynn, *Four Faces of Jesus: The Uniqueness of the Gospel Narratives* (Michigan: Kregal Publications, 1993), 84. Cf. also Vincent Taylor, *The Gospels: A Short Introduction* (London: The Epworth Press, 1962), 26f.

[59] Such parables may have been spun out of ideas known from the Old Testament. The prodigal son reflects the injunctions of Deut 21 and the Jewish fondness for younger brothers and distrust of older brothers. The Good Samaritan catches up Hosea 6; 1 Kings 13:11-32 and 2 Chr 28: 8-15. The unjust steward seems to continue the usage of presenting an immoral character as good example. Cf. G. J. Diamond, 'Reflections Upon Recent Developments in the Study of Parables in Luke,' *ABR* 29 (Oct, 1981): 3. Cf. also J. Duncan M. Derrett, 'Law in the New Testament: The Parable of the Unjust Judge,' *NTS* 18 (1971): 178ff.

[60] The term means the love of human kind. It is one of the methods used for the rereading of the ancient novels. This is evident in the parables of the Good Samaritan. Because the behavior of the Samaritan is a conventional manifestation of *Philanthropia* whose value does not require the degree of enmity between Jews and Samaritans posited by some scholars. The love expressed in this parable is the standard ancient way of describing a good person. Through this parable Luke moves in a broad Mediterranean context. Sarah Henrich, 'Embedded in the 1st Century elite in our own: Recent Research on Luke's Gospel,' *Currents in Theology and Mission* 33/6 (Dec, 2006): 483.

[61] Robert J. Karris, 'Poor and Rich: The Lukan *Sitz im Leben*,' *Perspectives on Luke-Acts,* edited by Charles H. Talbert (Edinburgh: T&T Clark, 1978), 112ff.

[62] C. T. Thomas, *Jesus and His Good News: A Lay Perspective* (Delhi: ISPCK, 2001), 109.

line with R. J. Raja,[63] Luke's Gospel and parable in particular highlights a life in close communion with God and faithfully serving him by serving those in need.

The ethical, rhetorical and theological directions attributed to the L parables belong to their Gospel narrative framing and resolution, not the parables plots,[64] which sustain metonymic density in their fluctuating points of reference. The L parables are frequently used to illustrate extravagant claims for parables as metaphors that dramatically shatter one's world to disclose the kingdom of God. However, without their frames, these stories can be interpreted in any direction.[65]

L parables give a clear insight into Luke's methods: his historical patterning, his human interest and his continuance which he inherited in addition to his own realistic narrative interests.[66] There are various characteristics of parables such as earthiness, conciseness, major and minor points, repetition, conclusion at the end, listener-relatedness, reversal of expectation, kingdom-centered eschatology,[67] kingdom ethics, God and salvation in the parables.[68]

There are five parables in Luke's presentation of the life of Jesus in Galilee and two in his description of Jesus' brief teaching in Jerusalem.[69] Whereas in the travel narrative, there are almost seventeen parables found

---

[63] R. J. Raja, "'Rich towards God:" Bhakti in the Gospel of Luke I," *VJTR* 59/4 (April, 1995): 233. He emphasizes the significance of Luke's Gospel as it represents *Bhakti* marga and R. J. Raja, "'Rich towards God:" Bhakti in the Gospel of Luke III," *VJTR* 59/6 (June, 1995): 389-399. Cf. also Norval Geldenhuys, *Commentary on the Gospel of Luke* (London: Marshall, Morgan and Scott Ltd, 1965); and Edward Schweizer, *The Good News According to Luke,* tr. by David E. Green (Atlanta: John Knox Press, 1984).

[64] Reversal of expectation is one of the plot in parable of rich man and Lazarus and Pharisee and tax-collector. Cf. Grant R. Osborne, *The Hermeneutical Spiral: A Comprehensive Introduction to the Biblical Interpretation* (Downers Grove, Illinois: IVP, 1991), 242.

[65] Cf. Stephen Curkpatrick, 'Parable Metonymy and Luke's Kerygmatic Framing,' *JSNT* 25/3 (2003): 289-307.

[66] John Drury, *The Parables in the Gospels: History and Allegory* (New York: Crossroad, 1985), 121

[67] Robert Maddox, *The Purpose Luke-Acts,* edited by John Riches (Edinburgh: T&T Clark, 1982), 100ff.

[68] Grant R. Osborne, *The Hermeneutical Spiral: A Comprehensive Introduction to the Biblical Interpretation*, 239f. John J. Kilgallen, "Parables in the Gospel of Luke," *Chicago Studies* 38/3 (Fall/Winter, 1999): 273.

[69] The parables in the Galilee period are important because they emphasize the distinctiveness of Jesus in the Jewish traditions; they insist on hearing well his word, with generous and noble heart and living it perseveringly. John J. Kilgallen, 'Parables in the Gospel of Luke,' 273.

in Luke's record. According to Richard N. Longenecker, "Possibly Luke also used a "parable-travel" source for the writing of his travel narrative (9:51-19:27)."[70] Luke's interest in the parables of Jesus was largely that of a literary stock with matchless stories of the new life in the kingdom of God.[71]

The parables are usually taken from everyday life, but they are not necessarily realistic and because of hyperbole or elements of improbability they often are pseudo-realistic and have elements that shock. The degree to which the theological referent is transparent of each of the parable varies from other parable.[72] The role of culture in the parable is one area worthy of attention in the study of it.[73]

In the parables of Jesus one of the characteristic features of parable is its contextual unity around some theme. The parables of the debtors (Lk 7: 41-43) is a unit within the larger context (7:36-50), and serves to establish a major point. The parable of the Rich Fool (12:16-21) is an interpretation of what precedes (12:13-15). The parable in Luke 16:19-31 (Rich man and Lazarus) belongs to the denouncements of chapters 14-18. The parable of the Good Samaritan (Lk 10:30-35) is framed by 10:29 and 10: (29-) 36, 37 also fits closely with the lawyer-Jesus dialogue (10:25-28).

7.2. Context of Lukan Parables

Joseph A. Fitzmyer[74] and R. A. Culpepper[75] divide the narrative structure of Luke into four sections, that is, prologue and infancy narrative (Lk 1:1-2:52), preparation and ministry in Galilee (Lk 3:1-9: 50), Jesus' journey to Jerusalem and ministry in Jerusalem (Lk 9:51-21:38) and Jesus' passion, resurrection and ascension (Lk 22:1-24:53). The parables such as the parable of the Good Samaritan (10:25-37); the parable of the Rich fool (12:16-21);

---

[70] Richard N. Longenecker, 'Taking up the Cross Daily: Discipleship in Luke-Acts,' *Patterns of Discipleship in the New Testament,* edited by Richard N. Longenecker (Michigan: W. B. Eerdmans, 1996), 51. One of the significant themes in the Gospel of Luke, particularly in the parables of the travel narrative is the emphasis on the discipleship. He also wants his readers to know that being a follower of Jesus requires 1. New attitudes toward poverty, wealth and the use of riches for the benefit of others and 2. A radical new type of life style that puts following Jesus before every other allegiance, so radical that every other allegiance, of whatever nature, can be characterized as 'hate' by comparison.

[71] A. T. Robertson, *Luke the Historian in the Light of Research* (Michigan: Baker Book House, 1977).

[72] K. R. Snodgrass, 'Parable,; *Dictionary of Jesus and the Gospels*, 594.

[73] Mike Graves, 'Preaching Lukan Parables: A Socio-Rhetorical Approach,' *SWJT* 40/1 (Fall, 1997): 19.

[74] Joseph A. Fitzmyer, *The Gospel According to Luke,* 28 A, The Anchor Bible, 134.

[75] R. A. Culpepper, 'The Gospel of Luke: An Introduction, Commentary and Reflections,' *The New Interpreter's Bible Commentary*, vol. 9, edited by Neil (Nashville: Abingdon Press, 1995), 10.

the parable of the Rich man and Lazarus (16:19-31); and the parable of the Pharisee and Publican (18:9-14) comes in the travel narrative. Each of these parables has a specific social context.[76]

7.3. Parables in the Travel Narrative

The main content of the travel narrative is structured of sixteen parables, sometimes two or three just strung together and they are framed by travel narrative. Parables in the travel narrative are addressed either to crowd or to opponents.[77] They tend to be brief and symmetrical. In the travel narrative, they make use of balanced structures involving two or three movements. They typically omit unnecessary descriptions and frequently leave motives unexplained and implied questions unanswered.[78]

The central section of the Gospel of Luke is called as the travel narrative (9: 51-19: 28). This is a journey[79] from Galilee to Jerusalem.[80] Luke has his own source[81] for the Gospel tradition which is called as L and the travel

[76] Those context will be dealt with in details in Chapter 5 of this work.

[77] The parables in the travel narrative are instructional for how believers should live their lives here and now-and so function as parables of the Christian life. They have often used for devotional and homiletical purposes. That is not only because of their multivalent imagery, but also because they have been tailored by Luke for easy application to living as a follower of Jesus. Luke has given the parable with different topics. They are 1. Loving and helping others (the good Samaritan 10:25-37), 2. Prayer (11:15-13; 18:1-8), 3. Possessions and true riches (12:13-34; the rich man and Lazarus (16:19-31), 4. Service to God (13:1-9; 17:7-10; 19:11-27), 5. The importance of response to God (14:15-24; 16:19-31), 6. God's love for the lost (15), 7. Humility (18:9-14), 8. Shrewdness in one affairs (16:1-12). Cf. Richard N. Longenecker, 'Taking up the Cross Daily: Discipleship in Luke-Acts,' 65ff.

[78] K. R. Snodgrass, 'Parable,' *Dictionary of Jesus and the Gospels*, 596. The authority of the teaching of Jesus is reveled in the parables. (1) The parables reflect the clarity and eschatology of Jesus' preaching and his conflict with Jewish authorities. (2) They reflect daily life in Palestine. (3) Little evidence exists that parables were used frequently prior to Jesus. (4) In view of the fact that parables do not appear in the NT outside the Gospels and rarely in other early Christian literature, the early church shows no propensity for creating parables.

[79] Luke probably used an extensive travel report in Luke-Acts. Cf. David E. Aune, *The New Testament in its Literary Environment*, edited by Wayne A Meeks (Philadelphia: The Westminster Press, 1997), 122. The chronological order of the travel narrative has brought many issues. Various arguments are made. It is an account not only of the last journey of Jesus to Jerusalem but also of one or two other journeys which made to that city after completing his ministry in Galilee. Cf. George Ogg, 'The Central Section of the Gospel According to St. Luke,' *NTS* 18 (1971): 39.

[80] This journey to Jerusalem is the way to glorification and suffering. Helmut Flender, *St. Luke: Theologian of Redemptive History*, tr. by Reginald H and Ilse Fuller (London: SPCK, 1967), 73.

[81] Apart from L he might have also used the Q source. For details of the Q source. cf. F. Gerald Downing, 'A Genre for Q and A Socio-Cultural Context for Q: Comparing Sets

narrative is unique in it. He has also been influenced by sources common to one or the other Gospel. In any cases, Lukan Gospel tradition is unique because he authors the matter in his own characteristic ways and introduces many incidents which are found only in this Gospel. This special Lukan characteristic of the life of the disciples in the 'travel narrative' gives some insights into the person of Jesus.

The travel narrative includes Samaritan descriptions (Lk 9:51ff; 10:10; 17:11). The parable of the Good Samaritan is an example for the third Gospel's openness to the gentile mission and the opening of the kingdom of God to the Samaritans.[82] The journey to Jerusalem is the time when Luke cites almost majority of parables.[83] The narrative parables in particular are found in the same section.[84]

In this section, Jesus is seen as a teacher who "educates his disciples into the cost and the way of discipleship and forms them into his community which is characterized by perseverance, ceaseless prayer, a sense of love and sharing."[85] The parables in the travel narratives set out lessons, such as loving and helping others (Lk 10:25ff); prayer (11:5ff;18:1ff); possessions and true riches (12:13ff; 16:19ff); service to God (13:1ff; 17:7ff; 19:11ff); the importance of response to God (14:15ff;); God's love for the lost (15:1ff); humility (18:9ff); and shrewdness in one's affairs (16:1ff) to the disciples.[86]

7.4. Women in Lukan Parables

In the Gospel of Luke, Jesus is frequently portrayed as in solidarity with the disenfranchised and outcasts of society with a specific concern towards women. This is evident even in the parables. Number of women depicted in the Gospel of Luke and the emphasis on their presence in the narrative are

---

of Similarities with Sets of Differences,' *JSNT* 55 (Sep, 1993): 3-26. For the tradition and redaction of parables especially on Luke 15. See J. T. Sanders, 'Tradition and Redaction in Luke XV.11-32,' *NTS* 15 (1969): 433-438.

[82] Matthew Black, *The Gentiles and Gentile Mission in Luke-Acts* (Cambridge: Cambridge University Press, 1973), 43.

[83] The journey to Jerusalem is the time when Luke cites almost 17 parables. There are at least 24 parables in the Gospel of Luke (though not all that can recognize as parable is called parable). Luke used five parables in the life of Jesus in Galilee and two parables in the teaching in Jerusalem. cf. John J. Kilgallen, 'Parables in the Gospel of Luke,' *Chicago Studies* 38/3 (Fall/Winter, 1999): 273. John Drury finds thirty out of fifty parables in the travel narrative. Out of thirty fourteen parables are peculiar to Luke. Cf. John Drury, *The parables in the Gospels: History and Allegory*, 111f.

[84] Paddy Meagher, *Paddy Fields and a Grain of Rice*, 160.

[85] J. P. Kealy, *The Gospel of Luke* (Denville: Dimension Books, 1979), 266f.

[86] Richard N. Longenecker, 'Taking up the Cross Daily: Discipleship in Luke-Acts,' *Patterns of Discipleship in the New Testament*, 66f.

surprising.[87] The Gospel of Luke shows the greatest interest in women in the life and ministry of Jesus, including various accounts and stories[88] about women unique[89] to its presentation.

Luke also gives the specific names of more women in Jesus' life than do the other Gospels. This interest is continued in Acts (cf. Acts 1:14). Luke relates stories to the healing (Lk 4:38-39; 8:1-3, 40-56; 13:11-17; 17:11-17) and faith (Lk 4:26; 7:36-50; 8:48; 18:1-8; 21:1-4) of women, many of which are unique to Luke. Women are important in two parables and they are unique to Luke (Lk 15:8-10; 18:1-8) and are mentioned in two stories about the kingdom of God (Lk 13:20-21; 17:35).

The parables of women are peculiar in Lukan parables. They are the parable of the lost coin and widow and the unjust judge.[90] These parable shows that women and men both act in the divine image to bring about the realm of God.[91] In the Gospel of Luke, both men and women are mentioned as pairs,[92] with some exceptions, this is not done by way comparison or

---

[87] Jane Schaberg, 'Luke,' *The Women's Bible Commentary*, edited by Carol A. Newsom and Sharon H. Ringe (London: SPCK, 1992), 278.

[88] The place of women in discipleship is particularly stressed by Luke, both in general statements (Lk 8:19-21; 11:27-28), in the story of Mary and Martha (Lk 10:38-42) and in the reports of the female disciples who traveled with Jesus (Lk 8:1–3) and are described in the passion and resurrection narratives (Lk 23:49; 23:55-24:12). Again, some of these accounts are unique to Luke (Lk 8:1-3; 10:38-42; 11:27-28).

[89] Study on the role and position in the Gospel of Luke is interesting. Alfred Plummer remarks that the third Gospel has an especial sense the Gospel for women in *The Gospel According to St. Luke,* International Critical Commentary, 5th edition (Edinburgh: T&T Clark, 1981), xliiff. Robert O' Toole lists the passages which Luke has designed as parallel pairs of stories of men and women, that suggest an equality, and they receive the same salvific benefits in *The Unity of Luke's Theology: An Analysis of Luke-Acts,* Good News Studies 9 (Wilmington: Glazier, 1984), 118-26. Robert J. Karris, 'Women and Discipleship in Luke,' *CBQ* 56 (1994): 1-20 and Turid Karlsen Seim, *The Double Message Patterns of Gender in Luke-Acts* (Nashville: Abingdon Press, 1994) follows the same line. But recent feminist interpreters have noted, that Luke's portrait of women is ambiguous at best and dangerous at worst. See, Jane Schaberg, 'Luke,' *The Women's Bible Commentary*, 277. Mary Rose D'Angelo, "Women in Luke-Acts: A Redactional View," *JBL* 109/3 (1990): 441-461. Barbara E. Reid, *Choosing the Better Part? Women in the Gospel of Luke* (Collegeville: The Liturgical Press, 1996) and Elisabeth Schüssler Fiorenza, *In Memory of Her: A Feminist Reconstruction of Christian Origins* (New York: Crossroad, 1983).

[90] For a detail analysis of this parable see, Barbara E. Reid, "Luke's Mixed Message for Women," *Chicago Studies* 38/3 (Fall/Winter, 1999): 287ff.

[91] Barbara E. Reid, *Choosing the Better Part ? Women in the Gospel of Luke,* 176.

[92] Cf. Zacharia and Elizabeth, Joseph and Mary, Simon and Hannah (2:25-38), widow of Zarephath and Naaman (Lk 4:25-28), Healing of Peter's mother-in Law and demoniac (Lk 4:3). Centurion of Capernaum and widow of Nain (Lk 7:1-7), Simon the Pharisee and the sinful women (Lk 13: 18-21), Jairus and women with issue of blood (Lk 8:40-41; 43-48; 49-56), Good Samaritan and Mary/Martha (Lk 10:29-42), Men healed on Sabbath and

contrast, but rather to suggest a measure of equality that was unexpected in the time of Jesus.[93]

8. Types of Parables

Parables are concise narratives that convey moral or spiritual lessons through relatable scenarios, often featuring everyday characters and situations. Distinct from fables and metaphors, parables utilize storytelling to illustrate deeper truths, encouraging reflection and insight. While fables typically feature anthropomorphized animals to impart a moral lesson, parables focus on human experiences and relationships. Additionally, metaphors serve as figurative language that compares two unlike things to highlight similarities, often without a narrative structure. This distinction enhances our understanding of how parables function within literature, religion, and ethical teachings, making them a vital tool for conveying profound concepts in an accessible manner.

8.1. Example Parable

The parable is a negative example story which tells how not to act.[94] A parable has two points, one in a literal level which stems from the surface level and a metaphorical point, which is based on a deeper level. An example story has one point and one level. This parable is one of such in the Gospel of Luke and such parables are whose deeper level and metaphorical point have been missed out. "The metaphorical point is that similarly the kingdom of God abruptly breaks into persons consciousness, overturning prior and established values and conclusions."[95]

Parables are authentic piece of Jesus tradition and they are told to offer moral examples.[96] The parables such as the Good Samaritan (Lk 10:25ff), the Rich Fool (Lk 12:16ff), the Rich Man and Lazarus (Lk 16:19ff) and the Pharisee and Tax-Collector (18:9ff) come under this category. Arland J.

---

woman healed on Sabbath (Lk 13:10-17; 14:1-6), man with a hundred sheep and women with ten pieces of silver (Lk 15:4-10), sleeping man and women at the grinder (Lk 17:34-35), Abraham's daughter (Lk 19:9; 13:16). Unfortunate widow and the publican (Lk 18:1-14), women at the tomb and Emmaus disciples (Lk 23:58-24:35), Peter at the tomb and women at the tomb (Lk 24:12).

[93] Constance Parvey, 'The Theology and Leadership of Women in the New Testament,' *Religion and Sexism,* edited by Rosemary R. Ruther (New York: Simon and Shurter). Cited by Jane Kopas, 'Jesus and Women,' *Theology Today,* 46/2 (July, 1986): 193.

[94] John Dominic Crossan, 'Parable and Example in the Teaching of Jesus:' 78.

[95] John Dominic Crossan, 'Parable and Example in the Teaching of Jesus.' Cited in Dan O. Via, "Parable and Example Story: A Literary-Structuralist Approach": 105ff.

[96] This classification has begun with Adolf Jülicher, *Die Gleichnisreden Jesu,* 1888, 112ff; Rudolf Bultmann, *The History of the Synoptic Tradition,* tr. by John Marsh (New York: Harper and Row Publishers, 1963), 177-179.

Hultgren explains this form of parables as the most characteristic about them is that they set forth examples of human conduct for the disciple of Jesus to follow or to avoid. These parables are classified as "example stories."[97]

8.2. Parable and Fable

The parable-proper (narrative parable) is equated with the Greek fable. It is limited to those narratives in which the characters are usually animals, plants or inanimate objects and they have a prudential lesson. Whereas, by using the term parable indicates the narratives in which the characters are human beings which have a religious or moral lesson.[98] Parables and fables are "brief, invented narratives about incidents which shed light on certain aspects of human experience and behavior."[99] Generally, the supernatural does not figure directly in the parables. The two exceptions are the parable of the rich fool (Lk 12:13-21) and the rich man and Lazarus (Lk 16:19-31). Parables which narrate the relationship between humans and God have an element of reversal of fortune.

8.3. Parable and Metaphor

According to Adolf Jülicher the synoptic simile narratives are not expanded metaphors[100] where as Sallie McFague is of the view that the synoptic parables are expanded metaphors.[101] In the view of Dodd and Funk,[102] the inclusively disjunctive definition of the synoptic simile narratives as expanded comparisons or metaphors.[103] And "a metaphor or simile drawn

---

[97] Arland J. Hultgren, *The Parables of Jesus: A Commentary* (Michigan: W. B. Eerdmans, 2002), 92ff, classifies these parables in the third chapter. Parables of Exemplary Behavior.

[98] M. Boucher, *The Mysterious Parable: A Literary Study* (Washington: Catholic Biblical Association of America, 1977), 13.

[99] Mary Ann Beavis, 'Parable and Fable,' *CBQ* 52/3 (July, 1990): 480.

[100] Adolf Jülicher, *Die Gleichnisreden Jesus* (Tübingen: Mohr, 1910), 25-118.

[101] Cf. Sallie McFague, *Metaphorical Theology. Model of God in Religious Languages* (Philadelphia: Fortress Press, 1982).

[102] C. H. Dodd, *The Parables of the Kingdom*, 18, 19. And R. W. Funk, *Language, Hermeneutic and the Word of God: The Problem of Language in the New Testament and Contemporary Theology* (New York: Harper and Row, 1966), 136-137.

[103] There is a long history for the analysis of the parable as metaphor, especially by, Adolf Jülicher, *Die Gleichnisreden Jesus;* C. H. Dodd, *The Parables of the Kingdom*; Amos N. Wilder, *Early Christian Rhetoric: The Language of the Gospel* (Hendrickson Publishers: New York: 1964); R.W. Funk, *Language, Hermeneutic and the Word of God;* Dan O. Via, *The Parables: Their Literary and Existential Dimension*; John Dominic Crossan, *In Parables. The Challenge of the Historical Jesus*; Philip Wheelwright, *Metaphor and Reality* (Bloomington: Indiana University Press, 1962); and Sallie McFague, *Metaphorical Theology: Model of God in Religious Languages.* For more details of analysis on metaphor see, Mogens Stiller Kjargaard, *Metaphor and Parables: A Systematic Analysis of the Specific*

from nature or common life arresting the hearer by its vividness or strangeness, leaving the mind in sufficient doubt about its precise application to tease it into active thought."[104] According to J. D. Crossan,[105] there are two use of metaphor. The metaphors are not ones that simply illustrate information, but those in which participation precedes information. Similes and parables are to be found in the diachronic continuum between the present and imperfect metaphors.[106]

9. Narrative Laws of the Parables

In the narrative[107] parables, the comparisons made include narration; these parables have the quality of the particularity of stories set in past.[108] Among the L parables, according to the scholars[109] four parables come under the category of narrative parables.[110] They are the parable of the Good Samaritan (10:25-37); the parable of the Rich fool (12:16-21); the parable of the Rich man and Lazarus (16:19-31); and the parable of the Pharisee and Publican (18:9-14).[111] Arland J. Hultgren calls these parables as exemplary

---

Structure and Cognitive Function of the Synoptic Similes and Parables qua Metaphors (Leiden: E. J. Brill, 1986).

[104] C. H. Dodd, *The Parables of the Kingdom*, 4.

[105] John Dominic Crossan, *In Parables: The Challenge of the Historical Jesus*, 9-22.

[106] Mogens Stiller Kjargaard, *Metaphor and Parables: A Systematic Analysis of the Specific Structure and Cognitive Function of the Synoptic Similes and Parables qua Metaphors,* 239.

[107] Narrative is the normal human means by which one can describe existence in time, for human experience has a narrative quality. Plot is an important element in the narrative reading. *Point of view* in the narrative is often spoken of as the filter through which the narrator presents his narration. Those who read or hear a narrative depend on the narrator's viewpoint for how they perceive the story. Cf. William S. Kurz, "Narrative Approaches to Lk-Acts," *Biblica* 68/2 (1987): 196, 203.

[108] Arland J. Hultgren, *The Parables of Jesus: A Commentary*, 3.

[109] Adolf Jülicher, *Gleichnisreden*, 1:114; 2: 585-641; R. Bultmann, *History of the Synoptic Tradition,* 177-79; B. Smith, *Parables*, 18 cited in Arland J. Hultgren, *The Parables of Jesus: A Commentary*, 4.

[110] In other words exemplary Narrative (German: *Beispielerzählung*). According to Greg W. Forbes, there are at least nine parables unique to Luke's Gospel and of that occurs in the Travel Narrative. Cf. *The God of the Old: The Role of the Lukan Parables in the Purpose of Luke's Gospel* (Sheffield: Sheffield Academic Press, 2000).

[111] These four parables are narrative parables. For more detail on the narrative parables see, Robert W. Funk, *Parables and Presence: Forms of the New Testament Tradition* (Philadelphia: Fortress Press, 1982), 35. Narrative parables are clear and transparent. Cf. Jeffrey T. Tucker, *Example Stories: Perspectives on Four Parables in the Gospel of Luke*, JSNT Sup. Series, 162 (Sheffield: Sheffield Academic Press, 1998), 396-418 cited in Arland J. Hultgren, *The Parables of Jesus: A Commentary*, 4. In the narrative parables, the characters

narratives.[112] Jeffrey T. Tucker calls these four parables as *narrative parables*.[113]

Narrative parables are different from others in that they provide examples of human conduct to follow or examples to avoid. They are clear and transparent and calls for practical application. According to Philip Sellew, Parables of Luke uses a narrative device: when faced with a moment of decision, usually in a moral crisis, the central characters in each of these little stories address themselves through the use of the literary technique of interior monologue.[114]

In the view of Madeleinel I. Boucher, in the narrative parables persons are usually characterized by what they say or do.[115] C. H. Dodd opines that a narrative parable has a series of verbs in historical tense.[116] According to Robert W. Funk, a narrative parable has at least three major participants, and the narrative parables may also have at least two scenes.[117] Narrative parable has a sender, object and a receiver; in other words, helper, subject and opponent.[118]

Narrative always has to do with action or events. "Narrative parables share in common the obvious fact of narrativity."[119] It is, therefore, a dynamic form of speech.[120] Narrative parables have at least three principal characters and comparable plot structures and these parables are carefully composed and constructed.[121] In the narrative parables, simple and familiar vocabularies are used. There are fewer descriptions and adjectives are used, feelings and emotions are rarely mentioned and direct speech is preferred to

---

are stock characters, the plots are stock plots, see Bernard Brandon Scott, *Hear Then the Parable: A Commentary on the Parables of Jesus* (Minneapolis: Fortress Press, 1989), 36.

[112] Arland J. Hultgren, *The Parables of Jesus: A Commentary*, 125.

[113] Jeffrey T. Tucker, *Example Stories: Perspectives on Four Parables in the Gospel of Luke*, 396-418.

[114] Cf. Philip Sellew, 'Interior Monologue as a Narrative Device in the Parables of Luke,' *JBL* 111/2 (1992): 239-253.

[115] Madeleinel I. Boucher, *The Parables: A Biblical Theological Commentary*, New Testament Message, vol. 7, edited by Wilfrid Harrington and Donald Senior (Wilmington, Delaware: Michael Glazier Inc., 1981), 24.

[116] C. H. Dodd, *The Parables of the Kingdom*, 18. With the assistance of discourse structure, a new form of linguistic analysis, it helps to plot new and precise grids for the definitions of parables and other types of narrative.

[117] Robert W. Funk, *Parables and Presence: Forms of the New Testament Tradition*, 35f.

[118] Bernard Brandon Scott, *Jesus Symbol-maker for the Kingdom*, 99.

[119] Bernard Brandon Scott, *Jesus Symbol-maker for the Kingdom*, 98.

[120] Madeleinel I. Boucher, *The Parables: A Biblical Theological Commentary*, 22.

[121] Robert W. Funk, *Parables and Presence: Forms of the New Testament Tradition*, 19, 20.

third-person narration. There, are two sets of relationships which developed within the narrative.

Parables can be distinguished from other literary figures in that they are narrative in form but figurative in meaning. A parable may be briefly defined as a figurative narrative which is true to life and is designed to convey through analogy. In a parable there may be both similes and metaphors to make their analogies, and the rhetorical purposes of parables are to inform, convince, or persuade their audiences.

Pedagogically, Jesus used parables to motivate his hearers to make proper decisions. The parables revealed and concealed new truths regarding God's kingdom program to the original audiences of Jesus. Those who responded positively were called disciples and to them it was granted to understand the mysteries of the kingdom. The same truth was concealed from those who did not respond positively because of hardened hearts which were unreceptive to the message of Jesus.[122]

Narrative parable has the forms of rhythm and assonance and it endows the prose of the parables with certain poetic qualities.[123] In the narrative parables, the narrator gives the correspondences between picture and reality depend for the evaluation of his listeners. The narrator concedes them to the audience in order to establish the connection between the parable and the point in dispute.[124] "Contemporary literary criticism agrees with the Greco-Roman tradition in emphasizing the narrative element in parable, but with the Hebrew tradition in allowing both impossible and possible stories into the genre."[125] Studies show that Jesus was the first teacher in the Jewish tradition who made use of narrative parables for instruction.[126]

---

[122] Mark L. Bailey, 'Guidelines for Interpreting Jesus' Parables,' *Bibliotheca Sacra* 155 (Jan-Mar, 1998): 30.

[123] Robert W. Funk, *Parables and Presence: Forms of the New Testament Tradition*, 20.

[124] Eta Linnemann, *Jesus of the Parables: Introduction and Exposition* (New York: Harper and Row, 1966), 27.

[125] John Dominic Crossan, 'Parables,' *ABD,* 149. In modern parabolic theory, three elements are taken for consideration. They are the qualities of narrative, metaphor and brevity. Lukan parables reflect the conflict in the parable. The persistent man in conflict with his friend who had already gone to bed (Lk 11:5-8), the persistent widow and the judge (18:1-8), the conflict between the rich man and Lazarus, the prodigal son and his older brother (15:11-32) and so on. For the study of the parable of the Judge and the widow cf. Edwin D. Freed, 'The Parable of the Judge and the Widow (Luke 18:1-8),' *NTS* 33/1 (1987): 38ff.

[126] Cf. J. Jeremias, *The Parables of Jesus,* 12; Jacob Neusner, 'Types and forms in ancient Jewish Literature: Some Comparisons,' *HR* 11 (1972): 376; David Stern, "Jesus' Parables from the perspective of Rabbinic Literature: The Example of the Wicked Husbandmen," *Parable and Story in Judaism and Christianity,* edited by Clements Thoma and Michael Wyschogrod (New York: Paulist Prfess, 1989), 43; idem, *Parables in Midrash* 5 and H.

In the narrative parables, the characters of the narrative are understood by characteristics which are attributed to them. There are different kinds of characters based on their traits. It is related to the telling and showing of the characters. On the basis of such difference the distinction is made between *round characters*, who possess a variety of potentially conflicting traits, and *flat characters*, whose traits are all consistent and predictable...[and] *stock characters* for those who with a single trait.[127] The major characters are the center of the narrative and there are minor characters with variant purposes. Sometimes these minor characters are placed in the margin and required to be read them by bringing them into the front. They perform a perfunctory role in the narrative.

In every narrative, there are different characters with different purposes. Each character carries its own role within the story or the discourse. A story is about someone that is the character. The actions are carried out by someone: the character. In biblical narratives, the characters are introduced to the reader by four ways such as the character's own actions, interactions with others, character's own speech, through the speeches of the characters about the special character and through the narrator's specific comments about the character.[128] They are the living beings that actualize the meaning for the events. In the parables of Luke, one could come along with such presentation of characters.

Narrative parables of Luke have a modest plot, with an element of conflict, and that leads to a resolution. The conflict is not the disagreement in theology, but in the behavior and ideology of the characters. Through the parables, Jesus questions the dispositions and conduct of characters who personify Greco-Roman social values and structures.

Lukan parables function as a counter-narrative that sets an alternative vision of life that challenged the foundational values and structures of Greco-Roman society. Through the reading of the Gospel as a counter-narrative, the reader understands the Gospel to advocate certain perspectives, structures and practices associated with Jesus and God, while rejecting those associated with the religious leaders and the devil.

McArthur and R. Johnson, *They also Taught in Parables,* 106f, Cited in Arlund J. Hultgren, *The Parables of Jesus: A Commentary*, 7.

[127] Cf. Mark Allan Powell, *What is Narrative Criticism?* (Minneapolis: Fortress Press, 1953), 55.

[128] Cf. Richard G. Bowman, 'Narrative Criticism: Human Purpose in conflict with Divine Purpose,' *Judges and Method: New Approaches in Biblical Studies*, edited by Gale A. Yee (Minneapolis: Fortress Press, 1985), 30.

Narratives are stories which may be historical or fictional. They have characters,[129] plot, point of view, rhetorical devices and setting.[130] These parables are subject to the laws of popular narrative.[131] There is *conciseness* in the narrative and only necessary persons appear. *Feelings and motives* of the characters are mentioned when they are essential for the action or point. Descriptions of the *events and actions* are also limited to the requirements. Parables carry *direct speech*[132] *and soliloquy.*[133]

There are two types of narratives: dramatic and non-dramatic. In the dramatic narratives, the narrator emphasizes a certain conflict which motivates the events that s/he is telling or writing and directs them to some sort of resolution. "This general progression from conflict to resolution may involve different types of crisis situations, whether major or minor, from the perspective of the participants involved as well as the storyteller."[134] There are conflicts between Jesus and the Pharisees, religious leaders[135] of his day. Plot is a significant element in the interpretation because it is a story that begins with a stable condition, goes through some sort of disequilibrium, caused by conflict[136] and concludes with a resolution, a new stable condition.

---

[129] Characters in a narrative are persons with moral, dispositional and emotional qualities that are expressed in what they say and do. A narrator may either show (the character is talking or acting) or tell (intervene authoritatively to describe or evaluate the character). Characterization is used to identify the main traits, the defining characteristics of a character. James L. Resseguie, 'Literature, New Testament as,' *Eerdmans Dictionary of the Bible,* edited by David Noel Freedman (Michigan: W. B. Eerdmans, 2000), 816.

[130] The setting of a narrative: the historical time, social circumstances and general locale in which its action occurs. James L. Resseguie, 'Literature, New Testament as,' *Eerdmans Dictionary of the Bible,* 816.

[131] Rudolf Bultmann gives it in detail in *The History of the Synoptic Tradition.*

[132] Lost sheep and the Lost coin (Lk. 15:4-10), parable of the Master and the servant (17:7-10), the parable of the Barren Fig Tree (13:6-9) and parable of the great supper (14:15-24). For the details of the parables in Luke ch. 15 see, Charles E. Carlston, "Reminiscence and Redaction in Luke 15:11-32," *JBL* 94/3 (Sep, 1975): 368ff.

[133] It can be seen in the parables of the Prodigal son (15:12ff), the Unjust Steward (16:21), the unfaithful servant (12:45), the Wicked Husbandman (20:13ff) and Pharisee and Publican (18:9ff).

[134] Ernst R. Wendland, 'A Tale of Two Debtors: On the Interaction of Text, Context, and Context in a New Testament Dramatic Narrative (Luke 7:36-50),' *Linguistics and New Testament Interpretation: Essays on Discourse Analysis,* edited by David Alan Black (Nashville, Tennessee: Broadman Press, 1992), 101.

[135] J. B. Tyson, 'Conflict as a Literary Theme in the Gospel of Luke,' *New Synoptic Studies,* edited by W. Farmer and Macon (GA: Mercer University Press, 1983), 320-26.

[136] There are conflict with the supernaturals, nature, characters or within oneself. James L. Resseguie, 'Literature, New Testament as,' *Eerdmans Dictionary of the Bible,* 817.

There is an interpretive introduction in each of the Lukan parable. Luke uses a narrative audience. Lukan parables are used to chasten the narrative audience and to correct a mistaken supposition.[137] Lukan parables also give a vivid counterpoint to the assertion or question of the listener. "Luke's audiences are the characters immediately identified as the listener."[138] Lukan parables are narrative collocation which collocates in relation either to each other or to the surrounding narrative such that they draw on their context for meaning.[139]

9.1. Characters in the Parable

The parables in Jesus' parables are detailed enough to allow its readers to identify with them.[140] Parables in the Gospel of Luke present memorable and realistic characters and they "embody the "concrete universal" distinctive and memorable while appealing to people across cultures and time.[141]

According to Garwood P. Anderson, the characters in the Lukan parables are some or other way in crisis.[142] The plot of, almost, all the parable turns on a crisis, not merely in the general sense in which all narratives are propelled by conflict, but in a more personal sense as characters face shame, marginalized, destitution or judgment, where they must improvise a response.[143] Lukan parables are sometimes seen as stories with ambiguity.

Varieties of characters are seen in the Lukan parables. Very rich joint family with six wealthy brothers insensitive to the poor at their gate. The fraudulent manager, shrewd and smart (16:1-11). The self righteous group, the unprincipled judge who scare cared for God or for what others thought (18:1-8). The absentee landowner confronted with scheming and violent tenants (20:9-15). Systems for banking and making money multiply without the stock exchange (19:11-27). The wasteful son savoring life overseas[144] (15:11-20). The schemers who attempted to destroy with duplicity (20:

---

[137] Garwood P. Anderson, 'Seeking and Saving What Might have been Lost: Luke's Restoration of an Enigmatic Parable Tradition,' *CBQ* 70/4 (Oct, 2008): 735.

[138] Garwood P. Anderson, 'Seeking and Saving What Might have been Lost: Luke's Restoration of an Enigmatic Parable Tradition:' 737.

[139] Garwood P. Anderson, 'Seeking and Saving What Might have been Lost: Luke's Restoration of an Enigmatic Parable Tradition:' 743.

[140] Mike Graves, 'Preaching Lukan Parables: A Socio-Rhetorical Approach:' 26.

[141] John R. Donahuse, 'The Parable of Luke,' *BT* 41/5 (Sep, 2003): 283.

[142] Garwood P. Anderson, 'Seeking and Saving What might have been lost: Luke's Restoration of an Enigmatic parable Tradition:' 729f.

[143] Garwood P. Anderson, 'Seeking and Saving what Might have been Lost: Luke's Restoration of an Enigmatic Parable Tradition:' 731.

[144] Charles Homer Giblin, 'Structural and Theological Considers on Luke 15,' *CBQ* 24/1 (Jan, 1962): 15-31.

20-26). Brothers fighting over inheritance (12:13-15), the banquets of the wealthy (14:12-13, 16), the hypocrisy of religious leaders (11:42-52; 20:45-47) and the prostitutes and a society marked by immorality (17:26-30).[145]

9.2. Characterization in the Parable

In the parables, the character's speech is shown in a subtle way to enhance characterization. "Most of the characterization in the Gospel of Luke takes place through indirect presentation, which may take the form of speech, action, external appearances, or environment."[146] In the parable of the prodigal son, the elder brother replies to his father and telling refer to his younger brother as "This son of yours..." (15:30). This subtle use of dialogue indicates his feelings toward his brother; he rejects any familial relationship with him. Another example of this type is found in the speech of the rich man in the parable of the Rich man and Lazarus. The rich man considers Lazarus to be inferior (16:24, 27) even when he is in hades and Lazarus in the bosom of Abraham.

Some characters spoke nothing but their actions are louder than words. The altruistic actions of the Good Samaritan (10:29-37) is an example.[147] The rich fool contemplated a life of ease (12:16ff). "If a character's external appearance is described, that information–physical features, clothing, movements, gestures–also needs to be processed as far as characterization."[148] In the parable of the rich man and Lazarus, the rich man is "clothed in purple," but Lazarus was covered with sores (16:19-20). The environment of the character, when described, also important in the characterization. The tax-collector in the parable of the Pharisee and the tax-collector is portrayed as "in the temple....standing far off," an illustration of his feeling of unworthiness (18:13). Characterization is also enhanced by comparing or contrasting one character with another. The Samaritan is favorably contrasted with the priest and the Levite in the parable of the Good Samaritan (10:29-37), the contrast made between the rich man and Lazarus exemplifies the power of this literary technique (16:19-31).

---

[145] Paddy Meagher, *Paddy Fields and a Grain of Rice,* 161.

[146] David B. Gowler, 'Characterization in Luke: A Socio-Narratological Approach,' *BTB* 19/2 (1989): 56.

[147] A routine act carries more weight than a one-time, as seen in the continual conflicts between Jesus and the Pharisees. The narration of these conflicts reinforces the predominantly negative picture of the Pharisees. Their challenges to Jesus about his authority to forgive sins (5:17-26), his disregard for purity rules (eg. 5:29-32; 7:39) and Sabbath observances (eg. 6:11; 14:1-6) characterize them as members of the opposition. The mere telling of these repeated conflicts helps both the character of the Pharisees and the character of Jesus. Cf. David B. Gowler, 'Characterization in Luke: A Socio-Narratological Approach:' 56.

[148] David B. Gowler, 'Characterization in Luke: A Socio-Narratological Approach': 56.

9.3. Conflicting Character-Types

The device of conflict character is presented with the purpose to sharpen the point being made. The contrast is between two figures in the two debtors, the prodigal son and his brother, the rich man and Lazarus, and the Pharisee and the tax collector. In the parable of the Good Samaritan, one figure (the Samaritan) is in conflict with two (the Priest and Levite). In the parable of the Good Samaritan, the contrast made between good and best. In the rich man and Lazarus contrast made between rich and poor. In the Pharisee and the tax collector the conflict can be seen between repentant and unrepentant.

10. Narrative Devices in Lukan Parables

Lukan parables have narrative devices in its structure. "Narrative exists as two levels or dimensions. As *story* it is objective statement creating a world of events and persons who are real from the view point of that created world."[149] A narrative also could be a story and discourse at the same time with the discourse level being signified in various ways along the story line.[150] "The narrative parables are metaphors of the kingdom: they give a new vision of every existence as transected by the surprising incursion of the transcendent. The metaphoric tenor is the kingdom of God (heaven), and the vehicle is the narrative."[151]

It is the narrative message rather than the underlying code that is of value to be drawn out. Hence, the narrative structure that needs to be studied by the interpreter is the *surface structure* of the story, for this surface structure embodies the message of the parable.[152] One needs to find out the patterns and structures embodies the message of the parable.[153] Parabolic narrative is a way of understanding one thing in terms of another, the metaphorical network exposes both similarities and differences.

10.1. Plot of the Parable

Plot is the structure of a narrative's actions that are directed toward an intended effect. A plot has a beginning, a middle and an end. The beginning initiates the main action that causes the reader to look forward to something more. The middle presumes that something precedes and more will follow.

[149] Dan O. Via, 'Parable and Example Story: A Literary-Structuralist Approach:' 107. Cf. Mark Allan Powell, 'Toward a Narrative Critical Understanding of Luke,' *Interpretation* 48/4 (Oct, 1994): 341-346.

[150] Dan O. Via, 'Parable and Example Story: A Literary-Structuralist Approach:' 107.

[151] Dan O. Via, 'Parable and Example Story: A Literary-Structuralist Approach.' 118

[152] Paul Ricoeur, 'Biblical Hermeneutics,' *Semeia* 4 (1975): 65.

[153] Mary Ann Tolbert, *Perspectives on Parables: An Approach to Multiple Interpretation* (Philadelphia: Fortress Press, 1979), 74.

The end follows what has gone before and requires that nothing follows.[154] In the parables, plot is the element of conflict. There are two aspects for a narrative. They are the discourse and the story. Story refers to the content of the narrative, what it is about.

A story consists of such elements as events, characters and setting and the interaction of these elements comprises the plot. The rhetoric of the narrative, the way it is told is the discourse. Plot is an essential part of a narrative. A Plot is the outline or framework of events that happen in the story. The story is where the characters interact; the discourse is where the implied author and the implied reader interact. Story and discourse are inseparable.[155]

10.2. Point of View

Point of view signifies the way a story is told. The actions, setting and events are mediated through the narrator's perspective which is expressed in terms of space, time, phrases and words, insights into a character's thoughts and feelings and the beliefs, values and norms of the narrator.[156] In the Lukan parables one can find these features.

10.3. Soliloquy

There is the inner dialogue or soliloquy in L parable. They are evident in the parable of the foolish rich man, the prodigal son and his brother, the unrighteous Judge, and the pharisee and the tax-collector. These soliloquies of various characters reveal the true character and motivation of the speaker, which is crucial for understanding and interpreting the characters in the parable. It is a natural device of a parable. Because it helps the narrator to make the point clearly, quickly and, thus, avoids using the more lengthy discourse device of description of activity.[157]

10.4. Concluding With a Question

This can be seen in the parable of the two debtors as "Which of them will love him more?," in the parable of the Good Samaritan as "Which of these three, do you think, proved neighbor to the man who fell among the robbers?", and in the parable of the rich fool, "and the things you have

---

[154] James L. Resseguie, 'Literature, New Testament as,' *Eerdmans Dictionary of the Bible,* 817.

[155] Mark Allan Powell, *What are they Saying about Luke* (New York: Paulist Press, 1989), 23.

[156] James L. Resseguie, 'Literature, New Testament as,' *Eerdmans Dictionary of the Bible,* 816f.

[157] Douglas M. Parrott, 'The Dishonest Steward (Luke 16:1-8a) and Luke's Special Parable Collection,' 510.

prepared, whose will they be?" The purpose of these question to the listeners to make an answer which is implicit in the parable or obvious from the question.[158] The answer they make definitely gives the value of the Kingdom.

11. Conflict in the Gospel of Luke

Several scholars have made the contributions in the area of conflict in the Gospel of Luke. According to J. B. Tyson,[159] there are different conflicts in the Gospel of Luke, which were conflicts between incompatible systems: Jesus, the Roman aristocracy, the Jewish elite and the Jewish peasantry. J. D. Kingsbury[160] simply focuses on the description of these conflicts without indicating its further implications, while R. T. France and M. Desjardins[161] argue that Jesus faced conflict because of his arrogant attitude. According to B. J. Malina,[162] the conflict Jesus endured was because he stood against the powerful elite who perpetrated injustice by labeling and thus marginalized those who did not adhere to the accepted social norms of the day.[163]

R. J. Cassidy[164] and M. Desjardins[165] have argued that Jesus stood against religious abuse, the down-play of women and social status and the misuse of political structure. R. J. Cassidy[166] had observed that Jesus' conflict-ridden public ministry was due to the fact that first-century Palestine was essentially an agonistic society.[167]

---

[158] Douglas M. Parrott, 'The Dishonest Steward (Luke 16:1-8a) and Luke's Special Parable Collection,' 510.

[159] J. B. Tyson, 'Conflicts as Literary Theme in the Gospel of Luke', *New Synoptic Studies*, cf. also K. E. Boulding, 'Organization and Conflict': 129.

[160] J. D. Kingsbury, *Conflict in Luke: Jesus, Authorities, Disciples* (Minneapolis: Fortress Press, 1991).

[161] R. T. France, *Jesus the Radical: A Portrait of the Man they Crucified* (Leicester: IVP, 1990), 22, and M. Desjardins, *Peace, Violence and the New Testament* (Sheffield: Sheffield Academic Press, 1997), 75.

[162] B. J. Malina, 'Reading Theory Perspective: Reading Luke-Acts', *The Social World of Luke-Acts: Models of Interpretation* edited by J. H. Neyrey (Peabody, MA: Hendrickson Publishers, 1991), 99.

[163] Adolf Harnack, *What is Christianity* ([illegible]: Book Tree, 2006), 103,104. Agrees with Malina that those in power like the priests and the Pharisees held the Jewish nation in bondage and murdered its soul. He then argues that Jesus responded to such an unconstitued 'authority' by showing a really emancipating and refreshing disrespect.

[164] R. J. Cassidy, *Jesus, Politics and the Society: A Study of Luke's Gospel* (Maryknoll: Orbis Books, 1980), 35.

[165] M. Desjardins, *Peace, Violence and the New Testament*, 78.

[166] R. J. Cassidy, *Jesus, Politics and the society: A Study of Luke's Gospel*, 124.

[167] There are also studies on the conflict in other Gospels too. In the development of plot in the respective Gospels, the Jewish leaders play a more significant role than do the disciples. The reason is that the element of conflict is of the essence of Gospel's-plot, and

The *Journey to Jerusalem*[168] is the large portion of Jesus' ministry which contributes to the conflict between Jesus and people, and the parables reflect these conflicts, and through the presentation of the kingdom values and the resolutions were also made. In the journey section, the narrator makes use of a series of discourses to describe the ideological conflict between Jesus and people,[169] a conflict which revolves around the presence of the kingdom of God, the need for repentance, the correct use of possessions and ritual purity and so on and the kingdom values which give the resolutions to those conflicts.

In the Gospel of Luke, one can find that the religious groups such as the Pharisees, Sadducees, Scribes and Chief Priest are in conflict with Jesus, and sometimes the people and crowd are in conflict with Jesus, sometimes the disciples are in conflict with Jesus. Luke has presented a theological interpretation of the inescapable enigma that Israel, as a whole, had rejected its messianic fulfiller of salvation.[170] Jesus speaks the parables in the context of such conflicts and he also presents the Kingdom values which can ease the conflict by applying those values in it.

In the Gospel of Luke, one could find that Jesus was opposed by his contemporaries because of the goal and the content of His mission, as well as the way in which they understood His identity. Jesus worked at the margins of society, that is, His actions were seen as going against the grain of accepted societal norms. He mingled with those who were considered outsiders and did not operate in conformity with the goals and interests of his opponents. His identity revealed in his message was an open challenge to the status quo. He challenged the social order by x-raying societal abnormalities such as injustice, oppression, exploitation and racism and stood for an alternative that consisted of justice, love, equality and peace, all virtues of the kingdom. The rich are in a position to relax and enjoy their good fortune. All their responsibilities in life will have now been met, and all the needs of their life will now be satisfied, or so they think.

---

at the human level it is particularly with the Jewish leaders that Jesus becomes embroiled in moral struggle. Cf. Jack Dean Kingsbury, 'The Developing Conflict between Jesus and the Jewish Leaders in Matthew's Gospel: A Literary-Critical Study,' *CBQ* 49/1 (1987): 57-73.

[168] On travel narrative and its relation to Moses of Deuteronomy and various issues related to it are discussed in David P. Moessner, 'Luke 9:1-50: Luke's Preview of the Journey of the Prophet Like Moses of Deuteronomy,' *JBL* 102/4 (Dec, 1983): 575-605.

[169] Frank J. Matera, 'Jesus Journey to Jerusalem (Lk 9:51-19:46): A Conflict with Israel,' *JSNT* 51 (Sep, 1993): 77. According to Matera, The journey narrative is the best expression of the why and how Jesus came into conflict with Israel.

[170] David P. Moessner, 'The Leaven of the Pharisees' and 'this Generation': Israel's Rejection of Jesus According to Luke,' *JSNT* 34 (Oct, 1988): 42.

12. Lukan Parables and Conflict

There are themes such as repentance, kingdom of God, forgiveness, reversal of fortune and so on can be found in the parables of Luke. But one can find some kind of conflict presented in all the parables of Luke. It may be the creation of Luke which, he may be also part of, the Jewish-Christian conflict in the first century Christianity. The whole collection of Luke, as he edited it, might have taken on allegorical overtones relating to that conflict,[171] especially in parables. Generally, in the Gospel of Luke, conflict seems to revolve around two aspects of Jesus' ministry. First, it is about the authority of Jesus. Second, the conflict lies in the message of Jesus.[172]

There are two major strands of conflict theory according to the kinds of social cleavages, they also emphasize the historical role that conflict plays in them. The conflict theory is more or less directly hailing from the Marxist tradition. These theories focus on the fundamental material interests of different groups as they become intertwined with political forces. These conflicting interests are ultimately based in the mode of production, which creates two main classes in the case of capitalism, labor and capital.

It is the conflict or struggle between these two primary classes, and the organizations representing their interests that is thought to provide the fundamental key to explaining political outcomes. Adam Smith and Max Weber follow the same method. It was raised in 1960s as a reaction set against the value consensus approach under the label of conflict theory. Conflict theories emphasize the importance of social cleavages generating social conflict that in turn account for political outcomes.

L. A. Coser[173] criticizes this understanding of conflict which seems to draw a distinction between conflict and other related terms such as hostility, tension, disputes, contest, and competition. Conflict, thus, has both physical and emotional elements. In broader terms, R. Dahrendorf defines conflict as "all relations between sets of individuals that involve an incompatible difference of objective."[174] This definition seems more inclusive. For J. H. Turner, it is "a process of events leading to overt interaction of varying degrees of violence among two parties."[175] Here, conflict is understood

[171] Douglas M. Parrott, 'The Dishonest Steward (Luke 16:1-8a) and Luke's Special Parable Collection,' 508.

[172] Stevon M. Sheeley, *Narrative Asides in Luke Acts*, JSNT Supplement Series, 72 (Sheffield: Sheffield Academic Press, 1992), 141, 142. For various aspects related to the literary criticism, narrative elements in particular are discussed in this work. Cf. Jack Dean Kingsbury, 'The Plot of Luke's Story of Jesus,' *Interpretation* 48/4 (Oct, 1994): 369-378

[173] L. A. Coser, *The Functions of Social Conflict* (Glencoe: The Free Press, 1956), 135.

[174] R. Dahrendorf, 'Towards a Theology of Social Conflict': 135.

[175] J. H. Turner, *The Structure of Sociology Study*, 183.

as an eruption resulting from an impending unresolved problem or its manifestation or open confrontation.

Once more, both physical and psychological or emotional conflict comes into play. The way in which K. E. Boulding defines conflict, namely as a "system of interacting systems, each party to the conflict being a system in itself, bound, however, to the other party by a system of communication, information, subjective knowledge, and behavior reactions."[176] Boulding's definition is important for the study of Lukan parable, such as Jesus and other independent systems such as those of the Roman aristocracy, the Jewish elite, and the Jewish peasantry. It leads one to analyze the conflict in the Lukan parables.

Summary of Findings

This chapter has discussed the characteristics of the parables. Parables of Jesus were always with some application. With unique qualities, parable reflects new kingdom program through parables. Parables of Luke are designed with various literary characteristics to challenge its audience. There are various kinds of parables, example parables, parable and fable, and parable and metaphor. In the Gospel of Luke, narrative laws are applied in the parables, characterization and conflicting character–types, plot, point of view and rhetorical devices. This study shows that the contextual needs direct one's attention to the study of parable on the basis of its needs. One needs to understand, examine, evaluate, interpret and apply the parable only after examining the context of the parable. In other terms, one must understand the context within the literary and theological context of the parable before giving any interpretation to it.

---

[176] K. E. Boulding, 'Organization and Conflict,' *Journal of Conflict Resolution* 12 (1957): 122, 129.

6

Theology of Miracles

Introduction

The Gospel of Luke is unique among the Synoptic Gospels for its emphasis on the humanity, compassion, and inclusiveness of Jesus. One of the key ways Luke highlights these characteristics is through the recording of miracles. The miracles in Luke's Gospel serve as signs of God's intervention in human history, revealing Jesus' divine authority and His compassion for those who are marginalized. These miraculous acts also affirm Jesus as the promised Messiah, fulfilling Old Testament prophecies. This essay will explore the various miracles presented in the Gospel of Luke, analyzing their theological significance and their role in emphasizing Jesus' mission to bring salvation and healing to all. Illness and healing are fundamental concerns for all humankind. The term "healing" today is often used to describe non-medical treatments for disease, frequently referred to as faith healing, divine healing, or spiritual healing. This understanding is based on a fragmented view of the human person, where the doctor cares for the body and the church cares for the soul. However, all healing ultimately comes from God, whether through creation, providence, or redemption. God created the body and mind with a limited capacity for self-healing and placed healing agents in our environment.

In the narratives of the Synoptic Gospels, we frequently encounter depictions of the earthly Jesus, who not only preached but also performed miracles that evoked astonishment. The Gospels contain numerous miracle stories, affirming that Jesus brought about remarkable changes in both bodies and souls. He exercised His authority and extraordinary power over nature.

1. Meaning and Definition of Miracle

Healing may be described in terms of the curing or restoring to health of a sick person, whether by promoting the closure of wounds, repairing the results of accidents or surgical disease, or administering effective treatment for specific pathological conditions of the body or mind. Health is frequently given the minimum definition of the absence of disease, but a state of clinical health involves definite positive considerations also. A person may be described as healthy when he exhibits that state of body and mind in which all the functions are being discharged harmoniously.[1]

The word "heal" is used in several ways in the Bible:

1. **Physical Healing:** It commonly means to make whole or well, as seen in *Ecclesiastes 3:3*. This sense of healing appears in prayers for health restoration (*Numbers 12:13; Psalm 6:2; Jeremiah 17:14*) and in declarations of God's power to heal physically (*Deuteronomy 32:39; 2 Kings 20:5-8*).
2. **Spiritual Restoration:** "Heal" is also used metaphorically to describe the restoration of the soul to spiritual health, addressing the wounds caused by sin (*Psalm 41:4; Jeremiah 30:17*).
3. **National Restoration:** The term conveys the healing and deliverance of an afflicted land in passages like *2 Chronicles 7:14* and *Isaiah 19:22*.
4. **Forgiveness of Sin:** "Heal" is used to signify the forgiveness of sins, as in *Jeremiah 3:22*.[2]

Healing occurs throughout a person's life journey as well as across generations. It can be experienced in many forms restoration. Mostly, however, it is about renewal. Leaving behind those things that have wounded us and caused us pain. Moving forward in our journey with hope for the future, with renewed energy, strength and enthusiasm for life.

There are different words used for healing both in Hebrew and Greek. The English word heal once has a much broader meaning than it has now *Arukhah* (from *arakh* 'to be long') primarily meaning the new flesh that

---

[1] George Arthur Buttrick, 'Health, Healing,' *The Interpreter's Dictionary of the Bible* (Nashville: Abingdon Press, 1962), 541.

[2] James Orr, 'Heal,' *International Standard Bible Encyclopedia* (Grand Rapids: WM.B. Eerdmans Publishing Co., 1915), 1349.

gradually forms in the case of a wounds, then healing, or health.[3] There is another word *Rapha,* this is central to the OT language of healing, a root meaning for *Rapha* "to bring together, draw near, or "to Heal" (physical illness and disease).[4] It is commonly used for healing. Other word *haya* means to revive and *sub* restore.[5]

The English word "miracles" comes from the Latin word *miraculum*, meaning "something to be wondered at." According to traditional theory, the purpose of miracles was evidential—Jesus performed miracles to prove Himself as the Divine Son of God and to demonstrate the arrival of the Kingdom of God. His miracles were intended to invoke faith and challenge people's understanding. These mighty works were performed not only to inspire faith but also to meet the immediate needs of human beings.

Jesus' miracles are closely tied to His proclamation of the coming Kingdom of God. A comparison of Mark 1:21-27 with 14-15 and 1:39 reveals that Jesus repeatedly taught about the Kingdom of God in various synagogues and performed exorcisms. Similarly, Mark 3:20-29 implies that Jesus' exorcisms should be understood as successful attacks by the reign of God against the kingdom of Satan.

2. Types of Miracles in Luke

Luke's Gospel contains several types of miracles, including healings, exorcisms, resurrections, and nature miracles. Each category of miracles serves to reveal different aspects of Jesus' divine mission. Luke's Gospel is mainly historical. No other writer gives dating for his narrative as Luke does[6] Luke aimed in his gospel chiefly at the Gentiles and stressed Jesus' compassion for the troubled and vulnerable. Thus, like Mark and Matthew, Luke expects that healings will continue in the apostolic age and beyond, but he recognizes their limited value in creating faith (16.31) and subordinates them to conversion and salvation in importance (10:20).

The Gospel of Luke narrates fourteen healing miracles including exorcisms. One can read about two general references to healings without specific descriptions, two resuscitations, the commissioning of the twelve Apostles "to preach and heal" (Lk 9:1). And sending forth of the seventy Disciples "to preach and heal" (Lk 10:9)

[3] Melancthon W. Jacobus, 'Health,' *Funk and Wagnall's New Standard Bible Dictionary* (New York: Funk and Wagnall's Company, 1936), 333.

[4] Michael L. Brown, *Israel's Divine Healer* (Michigan: Zondervan Publishing House, 1995), 25.

[5] J. D. Douglas, 'Disease and Healing,' *The New Bible Dictionary* (Michigan: William B. Eerdmans Publishing Company, 1962), 313.

[6] Merrill C. Tenney, *New Testament Survey* (Michigan: Wm. B. Eerdmans Publishing Co., 1961), 164.

2.1. Healings: Many of the miracles in Luke involve physical healing, showing Jesus' compassion and power over illness. Notable examples include the healing of Peter's mother-in-law (Lk 4:38-39), the healing of a centurion's servant (Lk 7:1-10), and the cleansing of the ten lepers (Lk 17:11-19). These healing miracles highlight Jesus' concern for individuals across social and ethnic boundaries, including Jews, Gentiles, and Samaritans. The healings also symbolize spiritual restoration and the breaking of barriers, as seen when Jesus touches the leper, a socially excluded person (Lk 5:12-16).

Healing of a demon-possessed man in Capernaum (Lk 4:31-37)
Healing of Peter's mother-in-law (Lk 4:38-39)
Healing of many people at sunset (Lk 4:40-41)
Healing of a leper (Lk 5:12-16)
Healing of a paralytic (Lk 5:17-26)
Healing of a centurion's servant (Lk 7:1-10)
Healing of the woman with the issue of blood (Lk 8:43-48)
Healing of a demon-possessed boy (Lk 9:37-43)
Healing of a crippled woman on the Sabbath (Lk 13:10-17)
Healing of a man with dropsy on the Sabbath (Lk 14:1-6)
Healing of ten lepers (Lk 17:11-19)
Healing of a blind man near Jericho (Lk 18:35-43)

2.2. Exorcisms: Jesus' authority over evil spirits is demonstrated through exorcisms, which emphasize His divine power over the forces of darkness. In Luke 4:31-37, Jesus casts out a demon from a man in Capernaum, and the people are astonished at His authority. The exorcisms signify the arrival of the Kingdom of God, where evil is confronted and overthrown by Christ's power. The exorcism of the Gerasene demoniac (Lk 8:26-39) further illustrates Jesus' ability to liberate people from spiritual bondage, revealing His mission to set captives free.

Exorcism of a demon-possessed man in Capernaum (Lk 4:31-37)
Exorcism of many demons from the Gerasene demoniac (Lk 8:26-39)
Exorcism of a mute demon (Lk 11:14)

There are eight miracles of exorcisms mentioned in the Gospels, in the eyes of Jesus, the deliverance of possessed persons is as important as the healing of the sick. Frequently, Jesus casts one or more demons out of individuals who have been possessed by them, the demons regularly demonstrate that they know who Jesus is, even when most or all of the human onlookers do not (Mk 1:24; 5:7). They use this knowledge to try to gain mastery over Jesus. But in every instance they fail. Jesus proves his superiority over Satan.[7] The people were amazed that Jesus simply commanded the demons and they obeyed (Lk 4:36). The ministry of Christ is in casting out evil spirits since He did so by His power and authority. When His disciples cast them out in His name, they were depending upon this same power and authority (Act 3:6). Jesus interprets his exorcisms as a sign of the work of the Spirit in his mission and as a demonstration of God's kingdom at work among them (Matt 12:24-33; Mk 3:22-30; Lk 11:14-26).[8]

2.3. Resurrections: Luke records two notable resurrection miracles, the raising of the widow's son at Nain (Lk 7:11-17) and the raising of Jairus' daughter (Lk 8:40-56). These miracles demonstrate Jesus' authority over death and serve as a foretaste of His own resurrection. They also point to the ultimate promise of eternal life, underscoring the Gospel's theme of hope and salvation for all.

It is surprising to see that all the Gospels contain only three resuscitation miracles, in which Jesus brings dead people back to life again. The only explanation for this might be the Jesus brought only three people back to life during his public ministry! But this would be unconvincing because the Gospels themselves state that they only contain a small section of the miracles Jesus had worked (Lk 7:11-17; Mt 9:18-26; Mk 5:21-43; Lk 8:40-56; Jn 11:1-44). Some writers prefer to speak of these as resuscitations to distinguish them from the resurrection of Jesus and from the coming resurrection of all believers which is a restoration to life without death ever again intruding. But inasmuch as these terms suggest a non-miraculous procedure, they do not correspond to what the Gospels describe. For critics who are inclined to disbelieve the miraculous, the resurrections are the most incredible of all of Jesus' healing miracles. Ultimately their credibility depends on the evidence for the resurrection of Jesus.

2.4. Nature Miracles: Nature miracles, such as the calming of the storm (Lk 8:22-25) and the miraculous catch of fish (Lk 5:1-11), emphasize Jesus' control over creation. These miracles not only demonstrate His divine power but also reinforce the theme of discipleship, as seen in Peter's response to the miraculous catch of fish, where he recognizes his unworthiness and is called to follow Jesus. The miraculous catch of fish (Lk 5:1-11), Calming of the storm (Lk 8:22-25), Feeding of the 5,000 (Lk 9:10-17) and Jesus walking on water (implied in Luke 9:17; mentioned in Matthew and Mark) are the nature miracles found in the Gospel of Luke.

---

[7] Joel B. Green, Scot McKnight. 'Healing,' *Dictionary of Jesus and the Gospels* (Illinois: Inter Varsity Press, 1992), 300.

[8] T. Desmond Alexander, 'Healing,' *New Dictionary of Biblical Theology* (Leicester: Inter-Varsity Press, 2000), 538-39.

3. Types of Healing

Five major kinds of healing miracles occur in the Gospels. Each requires slightly different interpretation and some scholars would evaluate the historical reliability of the various categories differently as well. The provision, prevention and the permission of diseases also related to the Biblical miracles. There are sixteen healings without any mention of demonic possession. Out of these healings, nine refer to the cure of impaired faculties: blind people to see (Mt 9:27-31), the deaf to hear (Mk 7:32-37), and the lame to walk (Jn 5:1-5). He cleansed leapers (Lk 5-12-16), cured fevers (Jn 4:43-53), stopped a hemorrhage (Mk 5:24-34), restored a withered hand (Mk 3:1-6), replaced a cut-off ear (Lk 22:51), and healed a wide variety of unspecified illnesses. He healed with a word without praying to God or invoking his name. Luke says that Jesus had the power of the Lord with him, to heal. His enemies attributed this power to Satan.[9] He sent forth his disciples with authority to heal every deceases and infirmity. Early Christianity also possessed miraculous powers, including the power to heal (Act 2:22; 3:16: 4:30).[10] Here faith plays a mediating role in relation to the power Jesus exercises of establishing the kingdom.

3.1. Divine Healing

Divine healing is different from the natural, medical, psychology, demonic healing. Basically they have nothing in common with the divine healing which God performs on a human body, through the merit of the atonement of Jesus Christ on Calvary, and through the power of the Holy Spirit. The divine healing is for the total personality of man body, soul and spirit. All the examples of Biblical Divine Healing in the Bible were accomplished by the power of God instantaneously. They were not done by the person but were done through the person by the Holy Spirit. God is the only one who can do creative healing. They lasted for the rest of the person's natural life. The person that was healed did not have to come back for repeated treatments or healings.[11]

3.2. Natural Healing

Natural healing is the type of healing that occurs most often. Natural Healing is, for many reasons, a slow process. Over time the body heals itself, giving itself time to rest and recover. Natural Healing usually lasts until the

---

[9] E, Andrews, 'Healings, Gift of,' *The Interpreter's Dictionary of the Bible* (N.p.: N.p, 1994), 549.

[10] Letter and Hill, 'Christian Healing,' *New Catholic Encyclopedia* (Grand Rapids: Zondervan Publishing House, 2003), 678.

[11] Sandy Simpson, *Biblical Divine Healing Versus Others of Healing*. 22.

next sickness, injury or other problem presents itself. But Natural Healing is not always a cure all. There are times when the body is overwhelmed and, without outside help, it cannot heal itself. Also, if the body becomes weakened, such as a weak immune system, the body may no longer be able to repair itself and disease may continually reoccur. Natural Healing happens over and over through the lifetime of the individual.

3.3. Medical Healing

The human body has all the chemical elements that are found in the earth. If a man is sick due to lack of certain chemicals, vitamins, protein and bacteria, they can be replaced by the chemical values collected from nature's herbs, fungi, chemicals and bacteria. Surgery helps to remove any dead tissues or poison and to set the broken bones in their places etc. So the medical practitioners and surgeons do their best to extend the natural means of healing to restore health to the patient. It should be borne in mind that the healings is not in medicine, but it only co-operates with the self-healing qualities of the human tissues, skin, bones, and nerves. Medical healings cannot cure the mind and soul.

3.4. Psychological Healing

Psychological healing can be achieved swiftly through modern therapeutic techniques rooted in energy psychology and strategic psychotherapy. This healing journey begins with a commitment to uncover the hidden truths about oneself, often involving a deep exploration of thoughts, emotions, and past experiences. As individuals engage in this process, repressed or forgotten feelings and memories resurface, allowing them to confront and process unresolved issues. This awareness is crucial, as it enables individuals to understand the underlying factors contributing to their emotional pain and psychological distress. By addressing these aspects, therapeutic methods can facilitate healing, promote emotional resilience, and foster a greater sense of self-awareness and well-being.

3.5. Demonic Healing (Paranormal)

Demonic Healing has been in existence in the world practically since the creation. It is the oldest healing art. There are many branches of demon healing cults, who invoke the spirits to heal the sick. But the problem with this type of healing is that it is a lying wonder and opens the door to demonic influence, demonization, even possession. In the demonic healing the patient is made to surrender himself to the evil spirit which afflicted him/her, whereby he/she is relieved of his sickness, but in fact, being now possessed by the demon, he/she is liable to suffer more in the future, though he/she might experience a temporary relief. This healing claimed to be from God but whose source is really from the devil. There is much evidence also that suggests that this type of healing is a shell game of the enemy.

4. The Purpose of Healing

Purpose of healing is not merely to meet a human need. It is ultimately to bring glory to God. When healing comes, it is not simply because someone has a need. The ultimate purpose of healing is to bring the person into a closer, a more intimate relationship to God and fellow human beings. Healing is not an end in itself, but a means to an end to be a better person and to do good in the world in which he lives.[12] To cure the ailments of one's body and to cure the maladies of men's souls, by forgiving their sins, turning them from sin to God and filling them with spiritual comfort.[13]

The purpose of the healing was theological, not medical. It is clear that the works of healing demonstrated and proved that He was the son of God. He performed them in His own peculiar power and that of the Holy Spirit which He possessed without measure. They confirmed His person as well as His power.[14] And also it is portrayed as a sign of breaking the kingdom of God, as the divine blessings of salvation (Lk 4:18-19; Is 58:6; 61:1-2; Matt 8:14-17; Is 53:4).

The purpose of healing is to fulfill the purposes of the kingdom of God. Jesus always combined healing with proclaiming the kingdom of God. Through healing the sick Jesus defeated Satan and demonstrated his rule.[15] Sin, the origin of sickness, originates in evil and Satan's kingdom; therefore, sickness proceeds from Satan. Healing is a pronouncement of victory over the kingdom of Satan. Further, it is a foreshadowing of the fullness of the kingdom of God. In this sense, the focus of healing is eschatological.

5. Foundation for Healing

The foundation for understanding the concept of biblical healing is found in the Torah (the books of the law) and the Tanakh (the Old Testament). Without this foundational perspective on healing, it is impossible to understand the holistic nature of healing as presented in the Scriptures. Yehovah Rapha is one of YHVH Elohim's covenant names. Rapha is a Hebrew word that means "to heal, make healthful" and can refer to Elohim, a healer or physician and involves being healed from individual distress, national hurts or defects.

---

[12] Lars Wilhelmsson, *Divine Healing Life, Death, Illness & Healing*, 45.

[13] Samuel Fallows, 'Heal,' *The Popular and Critical Bible Encyclopedia and Scriptural Dictionary* (Chicago: The Howard-Severance Company, 1908), 772.

[14] Charles F. Pfeiffer. 'Healing, Health,' *Wycliffe Bible Encyclopedia* (Chicago: Moody Press, 1975), 766.

[15] John Wimber, *Power Healing* (New York: Harper & Row, 1987), 36.

One view maintains that the privilege of physical healing is governed by the will and sovereignty of God. God heals whomever He wills. Most supporters of divine healing, however, believe that physical healing, like salvation.[16]

6. Nature of the Healing

God created human beings perfectly. By hoping to become better than God's creation, humans became slaves to Lucifer. Their bodies were affected by sickness and death, their minds became confused regarding right and wrong and their wills were no longer able to recognize and resist sin. But God stepped in and began the work of restoration.

Healing is not the by-product of emotion and healing does not happen just because human need one. Healing is the by-product of meeting God's conditions. God does not respond to emotional intensity and He does not respond because it is urgent. God responds when a person meets his spiritual conditions for healing to be happened.[17] There are physical laws in the natural realm. There are spiritual laws in the supernatural realm. Physical laws govern how things work in the natural and spiritual laws govern how things work in the supernatural. Physical laws, however, are subject to spiritual laws and a healing occurs when supernatural forces are brought to bear on the natural realm. The healing of the sick can in no way be termed against nature, seeing that it is sickness which is abnormal and not health. The healing is the restoration of the primitive order.[18]

7. The Source of Healing

In the OT, Yahweh alone was the source of healing, just as He was considered the source of sickness. Summarizing the basic OT attitude concerning sickness and healing, (Deut 32:30), portrays God as the direct dispenser of sickness and disease as punishment for man's sin (Num 12:9-15; 2 Chro 21:18-19; 26:16-21), while healing is a reward for obedience, a manifestation of God's forgiveness, mercy and love.[19]

Illness touches everyone in one way or another. When a person gets sick, it is only natural that he/she wants to get well. All ways human being are trying to find ways and means to remain happy and healthy. Healing is not just an absence of disease. It has much wider meaning; it is a positive feeling of wellbeing, physically, emotionally, socially and spiritually. The

---

[16] Walter A. Elwell, 'Heal, Healing,' *Evangelical Dictionary of Theology*, 539.

[17] John Hagee, *The Power to Heal* (Texas: Horticultural Printers, 1991), 14.

[18] Richard Chenevix Trench, *Notes on the Miracles of Our Lord* (Grand Rapids: Baker Book House, 1949), 12.

[19] Walter A. Elwell, 'Heal, Healing,' *Evangelical Dictionary of Theology* (Michigan: Baker Books House Company, 2001), 539.

healing miracles in the Bible it is not something everyone can do, but it is a mighty act of God in believer's life. God is not only creator of mankind but also He is able to heal all diseases which men/women are going through. He has the power to control and change it. God is the source of healing. Scriptural evidence underlines the identity and role of Yahweh as original giver and restorer of human life. This is true for individuals and also for the people of God, who depend upon him for renewal.

8. Understanding on Healing in the Bible

Bible has much to say about healing. In order to have a clear understanding of divine healing and to claim personal healing, writer would like to turn to the bible and study the healing wrought both in the Old Testament and in the New Testament and the various promises of God by which God revealed his healing power proving His faithfulness. God has not changed. He says, for I am the lord, I change not' (Mal 3:60). In the gospels, the work of physicians on the basis of creation is recognized (Mk 2:17; Lk 4:23), but much more is said about miraculous healing and healing on the basis of redemption. Right through the Bible, from Genesis to Revelation, one can see God who is anxious to manifest His healing power, both among His own children and the heathens.

8.1. Understanding on Healing in the Old Testament

The OT provides the proper background for a Christian understanding of the concept of healing. And the basic point is made that God is the healer of his people (Ex 15:22-26). God speaks of himself as their healer. This refers primarily to physical sustenance, but it points to the more encompassing concept of God sustaining his people in an eternal relationship with himself. Therefore the writer trying to have glance through the Bible, starting from the Book of Genesis, gathering some of the healings wrought by God without any form of medical aid.

8.2. Understanding on Healing in the New Testament

The New Testament Gospels document numerous miraculous healings performed by Jesus, demonstrating his compassion and authority over physical and spiritual afflictions. These miracles served to reveal his identity as the Son of God, bringing hope to those who were marginalized, suffering, or oppressed. Jesus healed a wide range of people, from lepers and the blind to the paralyzed and demon-possessed, showcasing his power to bring wholeness and restoration in every aspect of life. His miracles were acts of love and mercy that fulfilled people's immediate needs while also pointing to a deeper spiritual transformation.

In the Gospel accounts, Jesus' healing ministry is often connected with faith. Many instances highlight the faith of the person being healed or of those interceding on their behalf. For example, in Mark's Gospel, the healing of the paralytic lowered through the roof emphasizes both the faith of his friends and Jesus' authority to forgive sins, tying physical healing to spiritual renewal. Similarly, the healing of the woman with the issue of blood illustrates how personal faith in Jesus' power brings restoration, even when cultural barriers and isolation stand in the way.

Beyond individual healing, Jesus' miracles symbolized the broader purpose of his mission: to bring liberation, restoration, and hope to a broken world. His actions were not just isolated acts of kindness but were signs of the coming of God's kingdom, where suffering, sickness, and sin have no power. Each healing points to the ultimate hope of a future where all pain and suffering are removed, reflecting Jesus' role as the one who mends lives, restores dignity, and promises an eternal, healed life for all who believe.

8.3. Emphases of the Gospel Writers on Healing

The four Gospels in the New Testament document numerous miracles performed by Jesus, particularly his healings of the sick who sought him. Though these accounts include historical elements, the Gospels were not primarily written as detailed histories or biographies; rather, they were intended to inspire faith in Jesus Christ as the Messiah. Each Gospel writer portrays Jesus' life and ministry from a distinct perspective, with unique emphases on his healing works.

Matthew highlights Jesus' healings as a fulfillment of Old Testament prophecy, underscoring his identity as the promised Messiah. Mark, with a focus on action and immediacy, often depicts Jesus' healings as powerful acts of compassion, demonstrating his authority over sickness and evil. Luke, the physician, emphasizes Jesus' deep compassion for marginalized and suffering people, presenting him as the healer for all humanity. John, meanwhile, focuses on healing miracles as "signs" that reveal Jesus' divine nature, encouraging belief in him as the Son of God. Together, the Gospel writers offer a rich and varied portrait of Jesus' healing ministry, inviting readers to deepen their faith in his redemptive power.[20]

8.4. Healing in the Life of Jesus Christ

For Jesus, healing was a profound expression of God's compassion toward both the sick and the sinful. His healings were not simply acts of mercy; they were integral to his proclamation of the Good News. Through each healing, Jesus revealed God's love and care, offering people both

[20] James Harpur, *The Miracles of Jesus* (New York: The Reader's Digest Association, Inc., 1997), 7-8.

physical restoration and a glimpse of spiritual renewal. Healing became a sign that God's kingdom was breaking into the world, demonstrating that God's grace was accessible to all who sought it.

Moreover, Jesus' healings were part of his active struggle against the forces of evil. In healing those oppressed by sickness and demonic forces, he confronted the brokenness and suffering that had taken hold of the world. His miracles displayed his authority over both natural and supernatural forces, revealing his power to overcome darkness and liberate humanity. Each act of healing pointed to a larger victory over the powers that sought to harm and enslave.

Ultimately, Jesus' healings were only the first step toward the final defeat of evil. His ministry set the stage for his ultimate act of salvation on the cross, where he would decisively overcome sin and death. His healings offered a foretaste of the complete restoration promised to those who would believe, embodying God's promise of eternal wholeness and liberation from all suffering in the life to come.

8.4.1. Jesus is the Man of Healer

Jesus is the great Physician or He is the man of Healer throughout the four Gospels it is very clear. Jesus performed a variety of miracles, Healings are the most numerous type of miracle and healing was a central activity of Jesus in the Gospels. The activity of Jesus as a healer is distinctive in two ways, one is the degree to which healing was central to or typical of his ministry and second, his unmediated exercise of the saving power of God. He did not ask God to intervene on behalf of the sick, but pronounced healing directly, in speech acts that assumed his possession of divine authority to do so.

Jesus heals the person using word, touch, or technique, a cure occurs suddenly and visibly and onlookers express amazement and wonder.[21] Jesus heals every sickness and disease, no matter what the cause. If it is caused by sin, Jesus heals it. If it is caused by an evil spirit, Jesus heals it.[22] He broke the yoke of Satan's oppression wherever He found it.[23] The blood of Jesus also has the power to heal any man or woman who comes to him with faith in the blood covenant.[24]

---

[21] Kris D' Atri, *Health and Healing in the New Testament* (New York: Baker Book House, 1976), 45.

[22] John Hagee, *The Power to Heal* (Texas: Horticultural Printers 1991), 43.

[23] Gloria Copeland, *God's Will for your Healing* (KCP Publication, 1987), 21.

[24] David R. Nichols, *The Healing Presence of Jesus* (Hyderabad: A.P Bible College, 2003), 4.

8.4.2. Healing is an Important Part of Jesus Christ's Ministry

In the ministry of Jesus of Nazareth, healing the sick plays a part of primary importance. The first is that healing is a gift, which is given by our loving heavenly Father. The compassion that Jesus showed during His ministry on the earth is the expression of the nature of our Father's mercy and compassion for His children. The second issue is this: physical healing is one of the signs of the Kingdom of God. When God the Father wanted the fullness of His Kingdom to be known, He demonstrated it. One of the signs of this heavenly kingdom is the healing of bodies. Jesus did not expect people to believe His message of salvation and deliverance without proof. That's why He cast out demons and healed the sick and weak bodies of many people. Often in His teaching Jesus links these two aspects of the task He came to fulfill on earth, and which consists in "destroying the works of Satan" (1 John 3:8).

In all the healing miracles the healing took place all of a sudden and it caused amazement and wonder among the spectators. These sudden healing manifested God's glory revealed through Jesus.[25] And also it is only a step toward the final defeat of evil. The total victory over Satan takes place only with death of Jesus on the cross and his resurrection on the third day by the power of his cross and resurrection.[26] Jesus' ministry was spent in serving people by preaching, teaching and healing them. He mixed with all sorts of people.[27] The healing ministry of Jesus was continued through his commissioning and sending out of the twelve (Matt. 10:1-5; Mark 6:7-13; Lk 9:1-6) and the seventy (Lk 10:9).[28] Therefore, It is evident that in the ministry of Jesus, His work of physical healing plays a role of first importance, not apart from or inferior to His work, but parallel with it.[29]

8.4.3. Jesus Healed Both Physical and Spiritual Sickness

In the first instance, Jesus was firmly convinced of his Father's purpose for human wholeness and salvation (Jn 3.16, 10.10).[30] Jesus was a healer of body, mind and soul. Jesus saw wholeness as the wellbeing of the total person. There was no separation of body and soul because Jesus expressed

[25] K. K. George, *Jesus Christ Life and Teachings* (Thiruvalla: Christava Sahitya Samithi, 2002), 65.

[26] Bridget Meehan, *The Healing Power of Prayer* (Mumbai: St Paul's, 2005), 19.

[27] Margaret Baxter, *Jesus Christ: His Life and His Church* (Delhi: ISPCK, 2003), 30.

[28] Walter A. Elwell, 'Healing,' *Evangelical Dictionary of Theology* (Michigan: Baker Academic, 2001), 540.

[29] Bernard Martin, *The Healing Ministry in the Church* (Richmond: John Knox Press, 1960), 20.

[30] George Arthur Buttrick, 'Healing,' *The Interpreter's Dictionary*, 546.

them as something bound together in a living unity. Jesus cares for the soul as well as the body. Both sin and sickness came into the world through the fall of the human race. Therefore, the healing of both is provided in the redemption of humankind.[31]

9. The Meaning of Jesus' Healing

The healings performed by Jesus reflected God's transformative power to restore lives and renew hope. Each act of healing went beyond physical relief; it reconnected individuals to their communities and offered them a new sense of worth and belonging. Jesus' healings were deeply personal, often reaching those marginalized by society, and they conveyed God's inclusive love. His miracles embodied the message that God's care was not distant or theoretical but present and active in the lives of ordinary people. Through healing, Jesus unveiled the closeness of God's kingdom, showing that liberation and wholeness were within reach for all.

9.1. Teaching about Faith

Faith is the most recorded quality connected with the impartation of healing power. Jesus seemed to be more able to heal in the presence of faith, as illustrated by his experience in his own home town (Lk 4:23-28 and at Nazareth Mk 6:1-6; Lk 4:23-28). He was especially moved by the "great faith" of the centurion (Mt 8:5-13). He observed supernaturally the faith of the "stretcher carriers" as they carried the paralytic and lowered him into the room where Jesus was preaching (Mk 2:1ff). He was always willing to heal those who came to him with faith (Mt 8:1-4, 8:5-13).[32] Many of the healing cases show that one of the essential elements in the acts of healing accomplished by Jesus Christ was faith in Him.

9.2. Jesus' Compassion

In His earthly ministry, He was often challenged by pain, sickness and disease in every conceivable form widow at Nain who lost her only son (Lk 7:11-20), He had compassion toward the two blind men at Jericho and so he gave them sight (Mt 20:34), when he crossed the sea of Galilee to a lovely place he saw a big crowd and had compassion on them and healed their sick (Mt14:14). These show that, the reason for the healing miracles was Jesus' compassion towards people who were suffering. In every case He was moved with compassion.[33] One of the main motives of Jesus' for healing people would be his compassion for the sick. He met people where

---

[31] T. L. Osborn, *Biblical Healing* (Tulsa: Global Publishers, 2004), 8.

[32] Tony Cauchi, *Healing in the Gospel* (Revival Library, 2011)

[33] Kathry N. Kuthlman, *Victory in Jesus and the Lord's Healing Touch* (Pittsburgh: The Kathryn Kuhlaman Foundation), 26.

they were and He took them as he found them.[34] Right from the outset Jesus compassion is highlighted at a motivating factor in Jesus ministry of healing.

9.3. Breaking Down the Social Barriers

The healing miracles of Jesus Christ were a way as to incur the anger of the Jewish leaders. He does not have to touch the leaper to cleanse him, but He does so purposefully to show that he is unconcerned with the ritual taboos that separated classes of people (Mk 1:14). In another occasion He sends ten lepers to the priest for their cures to be confirmed, but only a Samaritan returns to give thanks. Jesus declares that one clean, leaving open the question of what happened to others nine (Lk 17:11-19). Here it is clear that the despised, outcast Samaritan is the hero the social barriers Judaism had erected is being destroyed. And also in (Mk 7:24-30) Jesus praises a Syro-Phoenician woman for her faith and heals her daughter, demonstrating that his saving power is not to be limited to Israel. In each of these instances Jesus is preparing the way for the establishment of a broadly inclusive religious movement not bounded by barriers of race, sex or nationality?

9.4. Teaching about Sin

He taught forgiveness of sin and healing together. Sometimes He healed first, then forgave sin (Lk 17:9 and John 5:14). Other times He forgave sins first, then healed (Mark 2:1-12). Before healing the paralytic, Jesus tells him that his sins are forgiven. Then He commands him to rise and stresses that this act of healing is a proof that He has the power of forgiving sins. After healing the man who had been an invalid for thirty eight years, Jesus tells him, stop sinning or something worse may happen to you (Jn 5:14). Here Jesus presumes the common Jewish view that illness was a punishment for sin. Sometimes healings undo a punishment for sin other times there is no relation between health and obedience, or between sin and sickness, beyond the general observation that all evil came into the world through original sin. The intention of the healing miracles is to display Jesus authority to forgive sin of mankind.

9.5. It is Signs of the Kingdom and of the Messiah

Healing and the preaching of the Kingdom are tied together in Jesus ministry. In gospel of Luke it has mentioned that after healing the sick and says to them the kingdom of God has come near to you (Lk 10:9). The Presence of the Kingdom is graphically demonstrated when the imprisoned John the Baptist sends his disciples to Jesus (Lk 7:19-23).[35] When Jesus

[34] Derek Prime, *Jesus His Life and Ministry* (London: Thomas Nelson Publishers, 1995), 51.

[35] John Edmiston, *Healing* (AIBI International Publishers, 2010), 14.

extends help, the kingdom of God is achieved at a specific point each partial victory is a foretaste and guarantee of the final victory. He conquers, and nothing can resist Him even though He is put to death, the kingdom of God comes thereby.[36] Jesus saw healing as a demonstration of the real Presence of the Kingdom that would encourage those who struggled to believe.

10. The Kinds of Healing

Jesus' healings in the Gospels reveal a variety of methods, each emphasizing different aspects of his compassionate and powerful ministry. These methods include healing by touch, by faith, by prayer, and by word, each highlighting unique interactions with those he healed and underscoring diverse expressions of God's power at work. Healing by touch demonstrates Jesus' willingness to reach out physically to the afflicted, often to those considered untouchable. Healing by faith emphasizes the trust and belief of those who sought him, where their faith became a key element in their restoration. Healing by prayer illustrates Jesus' connection with the Father, showing dependence on divine will in bringing about healing. Healing by word reflects the authority of Jesus' spoken commands, where even his voice could banish sickness and affliction. Together, these types of healing paint a multifaceted picture of Jesus' ministry, revealing both his approachability and his authority over every form of human suffering.

10.1. The Healing by Touch

There is power in the touch of Jesus to heal all physical and the spiritual infirmities cause by human depravity and the effects of sin. The idea that a touch of Christ is enough to accomplish a healing miracle or a resurrection from the death occurs several times in the gospels.[37] Sometimes Jesus Christ allows the sick to come and touch Him, either His own person or His garment (Mk 5:25-34; 3:10). On other occasions, Jesus Himself touches the sick (Matt 9:27-31). When the sick with divers diseases were brought unto Him at sunset He laid His hands on every one of the sick and healed them (Lk 4:40). Physical disease, blindness, disturbed minds, guilt-burdened souls, sorrowful hearts all were miraculously healed by the touch of Jesus Christ.[38]

---

[36] Gerhard Kittel, 'νΙαοµια,' *Theological Dictionary of the New Testament* (Michigan: Wm. B. Eerdmans Publishing Company, 1965), 213.

[37] Pieter J. Lalleman, *Healing by a Mere Touch as a Christian Concept* (N.p.: N.p., 1997), 354.

[38] Charles L. Allen, *The Touch of the Master's Hand* (USA: Felming H. Revell Company, n.y), 9.

10.2. The Healing by Faith

In Jesus healing miracles there were occasions when his opponents demanded healing miracles as the condition for their believing in him. Jesus consistently refused to respond positively to such demands.[39] Jesus stressed the role of faith as the key to the healing. All the books on healing the New Testament emphasize the role that faith plays in healing. "Go in peace, your faith has made you whole", is a constant saying of Jesus.[40] If the sick can be led to fix their eyes in faith upon the Mighty Healer, one shall see wonderful results. It will bring life to the body and to the soul.

10.3. The Healing by Prayer

Prayer is the one of the special theme throughout the Bible. The four Gospels have emphasis number of times that Jesus prayed. For instance, Jesus once healed a leper. This event drew crowds that came to hear and to be healed (Lk 5:15), but Jesus chose to withdraw into the wilderness to pray. One must suppose from this that prayer was an essential element in the ministry of Jesus. In another event that He was talking to a massive congregation and when He pronounced a healing prayer they began to get well (Mt 8:16).[41]

10.4. The Healing by Word

Speaking the right words was another important factor in the healings Jesus accomplished. In his ministry Jesus took the power of words with utmost seriousness.[42] Usually the words used for healing were in connection with casting out an unclean spirit. Sometimes he healed with his word and not his hands.

Healing reported in the OT are few compared with those of Gospel narratives. In general, it is true to say that the healing is not fundamentally different from that of other miracles. Both in the OT and NT miracles in particular healing are the display of God's power over the evil or its effects upon individuals. The cure of illness was often considered miraculous and obedience to God in both the OT and the NT. Physical healing is a dramatic demonstration of God's power and love for human beings. It also reveals the depth of his involvement in the lives of people. However in the OT and as well as in the NT divine healing begins with searching of heart and confession

[39] Brian C. Wintle, *Synoptic Studies A Primer* (Bangalore: Theological Book Trust, 2007), 66.

[40] Francis Mac Nutt, *Healing* (New York: Bantam Books, 1980), 99.

[41] John Hagee, *The Power to Heal* (Dallas: Hagww Ministries, 1991), 41.

[42] Thomas and Sharon Neufer Emswiler, *Wholeness in Worship* (New York: Harper and Row, 1980), 21.

of sins through the response of person faith in God. Because God is the main source of healing (I am the Lord, who heals you Ex 15:26), when a person cry to God or call the name of God, the Lord's has gracious response for mankind to receive healing, it shows the love of God has displayed in the lives of people in OT and NT too.

11. Theological Significance of Miracles in the Gospel of Luke

Luke has the same number of healing stories as Matthew (twenty-five), but is far more specific in his accounts of them. When Jesus Christ healed the sick and raised the dead, He manifested His sovereign power over the spiritual poverty of depraved humanity.[43] It also includes five healing miracles, the raising of the son of the widow of Nain (7:11-16), woman bowed together (13:11-16), ten lepers (17:12-19) and the Malchus Ear (22:50, 51), these were not recorded by the other Gospel writers Matthew, Mark and John. However, more details of it, given below with the event, place, character, and its theological significance.

11.1. The Raising of the Son of the Widow of Nain (Lk 7:11-16)

One such instance of this is the raising of a widow's son a narrative of tremendous importance in the understanding the nature of God and God's redemptive action through Jesus. This miracle falls under the category of resuscitation, a specific kind of miracle which is fairly rare in biblical literature. The account of resuscitation of the son of a widow of Nain is unique to Luke because it has no parallel in other Gospels.

Luke emphasizes that, when Jesus sees widow of Nain situation, "His heart went out to her" (7:13). Three times Luke inserts the feminine pronoun into this single verse. Jesus' compassion is fueled by the widow's plight. In the ancient world much more than in contemporary Western settings, it was the case that people's children were their retirement. Jesus' compassionate restoration of this widow's son may have meant the difference between survival and destitution. This evidently the first time the Lord had restored a dead person to life. As a result, great fear came on all the people. They acknowledged that Jesus was a great Prophet, affirming that "God had visited His people."[44] The conquest of death in this instance served several purposes, that is; it united a mother and her son, and it brought glory to God.

The conclusion to this healing story is important to Luke's theological message is; when the crowds saw this there were filled with awe and praise God, saying, "God has come to help his people" (7:16). Jesus' healing

[43] W. E. Best, *Studies in the Person and Work of Jesus Christ* (USA: South Belt Assembly of Christ, 1975), 150.

[44] G. Coleman Luck, *Luke: The Gospel of the Son of Man* (Chicago: Moody Press, 1960), 63.

actions point to God's restoration now begun in Jesus. Luke frequently highlights responses of the crowds to Jesus' healing activity. Having power to raise the physically dead, Christ is well able, in virtue of His own death and resurrection, to raise the newness of life those who are dead in their sin and trespasses.

11.2. The Healing of the Woman 'Bowed Together' (Lk 13:11-16)

This story, unique to Luke's Gospel, explains what it precedes and introduces what it follows. It is a healing story which leads into a conflict between the leader of the synagogue and Jesus and which culminates in a pronouncement by Jesus.[45] It is interesting that woman condition was caused by a demon. There are many different symptoms mentioned in the Bible that were caused by demon activity (Mat 9:32-33), dumbness (Mat 12:22), blindness (Mat 17:14-18), seizures (Lk 4:33, 8:26), mental disorders, insanity, and abnormal strength. This of course does not mean that these conditions are always demonic in source. But the Bible clearly says that this condition was. This should teach us that Satan is a real and very busy enemy. Over and over it is recorded that Jesus cast out demons of all kinds. He came to defeat Satan and to make him powerless against believers, and he clearly demonstrated his ability to do this while here on earth.

While Jesus was teaching, He noticed a pitiful woman in the synagogue. Cripple for eighteen years, she was bent over and unable to walk erect. This woman graphically portrayed Israel's condition in the sight of God. The law has been given to that nation to reveal the demands of the holiness of God so that people might walk uprightly before Him. But Israel had ignored the law, and their walk was displeasing to Him. But that the nation's condition was not hopeless is seen in what Christ did for this cripple. Calling her to Himself, Christ set her free from her infirmity. He touches her and immediately her stooped, bent body was made straight so that she could stand erect again. Christ has been calling the nation to Himself, even as He had called this woman to Himself. He offered to make the nation whole again so that they could walk uprightly before God. But the nation would not come to Him. Thus this was a revelation of Israel's need and an indication of how that need could be met.[46]

11.3. The Healing of the Ten Lepers (Lk 17:12-19)

The healing story of ten lepers is unique to Luke's Gospel, because the number of the lepers has been increased from one to ten. The healing miracle

---

[45] I. H. Marshall, *The Gospel of Luke* (Grand Rapids: W. B. Eerdman's Publishing Co., 1978), 556.

[46] J. Dwight Pentecost, *The Words and Works of Jesus Christ: A Study of the Life of Christ*, 329-321.

is effected at a distance[47] a Samaritan has been included in the leper group. Luke made a place for the story in his narrative to show that an incident in Jesus' own ministry had foreshadowed the acceptance of the gospel by Gentiles and its rejection by Jews.

There is one lesson in the exchange between Jesus and the Samaritan man. God's grace is extended to all. God blesses humanity in a general way, but only the responsive who appreciate what he has done in Christ receive his full blessing and acceptance. Among the ten former lepers, only the Samaritan hears the comforting words "your faith has made you well." His gratitude has revealed his faith. Jesus commends him for his response and assures him that the appreciation he expressed is also appreciated. God is thanked for his deliverance (Ps 35:18), for loving us and being faithful (Ps 52:9; 107:8), for hearing our cry (Ps 118:21), for safe arrival after a long, arduous journey (Acts 28:15), for other believers and for the testimony of their faith (Rom 1:8), for the gift of salvation that enables one not to sin (Rom 6:17), for delivering us from our tendency to sin (Rom 7:25), for the spiritual gift of being able to address God (1 Cor 14:18), for resurrection hope (1 Cor 15:57), for testimony, deliverance and victory in the midst of persecution (2 Cor 2:14), for the support of a colleague in ministry (2 Cor 8:16), for other believers (Phil 1:3; Col 1:3; 2 Tim 1:3; Philem 4), for those who respond to God's Word (1 Thess 2:13), for being able to serve others for God (1 Tim 1:12) and for his attributes (Rev 4:9). Therefore, Salvation is effected by one's continued profession of faith in Jesus.[48]

Theologically viewing that, this incident Peter failed to understand the sweep of the entire plan of God. He did not fail to hear the change in procedures but tried to put instructions, which were still for the future, into operation before the proper time. A similar mistakes is being made today by Christians who try to put into operation now ethics that apply to the coming kingdom. Its ethical requirements focus mainly, though not exclusively, on helping and relating to the body of Christ (Gla 6:10). But in the coming kingdom all people will live in a friendly, a righteous world and ethical principles will be concerned with all humankind.

Balancing is the key idea for followers of Christ today. Providing for the servant of God is entirely in order. The life of faith does not exclude purses and swords (though only in self-defense, never to commit murder). Insisting rights may be proper (Acts 16:37). But it is also necessary to suffer wrong,

---

[47] T. S. Abraham, *General Survey of New Testament History* (Kerala: K. E. Abraham Foundation,), 71.

[48] Robert J. Karris, *Invitation to Luke: A Commentary on the Gospel of Luke with Complete text from the Jerusalem Bible* (Garden City, New York: A Division of Doubleday & Company, 1991), 199.

as our Lord did, and not to insist on our rights as he did not (I Pet 2:21-23).[49] Though all four gospel writers narrated this story, only Luke recorded the actual miracle of restoring Malchus's ear to normalcy. His being a doctor undoubtedly accounts for this detail.

Like Matthew, Luke commences with birth narratives which relate angelophanies and the virginal conception. Gabriel, in fact, draws a direct link between this generation by the Holy Spirit and Jesus' identity as "Son of God" (Lk 1:35). Luke makes use of the miracle stories in the frame work of his history of salvation and with a missionary aim. He depicts Jesus as the messianic prophet who brings deliverance and salvation. To analyze Jesus' miracles, they can be categorized into five groups based on their thematic focus and narrative context:

1. **Miracles in the Early Galilean Phase (Lk 4:14–5:2):** This phase includes three miracles that reveal both the deliverance and salvation Jesus brings and the dramatic rejection he encounters. These miracles set the tone for the nature of Jesus' ministry: one that meets human needs with divine power but also faces significant opposition.
2. **Salvation in Jewish Towns (Lk 5:12–7:17):** In this segment, Jesus performs miracles that showcase salvation offered to Jewish communities. The series culminates in Jesus' response to John the Baptist's emissaries *(Lk 7:18–23)*, reaffirming his role as the Messiah through acts of healing and deliverance as signs of God's kingdom.
3. **Salvation for the Apostles and Christological Revelation:** These miracles provide insight into the identity of Jesus and the apostles' growing understanding of him. Through these acts, Jesus not only delivers individuals from physical and spiritual afflictions but also reveals his divine authority, shaping the apostles' faith and comprehension of his messianic role.
4. **Miracles on the Journey to Jerusalem (Lk 11:14–18:43):** This group includes five miracles performed as Jesus journeys toward Jerusalem. These miracles embody the salvation Jesus offers and foreshadow his impending sacrifice, emphasizing themes of healing, repentance, and the invitation to follow him as he approaches his final mission.
5. **Healing during the Passion (Lk 22:47–53):** During his arrest, Jesus heals the servant of the high priest, a profound act that highlights his compassion even in moments of betrayal and violence. This

[49] Charles C. Ryrie, *The Miracles of Our Lord,* 175.

miracle underscores Jesus' commitment to reconciliation and mercy, even as he faces his own suffering and death.

Luke's presentation of Jesus' miracles largely corresponds to those of Mark and Matthew, yet there are interesting modifications. All of the Markan miracles appear in sequence in Luke save the cursing of the fig tree (cf. Lk 13:6–9) and the five miracle stories within Luke's so-called great omission (Mk 6:45–8:26). Luke also included a healing (Lk 7:1–10) and an exorcism (Lk 11:14) belonging to the Q material. And finally, Luke contains seven specific miracles unique to this Gospel, including the notice concerning the exorcism of seven demons from Mary Magdalene (Lk 8:2) and a report of the healing of the ear of the high priest's servant (Lk 22:51; cf. also 5:1–11; 7:11–17; 13:10–17; 14:1–6; 17:11–19). It has long been recognized that Luke redacted his sources to emphasize the praying of Jesus, and twice this motif appears in Luke's miracle stories (Lk 5:16; 9:29; cf. 3:21).

12. Theology of Miracles

12.1. The Kingdom of God: The miracles in Luke are central to Jesus' proclamation of the Kingdom of God. They serve as signs that God's reign has broken into human history through Jesus. In Luke 11:20, Jesus declares, "But if I drive out demons by the finger of God, then the kingdom of God has come upon you." The miracles reveal the power of the Kingdom and its liberating effect on those oppressed by sin, sickness, and evil.

In Mark the miracles are closely connected with the proclamation of the good news of the kingdom and with the person of Jesus. There are epiphanies of his person and mysterious power. He shows Jesus as the eschatological Saviour who destroy the kingdom of Satan and establish the kingdom of God. Miracles are signs because the demon himself is a sign. There are three stages can be discerned in the economy of the miracles. In the first (MK. 1:14-37) Jesus makes himself known to the crowds.

12.2. Compassion and Inclusivity: A distinctive feature of Luke's presentation of miracles is the emphasis on Jesus' compassion for the marginalized, including women, Gentiles, and the poor. For example, the healing of the bleeding woman (Lk 8:43-48) and the raising of the widow's son (Lk 7:11-17) highlight Jesus' concern for those who are socially vulnerable. These miracles affirm that the Kingdom of God is open to all, regardless of social status or ethnic background, reflecting Luke's broader theme of God's universal salvation.

12.3. Faith and Discipleship: In Luke, miracles often occur in the context of faith. Jesus frequently commends individuals for their faith, as in the case of the centurion whose servant is healed (Luke 7:9) and the sinful woman who anoints Jesus' feet (Lk 7:50). The miracles invite a response of faith, leading to deeper discipleship. This is exemplified in Peter's call to follow Jesus after the miraculous catch of fish (Lk 5:1-11), where the miracle leads to Peter's recognition of Jesus' divine authority and his willingness to leave everything behind.

12.4. Salvation and Restoration: Miracles in Luke are not merely acts of physical healing; they symbolize the broader theme of spiritual restoration and salvation. The healing of the paralytic (Lk 5:17-26), where Jesus first forgives the man's sins before healing his body, illustrates the connection between physical healing and spiritual salvation. Jesus' miracles thus function as visible manifestations of His mission "to seek and to save the lost" (Lk 19:10).

12.5. Miracles and Mission: Exorcisms and healings are a part of his mission and the establishment of the kingdom. The second stage Jesus devotes himself to disciple in order to form them and prepare them to widen the field of his action. He sends to preach and gives them power to cast out demons (Mk. 3:14). The third stage is dominated by the martyrdom of John the Baptist and the two multiplications of loves (Mk 6:6-8:30). The food given represents the abundance of messianic blessings; interprets the eschatological banquet and the Eucharist which prepares the way for it. Miracles are illustrations of Christ's power over typical diseases like leprosy, paralysis and so on. They show Christ to be all powerful over the realm of nature, the spiritual world and the power of sin. They further show that Christ is the conqueror of death as well as the restorer of disordered and defective faculties. The miracles of Jesus have a two fold value, a physical and spiritual, a temporal and an eternal.

Summary of Findings

The miracles in the Gospel of Luke are not only demonstrations of Jesus' divine power but also profound expressions of His compassion and mission. They point to the arrival of the Kingdom of God, where the forces of evil, sickness, and death are overthrown, and people are restored to wholeness. The miracles reveal the inclusivity of Jesus' ministry, extending God's grace to those on the margins of society. They also invite faith and discipleship, calling individuals to respond to Jesus' authority and follow Him. Ultimately, the miracles in Luke serve as signs of God's salvation, offering a glimpse of the restoration and hope that Jesus brings to all who believe in Him.

Throughout this chapter it is very much clear about the healing ministry of Jesus Christ with the biblical terms that were used by the Luke. In Lord's ministry the physical and the spiritual were closely associated. And He has shown that, for Him, the demands of physical life are worthy of His concern as well as the spiritual needs of the soul. His compassion and divine power embrace the whole man. In all the healings, compassion and love always presented. Divine healing is not only for some people or only some diseases but it is a promise of God for his children's to glorify his name. But Luke makes it clear that faith is the essential element not magic (8:48), or not by any traditional practices. No matter what diseases is or no matter what cast is. Jesus is willing to heal all mankind even his enemies too (Lk 22:51). Faith, obedience and God's mighty power is the key for healing. The God's grace is extended to all. Jesus is the healer, healing in him, healing in his name, healing in his word. Moreover with special emphasis on the four, Jesus' healing stores have played their unique theological significance is that Jesus healing activities were never effects only the body it also restores the soul. It is always about the whole person, about its again assuming the form that it has received from God. It is all because real faith, trust, obedience, submits to His will and expects mercies from Lord Jesus Christ.

7

Luke's Model of Discipleship and Leadership
Lessons from the Gospel of Luke

Introduction

Discipleship is one of the core Christian beliefs and it is grounded in biblical, theological, and historical contexts. Disciple-making concept is echoed both in the Old Testament and the New Testament. Jesus spent about thirty-three and half years on the earth. During the last three and half years, He was intensely involved in the task of discipleship; He called twelve people and taught, trained and influenced them through His own life and teachings. Undoubtedly, Jesus was the greatest disciple maker and powerful model of making disciples in history. Jesus before ascended to Heaven, He commanded to His disciples to go and make disciples of all nations and baptize them in the name of the Father, of the Son and the Holy Spirit and teaching everything He taught them.

In the Gospel of Luke, discipleship and leadership are intricately woven into the fabric of Jesus' ministry, presenting a model that continues to inspire and challenge believers today. Luke's narrative reveals a unique emphasis on Jesus' interactions with His disciples and the broader community, offering insights into His call for transformative discipleship. Through parables, teachings, and practical examples, Luke highlights qualities such as humility, compassion, and sacrificial love as essential for true followers and leaders within the Kingdom of God. This chapter explores Luke's portrayal of discipleship and leadership, focusing on the characteristics and actions that define a faithful disciple and leader, drawing out lessons for contemporary

Christian life and ministry. It examines how Luke's themes of inclusivity, servant leadership, and commitment to God's mission shape an understanding of discipleship that transcends cultural boundaries and endures through time.

The importance and urgency of making disciples remain unchanged. God has given an incredible plan to make disciples of all nations with the preaching of the Gospel. Somehow the value and the effect of the concept of discipleship is not fully understood and followed in the churches to the extent they should have been. As a result, disciples of all nations has been rather slow. It is the time that Christians to fully understand God's plan of discipleship.[1] In addition, "there is a discipleship deficiency in most churches resulting in a lack of transformation."[2] The church's loss of focus of its primary responsibility, and its shoddy attitude in raising true disciples has culminated in the loss of its vibrancy and relevance in the society.[3] This paper, therefore, accentuates definition and development of discipleship concept; Jesus' teachings on discipleship in the Gospels; the issues and challenges of discipleship-making in India; and the implication of Jesus' teachings to disciple making in the 21st century.

1. Definition of Leadership and Discipleship

The word leader means "a person who leads commands or preside a group organization or country."[4] Leadership in the Gospel of Luke can be defined as the exercise of influence, authority, and responsibility in a manner that aligns with the teachings and example of Jesus Christ. It involves guiding and serving others with humility, compassion, and a deep sense of responsibility, all within the context of responding to God's call. Regarding leadership, Charles R. Swandoll says "Leadership is not optional; it is essential for motivation and direction. Essential for evaluation and accomplishment. It is more than not elusive. In the context of influence it is an "inspiring influence."[5]

In Webster's Universal Encyclopedia Dictionary, describes a disciple as "a pupil or follower of any teacher or school of religion, learning, art, etc."[6] Christian disciple follows Jesus. A Christian disciple is one who loves God with everything one has. A Christian disciple, by God's grace, becomes more

---

[1] John William, *Discipleship* (Chennai: IICM, 1997), 9.

[2] Eric Geiger, Michael Kelley, and Philip Nation, *Transformational Discipleship: How People Really Grow* (Nashville: B&H, 2012), Kindle, 16.

[3] Aubrey Malphurs, *A New Kind of Church: Understanding Models of Ministry for the 21st Century* (Grand Rapids: Baker Books, 2007), 75.

[4] Judy Pearsal, *Oxford Dictionary* (New York: Oxford University Press, 1999), 806.

[5] Charles R. Swandoll, *Leadership* (Texas: Word Books, 1985), 38.

[6] Merriam Webster, *Webster's Universal Encyclopedia Dictionary* (London: Barnes and Noble Books, 2009), 206.

and more like Christ through a life of faith and obedience. Discipleship in the Gospel of Luke refers to the process of following and learning from Jesus Christ as a devoted student and follower. It involves not only a commitment to Jesus as a teacher and Lord but also an active and transformative journey of faith, growth, and service. The ability of management to make sound decisions and inspire others to perform well. Effective leaders are able to set and achieve challenging goals, to take swift and decisive action even in difficult situations, to outperform their competition, to take calculated risks and to persevere in the face of failure. Strong communication skills, self-confidence, the ability to manage others and a willingness to embrace change also characterize good leaders. "Leadership is the capacity and well to rally men and women to a common purpose, and the character which inspire confidence."[7]

The word "Discipleship" does not occur in the New Testament. "The idea of disciple, however, is expressed by the term disciple some 261 times, with the references occurring in the Gospels and the book of Acts. To make someone a disciple is mainly indicated by the verb ματηετευο, although the word disciple ("to follow after") is also used some 90 times mainly in the Gospels and Acts."[8] The suffix "ship" in the word the exclusive use of the word "disciple" in the Gospels and book of Acts has led some to raise the question whether the term may not be the best to use for believers today. If discipleship is "derived from the Old English "disciple," meaning "the state of," "contained in," or 'condition' The usage of the word ματηthς and its verb, however, makes the meaning of the term discipleship, which is derived from them, a little difficult to ascertain. When ματηthς is used in an educational, intellectual sense (Matt 10:24; 13:52), discipleship may be understood as the process of being educated by a teacher.

Discipleship is very important theme in the bible, it is clearly explains about this concept. Myers confirms by adding that "becoming a disciple of Jesus in general meant a transformation of a person's lifestyle."[9] Jesus made no secret of what He intended for His disciples. He made it clear that they were to deny themselves and to take up His cross and to follow Him (Matt 16:24). He also mentioned that to be a disciple meant to be a servant δουλος of others (Matt 23.11). Nancy Guthrie argues that "the only privilege that could be claimed by any of His disciples was that of service and sacrifice. Furthermore, His disciples were also to be obedient and to follow His

---

[7] J. Oswald Sanders, *Spiritual Leadership* (Secunderbad: O.M Books, 1967), 28.

[8] James G. Samra, *A Biblical View of Discipleship* (Bibliotheca Sacra 160), 2003), 219 220.

[9] Myers Ched, *Say to This Mountain: Mark's Story of Discipleship* (U.S.A: Orbis Books, 1996), 28.

example."[10] She concludes by stating that a disciple is an active follower of Jesus Christ and to further participate in His mission to the world.

2. Discipleship in Gospels

The word "disciple" occurs at least 230 times in the Gospels and 28 times in Acts. the Greek word μαθητής (mathētēs) is the root of our word mathematics, which means "thought accompanied by endeavor."[11] Disciples think and learn, but they also move beyond learning to doing the effort. Even in Jesus' time, disciples were those who were more than pupils in school, they were apprentices in the work of their master. The essence of the word disciple changed from the first time it is used in Matthew 5:1 to the last mention in Acts 21:16.

In the gospels, disciple already had a meaning before Jesus used the word. In the first century, the cultural understanding of a disciple was one who was more than just a learner; the disciple was also a "follower" (once again we see the connection between thinking and doing)."[12] Throughout the Greco-Roman world, great teachers were making disciples. Philosophers like Socrates had devoted followers who were trained under the guidance of an exemplary life. Disciples spent time with their master and became learning sponges, soaking up the teaching and example of the one from whom they were learning. Rabbis like Hillel and Shammai had disciples who learned how to interpret the Scriptures and relate them to life. "The Bible also tells us that there were disciples of the traditions of Moses (Jn 9:28) and that John the Baptist had disciples (Matt 9:14, 11:7, 14:2), some of whom joined Jesus' mission."[13]

At this juncture there are some very important distinctions that need to be made. This will be helpful in order to establish the principles that will define the working understanding of who a disciple is. Ogden urged that "a definition of discipling is important as the guiding vision for the nature of the discipling relationship. One must, therefore, have an appreciation for the different nuances of disciple as it is being used in the Bible."[14]

[10] Nancy Guthire, *Biblical Theology in Discipleship* (Carol Stream, IL: Tyandle Publishing House, 2007), 67.

[11] Gary C. Newton, *Growing Toward Spiritual Maturity* (Wheaton, IL: Evangelical Training Association, 1999), 15.

[12] Michael J. Wilkins, *The Concept of Disciple in Matthew's Gospel As Reflected in the Use of the Term Mathetes*, Novum Testamentum Supplements 59 (Leiden, The Netherlands: Brill Academic Publishers, 1988), 51.

[13] Bill Hull, *The Complete Book of Discipleship: On Being and Making Followers of Christ* (Colorado Springs: NavPress, 2006), 53-54.

[14] Greg Ogden, *Transforming Discipleship* (Downers Grove, IL: Inter Varsity Press, 2003), 130.

The study of discipleship in the New Testament will reveal clear similarities as well as differences. Malphurs underscored that "each New Testament author wrote to a specific audience with unique backgrounds and different needs."[15] This demanded the adaptation of the presentation of the gospel in a way that would meaningfully engage the various audiences. Longenecker pointed out that the various New Testament authors each had unique and characteristic ways of portraying authentic discipleship but, in spite of the variant approaches, there is still a certain "sense of center."[16]

The four Gospels, with the exception of the Gospel of Mark, used the word "disciple" to mean a believer who has confessed that Jesus is Lord, and a believer who came back to the church. However, as the church grew in hierarchical differentiation, the word "disciple" became ancient, and was replaced by "Christian" (Acts 11:26). In the Epistles, the word "disciple" disappeared and somewhat reappeared as the word "Saint." Why did the word "disciple" disappear. The word "disciple" had been used as a student who was learning secular wisdom in the Gentile areas, and the philosophers especially had been using this word for their followers."[17] Discipleship was practiced by Jesus (Matt 4:19). It was focused not on His teaching, but on His personality. So "being a disciple in Jesus Christ" means a holistic changed.

Biblical and Theological basis of the idea of discipleship is deeply rooted in New Testament writings. It can even be argued that discipleship is not an optional task for Biblical Christians. As one reads the New Testament it is clear that discipleship is the task of every believer and follower of Jesus Christ. While he was on earth, Jesus spent the majority of his time pouring his life into twelve young men. At the end of his time on earth Jesus commanded these men to go and make disciples. In Acts 2 "the Holy Spirit came down in a powerful way. On that day the church began to multiply and there is a beautiful picture of discipleship. The followers of Christ devoted themselves to the apostles teaching and fellowship, to the breaking of bread and prayers."[18] Acts 2:41 the early believers found themselves in discipleship.

2.1. Cost of Discipleship

The call is given, and it is immediately followed by the response of obedience. The disciples' response is an act of obedience, not a confession of

[15] Aubrey Malphurs, *Strategic Disciple Making: A Practical Tool for Successful Ministry* (Grand Rapids: Baker Books, 2009), 51.

[16] Richard N. Longenecker, *Patterns of Discipleship in the New Testament* (Grand Rapids, MI: Eerdmans, 1996), 6.

[17] John H. Oak, *Called to Awaken the Layman* (Seoul: Tyrannus Press, 1984), 98.

[18] John F. Walvoord and Roy B. Zuck, *The Bible Knowledge Commentary: New Testament edition* (Colorado Springs: Water Brook Press, 2000), 93.

faith in Jesus. How could the call so instantly prompt obedience? "The story is a stumbling block for the natural reason, and it is no wonder that anxious attempts have been made to separate the two events. Something must have happened in between, some psychological or historical event. Surely the publican must have known Jesus before, and that previous associate explains his readiness to hear the Master's call."[19] Unfortunately, our text is ruthlessly silent on this point, regarding the immediate sequence of call and response as a matter of crucial importance.[20]

It shows no interest in the psychological reasons behind a person's religious decisions. It is Jesus who calls, and as Bonhoeffer notes, this encounter testifies to the absolute, direct, and unaccountable authority of Jesus. No preliminaries are needed, and the only appropriate response is obedience to His call. Because Jesus is the Christ, He has the authority to call and to demand obedience to His word. "Jesus summons men to follow him not as a teacher or a pattern of the good life, but as the Christ, the Son of God. In this short text Jesus Christ and his claim are proclaimed to men. Not a word of praise is given to the disciple for his decision for Christ."[21] It is not the disciple who is to be contemplated, but the one who calls and His absolute authority. According to the text, there is no path to faith or discipleship other than obedience to the call of Jesus.

Discipleship means devotion to Christ, and, because Christ is the object of that devotion, it must take the form of discipleship. N. T. Wright says that "A theoretical Christology, a doctrinal system, a general religious knowledge on the subject of grace or on the forgiveness of sins, render discipleship surplus, and in fact they positively eliminate any idea of discipleship whatever, and are essentially inimical to the whole conception of following Christ."[22] With an abstract idea it is possible to enter into a relation of formal knowledge, to become enthusiastic about it, and perhaps even to put it into practice; but it can never be followed in personal obedience.

Christianity without the living Christ is inevitably Christianity without discipleship, and Christianity without discipleship is always Christianity without Christ. It becomes merely an abstract idea, a myth that acknowledges the Fatherhood of God but omits Christ as the living Son. Such a version of Christianity is, ultimately, the end of discipleship. Craig S. Keener observes, 'In such a religion, there is trust in God but no following of Christ. Because

---

[19] Craig Bloomberg, *The New American Commentary Volume 22 - Matthew* (Nashville: Broadman Press, 1992), 102.

[20] Smither Edward, *Augustine as Mentor: A Model for Preparing Spiritual Leaders* (Nashville: B&H Publishing Group, 2008), 108.

[21] Dietrich Bonhoeffer, *The Cost of Discipleship* (United States: Touchstone, 1995), 59.

[22] N. T. Wright, *Simply Jesus* (London: SPCK, 2011), 7.

the Son of God became man and is our Mediator, our only true relationship with Him is to follow Him. Discipleship is bound to Christ as the Mediator, and, where properly understood, it necessarily implies faith in the Son of God as Mediator. Only the Mediator, the God-Man, can call people to follow Him. Discipleship without Jesus Christ is a way of our own choosing.[23]

2.2. The Characteristics and Principles of Discipleship

Following Jesus: One of the central characteristics of discipleship in Luke is the act of following Jesus. Discipleship begins with the decision to leave behind one's former way of life and to walk in the footsteps of Jesus. This commitment involves being present where Jesus is, listening to His teachings, and closely observing His actions. Learning and Teaching: Discipleship in Luke also entails a dedication to learning from Jesus. Disciples are students who actively engage with His teachings, parables, and wisdom, seeking to understand His message and apply it to their lives. Furthermore, disciples are called to share what they have learned with others, thereby participating in a continuous cycle of teaching and learning. Personal Transformation: In Luke, discipleship is not merely an intellectual exercise; it is a journey of personal transformation. Disciples are called to undergo a change of heart, turning away from sin and self-centeredness, and moving toward God and others. This transformation is manifested in actions of love, mercy, and compassion.

There are principles in the process of discipleship. 1) Biblical discipleship is reproductive: Being productive is not a goal of biblical discipleship. Businessmen, sportsmen, professionals, even pastors and evangelists, are usually considered productive when they accomplish a quantitative goal. Biblical discipleship, however, emphasizes: (a) multiplication, not addition (b) quality, not quantity (c) the potential people have, not the positions they hold. 2) Biblical discipleship invites personal discovery. A disciple has to discover truth for himself. "The disciple's job, then, is to present truth that must be self-discovered. Jesus often presented things in such a way that people had to look beyond the obvious and make the effort to discover what He meant."[24] 3) Biblical discipleship reasons, persuades, and gives evidence, 4) Biblical discipleship counts the cost, 5) Biblical discipleship is giving, 6) Biblical discipleship has an eternal perspective.

[23] Craig S. Keener, 'Matthew,' *The IVP New Testament Commentary Series* (Downers Grove, IL: InterVarsity Press, 1987), 97.

[24] Bill Donahue and Russ Robinson, *The Seven Deadly Sins of Small Group Ministry* (Grand Rapids: Zondervan, 2002), 67.

2.3. The Conditions of Discipleship

The Conditions of Discipleship is found in Gospels. The basis for the parable is that Jesus stated what one must do to consider themselves a disciple of Christ. But what is a disciple and what does a disciple follow? Moreover, who is considered worthy to be a disciple? These questions are thoroughly answered in Mark 8:34-9:1. The inclusion of the crowd is of "vital" importance according to Lane "suggests that when Jesus called the crowd and his disciples, he was indicating that anyone could be his disciple. Frances Andrews however, suggests that the calling of the crowd implied that Jesus was speaking to all his disciples, not just the Twelve. Lane is correct, however, in saying that Jesus was speaking to the whole crowd."[25] In v. 34 Mark wrote that he called the crowd with his disciples. The inclusion of with declares that he was calling everyone. It also indicated that his formal disciples are not the only ones who need to, "take up their cross and follow me." This would also be of utmost importance to Mark's audience. To them, it declared that discipleship is not just exclusive to Church leaders, but to anyone who follows Christ.

That discipleship is not just a matter of learning particular facts, but rather, is a way of living. So then simply listening to the words of a teacher, does not mean that one is his disciple. One has to be firmly grounded in his teaching. "This means converting the teacher's words into a life, so that they become principles that are firmly established in the one who is learning. So true discipleship, then, is a discipleship of life which is manifested in a practical way in a person's way of living."[26] It also reveals itself as being a discipleship according to a particular teacher who was himself distinguished by that quality of life and type of teaching.

2.4. Methods of Discipleship

A strict one to one program is emphasized. Based on Christ's last and greatest commission, the goal is to make disciples of all nations. However, "the weaker point of the studies is that they have either omitted or only briefly mentioned the praise and worship service and the Holy Communion."[27] This causes great concern. The community of disciples requires the learner's ability of memorizing verses, and they act out II Timothy 2:2 literally. The few methods of Discipleship which is very much used in few decades, James

---

[25] Frances Andrews, *The Early Humiliati* (Cambridge, UK: Cambridge University Press, 1999), 41-42.

[26] William L. Lane, 'The Gospel of Mark,' *The New International Commentary of the New Testament* (Grand Rapids, MI: Eerdmans, 1974), 17.

[27] William R. Estep, *Renaissance and Reformation* (Grand Rapids: William B. Eerdmans Publishing Company, 1986), 46.

Montgomery Boice mentioned in his book "The Bible study books use inductive methods and have many volumes; in fact, these books are used also for quiet times, making them a transcendental book. The reason for writing in an inductive way is so that the learner can find the truth himself through verse by verse analysis. One can easily find that the Bible is truly the Word of God. This is a good text for college level students."[28]

2.4.1. Call to Commitment and Loyalty

The Lord Himself tells us in Luke 9:23, "if anyone wishes to come after Me, he must deny himself, and take up his cross daily and follow Me." This involves a resolution, a discipline and a trust. If one wants to be discipled by the Lord one must resolve to deny oneself. This bespeaks a consecration of your spirit, soul, and body (I Thess 5:23). A resolution must be made to allow one's being to be humbled under the mighty hand of God (I Peter 5:6). T. F. Torrance explains "God dwells with one who is of a broken and contrite spirit (Ps 34:18; Isa 57:15). One must be willing to renounce the things of the world, not conforming one's soul to all that the world has to offer (Rom 12:2), but learning not to love the world or the things in the world (I Jn 2:15-16)."[29]

2.4.2. Call to Relational Integrity

The words of Jesus in John 15:4 serve as an anchor for establishing the organic relational approach that Jesus takes in the discipleship process. Ellen White cites, "Abide in me, and I in you. As the branch cannot bear fruit of itself, except it abide in the vine; no more can ye, except ye abide in me." This verse perfectly sets the stage for advancing her position on the mutual responsibility shared between Christ and the disciple, illustrating how this relationship contributes to the disciple's maturation. Discipleship is not confined to an internal, invisible process; rather, it is clearly manifested in the daily life of the disciple, as the fruit produced serves as evidence of the depth of their spiritual experience. Ellen White further emphasizes this point by stating, "If the heart has been renewed by the Spirit of God, the life will bear witness to the fact."[30]

The greatest proof of discipleship was not limited to one's relationship or interaction with God; For Ellen White, "it is also demonstrated in his human relationships. She asserted that as we live in close fellowship with God, we will love one another in the same way Christ has loved us. This is the identifying mark and signal to the world that we are indeed Disciples of

[28] James Montgomery Boice, *Christ's Call to Discipleship* (Chicago, IL: Moody Press, 1986), 123.

[29] T. F. Torrance, *Service in Jesus Christ* (Grand Rapids: Eerdmans Press, 1975), 1.

[30] Ellen G. White, *Steps to Christ* (Mountain View: CA: Pacific Press, 1956), 57.

Christ."[31] The reason for this impact and its convincing power to the world is the fact of its being so contrary to our natural inclination. This would suggest an outside force at work within us. Ellen White put it this way, "When men are bound together, not by force or self-interest, but by love, they show the working of an influence that is above every human influence."[32]

Discipleship is this intimate relational process which Jesus defined by his person and words, and which his Spirit helps us live and experience to its fullness. When we see the incarnation, we can never get away from Jesus' words to "Follow me." Likewise, along with his person we can never get away from relationship. Mark Driscoll says that "Relationship is basic to Jesus Christ, it is God's nature. The relational significance of this process of intimate relationship is not readily apparent in the pursuit of discipleship if we are predisposed to define ourselves by what we do and to do our relationship based on this "outside-in" approach."[33] As Jesus vulnerably opened his heart and made himself relationally accessible, he called persons to be intimately involved with him and their lives will be changed. But such transformation doesn't take place apart from the relationship.

2.4.3. Call to Integral Mission

The disciples' mission is described in a similar way to Jesus' mission. Note the similarities between Matthew 4:23 and 10:7–8. They are sent out in a mission of preaching and healing. Here in the gospels Jesus passes on his authority of word and deed to his apostles. The personal authority of Jesus is behind and is carried through in the words and deeds of the disciples. Leroy Eims, says that "Holistic mission has been around for a while. It emphasizes that in our mission activities we must address the whole of human need physical, material, intellectual, emotional, social, and spiritual not just the last of those. This is certainly an important corrective to narrowing mission down to a single task."[34]

At the start of this discourse, Matthew distinguishes between the crowd and the disciples. In the preceding periscope 9:36–37 instead of following Mark who records Jesus teaching the crowd, Matthew records Jesus exhorting the disciples to pray for labourers. In 10:1 Jesus calls the disciples and sends them out to the lost sheep of the house of Israel (10:6), already referred to in 9:36. Mark's account of Jesus teaching the crowd and

---

[31] Ellen G. White, *Testimonies for the Church*, 9 vols. (Mountain View, CA: Pacific Press, 1949), 219.

[32] Ellen G. White, *Desire of Ages* (Mountain View, CA: Pacific Press, 1940), 677-678.

[33] Mark Driscoll and Gerry Breshears, *Doctrine: What Christians Should Believe* (Wheaton: Crossway, 2010), 312.

[34] Leroy Eims, *The Lost Art of Disciple Making* (Grand Rapids: MI: Zondervan, 1980), 28.

ministering directly to them is contrasted in Matthew where Jesus ministers to the crowd through the disciples. Matthew is immediately signaling to his readers that the keynote of this mission discourse is the disciples as Jesus' fellow workers in the mission harvest.

3. Characteristics of Leadership in Luke

Luke's Gospel places a strong emphasis on servant leadership, a concept in which leaders see themselves as servants first, prioritizing the needs of others over personal gain or power. This model is vividly illustrated through Jesus' acts of humility, most notably when He washes the disciples' feet (Lk 22:24-27). In this act, Jesus redefines leadership, challenging the prevailing notions of authority and dominance. By adopting the posture of a servant, He teaches that true leadership is grounded in love, humility, and a commitment to the welfare of others. This countercultural approach serves as a foundational principle for discipleship, urging leaders to serve rather than to be served.

Compassion is another central characteristic of leadership in Luke. Throughout the Gospel, Jesus consistently demonstrates compassion by healing the sick, feeding the hungry, and reaching out to the marginalized. These acts of kindness reflect a deep empathy for human suffering and a commitment to justice. Leaders in Luke are called to emulate this compassion, understanding that effective leadership involves more than just authority; it requires a genuine concern for the well-being of those they lead. By fostering an environment of empathy and care, leaders can create a supportive community that reflects the love of Christ.

Furthermore, effective leadership in Luke involves empowering others to reach their full potential. Jesus invests significant time in teaching and mentoring His disciples, equipping them with the knowledge and skills necessary to carry out His mission. He encourages them to engage actively in ministry, thereby fostering their growth and confidence. This model of leadership emphasizes the importance of mentoring and supporting those under one's care, enabling them to contribute meaningfully to the community's well-being. By empowering others, leaders not only fulfill their responsibilities but also cultivate a culture of collaboration and shared purpose, reinforcing the values of love and service central to the teachings of Jesus.

3.1. Luke's Emphasis on Leadership as a Response to God's Call

Luke's Gospel contains several parables that emphasize leadership as a response to God's call and a responsibility to steward resources faithfully. The parable of the talents (Lk 19:11-27) illustrates the importance of using one's gifts and resources wisely in God's service. This parable underscores the idea that true leadership is not about accumulating power or wealth but about faithfully managing what has been entrusted to us for God's purposes. It challenges leaders to recognize their roles as stewards who must account for their actions and decisions, highlighting that our response to God's call involves a commitment to using our abilities and resources to further His kingdom. Through these teachings, Luke calls individuals to embrace a sense of responsibility and intentionality in their leadership, reflecting God's values in their actions and decisions.

Luke highlights the importance of faithfulness and integrity in leadership. Leaders are called to be trustworthy and responsible stewards of their positions and resources. The parable of the dishonest manager (Lk 16:1-13) illustrates the value of using one's influence and resources for good and for the kingdom of God. "Integrity is doing the right thing when no one is watching."[35] It emphasizes that leaders should act with integrity and accountability. There are two critical components of integrity that go beyond just doing the right thing when no one is looking. The first is the adherence to a moral or ethical principle. This isn't simple compliance to a rule; it implies a philosophical understanding of the reason it exists. The second is the pursuit of an undiminished state or condition.[36] Everyone makes mistakes, so being a person of integrity does not mean you haven't committed a moral or ethical violation, ever. It means having the strength of character to learn from those 'misbehaviors' and seek continual self-improvement.[37]

3.2. Jesus as the Ultimate Model of Discipleship and Leadership

Jesus serves as the ultimate model of leadership in humility and servanthood, consistently demonstrating that true leadership involves a willingness to humble oneself and serve others. A powerful example of this is when He washes the feet of His disciples (John 13:1-17), a task typically reserved for servants. This act not only symbolizes His servant leadership but also underscores the importance of humility in leadership. By taking on the role of a servant, Jesus teaches His followers that leadership is not about seeking status or power but about caring for and uplifting those around us. This selfless attitude encourages leaders to prioritize the needs of others, fostering a culture of respect and service.

Compassion and a commitment to healing are also defining characteristics of Jesus' leadership. Throughout His ministry, He exhibits

---

[35] A. R,Gostick, & D. Telford, *The Integrity Advantage* (Layton: Gibbs Smith Press, 2003), 120.

[36] MacArthur John, *Called to Lead: 26 Leadership Lessons from the Life of the Apostle Paul* (Nashville: Thomas Nelson, 2004), 23.

[37] Peter K. Nelson, *Leadership and Discipleship: A Study of Luke 22:24-30* (Atlanta, GA: Scholars Press, 1994), 114.

deep compassion for those who are suffering, whether physically, emotionally, or spiritually. His acts of healing and restoration reflect His profound concern for the well-being of others, emphasizing that effective leadership prioritizes the welfare of those being led. By actively engaging with the pain and struggles of individuals, Jesus models a leadership style that encourages empathy and action. Leaders today can learn from this example by being attentive to the needs of their communities and striving to create environments where healing and support are paramount.

Furthermore, Jesus' leadership is marked by inclusivity, breaking down social, cultural, and religious barriers. He actively reaches out to and embraces people from diverse backgrounds, including Samaritans, tax collectors, sinners, and the marginalized. This inclusive ministry challenges societal norms and models a leadership approach that seeks to include rather than exclude. By welcoming those who are often overlooked or shunned, Jesus demonstrates that true leadership involves recognizing the inherent worth of every individual. This emphasis on inclusion serves as a powerful reminder for contemporary leaders to cultivate diversity and foster a sense of belonging, ultimately enriching their communities and reflecting the broader values of the Kingdom of God.

3.3. Jesus' Call to Radical Discipleship and Leadership

Jesus calls His disciples to radical discipleship by urging them to take up their crosses and follow Him (Lk 9:23). This call challenges individuals to deny themselves, relinquish their own desires, and prioritize their commitment to Him. Taking up the cross signifies a willingness to endure suffering and sacrifice for the sake of the Gospel and God's kingdom. It requires a profound transformation in one's values and priorities, as disciples are asked to place their allegiance to Christ above all else. This act of self-denial is not merely a one-time decision but a continual process of aligning one's life with the teachings and example of Jesus, reflecting a deep commitment to His mission.

Moreover, Jesus emphasizes that discipleship comes with a cost, warning that following Him may lead to persecution, rejection, and hardships (Lk 9:57-62; Lk 14:25-33). This acknowledgment highlights the necessity for unwavering commitment and readiness to make sacrifices in the pursuit of godly leadership. Disciples must count the cost and be prepared to face challenges that may arise from their faithfulness to Christ. Such readiness not only strengthens personal faith but also serves as a testimony to others about the transformative power of the Gospel. By embracing this cost, disciples exemplify a profound trust in God's purposes, demonstrating that true leadership in the Kingdom of God is rooted in a willingness to endure and persevere for the sake of His glory.

In conclusion, Jesus serves as the ultimate model of discipleship and leadership. His leadership is marked by humility, compassion, and inclusivity. He calls His followers to learn from His actions and teachings, recognizing that discipleship involves growth and occasional failures. Jesus also issues a radical call to discipleship, emphasizing the importance of taking up the cross and being prepared to bear the cost of following Him. His example and teachings continue to inspire and challenge individuals in their own journeys of discipleship and leadership.

4. Theology of Discipleship

The theology of the discipleship is very important theme in the Bible, in the decades of the church history it is clearly seen as tool to implement in the church. Rick warren says that "One of the most interesting and intimate theological facts of being a disciple of Christ is that it begins with the personal call of Jesus."[38] Christ summarized the call to discipleship when He stood on the banks of the Sea of Galilee and called to Simon and Andrew, "Follow me." This was in severe contrast to the Early Jewish and Greek traditions of the First Century. In that culture, it was considered dishonorable for teachers to seek out their followers.

However, fearless by the rabbinical tradition and the social stigma, Jesus condescended and demonstrated the purpose of His incarnation (Lk 19:10). Michael Wilkins writes, "At the inauguration of his kingdom mission, Jesus establishes a new pattern (discipleship), because he is the one who takes the initiative to seek out and call these brothers to enter into a relationship with him."[39] Thus discipleship begins and rests with the sovereign call of God. Jesus explained this to His disciples. When He told them, "You did not choose me, but I chose you and appointed you that you should go and bear fruit and that your fruit should abide." The next distinctive element of discipleship is the radical nature of the call. Jesus summoned those who would follow Him to forsake everything.

This was made clear to a great crowd clamoring to follow Jesus during His ministry in Perea. Francis Chan, says that "If anyone comes to Me, and does not hate his own father and mother and wife and children and brothers and sisters, yes, and even his own life, he cannot be My disciple. By this, Jesus was not implying that devotion to family be discarded; rather, the

---

[38] Rick Warren, *The Purpose Driven Church: Growth Without Compromising Your Message and Mission* (Grand Rapids, MI: Zondervan Publishing House, 1995), 143.

[39] Michael J. Wilkins, 'Matthew,' *The NIV Application Commentary* (Grand Rapids, MI: Zondervan, 2004), 180.

closet human relationships, even family bonds, must never impede one from following Christ."[40]

4.1. The Heart of Discipleship

Discipleship should be outward focused. We don't invest in someone only for the sake of that individual, but we do so with the others so that they will impact their mind. We proclaim Jesus to men and women who will go onto proclaim Jesus to the world. Even if outwardly we are "proclaiming Jesus" in how we do discipleship, we must make sure that inwardly, our motive is to make much of Him, rather than to make much of ourselves. The concepts in the remainder of this article should fall under the umbrella of this first principle. "The reason we devote ourselves to all of the following principles is to bring fame and praise to the name of Jesus. Discipleship is purposeful, fun, and rewarding."[41] It is one of the greatest joys of my life. However, like most valuable things, discipleship also requires energy, time, and hard work. It is costly.

In this description of his ministry, "toil" and "struggle". "The Greek word which is translated as "toil" in this passage means "to grow weary, tired, exhausted", or "to labor with wearisome effort." And the word for "struggle" is often used to describe the strenuous exertion that goes into an athletic competition or a fight. Paul fought and labored to the point of exhaustion to present believers mature in Christ. Discipleship cost him greatly, and it should cost us as well.

4.2. Goal of Discipleship

The ultimate goal of discipleship is to mature in faith, a process fuelled by the Spirit's work in our lives and fostered within the community of believers. As we grow, discipleship calls us to intentionally invest in others, helping them deepen their faith and equipping them to disciple others in turn. Leroy Eims emphasizes the importance of this intentional approach to discipleship, encouraging believers to engage systematically and strategically in ministry, sharing their experiences and wisdom with the aim of guiding others toward spiritual maturity. This cycle of growth and mentorship ensures that each believer is not only nurtured in their own faith journey but also equipped to help others along theirs.

Jesus modelled this principle by empowering His disciples, ultimately sending them out to minister independently. By doing so, He entrusted them with the mission, allowing them to carry forward His work and experience the responsibilities of ministry firsthand. This method not only reinforced their

[40] Francis Chan, *Forgotten God: Reversing our Tragic Neglect of the Holy Spirit* (Colorado Springs: David C. Cook, 2009), 85.

[41] Michael J. Wilkins, 'Matthew,' *The NIV Application Commentary,* 181.

faith and skills but also laid the foundation for a self-sustaining community of believers, each equipped to pass on the "baton of faith" to others. In this way, discipleship becomes a continuous, generational process, with each believer prepared to nurture and guide others in the journey of faith, ensuring that the mission of Christ endures and grows.[42]

4.3. Re-Visioning Discipleship

Discipleship defined in new sense to build the kingdom of God on this earth. When Jesus was on this earth, He gave the vision to His followers. Disciples are called to bear witness to Christ and what he has done in their lives. This is a witness borne out of experience. According to Watson "Spiritual renewal always precedes effective evangelism'. It can be added that effective evangelism always follows spiritual renewal. 'It is the daily, unspectacular witness of Christians who are alive in Christ, that will most likely break into areas who are alive in Christ, that the church is not otherwise touching at all."[43] The 'silent witness' provides evidentiary support to the spoken witness. But the latter must not be downplayed, as the spoken witness played a key role in the early Christian church as recorded in the New Testament.

Luke's Gospel stands out for its emphasis on the inclusion of women and marginalized individuals as disciples of Jesus. It highlights the stories of women such as Mary and Martha, the women who supported Jesus' ministry financially, and the Samaritan woman at the well. Luke also portrays Jesus as reaching out to tax collectors, sinners, and other marginalized groups, inviting them to become His followers. This inclusivity challenges societal norms of the time and emphasizes that discipleship is open to all.

4.4. Radical Discipleship

In the biblical accounts of the gospel writers, they explained about discipleship in radical shift in one's life, sometimes they have to offer their life. Augsburger, says that "those who committed to being Jesus' disciples were asked and expected not only to leave their old life behind but also to begin to see the world and life through completely new lens. Now neighbors were not only those people with whom they shared common values but included those who seemingly held different value systems the Samaritans (Lk 10:29-37)."[44] If someone violated them in some fashion, instead of

---

[42] Leroy Eims, *The Lost Art of Disciple Making,* 28.

[43] David Watson, *Called and Committed: World-Changing Discipleship* (Wheaton, IL: Harold Shaw Publishers, 1982), 194.

[44] D. W. Augsburger, *Dissident Discipleship: A Spirituality of Self Surrender, Love of God, and Love of Neighbor* (Grand Rapids, MI: Brazos Press, 2006), 66.

seeking retaliation they were to seek reconciliation and turn the other check as well (Matt 5:39; Lk 6:29).

Rather than worrying about their lives, where their next meal would come from, or what they would wear, "Jesus advised them "strive first for the kingdom of God and his righteousness and all these will be given to you as well" (Matt 6:33). The Christian life call for sacrifice and suffering."[45] As simple as Jesus' description of discipleship is, the breadth and extent of its meaning for our lives and the demands of loving implied by all our heart, soul, mind, and strength is formidable. Bonhoeffer believed that the Christian life requires a willingness to sacrifice one's own interests and needs, for some this might mean life itself, as it eventually did for him. "He believed that only by being willing to suffer could we ever find true joy, or grace as he commonly defined it He believed the power of the Christian life is in the willingness to suffer, to "take up cross and follow" as Christ declared necessary for anyone who wished to follow him (Mk 8:34). He went as far as to proclaim suffering as the badge of true discipleship.

4.5. God's Way of Discipleship

God designed the entire mission and discipleship in the center of kingdom of God. Hyunbo Son says that "Discipleship was not designed to occur outside the context of the church (not to be mistaken with the building or organizational structure), but in the context of a relational community of faith. The attachment is to the person of Jesus, as well as to his body the church. Theologically the two cannot be separated."[46] It is here that makes an important point of clarification. Discipleship should not be seen as something that runs parallel to church membership, or as something optional, and supplementary, or that describes a more spiritual class of believer. Terms like 'church member' or 'Christian' should not be devalued when discipleship is spoken of Mission.

4.6. Stewardship Discipleship

Stewardship Discipleship is another aspect in the Bible. In the Old Testament there are different kind of stewardships given by God (Gen 1:26-28) and in New Testament it can be seen as stewardship Discipleship. Steward a person who cares for the property of another while acting on behalf of the owner, and is accountable and responsible for the property. Here in the context of the New Testament discipleship explained and given responsibility to every believer. So how are discipleship, stewardship, and

---

[45] D. W. Augsburger, *Dissident Discipleship: A Spirituality of Selfsurrender, Love of God, and Love of Neighbor,* 66.

[46] Hyunbo Son, *Pastor! It is Very Easy to Evangelize* (South Korea: Life Way Press, 2010), 4.

evangelization related? To be a disciple of Christ, we must live as He did and we must practice Christian Stewardship in response to His gifts. Parishioners share their time, talent, and treasure in joyful and grateful recognition that every blessing and gift we have is from God. "These resources shared with the parish are critical for faith formation, advocacy, outreach, liturgy, hospitality, and virtually all of our ministries. By sharing these gifts, you enable the Church to develop and implement evangelization programs within our parish and our community."[47]

Luke underscores the importance of radical hospitality and compassion in discipleship. The parable of the Good Samaritan (Lk 10:25-37) illustrates the concept of neighborly love and compassion transcending cultural and social boundaries. Disciples are called to imitate this compassion and to welcome the stranger and the outcast. Jesus' teachings on caring for the poor and the hungry (e.g., the parable of the rich man and Lazarus) underscore the ethical dimension of discipleship, emphasizing the need to care for those in need.

5. Missional View of Discipleship

Missional discipleship is the process of making all believers to do mission right where they are or abroad as obedience of Jesus' commendation of the Great Commission in order to expand the Kingdom of God. All churches must make all believers preach the gospel as missionaries, and all believers must go to all nations to preach the Gospel and make disciples. "Go and Make disciples" in Matthew 28:19-20 was not limited to twelve disciples of Jesus Christ in the Gospels alone. Therefore, all believers must be saturated with Jesus' final commandment to go and make disciples in all nations. Church leaders have to ask themselves this way: "Do we see an ever-expanding company of dedicated people reaching the world with the gospel as a result of your ministry."[48]

5.1. Discipleship to Continue Jesus Mission

Missional discipleship was the essential ministry of Jesus Christ in the world. Jesus met His disciples and gave the commandment, "As the Father sent me, I am sending you." John 20:19-23. God sent Jesus Christ on the earth to save the lost, so Jesus was incarnated in the world. On the earth, Jesus saved many people with the gospel."[49] And then, before He ascended into the heaven, He gave His disciples this message. "I am sending you." Robert E. Coleman says that "This co mission is the mission of individual

---

[47] Dietrich Bonhoeffer, *The Cost of Discipleship*, 88.

[48] Robert E. Coleman, *The Master of Evangelism* (Grand Rapids, MI: Revell, 1963), 13.

[49] Robert E. Coleman, *The Master of Evangelism*, 13.

Christian and all churches and provides it with direction and motivation to save the lost."[50] Here it is very clear that every believer or disciple is to continue his mission as shown in the Bible John 4:1-42 which accounts tells the story of Jesus Christ and a Samaritan woman. Jesus Christ went to a town in Samaria called Sychar to preach the Gospel to a Samaritan woman. It was not common for Jews to go through Samaria to Galilee because of the historical background.

Jesus told His disciples to do what He practiced. Luke 4:18-19 is known as the Nazareth Manifesto of Jesus. The quotation from Isaiah has the significance of the Lord's statements of His call to His saving ministry and as Luke's affirmation of this ministry as themes in his Gospel.[51] Jesus' manifesto is inclusive, not exclusive. It is not that God is interested only in the poor, not the rich. Jesus had the concerned for the poor, the prisoners, the blind, and the oppressed. He is concerned for whom other people regard as rejects, whether because of their ethnicity. Discipleship mandate has two components: social mandate[52] and disciple making mandate; both can be called the "mission mandate."

5.2. Discipleship to Plant Churches

It simply cannot be a disciple without being a missionary a sent one and for the purpose of church planting. Alan and Debra Hirsch asserts that we must, "take the missional agenda of the church with extreme seriousness. For way too long discipleship has been limited to issues relating to our own personal morality and worked out in the context of the four walls of the church with its privatized religion."[53] In doing this, it has severely neglected biblical mandate to go and "make disciples and plant churches." it has narrowed the gospel message to just being about us. "Here one should understand to balance the impotence of personal morality, To strive for holiness and maturity in believer's own personal lives is extremely important, but it is only half the picture; the other half is our God-given responsibility to the world around us."[54] The fact is that every Christian can't be a disciple without being a missionary = no mission, no discipleship. It's simple every believer and mission have to understand.

---

[50] Robert E. Coleman, *The Master of Evangelism*, 14.

[51] John Nolland, 'Luke 1-9,' *Word Biblical Commentary*, vol. 35A, edited by Bruce M. Metzger and Others (Dallas: Word Books, 1989), 196.

[52] Samuel Mathai, *A Guide to Church Ministry* (Bhopal: SSM, 2008), 1, He calls Matthew 25:42-46; Luke 18:20-21 'A Social Mandate.'

[53] Alan Hirsch and Debra Hirsch, *Untamed: Reactivating a Missional Form of Discipleship* (Grand Rapids, MI: Baker Books, 2010), 29.

[54] Alan Hirsch and Debra Hirsch, *Untamed: Reactivating a missional form of Discipleship*, 29.

All churches and believers need to grow personally as the disciples of Christ and to make new disciples through sharing the Gospel. Stetzer and Putman similarly shared, "Scripture teaches that the church is God's missionary in the world. If we are going to join God on his mission, we have to recognize that we are missionaries...wherever he places us just like the first disciples."[55] In this regard, missional discipleship is very important to obey Jesus' commandment of the Great Commission, and which expanded the Kingdom of God. Therefore, all churches and Missions have to consider missional discipleship as first priority.

5.3. Discipleship to Respond to Need

Another aspect of Missiological, workable and biblical discipleship model is Reaching to the lost and responding to the need of the situation, which means reaching out to the lost people with the gospel through a variety of ways. In order to reach out to the lost people unto salvation, the first thing that all believers have to do is to go to their neighbors who are not believers. Aubrey Malphurs, states that "The Great Commission in Matthew 29:19-20 relates this to going to the all nations in order to make disciples. Going is a prerequisite of making disciples and is essential in reaching out to the lost people. Jesus Christ reached out to many lost people to make multiplying disciples."[56] Churches must reach out to the lost people to Christ with the Gospel so that they can be made disciples and not wait for the lost to come to them. Jesus Christ came to the earth to seek out the lost people and give them salvation. He commanded all believers to go to the ends of the world to preach the Gospel. Discipleship in the Gospel of Luke is characterized by following Jesus, learning and teaching His message, and undergoing personal transformation. Luke's emphasis on the inclusive nature of discipleship challenges societal norms and calls for radical hospitality and compassion. Discipleship is not limited to a select few but is open to anyone who is willing to follow Jesus, learn from Him, and be transformed by His teachings and example.

Disciple-Making is a process and a life style. It takes time and continues for a life time; once one accepted the call to live as disciple, start looking for people to invite into the same type of discipleship relationships with Jesus. Jesus did not begin discipleship as a new ministry; much of how he conducted hid discipleship ministry was already known and accepted. Jesus made some remarkable changes for his way of discipleship and in particular He made

[55] Ed Stetzer and David Putman, *Breaking The Missional Code: Your Church Can Become a Missionary in Your Community* (Nashville, TN: Broadman & Holman Publishers, 2006), 13.

[56] Aubrey Malphurs, *Planting Growing Churches for the Twenty-First Century* (Grand Rapids MI: Baker, 1992), 42.

change the way He initiated His discipleship relationship. Jesus made changes to how He initiated the discipleship relationship, the emphasis, to the process of discipleship, and to the duration of discipleship relationships.

Discipleship is done in community and not in a weekend service; the process is not only preaching and teaching of the word of God but also meetings their social needs. Disciple-Making mandate, Jesus gave to His followers two thousand years ago remains unchanged for His followers today. "Jesus' commands have not been undated, nor have they been revoked."[57] Dietrich Bonheoffer rightly wrote, "Christianity without discipleship is always Christianity without Christ. It remains an abstract idea; a myth much has a place for the Fatherhood of God, but omits Christ as the living Son. And a Christianity of that kind is nothing more or less than the end of discipleship. In such a religion, there is trust in God, but no following Christ.[58]

Felix Wilfred has observed that "the social, political and cultural situation in India and Asia at large presents unprecedent challenges to our Christian mission praxis.[59] As David Shibley rightly states, that issues and challenges are nothing new. Therefore understanding those issues and challenges are important for one to do the task of disciple- making in an effective and sensitive ways because India represents a glittering array of different people and their cultures, religious, languages, customs and dress.

A pleasant political condition of a nation is very important for national peace and prosperity. It opens a wider way for religious tolerance. The preamble sets out the tone and tenor of the entire constitution. It declares India to be a sovereign, secular, democratic republic assuring liberty of thought, expression, belief, faith and worship to all its citizens, equality and justice to all the citizens.[60] Even after seven decades of independence, Muslims and Christians live with fear and are afraid to profess their faith and doing their religious duties publicly.[61] The constitutional right and freedom is not completely practiced by all the minority groups. Religious militants perpetuate communalism and distort peace among ethnic and religious groups. Communalism is not a new

[57] Win Arn & Charles Arn, *The Master's Plan for Making Disciples*, 2nd ed. (Grand Rapids: Baker Books, 1998), 9.

[58] Dietrich Bonheoffer, *The Cost of Discipleship* (New York: Touchstone, 1995), Kindle, 59.

[59] Felix Wilfred, 'Challenges of Contextual Mission Today,' *Energizing Challenges to Mission,* edited by Siga Arles (Delhi: ISPCK, 2012), 1.

[60] M. T. Cherian, *Hindutva Agenda and Minority Rights: A Christian Response* (Bangalore: Centre for Contemporary Christianity, 2007), 133-134

[61] C. Priyadarsani, '*Pseudo Secularism: A Threat to National Tranquility,*' *Mission Intelligence,* No.21 (Bangalore, Indian Christian Research Organization (April- June 201): 8-10.

phenomenon in India history. A large section of the Indian society is suffering from poverty and unemployment.

Poverty is a phenomenon which is objective as well a subjective. Objectively poverty implies a dehumanizing condition in which people are unable to look after the basic needs. Subjectively, poverty stands for perceived deprivation. Poor people lack the necessary resources and capacity to satisfy basic needs like food, shelter, health and education. They live under difficult conditions which are not conducive for development of their human potential. The Word Bank estimates that 41.6% or 456 million Indian lives below the International Poverty Line."[62] A significant number of people living below the poverty line, its impact on socio- economically marginal families in the form of poor quality of life, disease, low literacy, malnutrition, and child labor become a serious concern. Such issues do not create a conducive situation for the people to participate in Bible study and other spiritual activities.

The kingdom as God's will for this earth can be entered here and now through a transformed life style of horizontal sharing of possessions by the haves to the bottom of society and upwards. Teachings of Jesus[63] have the quality of presenting the values of the kingdom in the context of conflict. The poor in the Gospel of Luke, are the recipients of God's special blessings, because they are poor and needy.[64] Kingdom values[65] are in conflict with the normal/popular expectation of its disciples. One of major theme in the teaching of Jesus is the discipleship.

6. Case Studies: Discipleship and Leadership in Luke's Gospel

This section explores Luke's unique portrayal of discipleship and leadership as demonstrated through key moments in Jesus' ministry. The call of the first disciples, as described in Luke 5, reveals how Jesus invites ordinary individuals into a journey marked by sacrifice, faith, and a

[62] Robert Castellino 'Is Indian Really Shining?' *Indian Current*, vol. XXII, Issue No. 33, 09-15 (August 2010): 33.

[63] Parables in the Gospel Luke are interesting to note. One of the significant things in the parables of Luke is its presentation of various kingdom values. The parables of the Good Samaritan (10:25ff), the parable of the rich fool (12:13-21), like the anecdotes of the Unrighteous steward (16: 1-9) and the rich man and Lazarus (16:19-31) shows the futility of serving mammon, i.e., wealth or property; and the stories summon the hearer-reader to use what he has for the poor while there is still time, a theme common both to parables that refer explicitly to the kingdom. Cf. Richard H. Hiers, *The Kingdom of God in the Synoptic Tradition* (Gaineville: University of Florida Press, 1970).

[64] Philip van Linden, *The Gospel of Luke and Acts* (Wilmington: Michael Glazier, 1970), 81.

[65] Jesus taught about His Kingdom (ultimately God's Kingdom); the parables were the parables of the Kingdom. In the parables one could find the qualities one must possess to enter into the kingdom. Those qualities are commonly called as Kingdom values.

readiness to embrace a life of purpose beyond societal expectations. Through the parable of the Good Samaritan, Luke emphasizes a model of leadership grounded in compassion and inclusivity, challenging followers to extend love and mercy across social divides. Further, Luke highlights the critical role of women in Jesus' ministry, illustrating how they were empowered as leaders and active participants in the Kingdom of God. Together, these passages reflect a holistic view of discipleship[66]—one that blends humility, compassion, and an inclusive commitment to serve others.

6.1. The Call of the Twelve Disciples (Lk 5:1-11)

In Luke 5:1-11, the call of the Twelve Disciples marks a significant moment in Jesus' ministry, as He invites ordinary fishermen to become His closest followers. This passage highlights the initial encounter between Jesus and the future disciples, emphasizing their willingness to leave behind their livelihoods and step into a new life of purpose and faith. Through this call narrative, Luke introduces foundational themes of discipleship, such as trust, obedience, and the readiness to embrace the unknown for the sake of God's Kingdom. Jesus' interaction with these men not only signifies the beginning of their transformation but also sets the tone for a model of leadership defined by humility, sacrifice, and dedication to a higher calling.

In Luke 5:1-11, Jesus calls Simon Peter, James, and John to follow Him. The narrative features a miraculous catch of fish after a night of unsuccessful fishing. After witnessing this miracle, Peter recognizes his own unworthiness and Jesus' divine authority, leading him to leave everything and follow Jesus.[67] This account illustrates several lessons on discipleship and leadership. Jesus demonstrates His divine authority by commanding the fish to be caught. This underscores that discipleship is about following the authority of Jesus,[68] recognizing His lordship, and submitting to His leadership. Peter's decision to leave everything—his livelihood and possessions—reveals the sacrificial nature of discipleship. Discipleship often requires leaving behind comforts and security in pursuit of a higher calling. Peter's initial doubt and reluctance transform into faith and obedience through the encounter with Jesus. This highlights that discipleship is a transformative journey, where one's character

[66] Rosemary Radford Ruether, Eleanor McLaughlin, *Women of Spirit: Female Leadership in the Jewish & Christian Traditions* (New York: Simon & Schuster, 1979), 75.

[67] Benjamin Wing Wo Fung, *A Defense for the Chronological Order of Luke's Gospel: The Meaning of 'Orderly' (Kathexes) Account in Luke 1:3* (Eugene, OR: Wipf and Stock Publishers, 2019), 95.

[68] Tung Chiew Ha, *Biblical Narrative Learning: Teaching Adequate Faith in the Gospel of John* (Eugene, OR: Wipf and Stock Publishers, 2015), 112.

and faith develop as they follow Jesus.[69] Most of the biblical qualifications relate to each candidate's moral and spiritual qualities. The first, overarching qualification is that of being "above reproach."[70]

6.2. Interaction with the Fishermen

Jesus' interaction with the fishermen in Luke 5:1-11 offers profound lessons on discipleship and leadership, emphasizing trust, humility, and a willingness to embrace a higher calling. When Jesus calls Simon Peter and his companions, He meets them in the midst of their daily work, transforming an ordinary moment into one of divine purpose. Despite their unsuccessful night of fishing, Peter chooses to trust Jesus' instruction to cast the nets once more, resulting in a miraculous catch. This act of faith highlights that fruitful ministry flows from reliance on God rather than personal skill or expertise. By calling these fishermen, Jesus shows that discipleship is open to all who are willing to follow Him, regardless of background, and invites them to participate in a mission that transcends personal ambition. In this way, Jesus sets a model of leadership rooted in obedience, humility, and a commitment to serve others over oneself. Authority and Humility: Discipleship involves recognizing Jesus' authority and humbling oneself before Him, as Peter did when he acknowledged his own sinfulness. Sacrifice and Commitment: Leaders and disciples are called to make sacrifices for the sake of their calling and mission.[71] The disciples left their careers as fishermen to follow Jesus, demonstrating their commitment. Jesus' ability to transform the lives and perspectives of His disciples highlights the transformative power of effective leadership. Leaders should inspire growth and change in their followers.

6.3. The Good Samaritan Parable (Lk 10:25-37)

The parable of the Good Samaritan in Luke 10:25-37 stands as one of Jesus' most profound teachings on love, compassion, and neighborly responsibility. Presented in response to a lawyer's question about inheriting eternal life and defining "neighbor," this parable transcends cultural and social barriers, illustrating the depth of compassion that true discipleship requires. In the story, Jesus challenges prevailing biases by portraying a Samaritan—a figure typically despised by the Jewish audience—as the embodiment of mercy and kindness. This parable not only redefines neighborly love but also offers a model of compassionate leadership that calls believers to extend care and empathy to all, especially those outside their immediate circles or

---

[69] Dwayne H. Adams, *The Sinner in Luke* (Eugene, OR: Wipf and Stock Publishers, 2008), 105.

[70] R. L. Daft, *Leadership: Theory and Practice* (Orland: The Dryden Press, 1999), 176.

[71] Slawomir Szkredka, *Sinners and Sinfulness in Luke: A Study of Direct and Indirect References in the Initial Episodes of Jesus' Activity* (Tübingen: Mohr Siebeck, 2017), 18.

comfort zones.[72] Through the example of the Good Samaritan, Luke presents a vision of discipleship that embraces inclusivity, urging followers of Jesus to embody selfless love in their relationships and communities.

The Good Samaritan parable is a well-known story of compassion and neighborly love. In this parable, a Samaritan, traditionally seen as an outsider and enemy to the Jews, shows mercy to a wounded traveler ignored by a priest and a Levite. The parable teaches that true neighborliness involves caring for the needs of others, regardless of social or ethnic differences. It conveys lessons on compassionate leadership and inclusive discipleship. The Samaritan exemplifies compassionate leadership by stopping to help a stranger in need.[73] Leaders should prioritize empathy and care for the well-being of those they lead. The parable challenges preconceived notions and prejudices by portraying a Samaritan as the compassionate neighbor. This underscores the inclusivity of discipleship, where all are called to love and serve without discrimination.[74]

6.4. Lessons on Compassionate Leadership and Inclusive Discipleship

In the Gospel of Luke, Jesus exemplifies compassionate leadership and inclusive discipleship, calling His followers to embrace empathy and openness toward others, particularly those marginalized by society. The parable of the Good Samaritan (Lk 10:25-37) powerfully illustrates this, challenging cultural boundaries by portraying a despised Samaritan as a model of true compassion and neighborly love. Through this story, Jesus teaches that authentic discipleship is not confined by social or ethnic divisions but is marked by a genuine care for all people. His interactions with tax collectors, sinners, and the poor further demonstrate a leadership style rooted in compassion, showing that disciples are called to serve selflessly, without judgment. In this way, Luke presents a model of leadership that values every individual, urging believers to extend God's love and grace to those beyond their immediate circles and to cultivate an inclusive community that reflects the Kingdom of God. Compassion Across Boundaries: Compassionate leadership transcends boundaries and prejudices. Leaders should be willing to extend help and care to anyone in need, regardless of differences. Discipleship should embrace the principle of inclusive love, where followers of Jesus extend love and compassion to all, even those considered outsiders or enemies.

---

[72] Phillip C. Thrailkill, *Following Jesus: Discipleship in the Gospel of Luke and Beyond* (Eugene, OR: Wipf and Stock Publishers, 2022), 87.

[73] Efrain Agosto, *Servant Leadership: Jesus Andpaul - the Ultimate Mode P5021* (Manchester: Chalice Press, 2005), 58.

[74] Dave Heney, *Luke 10 Leadership: How to Succeed at Parish Ministry* (Notre Dame, IN: Ave Maria Press, 2020), 68.

6.5. The Leadership of Women Disciples (Lk 8:1-3)

In Luke 8:1-3, the leadership of women in Jesus' ministry is highlighted, offering a striking example of inclusivity and empowerment within the early movement of discipleship.[75] This passage names several women—Mary Magdalene, Joanna, Susanna, and others—who accompanied Jesus and provided essential support for His mission.[76] Their presence and active participation alongside Jesus and the Twelve signify a radical departure from the social norms of the time, where women were often marginalized in public and religious life. Luke's emphasis on these women's roles not only underscores their commitment and leadership but also reveals Jesus' acknowledgment of their contributions as vital to the advancement of His ministry.[77] By including women as integral followers and supporters, Luke paints a picture of discipleship that values diversity and elevates those who serve, setting an example for future generations of leaders in the Christian community.

In Luke 8:1-3, women are mentioned as active participants in Jesus' ministry. They provided financial support for His mission, and their names, including Mary Magdalene, are listed among His followers. This passage challenges traditional gender roles and highlights the leadership roles women played in Jesus' ministry.[78] Jesus' inclusion of women in His ministry and their active roles as financial supporters demonstrate His commitment to empowering women as leaders and followers. This challenges societal norms and underscores the inclusivity of His discipleship. Jesus' acknowledgment of the women's contributions by naming them as followers highlights the importance of recognizing and valuing the contributions of all disciples, regardless of gender.[79] The case studies from Luke's Gospel illustrate key principles of discipleship and leadership, including the recognition of divine authority, sacrificial commitment, transformational leadership, compassion, inclusivity, and empowerment of all, regardless of social or gender distinctions. These lessons continue to inspire contemporary discussions of discipleship and leadership within a Christian context.

---

[75] Myrtle Pellew, *Women Leaders in Ministry: From Bondage to Freedom at Last!* (Bloomington: Xlibris Corporation, 2011), 18.

[76] Mel Shoemaker, *The Theology of the Four Gospels* (Nashville, TN: WestBow Press, 2011), 125.

[77] Anthony B. Robinson and Robert W. Wall, *Called to Be Church: The Book of Acts for a New Day* (Grand Rapids, MI: Wm. B. Eerdmans Publishing, 2006), 38.

[78] Carroll D. Osburn, *Essays on Women in Earliest Christianity, Volume 1* (Eugene, OR: Wipf and Stock Publishers, 2007), 452.

[79] Frederick James Murphy, *An Introduction to Jesus and the Gospels* (Nashville, TN: Abingdon Press, 2005), 363.

7. Challenges and Obstacles to Discipleship and Leadership in Luke

The Gospel of Luke presents a realistic view of the challenges and obstacles that disciples face in their journey of faith and leadership. Through Jesus' teachings and parables, Luke addresses barriers such as materialism and self-centeredness, which often hinder believers from fully committing to God's Kingdom. He also warns of the dangers of pride and self-righteousness, showing how these attitudes can distort true discipleship and lead to spiritual stagnation.[80] Moreover, the fear of persecution and rejection stands as a common obstacle, testing the resolve of those who seek to follow Christ in a world that may oppose His message. In the Parable of the Sower (Lk 8:4-15), Jesus provides a vivid metaphor for these challenges, illustrating the importance of endurance and faithfulness amidst trials.[81] By addressing these barriers, Luke offers a framework for understanding the cost of discipleship and the steadfastness required to lead a life committed to Christ.

7.1. The Role of Materialism and Self-Centeredness

Materialism and self-centeredness emerge as significant challenges to discipleship and leadership in the Gospel of Luke, often diverting individuals from wholehearted commitment to God's Kingdom. Luke consistently emphasizes Jesus' warnings about the dangers of wealth and the pursuit of worldly possessions, which can entangle the heart and diminish one's reliance on God. Parables such as the Rich Fool (Lk 12:13-21) and the Rich Man and Lazarus (Lk 16:19-31) illustrate the spiritual risks associated with prioritizing material wealth over compassion and humility. Jesus calls His disciples to forsake self-centered ambitions and instead adopt a lifestyle of generosity and service, warning that one cannot serve both God and wealth. Through these teachings, Luke presents materialism and self-interest as direct obstacles to the sacrificial love and humility required for true discipleship, challenging followers to embrace simplicity and selflessness as foundational qualities of their faith journey.[82]

In Luke's Gospel, materialism is depicted as a barrier to discipleship. The story of the rich young ruler (Lk 18:18-30) illustrates how attachment to wealth and possessions can hinder one's willingness to follow Jesus. The rich young ruler is unwilling to part with his wealth, and this prevents him from becoming a true disciple. This challenge reminds leaders and disciples

[80] Darrell L. Bock, *Luke: 2 Volumes (Baker Exegetical Commentary on the New Testament)* (Grand Rapids, MI: Baker Academic, 1996), IV.

[81] Gary M. Burge and Gene L. Green, *The New Testament in Antiquity, 2nd Edition: A Survey of the New Testament within Its Cultural Contexts* (Grand Rapids, MI: Zondervan Academic, 2020), 258.

[82] Cynthia A. Jarvis and E. Elizabeth Johnson, *Feasting on the Gospels--Luke, Volume 2: A Feasting on the Word Commentary* (Louisville: Presbyterian Publishing Corp, 2014), 49.

to prioritize spiritual values over material gain.[83] Self-centeredness, or a focus on one's own desires and interests, can also obstruct discipleship and leadership. When individuals place their own ambitions and priorities above those of Jesus, they may fail to fully embrace His teachings and mission. Jesus calls for self-denial and carrying one's cross, emphasizing the need to relinquish self-centeredness in favor of a commitment to His lordship and service to others.

7.2. The Dangers of Pride and Self-Righteousness

Pride and self-righteousness are depicted in the Gospel of Luke as substantial obstacles to authentic discipleship and effective leadership, creating barriers between individuals and God, as well as between leaders and the people they are called to serve. Jesus addresses these issues through stories like the Parable of the Pharisee and the Tax Collector (Lk 18:9-14), where He contrasts the humility of the tax collector with the Pharisee's self-righteousness.[84] The Pharisee's attitude reflects an inflated sense of spiritual superiority, relying on external appearances rather than a humble heart. Jesus consistently teaches that true discipleship demands humility, a willingness to recognize one's shortcomings, and reliance on God's grace. By exposing the dangers of pride, Luke warns that self-righteousness can distort one's perception of God and others, leading to judgmental attitudes and a lack of compassion.[85] Thus, humility, not pride, becomes the hallmark of discipleship, guiding leaders to serve with empathy, authenticity, and a focus on God's grace.

Luke's Gospel warns against pride through various encounters with Pharisees and religious leaders who exalted themselves. The parable of the Pharisee and the tax collector (Lk 18:9-14) illustrates the danger of prideful self-assurance in one's righteousness. Pride can blind individuals to their need for God's grace and mercy, hindering genuine discipleship. Self-righteousness, a belief in one's own moral superiority, can lead to judgmental attitudes and a lack of empathy for others. In the story of the woman who anointed Jesus' feet (Lk 7:36-50), the Pharisee's self-righteousness prevents him from recognizing the woman's repentance and Jesus' forgiveness. Leaders and disciples must guard against self-righteousness and cultivate humility and compassion.

---

[83] John Phillips, *Exploring the Gospel of Luke: An Expository Commentary* (Grand Rapids, MI: Kregel Academic, 2005), 112.

[84] Philip Schaff, *Introduction, and the Gospels of Matthew, Mark, and Luke* (New York: C. Scribner's sons, 1889), 187.

[85] Mark L. Strauss, *Four Portraits, One Jesus, 2nd Edition: A Survey of Jesus and the Gospels* (Grand Rapids, Michigan: Zondervan Academic, 2020), 543.

7.3. The Fear of Persecution and Rejection

The fear of persecution and rejection poses a serious challenge to discipleship and leadership in the Gospel of Luke, as it can discourage individuals from fully committing to Jesus' call. Jesus frequently reminds His followers of the costs associated with discipleship, preparing them for the potential hardship, isolation, and even hostility they may face. In passages such as Luke 6:22-23 and Luke 9:23-26, He emphasizes that following Him often means standing apart from societal norms and enduring misunderstandings or criticism from others.[86] Despite these challenges, Jesus calls for courage, encouraging disciples to take up their cross daily and to find strength in their identity in God's Kingdom rather than seeking approval from the world. By addressing the fear of persecution and rejection, Luke underscores the necessity of resilience and faith, presenting discipleship as a commitment to the truth that transcends worldly acceptance and affirms the enduring promise of God's presence and reward.[87] Fear of persecution and rejection can deter individuals from embracing discipleship and leadership:

Jesus frequently warns His disciples about the possibility of persecution due to their association with Him (Lk 21:12-19). Fear of persecution may cause some to conceal or compromise their faith. Effective leadership and discipleship require courage and a willingness to endure persecution for the sake of one's faith and commitment to Jesus.[88] The Gospel of Luke records instances where Jesus and His message faced rejection in various communities. The fear of rejection by family, friends, or society can discourage individuals from openly following Jesus or stepping into leadership roles. Discipleship often involves the challenge of accepting potential rejection while remaining faithful to one's calling.

7.4. The Parable of the Sower: Lesson on Endurance and Faithfulness

The Parable of the Sower in Luke 8:4-15 serves as a poignant lesson on the endurance and faithfulness required of disciples and leaders as they navigate the challenges and obstacles of their spiritual journey. In this parable, Jesus illustrates the various responses to His message through the imagery of seeds sown on different types of soil. Each type of soil represents distinct conditions of the heart that can hinder or nurture spiritual growth. The seeds that fall on the path are quickly eaten by birds, symbolizing those who hear the word but fail to understand it, the rocky ground represents those

---

[86] Martin W. Mittelstadt, *The Spirit and Suffering in Luke-Acts: Implications for a Pentecostal Pneumatology* (London: A&C Black, 2004), 61.

[87] Clifford Samuel, *Luke to Theo: Understanding Luke's Gospel in the World of the First Century* (London: Austin Macauley Publishers, 2024), 206.

[88] Darrell L. Bock, *Luke*, 338.

who initially receive the message with joy but fall away when faced with trials; the thorns depict individuals who are choked by worries and material concerns, preventing them from bearing fruit.[89] In contrast, the good soil signifies those who hear the word, retain it, and produce a bountiful harvest through perseverance. This parable emphasizes the importance of cultivating a receptive heart and the necessity of enduring faithfulness in the face of adversity, reminding disciples and leaders that true growth in faith is often tested by life's challenges. Through this teaching, Luke encourages followers to remain steadfast and committed, trusting in God's transformative power to produce lasting fruit in their lives and ministries. The Parable of the Sower in Luke 8:4-15 illustrates the challenges and obstacles disciples and leaders may encounter:

Some individuals receive the word of God with enthusiasm but lack depth, representing those who may initially embrace discipleship or leadership but quickly fall away when faced with difficulties or distractions. Other individuals allow the cares, riches, and pleasures of life to choke the word, symbolizing the impact of materialism and self-centeredness on discipleship and leadership. Those who receive the word with a noble and good heart represent individuals who endure and bear fruit, despite the obstacles and challenges they face.

This parable emphasizes the importance of endurance and faithfulness in the face of challenges. Leaders and disciples must strive to cultivate a receptive heart (good soil) that remains committed to God's word and mission, even when faced with obstacles such as materialism, self-centeredness, pride, self-righteousness, fear of persecution, and rejection.[90] Through endurance and faithfulness, disciples and leaders can overcome these challenges and continue to grow in their journey of discipleship and leadership.

8. Contemporary Relevance of Luke's Model of Discipleship and Leadership

The contemporary relevance of Luke's model of discipleship and leadership is profound, offering timeless principles that resonate with today's challenges and opportunities in ministry and everyday life. Luke's emphasis on humility, compassion, and inclusivity in discipleship serves as a crucial reminder for modern believers navigating diverse and often polarized communities. His teachings call for leaders to embody servant leadership,

[89] Franklin Scott Spencer, *The Gospel of Luke and Acts of the Apostles: Interpreting Biblical Texts Series* (Nashville, TN: Abingdon Press, 2008), 144.

[90] Richard N. Longenecker, *The Challenge of Jesus' Parables* (Grand Rapids, MI: Wm. B. Eerdmans Publishing, 2000), 130.

prioritizing the needs of others over personal ambitions, which is increasingly vital in a culture that often celebrates individualism and self-promotion.[91]

Moreover, Luke's portrayal of women as vital contributors to Jesus' ministry challenges contemporary church structures to embrace gender equality and empower all members of the community to take active roles in leadership. The lessons from the parable of the Good Samaritan resonate powerfully in today's context, encouraging individuals to break down social and cultural barriers and to practice radical compassion in their interactions with those who are marginalized or different from themselves.[92]

Additionally, the obstacles outlined in Luke, such as materialism, pride, and the fear of persecution, remain prevalent in contemporary society. Addressing these challenges requires a renewed commitment to spiritual growth and community engagement, fostering an environment where faith can thrive amidst adversity.[93] Ultimately, Luke's model serves as a guide for developing resilient, compassionate leaders and disciples who are committed to living out their faith authentically in a complex and changing world, advancing the mission of the Kingdom of God in their communities.

9. Application in Church and Ministry Settings

Applying the principles of radical discipleship in church and ministry settings involves fostering a community that encourages self-denial and prioritizes commitment to Christ. Leaders can cultivate an environment where individuals are taught the significance of taking up their crosses daily, emphasizing that true discipleship often requires personal sacrifice and a willingness to face challenges for the sake of the Gospel. This can be implemented through discipleship programs, workshops, and sermons that focus on the importance of following Christ's example in everyday life. By creating spaces for open discussion about the cost of discipleship, congregants can be better prepared to support one another through trials and encourage each other in their faith journeys.

Furthermore, ministries can actively engage in outreach that exemplifies compassion, inclusivity, and service to the marginalized, reflecting Jesus' call to radical love and acceptance. This might include community service initiatives, partnerships with local organizations, and support for those facing persecution or hardship. Encouraging church members to use their gifts and resources for the benefit of others reinforces the idea that leadership in the

[91] Barbara E. Reid OP and Shelly Matthews, *Wisdom Commentary: Luke 10-24* (Minnesota. Liturgical Press, 2021), 429.

[92] John T. Carroll, *Luke: A Commentary* (Louisville, Kentucky : Westminster John Knox Press, 2012), 463.

[93] Suzanne Watts Henderson, *Christology and Discipleship in the Gospel of Mark* (Cambridge: Cambridge University Press, 2006), 56.

church is about servanthood. When the church embodies these values, it not only nurtures a deeper sense of community but also equips individuals to lead by example, demonstrating that the call to follow Christ entails a commitment to love and serve others, even in the face of difficulties.

Additionally, providing opportunities for congregants to share their experiences of discipleship and the challenges they face can foster mutual accountability and support. Small groups, mentorship programs, and prayer circles can serve as platforms for individuals to express their struggles, seek guidance, and celebrate victories in their faith. By emphasizing the importance of community in discipleship, the church can create a culture that not only prepares members to take up their crosses but also rejoices in the journey together. This holistic approach to discipleship ensures that the church becomes a nurturing ground for leaders who are equipped to face the challenges of following Christ and impacting their communities positively.

9.1. Fostering Inclusive Leadership Structures

Luke's emphasis on inclusive discipleship offers valuable insights for contemporary church and ministry settings by advocating for the recognition and nurturing of diverse talents and gifts among all individuals. This approach emphasizes the importance of valuing every member's contribution, fostering leadership structures that prioritize inclusivity and active participation. By embracing the gifts of people from varied backgrounds, including those often underrepresented—such as women and marginalized groups—ministry leaders can create a space where everyone feels valued and empowered to contribute. This model of leadership not only aligns with the spirit of Luke's Gospel but also strengthens the sense of community and belonging, enriching the faith experience for all involved.

Encouraging individuals from diverse backgrounds to assume leadership roles can bring a depth of perspective and experience that better reflects the broader community. As Luke's example illustrates, inclusive leadership is not simply about filling positions but about building a vibrant ministry that mirrors the diversity of God's people. Such representation fosters a richer, more dynamic faith community that is better equipped to meet the varied needs of its members. When leaders make inclusivity central to their mission, they enhance the church's capacity for outreach, growth, and resilience, ultimately creating a ministry that embodies compassion, unity, and the welcoming love reflected in the teachings of Luke.[94]

[94] David Gooding, *According to Luke: The Third Gospel's Ordered Historical Narrative* (Cincinnati, OH: Myrtlefield House, n.d.), 187.

9.2. Empowering Emerging Leaders

Luke's model of discipleship emphasizes empowering emerging leaders through growth opportunities and intentional mentorship, setting a framework that contemporary church and ministry settings can replicate to develop future leaders. In Luke's Gospel, Jesus' discipleship approach included both instruction and hands-on ministry experience, preparing His followers to carry forward His mission. Similarly, today's faith communities can build mentorship programs and leadership development initiatives that provide young and aspiring leaders with the skills, biblical knowledge, and practical experience necessary for effective service. This structured approach to leadership development nurtures a generation equipped to lead with confidence, compassion, and faith-centered conviction.

By fostering a culture of mentorship and empowerment, faith communities build a continuous and resilient leadership pipeline. Experienced leaders can actively pass down their wisdom and insight, while new leaders gain firsthand guidance and a network of support. Such an approach not only strengthens the immediate ministry but also ensures continuity and long-term stability. As seasoned leaders invest in the growth of emerging leaders, they create a legacy that honors their work and sustains the community's mission. This commitment to mentorship embodies the spirit of Luke's discipleship model, empowering each new generation to step forward with a sense of purpose and readiness to lead.[95]

9.3. Lessons for Leadership in Secular and Nonprofit Organizations

The Gospel of Luke offers valuable lessons on leadership that are highly relevant for both secular and nonprofit organizations, emphasizing qualities such as compassion, integrity, and servant leadership. Luke's portrayal of Jesus as a leader who prioritizes humility, inclusivity, and service to others provides a model for leaders seeking to create positive, ethical workplaces. For instance, the emphasis on compassionate leadership encourages leaders to put people before profit or position, fostering a workplace culture that values empathy and respect. Jesus' interactions with people from diverse social backgrounds highlight the importance of inclusivity, reminding leaders to build teams that reflect a range of perspectives and to treat every member as a valued contributor.

Moreover, Jesus' focus on mission-driven work, seen in His dedication to serving the marginalized, speaks to the core of nonprofit work, where purpose often outweighs personal gain. By leading with integrity and selflessness, as exemplified in Luke, leaders can cultivate trust and motivate

[95] Anthony J. Gittins CSSp, *Called to Be Sent: Co-Missioned As Disciples Today* (Eugene, OR: Wipf and Stock Publishers, 2018), 200.

their teams to pursue goals with dedication and unity. Overall, Luke's lessons on leadership encourage a style rooted in values, service, and community, offering a foundation for effective, ethical leadership across sectors.

9.4. Servant Leadership as a Model for Success

Luke's concept of servant leadership, as presented in the New Testament, provides a model of leadership that prioritizes the needs and well-being of others above self-interest. This approach to leadership is rooted in humility, empathy, and a deep commitment to serving one's community or organization. When leaders focus on serving their teams, clients, or beneficiaries, they foster an environment where individuals feel valued and supported. Such an approach not only builds trust but also encourages collaboration and loyalty within the organization. By putting the interests of others first, servant leaders create a foundation of respect and mutual support, which leads to more effective teamwork and a stronger sense of purpose among members.

In secular and nonprofit settings, embracing the principles of servant leadership can lead to significant improvements in organizational effectiveness and employee satisfaction. Leaders who exhibit humility and empathy often find that their teams are more engaged and motivated, as these qualities create a positive work culture that values personal growth and collective success. This people-centered approach can increase productivity, reduce turnover, and enhance overall job satisfaction, leading to a more resilient and adaptable organization. As Luke's concept of servant leadership illustrates, when leaders genuinely care for the well-being of those they lead, they inspire others to invest in the organization's mission, fostering a shared commitment to success and positive impact.

9.5. The Ethical Foundations of Leadership

Luke's emphasis on ethical leadership, compassion, and inclusivity offers a powerful framework for leadership within secular and nonprofit organizations. Leaders who prioritize ethical behavior, fairness, and justice create environments that promote trust and collaboration. By championing these values, leaders can inspire their teams to work together more effectively, fostering a culture where all voices are respected, and decisions are made with integrity. Luke's approach to ethical leadership goes beyond personal gain, challenging leaders to act in the best interests of their communities and to consider the broader social implications of their actions. This commitment to ethical principles cultivates a sense of belonging and purpose among employees, aligning them with the organization's mission in meaningful ways.

Incorporating the principles of ethical leadership from Luke's Gospel can significantly enhance an organization's reputation and create a lasting positive impact on society. When leaders embody compassion and inclusivity, they not only attract diverse perspectives but also demonstrate a commitment to social responsibility, which can inspire trust from stakeholders, beneficiaries, and the wider community. Such ethical leadership establishes a solid foundation for sustainable success, as organizations are better equipped to respond to challenges and changes with a clear moral compass. In this way, Luke's teachings on ethical leadership can help organizations make a genuine difference, building both internal resilience and external credibility in an increasingly interconnected and socially conscious world.[96]

9.6. Discipleship and Leadership in Social Justice Movements

The model of discipleship and leadership found in the Gospel of Luke offers profound insights for social justice movements, where the pursuit of equity, compassion, and solidarity with the marginalized are central. Jesus' ministry, as depicted in Luke, was marked by a commitment to addressing injustices and uplifting those who were oppressed or excluded, from His care for the poor to His defense of those shunned by society. His approach to leadership emphasizes humility and service, setting an example for leaders in social justice movements to prioritize the needs of the vulnerable above personal or political gain.

Luke's emphasis on compassionate and inclusive discipleship calls for movements to be rooted in love and empathy, fostering an environment where diverse voices and experiences are valued and upheld. This approach not only strengthens the movement's impact but also ensures it aligns with values of justice, respect, and unity. Through the lens of Luke's model, discipleship in social justice is an active call to seek transformation, address systemic inequities, and embody a commitment to justice and peace that reflects the ethics of God's Kingdom.

9.7. The Role of Compassion and Advocacy

Luke's Gospel places a strong emphasis on compassion and advocacy for the marginalized, highlighting Jesus' ministry to those often overlooked or oppressed. This message resonates deeply with contemporary social justice movements, offering leaders and activists a framework of empathy, courage, and proactive engagement. Luke's portrayal of Jesus as an advocate for the outcast provides a model of leadership rooted in humility and solidarity, calling leaders to stand with those who face systemic injustices. By championing the rights and dignity of all individuals, leaders can embody the compassionate, inclusive values that Luke highlights, aiming to create environments where everyone has the opportunity to flourish.

[96] M. Eugene Boring and Fred B. Craddock, *The People's New Testament Commentary* (Louisville, KY: Westminster John Knox Press, 2010), 259.

These principles from Luke's Gospel inspire a commitment to lasting change that prioritizes equity and justice in society. Leaders who embrace Jesus' example of compassion and advocacy can take practical steps to address inequalities and challenge the status quo. Whether by supporting fair policies, increasing representation, or fostering inclusive communities, such leaders actively contribute to a more just society. In this way, Luke's teachings empower individuals not only to recognize the needs of the marginalized but also to act in ways that promote meaningful change, aligning their efforts with a mission of universal dignity and fairness.

9.8. Models of Inclusive Activism

Luke's emphasis on inclusive discipleship aligns with the principles of inclusive activism in modern social justice movements. Advocates can draw upon Luke's model of including women, marginalized groups, and diverse voices in their advocacy work to ensure a more comprehensive and impactful approach to social change.[97] By promoting diverse leadership and collaboration, contemporary social justice movements can create a broader and more sustainable impact in the fight for justice and equality. Luke's model of discipleship and leadership has enduring relevance in various contexts, including church and ministry settings, secular and nonprofit organizations, and social justice movements. It offers valuable lessons on inclusive leadership structures, empowerment of emerging leaders, servant leadership, ethical foundations, compassion, advocacy, and inclusive activism. These principles can guide contemporary leaders and advocates in their efforts to create more inclusive, compassionate, and just communities and organizations.

Summary of Findings

Kingdom discipleship is the transformative journey of both being and making disciples who wholeheartedly submit to God, with the goal of cultivating a deep and abiding relationship with Him. At its core, the Kingdom represents God's rule, reign, and authority over all creation, and discipleship involves the intentional process of guiding others—or oneself—into a life of commitment and surrender to God's purposes. This path requires a self-sacrificing spirit, as disciples are called to align their lives entirely with God's will, reflecting His love and truth in all aspects of life. In essence, discipleship goes beyond mere belief; it's an active pursuit of God's Kingdom values that shape individuals into true followers of Christ.

This concept of Kingdom discipleship captures the very heart of Jesus' mission and serves as the foundation of the church's purpose as the body

---

[97] John MacArthur, *Luke 1-17 MacArthur New Testament Commentary Set* (Chicago, IL: Moody Publishers, 2011), 168.

of Christ. The church is not only a community of believers but a dynamic movement, tasked with expanding God's Kingdom on earth through dedicated discipleship. Just as Jesus invested in His followers, teaching them to embody His character and carry forward His message, the church is called to raise disciples who live out the values of the Kingdom in their everyday lives. By committing to this mission, the church fulfills its role in God's plan, embodying His reign in the world and inviting others to experience the transformative power of life under His rule.

This chapter has sought to affirm that the privilege of discipleship is extended to all individuals, emphasizing that the invitation to follow Christ is universal and inclusive. Christ initiates this call to Missiological Discipleship, providing all that is necessary to guide each disciple toward spiritual maturity and fulfillment of their purpose. Yet, this journey is not solely a divine work; it requires the individual's active choice and consistent commitment. Discipleship, in this sense, involves a partnership between God's initiating grace and the disciple's response—a dedication that deepens through a commitment to Christ's mission.

At the heart of Missiological Discipleship lies the profound truth of God's pursuit of humanity, with a purpose of reconciliation and restoration. This divine mission extends the privilege of being co-laborers with God, inviting all who accept the call to participate in a purpose that transcends individual lives and reaches toward the fulfillment of God's grand design. In joining this mission, disciples engage in a transformative partnership with God, working to bring His redemptive love and Kingdom to the world. Thus, Missiological Discipleship is not only an invitation to personal growth but a call to actively partake in God's unfolding plan since creation, making each disciple an integral part of this ultimate, redemptive mission.

8

Passion and Resurrection Narratives in Luke's Gospel The Culmination of Salvation

Introduction

The passion and resurrection narratives in the Gospel of Luke are central to the Christian faith and represent the culmination of the salvation story, with all four Gospel writers dedicating significant attention to it, making it the core of their accounts. These narratives recount the events leading up to Jesus' crucifixion, His death on the cross, His burial, and ultimately His triumphant resurrection from the dead. Here, we will delve into the significance of these narratives and how they form the climax of Luke's message of salvation. Luke's unique interpretive approach and creative contributions to the passion narrative can be readily identified and appreciated. However, the sources underlying Luke's passion narrative have been widely scrutinized. In this chapter, we examine the meaning and significance of the term "passion narrative" and its role within the Gospels. We also explore the genre, sources, and distinctive characteristics of the passion narrative, including the influence of the pre-Gospel passion traditions, the narrative's formation and development, and the role of the Old Testament within these accounts.

1. The Significance of the Passion and Resurrection Narratives

The passion and resurrection narratives within the Gospel of Luke hold profound significance within the Christian faith. These narratives chronicle the final moments of Jesus' earthly ministry, His crucifixion, burial, and the miraculous event of His resurrection from the dead. They are central to the Christian understanding of salvation, redemption, and the promise of eternal life. The passion narrative highlights the sacrificial atonement of Jesus, His willingness to bear the sins of humanity, and the unjust suffering He endured. The resurrection narrative, on the other hand, signifies the victory of Jesus over death and sin, offering hope, forgiveness, and the assurance of new life to all who believe. In this study, we will delve into the profound theological, historical, and spiritual dimensions of these narratives and their enduring relevance in contemporary Christian thought and practice.

2. Overview of Luke's Gospel and Its Unique Perspective

The Gospel of Luke, one of the four canonical Gospels in the New Testament, offers a distinctive perspective on the life and ministry of Jesus Christ. Unlike the synoptic Gospels of Matthew and Mark, Luke's Gospel is known for its attention to detail, historical accuracy, and emphasis on the compassion and inclusivity of Jesus. It presents a comprehensive narrative of Jesus' birth, ministry, teachings, and ultimate sacrifice. Luke's unique perspective on Jesus as the Savior of all, regardless of social or religious background, is evident throughout his Gospel and is especially poignant in the passion and resurrection narratives.

3. The Place of Passion Narrative in the Gospels

The sacredness of Jesus' passion and death had tended for a thorough instigation of these episodes[1] in the gospel accounts. The passion story is an oldest part of the gospel tradition to receive definite shape and it was the first portion of the gospel to acquire a set form and unity. It is probably the first proclamation[2] of the gospel consisted in the recital of the passion. The term *passion* is derived from the Latin term *Pati*: which means 'to suffer.'[3] The term mainly used to refer to the suffering of Jesus, to His crucifixion. The Greek term *paschō* sums up the sufferings that Jesus foretold and underwent and which Christians have interpreted as have redemptive worth for the liberation of wo/men.[4] The passion story as seen in the gospels is not with an

---

[1] Jerome Neyrey, *The Passion According to Luke: A Redaction Study of Luke's Soteriology* (NewYork: Paulist Press, 1985), 1.

[2] John L. McKenzie, ed., "Passion," *Dictionary of the Bible* (Milwaukee: The Bruce Publishing Company, 1965), 640.

[3] D. M. Beck, 'Passion', *The Interpreter's Dictionary of the Bible*, vol. 3, edited by George Arthur Buttrick (New York: Abingdon Press, 1962), 663.

[4] Xavier Léon-Dufour, 'Passion of Christ,' *Dictionary of the New Testament*, tr. by Terrence Prendergast (London: Geoffrey Champion, 1980), 313.

organic unity. Passion narrative was the group of the story which was bound up and embellished and became the kerygma[5] of the early church.

The suffering and the subsequent glory has been foretold in all four gospels by Jesus (Mt 16:21; Mk 8:31, 9:31, 10:33, 34; Lk 9:22, 44; 22:37; Jn 6:51; 10:11-18). Jesus emphasized the will of the Father and He Himself freely chose to suffer and die on behalf of the people[6] (Mk 10:45; 14:24; Jn 10:11-18). The story of the events of Jesus' last few days, culminating in the crucifixion, is given a considerable proportion of each gospel[7] (Mt 21-27; Mk 11-15 Lk 19-23 and Jn 12-19). The crucifixion was a torturous death prescribed by Roman law for those who were not Roman citizens,[8] together with the burial of Christ is described in all four gospels (Mt 26-27; Mk 14-15; Lk 22-23; Jn 12-19). These passages play a climax in presenting the Christology and Ecclesiology to the 1st century Christians. The passion narratives are also religious account that emphasize the theological meaning of the facts narrated in the context of the history of salvation.[9]

4. The Genre of the Passion Narrative

The word *genre* means the literary form of the narrative. The *genre* is a significant indicator of the passion narrative's meaning and antiquity. The centrality of the passion of Jesus to redemptive history is suggested not only by the use of the Old Testament in its interpretation, but also by the *genre* within which it is related. The studies in the *genre* have isolated the traditional literary schema known to some as the genre of "court conflict," to others as the "story of the vindication of the innocent sufferer."[10] Modern biblical scholarship agrees that there was a primitive narrative but there are divergent opinions on the *genre*, content and milieu of the formative of that narrative.[11]

---

[5] Rudolf Bultmann, *The History of the Synoptic Tradition*, tr. by John Marsh (New York: Harper and Row Publishers, 1963), 275.

[6] [illegible] J. D. Douglas (London: InterVarsity Press, 1962), 629.

[7] Joe M. Sprinkle, 'Death of Christ' *Baker Theological Dictionary of the Bible*, edited by Walter A. Elwell (Michigan: Baker Books, 1996), 156.

[8] John F. Walvoord, 'Jesus Christ', *Wycliffe Bible Encyclopedia*, vol.1, edited by Charles F. Pfeiffer, Howard F. Vos and Jon Rea (Chicago: Moody Press, 1975), 335.

[9] Jose Maniparampil, *Reading the Synoptic Gospels* (Bangalore: Clavetian Publications, 2004), 55.

[10] George W. E. Nickelsburg, 'Passion Narrative,' *The Anchor Bible Dictionary*, vol. 5, edited by David Noel Freedman, (New York: Doubleday, 1992), 172.

[11] M. Judge, 'Passion of Christ, (In the Bible),' *New Catholic Encyclopedia*, vol. x, edited by John P. Whalen (New York: McGraw Hill Book Company, 1967), 1052.

The protagonists in the passion narratives are recognized for their prominent qualities for a legal or royal setting. Their lives are involved by the evil schemes, innocent Jesus was persecuted and finally he was vindicated. Within the development of the *genre* of passion narrative (Isa 52:13–53:12), combines the twin motifs of vindicated innocence and vicarious death. This plays a pivotal role for the understanding of the whole meaning of the passion narrative.

Luke's passion narrative portrays Jesus as a model of patient and selfless suffering. In Luke's gospel, there are more characters than in other passion narrative. There are chief and high priests, the scribes, elders, the captions of the Temple, Judas, Sanhedrin, the multitudes, crowd, women, soldiers, people, their rules, Pilate and Herod.[12] According to Joel B. Green, the parallels between the Isaianic *genre* and the passion narratives of the gospels are exceptional. They demonstrate further the possibility of an earlier and self-contained passion narrative constructed along with this literary convention. Moreover, they emphasize the close relation of Jesus' passion with God's redemptive activity, and especially with the interpretation of innocent death found in Isa 52:13–53:12.[13]

5. Sources of Lukan Passion Narrative

Luke deviates more substantially from Mark in the passion narrative than does Matthew. According to R. E. Brown, Luke deletes some incidents (like the anointing at Bethany), transposes others (like the charge against the temple, which is applied to Stephen in Acts), adds still others (like Satan entering Judas' heart). The total settings are necessary to understand the passion message[14] with the exception of 23:13, Luke makes some fifteen small alterations in Mark to remove the people as far as possible from the proceedings against Jesus (cf.19:45-47; 20:1-2; 21:38; 22:2, 6, 47, 52; 23:1, 2, 27).

Characteristically, Mk 15:29 and Mt 27:39 have all the passersby mock Jesus on the cross. In contrast, Luke has only the rulers mock him (23:35). According to Etienne Troemé, "Mark was one of Luke's two or three main sources."[15] The Lukan story of the crucifixion (Lk 23:26-46) includes

---

[12] E. Jane Via, 'According to Luke, who put Jesus to Death', *Political Issues in Luke-Acts,* edited Richard J. Cassidy and Philip J. Scharper (NewYork: Orbis Books, 1983), 130.

[13] Joel B. Green, 'Death of Jesus', *Dictionary of Jesus and the Gospels,* edited by Joel B Green, Scot McKnight and Howard I Marshall (Downer's Grove, IL: InterVarsity Press, 1998), 161.

[14] Raymond E Brown, *Crucified Christ in Holy Week: Essays on the Four Gospel Passion Narratives* (Collegeville, Minnesota: The Liturgical Press, 1986), 47.

[15] Etienne Troemé, *The Passion as a Liturgy: A Study in the Origin of the Passion Narratives in the Four Gospels* (London: SCM Press, 1983), 28.

several anecdotes which are unknown to Mark and Matthew. They are (a) the encounter with the women of Jerusalem on the way to Golgotha (23:27-31), (b) The dialogue with the penitent thief (23:39-49) and (c) The repentance of the multitudes (23:48). The additional source (special Lukan source) of Luke gives the following information. A pre-trial hearing for Jesus before the Sanhedrin without any Jewish obligations related to the Jewish trail of Jesus.[16]

Luke was familiar with traditions of the passion other than that found in Mark.[17] Both Mark's and Luke's passion narrative is the contribution of roughly the same incidents but only 38 percentage is common with Marcan parallel. There was already the train of thought or the skeleton of the passion narrative in the early church tradition and both Mark and Luke made use of the same archetype.[18] It intertwines the Marcan material with the non-Marcan. There is other approach deals as Luke had copied almost verbatim from Mark's passion narrative, other times the author has copied from the special source and other times has interwoven in the same scene words from each. In the passion narrative as a whole Luke uses Marcan wording in a range of about only 30 to 10 percent.[19]

There is enough material in Luke almost certain to take the form of the meaning of these special traditions. Beginning at Chapter 22, which opens with the chief priests plotting in fear of the people. Luke's first 2 verses are like Mk 14:1-2, even if severely edited down. Then omits the anointing of Jesus at Bethany (Mk 14:3-9) and goes immediately to the betrayal by Judas. This he, attributes to Satan (22:3), it is unlike to Mark and Matthew. John follows the same (13:2, 27). Luke follows Mark in the saying that they agreed upon price is in 'money'[20] (22:5).

According to Frank J. Matera at least in one section of the Lukan passion narrative, the interpreter can explain Luke's divergence from Mark without recourse to a passion source addition to Mark.[21] The Lukan narrative of the last supper, passion and resurrection would be taken over from Mark,

[16] Joseph B. Tyson, 'The Lukan Version of the Trial of Jesus', [illegible] 258.

[17] Stephen J. Binz, *The Passion and Resurrection Narratives of Jesus: A Commentary* (Minnesota: The Liturgical Press, 1989), 71.

[18] Etienne Trocmé, *The Passion as a liturgy*, 36.

[19] Raymond E. Brown, *The Death of Messiah: From Gethsemane to the Grave: A Commentary on the Passion Narratives in the four Gospels*, vol. 1. (NewYork: Doubleday, 1994), 67.

[20] Geard S. Sloyan, *Jesus on Trial; The Development of the Passion Narratives and their Historical and Ecumenical Implications* (Philadelphia: Fortress Press, 1973), 90.

[21] Frank J. Matera, 'The Death of Jesus According to Luke: A Question of Source', *CBQ* 47/3, (July, 1985): 90.

but here the end product is different. Mixed in with passages that are very close to Mark and passages different or absent from Mark.[22] Although the Lukan passion narrative retains the genre, the general order, and the contents of Mark's narrative, its omissions, additions, and transpositions have led some scholars to conclude that Luke used a traditional passion narrative in addition to Mark's. He has written in the Semitized Greek where as in the gospel of Luke it differs. In the view of H. I. Marshall, although the story is essentially the same as that in Mark, Luke has added material from other sources, and has arranged it that various distinctive motifs stands out.[23]

According to Vincent Taylor, verses 15-18 are unique to Luke, suggesting a special source. Some authors think that on both linguistic (word use and word count) and structural grounds, there is good reason to trace verses 14-18 to a non-Marken source.[24] For Geard S. Sloyan, "All things considered, Luke's differences from Mark on the time of this inquiry and the order in which it appears in his narrative are such that he must have used another source."[25] Where as Hans Conzelmann says that although the use of new material by Luke cannot be disputed one may say that the most important alterations are due to the editorial work and are the expressions of his views.[26]

According to John Drury, Mark's version of the legal process against Jesus is thoroughly revised by Luke.[27] Luke chooses an alternative account and not any other source and to present a narrative in which the Jewish religious authorities with their temple police, actually carried out the crucifixion.[28] From the above discussion one can come to a conclusion that there were already a train of thought existed in the early church before any of the gospel narratives were in written form and both Mark and Luke might have made use of the same source. In addition to the Marcan source Luke might have used special source which also included the passion narrative more elaborately than that of Mark.

---

[22] Raymond E. Brown, *The Death of Messiah*, 64.

[23] Howard I. Marshall, *The Gospel of Luke: A Commentary on the Greek Text* (Exeter: The Paternoster Press, 1978), 785.

[24] Vincent Taylor, *The Passion of St. Luke: A Critical Historical Investigation,* edited by O. E. Evans (SNTSMS 19, 1972), 50. Cited in Geard S. Sloyan, *Jesus on Trial*, 91.

[25] Geard S. Sloyan, *Jesus on Trial*, 95.

[26] Hans Conzelmann, *The Theology of St. Luke,* tr., by Geoffrey Buswell (London: Faber and Faber, 1960), 200.

[27] John Drury, *Tradition and Design in Luke's Gospel: A Study in Early Christian Historiography* (London: Darton, Longman and Todd, Nd), 111.

[28] Jack Y Sanders, *The Jews in Luke-Acts* (Philadelphia: Fortress Press, 1987), 16.

6. Characteristics of Passion Narratives

The passion narratives as a first unit which took a final form in the early Christian proclamation of Jesus Christ, it has a pre-gospel passion narrative and there was a period of its development into a definite shape. In the passion narrative Christian interpreters found the Old Testament's or the First Testament's promise being full filled in Jesus' innocent suffering and death. These things are dealt below.

6.1. Pre-Gospel-Passion Narrative

Accounts of the sufferings and the death of Jesus gives the references to the passion of Jesus that are presented in canonical and extrabiblical early Christian writings are testimony to the importance of the passion narrative in the early life of the church.[29] The passion narratives in the present gospels (Mk 14-15; Mt 26-27; Lk 22-23; 2-23; Jn 18-19) are different "from the rest of the Gospel material in that they seem not to have been compiled from the individual, self-contains unites or stories, but presents a unified, sequential account of the final events in Jesus' life and ministry."[30]

Several arguments from the literary criticism support the hypothesis of such a primitive narrative more than any other part of the gospels; this division has the narrative of a connected historical account. Among all four gospels there are substantial arguments regarding the process of events of the passion. Although chronological agreements in earlier parts of the gospels reflect more freely the specific interests of the writers, the events of holy week seen to have been so fixed in the tradition and so respected as the record of the climax of Jesus' life that the order could not be freely changed. It might be abridged, expanded or supplemented, but in general the story was retained.[31]

6.2. Formation and Development of the Gospel Traditions

There are different facts which points to the formation of a narrative tradition older than the gospel accounts. Though there are differences in the accounts the four [illegible] follow the arrest (Mk 14:43; Mt 26:47; Lk 22:47; Jn 18:2). The traditions behind the formation of the passion narratives may be (a) a short kerygmatic account (cf. 1 Cor 11:23-26) (b) a little longer account (from arrest to crucifixion) (c) with which then added the incidents around passion narrative such as the Last supper, and the Gethsemane

---

[29] Marrion L Soards, 'Passion Narratives', *Eerdmans Dictionary of the Bible*, edited by David Noel Freedman (Michigan: W.B. Eerdmans Publishing Company, 2000), 1011.

[30] M. Judge, 'Passion of Christ, (In the Bible)', *New Catholic Encyclopedia*, 1052.

[31] M. Judge, 'Passion of Christ, (In the Bible)', *New Catholic Encyclopedia*, 1053.

experience and followed to this the (d) the gospel accounts as one finds today.[32]

While there is essential agreement among the four gospels on the important events of the passion, each of the accounts is a unique composition with its own literary characteristics and theological viewpoint.[33] The passion narrative can best be understood as salvation history. That history with a theological intent. In order to appreciate the narrative fully, one can be alert to the theological, missing and liturgical factors that influenced their information.

A study of similarities and differences among the four gospel passion narratives deepens appreciation of their significance and also reveals much about the way in which the early Christian community and evangelists understood them. Luke is a scene proper to his gospels, separates the mocking and scourging, he attributes the mocking to the court of Herod Antipas, where Jesus is treated with contempt because of His claim to royalty[34] (Lk 23:11).

In the third gospel the scourging alternative proposed by Pilate follows closely upon his scene at Herod's court. Luke's special dealings between Herod and Pilate, for the other gospel writers do not seem to knew of Jesus appearance before the Tetrarch of Galilee (Acts 4:24-30). As the mercenaries of Pilate took their clue from the charges of the court, ridiculing and maltreating Jesus as a religious leader, taunting Him to exercise now His power of prophecy.[35]

6.3. Old Testament in Passion Narrative

For the better understanding of the passion narrative one has to look at the role of Old Testament in the passion narrative. A widely held thesis maintain that the substance of the passion story derives from Christian reflection on the Old Testament, but Old Testament references play a crucial interpretative role in the story of Jesus' death.[36] In the process of viewing the significance of Jesus' death in a narrative context, early Christians employed the Old Testament at a number of levels. In some cases they incorporated *direct citations* of Old Testament materials into the passion story (Lk 22:37,

---

[32] J. R. Donahue, 'Passion Narrative', *The Interpreter's Dictionary of the Bible*, supp. vol, edited by Keith Crim (Nashville: Abingdon Press, 1976), 644.

[33] M. Judge, 'Passion of Christ, (In the Bible)', *New Catholic Encyclopedia*, 1053.

[34] M. Judge, 'Passion of Christ, (In the Bible)', *New Catholic Encyclopedia*, 1055.

[35] M. Judge, 'Passion of Christ, (In the Bible)', *New Catholic Encyclopedia*, 1053.

[36] Alan Richardson, *An Introduction to the Theology of New Testament* (London: SCM Press, 1958), 188.

citing Isa 53:12; Mk 15:34, citing Ps 22:1). In other instances *allusions* to Old Testament texts were woven into the narrative material.[37]

In Jesus' own teaching regarding His passion one of the most striking elements is His use of Old Testament allusions and His interpretation of the scriptures in function of His own person and mission in God's salvific plan. He is the climax toward which all of Israel's history has been moving. His doctrine is so firmly rooted in scriptural thought that one can have little understanding of it in less one knew the significance of the Old Testament references made. Not merely the passion as a whole, but also may individual happenings are seen as the fulfillment of scripture and God's fore ordained will.[38]

Luke included incidents and Old Testament allusions that contribute to the themes of his Gospel including Jesus as the chosen one of God, the Messiah (Lk 23: 35). He stress upon Jesus' fulfillment of the servant prophecy is apparent, for he includes the allusions of the other synoptics; and he makes a special point of emphasizing the realization of Isa 53:12, by alluding to it in three different verse [39] (Lk 12:37; 23: 32-33). On Calvary Jesus' last words as recorded in Luke expresses the filial obedience of the redeemer, the chosen one as He cries in words "father, into your hands…" (23:46). Jesus' death has a powerful effect on those who witness it, changing their assumptions about what has just transpired.[40] The open and watchful people had attentively and positively followed Jesus from the beginning of his Galilean ministry of justice and had momentarily shut down their quest for God under pressure, now beat their breasts. The have seen the faithful God's activities during Jesus' last moments has led them to faith in repentance[41] (cf. Lk 18:13). In the gospel, Jesus, the righteous one who proclaims in word and by life-style that God's kingly justice is for the outcasts, comes to fullness of narrative articulation as Jesus invites a condemned malefactor into paradise.[42]

7. Events in the Passion Narration

In the section of the prayer before the arrest (22:39 45), there is an entry into the Mount of Olives,[43] a preparation for the prayer, an actual prayer and

[37] Joel B. Green, 'Death of Jesus', *Dictionary of Jesus and the Gospels*, 161.

[38] M. Judge, 'Passion of Christ, (In the Bible)', *New Catholic Encyclopedia*, 1055.

[39] M. Judge, 'Passion of Christ (In the Bible)', *New Catholic Encyclopedia*, 1056.

[40] Robert C. Tannehill, *The Narrative Unity of Luke Acts: A Literary Interpretation* (Philadelphia: Fortress Press, 1986), 273.

[41] Robert Karris, Luke: *Artist and Theologian: Luke's Passion Account as Literature* (New York: Paulist Press, 1985), 112.

[42] Robert Karris, Luke: *Artist and Theologian*, 85.

[43] The Lukan account of the prayer before the arrest is shorter and the associates are ignored in the process. According to Mark (14:32-34), the place is Gethsemane and Jesus

there is an encounter with the disciples. Before bringing His appeal before God the Father, as a preparation for the prayer Jesus encourages the disciples to pray. In Luke's account of the prayer is shorter than other gospels (Lk 22:40). The structure of that scene is indicated by the narrator's concentration on movement. The encounter with the father is the central concept of the narrative. It helps to articulate Jesus' action in the trail (bringing appeal before God) and the reaction (saying to the disciples to "keep on praying so that they may not enter into temptation") to his disciples. The Passion Narration in the Gospel of Luke offers a distinctive portrayal of the final hours of Jesus' earthly life, presenting themes of compassion, forgiveness, and divine purpose. Found in Luke 22–23, this account emphasizes Jesus' unwavering commitment to God's plan, his empathy for others, and the profound mercy he extends even amid his own suffering. Unlike the other Gospels, Luke's narrative gives particular attention to Jesus' interactions with individuals, including his disciples, the women of Jerusalem, and even the thief on the cross, revealing Jesus' love and concern for humanity up until his final breath.

Luke's account of the Passion is characterized by unique elements such as Jesus' prayer for his persecutors, "Father, forgive them, for they do not know what they are doing" (Luke 23:34), and the compassionate dialogue with the repentant thief, who is promised a place in paradise. Throughout these chapters, we witness Luke's emphasis on Jesus as the righteous sufferer, fulfilling prophecy and demonstrating God's justice tempered by mercy. This portrayal invites readers to see the Passion not only as an event of suffering but as a profound manifestation of divine love and grace, underscoring the significance of Jesus' sacrifice in the broader narrative of salvation. In examining Luke's Passion Narration, we gain insights into the themes of forgiveness, redemption, and the Kingdom of God—a Kingdom extended to all who turn to God, even in their final moments. This study enriches our understanding of Luke's unique theological perspective, which frames the Passion as both a moment of deep sorrow and the dawn of hope for humanity.

7.1. The Prayer of Jesus (Lk 22:39-46)

This narrative terminates the transition from the last supper and trail. The narrator brings the attention of the readers to the arrival of Jesus and His disciples to a certain place: *Ορος τῶν 'Ελαιῶν*[44] (Mount of Olives). In Luke

gives a command to *sit* there while he pray and he takes Peter, James and John and opening up his bottled up emotions. In the gospel of Matthew, the Marcan source is followed.

[44] For the Greek Translations *The Greek New Testament,* edited by Barbara Aland, Johannes Karavidopoulos et al. Fourth Revised Edition. Edmonds, WA: United Bible Societies, 2001 is used.

22:39-46, the prayer of Jesus in the Garden of Gethsemane reveals a profound moment of vulnerability, surrender, and divine resolve as he prepares for the suffering he is about to endure. Unlike the other Gospels, Luke emphasizes Jesus' prayerful submission to the Father's will, highlighting his humanity and the depth of his inner struggle. This passage begins with Jesus instructing his disciples to pray that they will not "fall into temptation" (Lk 22:40), setting the tone for the urgency of spiritual vigilance in the face of trials.

As he distances himself slightly from the disciples, Jesus prays with intense emotion, asking, "Father, if you are willing, take this cup from me; yet not my will, but yours be done" (Lk 22:42). This prayer encapsulates Jesus' total submission to God's will, even as he contemplates the suffering he is about to face. Luke alone describes Jesus' agony so profoundly that "his sweat was like drops of blood falling to the ground" (Lk 22:44), possibly signifying the extreme emotional and physical toll of his impending passion.

Luke also uniquely mentions that an angel appeared to strengthen Jesus (Lk 22:43), symbolizing divine support and foreshadowing the victory that will follow his obedience and sacrifice. Despite the overwhelming pressure, Jesus' prayer demonstrates his unwavering commitment to fulfilling his redemptive mission. This moment of prayer in Gethsemane exemplifies his role as the obedient Son who embraces suffering, reinforcing Luke's portrayal of Jesus as the compassionate, righteous sufferer. The passage concludes with Jesus returning to his disciples, only to find them asleep from exhaustion, underscoring human frailty and the need for dependence on God in times of trial.

The prayer in Gethsemane invites readers to reflect on themes of surrender, obedience, and the courage to face suffering, trusting in God's ultimate purpose. There is an encounter between them before and after the actual prayer of Jesus.

7.1.1. Jesus with his Sleeping Disciples

The narrator gives the reason for the sleep of disciples that it was because of their grief. Jesus may well know what is to take place. But the call for prayer according to Luke is the prayer to, *ἵνα μὴ εἰσέλθητε εἰς πειρασμόν* (*not to lead into temptation* 22:46). So that they may be ready both spiritually and physically[45] for what is yet to happen. In Luke 22.45-46, following his intense prayer in Gethsemane, Jesus returns to find his disciples asleep, exhausted from sorrow. This moment captures a poignant contrast between Jesus' spiritual readiness and the disciples' vulnerability

[45] Raymond E Brown, *The Death of the Messiah From Gethsemane to the Grave: A Commentary on the Passion Narratives in the Four Gospels,* vol. 1 (London: Doubleday, 1994), 193.

Despite his earlier instruction for them to "pray that you may not enter into temptation" (Lk 22:40), the disciples are overcome by the weight of the moment and their own weariness.

Jesus' response is not one of frustration but rather of urgency and compassion. He asks, "Why are you sleeping? Get up and pray so that you will not fall into temptation" (Lk 22:46). His words underscore the importance of spiritual vigilance, especially in times of trial. In this scene, Jesus' loneliness in his hour of agony is palpable; he faces his impending suffering with only divine support, as his closest followers are unable to remain spiritually alert. This interaction with the sleeping disciples not only reflects human weakness and the disciples' struggle to comprehend the gravity of what is unfolding but also serves as a timeless reminder for believers to seek strength and resilience through prayer. Jesus' care and gentle rebuke to "get up and pray" reveal his pastoral heart, emphasizing the need for dependence on God amid challenges and the significance of remaining spiritually awake to align with God's will. It is a part of the trial which is close by as a part of the hour that is at hand. Jesus has received the power and energy after His appeal before God and He also command His disciples to taste the same thing.

7.1.2. Jesus Before Father

All three synoptists record the agony and repeated prayer. Luke alone presents the bloody sweat and the vision of the angel (22:43-44). Jesus began praying, Πάτερ, εἰ βούλει παρένεγκε τοῦτο τὸ ποτήριον ἀπ' ἐμοῦ (*'Father, if thou be willing take away this cup from me'*). This prayer to the Father is as an 'instigation of the devil' and the bloody sweat is the token of the un-human and superhuman effort to keep back his repetition of the prayer and limiting himself and gladly accepting the cup. Jesus' devout and reverent submission to the Father won victory. Jesus was saved from death, though not from dying.[46] There came angels from heaven not to minister to His exhaustion but to strengthen Jesus to pray earnestly to agonize so intensely as to produce that phenomenon.[47] Then soul of Jesus was agitated by a succession of deep and conflicting emotions. He was also wounded in the house of his friends when one of the twelve became the toll of his enemies and even Peter's faith failed more and more exclusively He felt himself thrown for sympathy on the unseen presence of the father.[48] The narrator shows the preparation of Jesus to the process of the next stage.

---

[46] Lonsdale Ragg, *St. Luke* (London: Methuen and co, 1922), 285.

[47] Lonsdale Ragg, *St. Luke*, 286.

[48] W. P. Paterson, 'Jesus Christ' *Hastings' Dictionary of the Bible*, edited by James Hastings 3rd Printing (New York: Hendrickson Publishers, 1996), 445.

7.2. The Arrest of Jesus (Lk 22:47-53)

After the prayer and the encounter with father now Jesus being ready for the arrest as well as for the further encounters. It is the initial encounter of Jesus with the disciple who became the betrayer, the narrator gives the reason for the betrayal as the work of satan inside Judas (Lk 22:3). There is also an encounter with the soldier, the disciple who took the path of violence and also with the spiritual authorities who came to Jesus in darkness to arrest him as the work of darkness. In Luke 22:47-53, the arrest of Jesus unfolds with a mixture of betrayal, confrontation, and profound restraint. As Jesus speaks to his disciples, Judas arrives, leading a crowd armed with swords and clubs. In a gesture of betrayal, Judas approaches Jesus to kiss him, symbolizing his treachery under the guise of friendship.

Jesus confronts Judas, asking, "Judas, are you betraying the Son of Man with a kiss?" (Lk 22:48), which underscores the pain of being betrayed by one of his closest followers. The disciples, in a moment of panic, ask if they should fight back, and one strikes the servant of the high priest, cutting off his ear. Yet, Jesus, refusing violence, heals the servant, demonstrating his commitment to peace even in the face of imminent danger. Addressing the chief priests, temple guards, and elders, Jesus highlights the irony of their actions, noting that they have come after him as though he were a criminal, yet he had been teaching openly in the temple daily. This arrest scene captures the tension between human hostility and divine restraint, as Jesus willingly surrenders to fulfill God's redemptive plan, embodying obedience and compassion amid betrayal and hostility.

7.2.1. Agreement of Friend with the Enemy

Judas' action as inside informer enabled the authorities to locate him among the thousands of pilgrims camping on the slope.[49] Knowing the place where Jesus could be found, Judas anticipated the place by leading the soldiers to catch him and with a hypocritical kiss he identified Christ to the soldiers.[50] With priestly party's officers, the subordinates like elders, captains of the temple, chief priests and Judas with [illegible] and [illegible] came to Jesus, though it was full moon, to prevent the possibility of escape under the shadow of the olive tree. Jesus in calm dignity came forth to meet them.[51] There were three things in the arrest of Jesus. 1. The attempt of Judas

---

[49] Howard I. Marshall, 'Jesus Christ', *The Illustrated Bible Dictionary,* edited by J. D. Douglas (England: IVP, 1980), 767

[50] G. Colman Luck, *Luke: The Gospel of the Son of Man* (Chicago: Moody Press, 1960), 115.

[51] A. R. Fausset, 'Jesus Christ', *Fausset's Bible Dictionary*, 14th print (Michigan: Zondervan Pub. House, 1949), 371.

to Kiss Jesus (22:47, 48). 2. The disciples' attempt for the defense (49-51). 3. The rebuke which Jesus administers to those who come to take Him (v. 52, 53).[52] Judas' existence and betrayal are historical because Christians would never have made up such a character as one of their own and especially as one of the inner circle of twelve apostles.[53] Judas gives the picture of extreme betrayal and hypocrisy. Jesus questions his attitude. Judas' abandonment of God's servant has led to an ironic act of betrayal. It is not only ironic but also tragic.[54]

7.2.2. Friend Becomes the Betrayer

Various reasons are given for Judas' betrayal of Jesus such as 'satan had entered into him' and simple greed for money grow out. Another speculation is that Judas was one of the militant zealots disillusioned with the non-violent line Jesus appeared to be taking and trying to put him to the test one way or the other.[55] *One of the twelve* is the common expression for the betrayer in the synoptics. It is said to specify the traitor as to throw his criminality into tragic relief. The purpose of drawing near Jesus was to kiss Him.

In Luke, there is no record of an actual kiss except (*ἤγγισεν τῷ Ἰησοῦ φιλῆσαι αὐτόν*) an attempt. As far as the narrative is concerned the following dialogue of Jesus might be taken as anticipating and avoiding the kiss. Greeting with a kiss was the customary form between the master and disciple.[56] According to the narrator, "Judas' betrayal was part of the plan of God so the forces at work behind the scenes in the arrest of Jesus are part of some great drama in which the cosmic of evil is temporarily in control of the situation."[57] In the gospel of Mark Judas actually kissed Jesus or that he called him 'master' whereas according to Luke Jesus ask a poignant question to Judas: *Ἰούδα (φιλήματι τὸν υἱὸν τοῦ ἀνθρώπου παραδίδως;* ('would you betray the son of man with a kiss?').

---

[52] F. Godet, *The Gospel of St. Luke, The Foreign Theological Library: A Commentary,* edited by MD. Cusin, 5th edition (Edinburgh: T&T Clark, 1976), 308.

[53] John Dominicrossan, *Who Killed Jesus: Exposing the Roots of Anti-Semitism in the Gospel Story of the Death of Jesus* (New York: Haper San Francisco, 1991), 71.

[54] Darrell L. Bock, *Luke*, IVP New Testament Commentary Series, edited by Grant R Osborne (England: IVP, 1994), 357.

[55] George Tybout Purves, 'Jesus Christ', *Davis Dictionary of the Bible*, 4th revised edition, edited by John D. Davis (Michigan: Baker Book House, 1980), 91.

[56] Lonsdale Ragg, *St. Luke*, 287.

[57] Duncan Mac Pherson, 'Luke', *Scripture Discussion Commentary*, vol. 8 edited by Laurence Bright (London: Sheed and Ward, 1971), 96.

7.2.3. Jesus and the Violated Soldier

There were no speeches between Jesus and the soldier but it is a typical act of mercy to an enemy. But the act of Jesus has got a clear practical bearing. Jesus did not wanted to be the leader of an armed band but He was treated like a robber. The response of the disciples to the situation was expressed through the way of violence by one of the disciples. According the gospel of John it was Peter who takes up the way of violence and cuts off the ear of the high priest's servant. The narrator also brings the attention of the readers that there is also an act of compassion by Jesus by healing the afflicted servant who has come as his enemy.[58] The encounter of Jesus with the soldier is an emphatic statement of the position of Jesus on violence. "Jesus meets violence not with counter violence but with compassion and healing; he puts together what has been torn apart."[59] By which the narrator bring out the theological significance of the encounter of Jesus.

7.2.4. Jesus and the Spiritual Authorities

According to Luke, chief priests, the officers of the temple police, and the elders had came to Jesus to arrest Him (ἀρχιερεῖς καὶ στρατηγοὺς τοῦ ἱεροῦ καὶ πρεσβυτέρους (22:52). In the passion narratives, the chief priests are seen as the most active opponents of Jesus. None of the gospel presents them as simple priests.[60] The chief priests deposed the high priest. The term chief priest designates to a Jerusalem priestly aristocracy with positions of privileged power over the temple and its treasury. Jesus had no encounter with the chief priests until in the passion narrative. *The chief priests, the officers of the temple police and the elders of the people* give the impression that these captains have military or policing function in relation to the temple and have the status of Sanhedrin.[61] Earlier in the gospel the plot of these group can be seen (Lk 22:2,4). The encounter of Jesus is not out of fear instead brings out their fear to approach Him in the light. The contrast is brought as *this is your hour and the power of darkness*. This is different from

[58] Denis McBride, *The Gospel of Luke: A Reflective Commentary* (Dublin: Dominican Publications, 1997), 294.

[59] Denis McBride, *The Gospel of Luke*, 294.

[60] There was only one high priest at a time in Judaism, with the incumbent theoretically determined by hereditary descent from Aaron through Zadok. This High Priest hood is for a lifetime. In the time of Jesus Caiaphas was the High Priest and the gospel of John gives the reference to Annas, the father in law of Caiaphas as High Priest. Cf. Raymond E Brown, *The Death of the Messiah from Gethsemane to the Grave: A Commentary on the Passion Narratives in the Four Gospels*, vol. 2 (London: Doubleday, 1994), 1425.

[61] Raymond E. Brown, *The Death of the Messiah From Gethsemane to the Grave*, vol. 2, 1430.

the other gospel narratives. Here Jesus directly encounters the authorities but indirectly views the power of darkness which is Satan.

7.3. Jesus and Peter (Lk 22:54-62)

He was first examined in the high priest Anna's house, during which Peter denied him, three times.[62] After the arrest of Jesus the narrator brings the attention of the readers to Peter. All the gospels follow the same sequence of the following of Peter with the arrested Jesus. The love toward the master made him to follow Him, but the fear made him to be far from Him. There was both bravery and loyalty seen in Peter's life. But it was not an act of faith. The details of Peter's denial are different in the account of each gospel writers. For Luke it was before a maid, then to a man and thirdly to another man. According to John, first denial was before a doorkeeper girl, then to the bystanders and then to Malchus (Jn 18:15-18, 25-27). Where as in Mark and Matthew follow the same sequence, firstly to a maid then to the same maid and then to the bystanders. According to Mathew and Mark, Peter began to curse and to swear.[63] But for Luke the look of the Master has soon brought him back soon by His compassion.

7.3.1. Warm Fire and Denial with Fear

Before narrating the trial of Jesus Luke brings the story of the denial of Peter. According to Luke, Peter follows the arresting party 'at a distance' (ὁ δὲ Πέτρος ἠκολούθει μακρόθεν). Peter first joins the circle where a fire is kindled in the center of the courtyard. But it did not give comfort for Peter, instead he rejected Jesus[64] (22:61, 62). At that moment, Jesus was in a place where Peter could see Him. When the guilty apostle looked up, Jesus looked at him, (καὶ στραφεὶς ὁ κύριος ἐνέβλεψεν τῷ Πέτρῳ) (22:61) and who can sound the depths of what passed in those moments in the mind of the tortured person or that His fallen apostle? In any case there is an unfathomable love for and sympathy with His disillusioned disciple spoke from His eyes.[65] The implications for Luke's readers are obvious: the story of Peter's denial warns of the dangers inherent in discipleship.[66] The first denial of Peter was in a place he was warming up himself with the enemies of Jesus.

---

[62] D. Guthrie, 'Jesus Christ', *The Zondervan Pictorial Encyclopedia of the Bible*, vol. 3, edited by Merrill C. Tenny (Michigan: Zondervan Pub. House, 1977): 556.

[63] Lonsdale Ragg, *St. Luke,* 290.

[64] Denis McBride, *The Gospel of Luke: A Reflective Commentary,* 295.

[65] Norval Geldenhuys, *Commentary on the Gospel of Luke* (London: Marshall, Morgan and Scott Ltd, 1965), 584.

[66] Brain E Beck, *Christian Character in the Gospel of Luke* (London: Westminister, 1989), 109.

The role of Simon Peter (22:54:61) is parallel to Mk 14:30. Perhaps the strong was preserved to show how Jesus was left his fate alone and to contrast Peter's refusal to own Jesus with his subsequent rock-like witness to him.[67] Peter's Galilean accent must have betrayed his origin (Mt 26:73). The Galileans pronounced Aramaic differently from their Jews in Judea.[68] Peter was a person who confessed that Jesus is the Christ and son of God. Whereas in the Garden of Gethsemane he sees Jesus overcome by weakness and he feels a tremendous uneasiness in his heart. Peter learned from the First Testament that God as great and powerful, he might have transferred all this power to Jesus but when he saw the weakness he could not understand the situation at all. He envisaged of the Kingdom of God as always victorious and it was the reason when Jesus foretold the passion, Peter refused to accept any such kind of understanding of the mission of Jesus.[69]

7.3.2. Repentance and Tears

There is a downward denial of Peter, walking, standing and sitting. While following Jesus he walked. He went into the court and stood among the people. Finally, he sat by the fire that the enemies of Christ had built. In the life of Peter luxury had taken the place of fidelity.[70] The encounter of Jesus with Peter has a long process. That included a prophecy, disillusionment, there is also a response of Peter to grace and there was also sorrow in his heart. The encounter of Jesus with Peter in the house of the High Priest is not a sudden or direct encounter.

While Peter was in the last supper, he was proud to die for Jesus but the significant thing in the case of Peter is the prophecy concerning his denial fulfilled here. It was the time for the crowing of the cock. Failure of Peter made him to depart from the sin and into painful tears. Peter's denials taken place before a porteress and a group gathered before the high priest's courtyard before common people those who were fire warming.[71] Firstly, the crowing of cock reminded Peter of the warning of Jesus (v. 34 cf 60). Secondly, while Jesus was standing shackled within the court was being led to the quarters of Caiaphas turned and looked Peter[72] (καὶ στραφεὶς ὁ κύριος ἐνέβλεψεν τῷ Πέτρῳ, v. 61). But it was foretold by Jesus himself and now it being fulfilled and the *look* of Jesus to Peter could communicate the message

[67] G. H. P. Athompson, *The Gospel According to Luke*, 264.

[68] G. H. P. Athompson, *The Gospel According to Luke*, 264.

[69] Carlo M. Martini, *Ministers of the Gospel* (Italy: Milano, 1981), 73.

[70] Fulton J. Sheen, *Characters of the Passion* (New York: Garden city Books: 1953), 16.

[71] Neil J. McEleney, 'Peter's Denials-How Many? To Whom?', *CBQ* 52/3 (July, 1990): 472.

[72] D. G. Miller, *Luke*, Layman's Bible Commentaries, (London: SCM Press, 1963), 159.

of the reality of the denial of Peter. It is not the crowing of the cock made Peter to be bitter in his experience instead the 'the Lord looked at him'. It lead him to repentance and tears, Peter ἐξελθὼν ἔξω ἔκλαυσεν πικρῶς. It was the outcome of Jesus' encounter with Peter.

7.4. Mocking Soldiers and Jesus (Lk 22:63-64)

Before the formal assembly of the Sanhedrin Jesus was with the soldiers who were in charge of the temple guard.[73] They used Jesus for their own entertainment. They mocked Jesus, beat him, blindfolded him and attacked him.[74] The Roman soldiers mocked Jesus after His trial before Pilate (cf. Mk 15:16-20). According to Luke, Jesus was mocked and beaten by the captors-perhaps the temple guards.[75] After the arrest of Jesus, the narrator narrates three events that occur in quick succession. They are the denials by Peter (vv. 54-62), the mocking (vv. 63-65) and the trial of Jesus (vv. 66-71). The trail of Jesus in the High Priest's house may be on the evening and on the Sanhedrin in the early morning[76] (vv. 54, 66). Firstly Jesus was brought before Annas immediately after his arrest (Jn 18:13; 14). Then, during night He was taken to the house of Caiaphas, the actual High Priest and examined there (22:54, 63-65). Early in the morning, the Sanhedrin proper met in order to carry out the official trial and arrive at the official condemnation (22:66-71). The trail began with a search for witness on whose evidence Jesus could be charged.[77]

7.5. Jesus before Sanhedrin (Lk 22:66-71)

The trail before the Sanhedrin is followed by the arrest and the trail of Jesus by the Jewish religious leaders of the day. He was sent bound, to the apartments of Caiaphas, where the Sanhedrin had hastily assembled. It was situated at Jerusalem. They are the supreme council[78] and they had legislative

---

[73] Ch. 22: [63] Now the men who were holding Jesus began to mock him and beat him; [64] they also blindfolded him and kept asking him, "Prophesy! Who is it that struck you?" [65] They kept heaping many other insults on him.

[74] Denis McBride, *The Gospel of Luke*, 294.

[75] Malcolm O. Tolbert, *Luke-John,* The Broadman Bible Commentary, edited by Cliffon J Allan (Nashville: Broadman Press, 1970), 174.

[76] Darrell L. Bock, *Luke*, 359.

[77] William Barclay, *Crucified and Crowned* (London: SCM Press, 1961), 61, 63.

[78] Luke Timothy Johnson, *The Gospel of Luke*, Sacra Pagina, edited by J. Harrington (Minnesota: The Liturgical Press, 1991), 361. There are different functions for this council. The Sanhedrin had the right to levy the death penalty for the blasphemy and other religious crimes. But the penalty for such were stoning. But in the case of Jesus he was executed by Romans and the penalty was also Roman penalty, crucifixion. Therefore the reasons for the death become political, not just religious. The Sanhedrin was the supreme Jewish court. It consisted of 71 members, drawn from the Pharisees, Sadducees, elders and priests. It met in

executive and Judiciary powers. No harmonious evidence of blasphemy, which was the crime they sought to prove against him, could be found so that the high priest was forced to solemnly adjure Him to say if He were a messiah.[79] The examination of Jesus before the Sanhedrin was not a proper trial according to the legal rules of procedure. The purpose of this trial was to build up a case that could be submitted to Pilate.[80]

7.5.1. The High Priest's Interrogation

When Luke speaks of the 'high priest' (τοῦ ἀρχιερέως) it may be Annas who was the high priest from 6-5 AD and who retained his influence up to 18th century when Roman Government had appointed his son-in-law Caiaphas to the office[81] (cf. Jn 18:12-23). Luke records only one meeting of the Jewish council at dawn. Luke's account has certain similarities with Mark's but in essentials differs widely.[82] In Luke 23:13, the public may have been 'packed' by the Jewish leaders to make a demonstration to influence the governor. Luke may also wish to show that the Jewish people bear some responsibility.[83]

In the passion narrative one could evaluate the participation of the priests in the crucifixion of Jesus Christ. "Luke goes beyond Mark in emphasizing the persistence with which the chief priests and their accomplices pursued Jesus and the intensity of the pressure they brought to bear upon Pilate."[84] The reaction was so strong against him and wanted to destroy him. According

---

the temple court under the chairmanship of the high priest. See, Edward H Patey, *A Doctor's Life of Jesus: St. Luke's Gospel* (London: SCM Press, 1965), 154. When the crucial decision is made the people support their leaders for the crucifixion of Jesus. From 23:13-25, the narrator places strong emphasis on the responsibility of both the leaders and the people as a reason for the death of Jesus. In the gospel of Luke, the religious leaders have repeatedly presented as people who exalt themselves (1:43; 14:7-11; 16:15; 18:9-14) and are greedy rich who neglect the poor (11:39-41; 14:12:-14; 16:14; 19-31). The rejection of the claim that Jesus is king, first, voiced by Pharisees and it is repeated by the chief priests, scribes and elder, i.e., the Sanhedrin.

[79] [illegible]

[80] Samuel P Dutt, "Pontius Pilate: In Search of Truth", *The Trial of Jesus*, edited by Satish C. Gyan (Raipur: Guru Sadan, Nd.), 25.

[81] Michael Fallon, *The Gospel to St. Luke: A Introductory Commentary* (Bangalore: Asian Trading Corporation, 2003), 333.

[82] G. H. P. Athompson, *The Gospel According to Luke* (Oxford: The Clarendon Press, 1972), 264.

[83] Josef Blinzler, *The Trail of Jesus*, tr. by Isabel and Florence Mc Hugh (Cork: The Mercier Press, 1959), 115.

[84] Richard J. Cassidy, 'Luke's Audience, the Chief Priests, and the motive for Jesus' Death', *Political Issues in Luke-Acts*, edited by Richard J. Cassidy and Philip J. Scharper (New York: Orbis Books, 1983), 148.

to Luke (19:47-48), the chief priests (ἀρχιερεῖς), the scribes (γραμματεῖς) and the principal men of the people (τὸ πρεσβυτέριον τοῦ λαοῦ) sought to destroy him, but they did not find anything in Him. Luke indicates that the chief priests and their associates challenged him publicly in three different instances.[85]

7.5.2. Jesus the Messiah/Son of Man?

The group of Jewish leaders who plot to kill Jesus gathered in the Sanhedrin and the temple and finally take action to get rid of him. Here (22:66), the narrator may be suggesting that the council or the official body has authority over the people and the right to act on their behalf.[86] The question asked in the Jewish trail "if you are Christ, tell us" (λέγοντες, Εἰ σὺ εἶ ὁ Χριστός, v. 67). Jesus did not give any yes or no answer. Because if he answer 'yes'- it could mean a sort of political messiah[87] equal to which the accusers thought of. If He answer 'no'- it would a false answer because He was the Messiah. On the other side if he argued or questioned any of their messianic expectations to correct them, they would not discuss with him (cf. 20:7; 41-44) or on the other hand, if He would have tried to explain the true nature of the messiahship, they may not be able to comprehend or believe

---

[85] Christ had the courage of conviction. Peter was probably his boldest disciple, yet he denied his Lord under pressure, where as Jesus confessed his own person and mission before the Sanhedrin even though it means His death Jesus stood alone as he faced his final ordeal. Cf. Everett F Harrison, "Christ Jesus", *The Zondervan Pictorial Bible Dictionary,* 13th printing, edited by Merrill C Tenney (Michigan: Zondervan Pub. House, 1972), 161. The council decided they had received all the testimony they needed in their view Jesus was guilty of blasphemy. So they were ready to hand him over to the Roman authorities. The council could give a guilty verdict, but the Jews at the time were not allowed to impose the death penalty. Only the Roman government could sentence one to death. Even though Jesus had performed messianic miracles, the leaders of the nation refused to believe. They acted on behalf of the nation rejecting Christ. See John A Martin, *Luke*, The Bible Knowledge Commentary: A Exposition of the Scriptures, edited by John F (Canada: Victor Books, 1983), 261. Richard J. Cassidy, "Luke's Audience, the Chief Priests, and the motive for Jesus' Death" 148.

[86] The concentration of Luke on Sanhedrin for the cause of the death of Jesus seems to harmonize perfectly with Luke's emphasis throughout that it is Israel's leaders and not the people as the opponents and is singled out as the perpetrators of Jesus' death. Robert L Brawley, *Luke-Acts and the Jews, Conflict, Apology and Conciliation* (Atlanta: Scholars Press, NY), 105. In Luke, the Pharisees provide a contrast with Jesus. Luke takes over the Pharisees in a historical cultural and religious context in which they demand admiration and assigns them as a commensurate role. Cf. David P. Mossner, 'The Leaven of the Pharisees' and 'this Generation': Israel's Rejection of Jesus According to Luke', 23. By referring to the council of the elders of the people (22-66), the narrator suggests that the official body has authority over the people and the right to act in their behalf. Robert C. Tennyhill, *The Narrative Unity of Luke-Acts,* 189.

[87] D. G. Miller, *Luke*, Layman's Bible Commentaries, 159.

it.[88] Therefore He answered "if I tell you, you will by no means believe" (Ἐὰν ὑμῖν εἴπω, οὐ μὴ πιστεύσητε· v. 67b).

There are two questions made by the Sanhedrin. One in relation to his sonship and the other is the messiahship. The narrator has clarified not only the political but also the religious dimension of the charges which were brought against Jesus. One need to distinguish between the 'son of God' (ὁ υἱὸς τοῦ θεου) and 'son of man' (ὁ υἱὸς τοῦ ἀνθρώπου). The leaders of the Sanhedrin had known it. Though they knew it, when they presented Jesus before Pilate the preference is given to the political aspect alone.[89] For the first question concerning the messiahship, Jesus' reply questions the court's ability and willingness to engage in a discussion which would make them to understand the true messiahship is seen impossible. There is a contrast brought between the 'son of man' and 'son of God.'[90]

There is a direct encounter can be seen in the trail before the Sanhedrin. He stresses his messiahship in one sense on the other he also gave the future glory which He is to enter into (ἀπὸ τοῦ νῦν δὲ ἔσται ὁ υἱὸς τοῦ ἀνθρώπου καθήμενος ἐκ δεξιῶν τῆς δυνάμεως τοῦ θεοῦ v. 69). "They would behold Him one day in the most honourable position in heaven, fulfilling the well-known prophecy of Daniel, with all judgment committee to His hands" (Dan 7:9, 10).[91] "Jesus' response to the council reveals that for Luke Jesus' only claim to leadership was a religious one."[92] The encounter of Jesus to the religious leaders led them to lead Jesus to political authorities.

7.6. The Trial Before Pilate (Lk 23:1-5)

Three episodes of passion make up narrative of the trail of Jesus include the initial interrogation by Pilate (23:1-5); the encounter with Herod (23:6-12); and the final Condemnation of Jesus (23:13-25). All four-passion narratives agree that the Roman governor Pilate Judged Jesus to be innocent and that his death was due to the Jewish insistence.[93] In the first encounter with Pilate there were the religious leaders brought a series of formal charges forward which were political in nature. These charges were contrast to the hearing before the Sanhedrin.[94]

---

[88] D. G. Miller, *Luke*, Layman's Bible Commentaries, 160.

[89] Paul W. Walaskay, 'The Trial and Death of Jesus in the Gospel of Luke', [illegible].

[90] Denis McBride, *The Gospel of Luke. A Reflective Commentary*, 297.

[91] J. C. Ryle, *Expository thoughts on the Gospels: Luke*, vol. 2 (Edinburgh: The Banner of Truth Trust, 1858), 443.

[92] Paul W. Walaskay, 'The Trial and Death of Jesus in the Gospel of Luke', 82.

[93] John Dominicrossan, *Who Killed Jesus,* 147.

[94] Donald Senior, *The Passion of Jesus in the Gospel of Luke* (Delaware: Michael Glazier Wilmington, 1988), 107.

First of all the charge against Jesus is that "He perverts our Nation" (Τοῦτον εὕραμεν διαστρέφοντα τὸ ἔθνος ἡμῶν 23:2). Secondly "He forbids us to give tribute to Caesar" (κωλύοντα φόρους Καίσαρι διδόναι 23:2). This charge against Jesus in relation to the poll tax is patently false. This charge was brought with a clever mind of the leaders. Because Pilate's major political responsibility is the tax collection for Rome. The other reason behind it is that taxes go to Caesar, raising the issue of Pilate's personal loyalty or disloyalty to the government.[95] Thirdly, he claims that he is 'Christ a king' (λέγοντα ἑαυτὸν Χριστὸν βασιλέα εἶναι 23:2). Here an explicit opposing of the ruler can be seen. Here, Jesus is pictured as a revolutionary and it is responsibility of Pilate to stop such people.[96] Finally, "He stirs up the people, teaching throughout all Judea, from Galilee even to this place" (23:5). The reason behind such accusations is that while the Jewish Sanhedrin would be concerned primarily with the religious claims of Jesus where as the Romans would care only about political charges.[97] Here the leaders are uncomfortable with Jesus and regard Him with contempt. They treated Jesus as a threat to their nation's tradition.

Luke stresses the initiative of the leaders in handing over Jesus to the Romans. Luke 22:66 considered critically as a writing obviously represents a combination of Mark 14:53 and 15:1(a). Luke's details of time are of only secondary importance when it is a matter of giving the historical combination of events.[98] The Sanhedrin has questioned the messiahship of Jesus and Jesus' answer to them can be clearly understood him the claim to be the messiah on this basis they proceed to accuse him before Pilate (22:70-23:2). "Thus the decision to seek Jesus' death from Pilate is specifically a rejection of Jesus as Messiah. However, the accusations made before Pilate are broader and reflects several issues which have previously emerged in the narrative."[99] After hearing the chief priests, Pilate challenged the accused to define His position, but to his astonishment the latter refused to express Himself concerning the charges brought against Him."[100] Pilate did not believe Jesus

[95] Darrell L. Bock, *Luke*, 365.

[96] Darrell L. Bock, *Luke*, 367.

[97] Donald Senior, *The Passion of Jesus in the Gospel of Luke*, 107.

[98] Josef Blinzler, *The Trail of Jesus*, 116.

[99] Robert C Tannehill, *The Narrative Unity of Luke-Acts*, 195.

[100] Josef Blinzler, *The Trail of Jesus*, 195. Pilate can be seen as the animus of the Jewish hierarchy who is convinced that Jesus is innocent. According to Mark, 15:10, 'he perceived that it as out of envy that the chief priests had delivered him up' (15:10) "I did not find this man guilty of any of your charges against him' (v. 14). Though he found Jesus innocent but failed to release him. The historical account also favorable to this. Philo of Alexandria records that Agrippa I passed a judgment on Pilate saying He was cruel by nature and in his hard-heartedness entirely lacking in remorse and Judaea of his day was marked by bribes,

to be guilty (Lk: 23:4). The anti-Jewish Pilate wished to show the Jewish leaders how little he thought of their evidence.[101]

Based on the ground of religious blasphemy one cannot be killed. The political reason were encouraging the people to sedition, forbidding the payment of the Roman tax and claiming to be a messiah and king.[102] Pilate was clearly unwilling to handle the case, a point made plain in all four gospels. He discerned that the Jews were implacable in their demand for the death of Jesus. But he was also that the prisoner had done nothing that Romans regarded as meriting that penalty. So Pilate wanted to do nothing with the case. It suited him to send Jesus to Herod.[103]

Luke presents Pilate as trying to strike a bargain with the Jewish leaders and the people. Although Jesus had been found to be guiltless, Pilate was willing to satisfy the Jews by flogging him before release. Thus, Luke subtly changes his picture of a Roman governor out of his own nation as guilty of sedition against Rome.[104] Pilate did not want to give Jesus to be crucified. Especially since he could not observe the savior's nobility of character, His fearlessness and His spiritual and moral superiority over His accusers, Pilate felt perhaps that this prisoner might possibly be a divine being who had come to the world and would eventually reveal His power.[105] "Here Luke has Pilate, the voice of Roman Justice, proclaim three times that there is no evidence to suggest that Jesus had done anything that deserve the death penalty."[106] Philip Esler uses the term social legitimization to describe the political and social motivations of Luke's project.[107] Pilate ignores the question whether Jesus being the Christ, which was irrelevant to him as a Roman. For Pilate, the only accusation that matters is whether Jesus is actually presenting himself as an earthly King.[108] Luke emphasizes the Roman declaration of Jesus'

vainglorious and insolent conduct, robbery, oppression, humiliations, men often sent to death untried, and incessant and unmitigated cruelty. Ernest Fremont Tittle, *The Gospel According to Luke: Exposition and Application* (New York: Harper and Brothers Publishers, 1957), 252.

[101] Josef Blinzler, *The Trail of Jesus*, 191.

[102] D. G. Miller, 'Luke', *Layman's Bible Commentaries*, 160

[103] Canon Leon Morris, *The Gospel According to Luke: An Introduction and Commentary* (Michigan: WB Eerdmans Publishing Company, 1974), 320.

[104] S. G. F. Brandon, *The Trail of Jesus of Nazareth* (London: B.T. Batsford Ltd., 1968), 173

[105] Norval Geldenhuys, *Commentary on the Gospel of Luke* (London: Marshall, Morgan and Scott Ltd, 1965), 595.

[106] O. C. Edwards, *Luke's Story of Jesus* (Philadelphia: Fortress Press, 1981), 90.

[107] Mark Allan Powell, *What are they saying about Luke* (New York: Paulist Press, 1989), 84.

[108] Eugene La Verdiere, *Luke: New Testament, A Biblical-Theological Commentary* (Veritas Pub.: Dublin, 1980), 272.

innocence because it is important for Roman Christians to know that Jesus did not contravene their Law.[109] Through the proclamation of the innocence of Jesus, by the Roman government for Luke "there is an apologetic aspect to this aspect of the characterization"[110] for the Christians.

Pilate questions the accused with regard to his political ambitions. When he asked Jesus 'whether He is king of the Jews', He really means, "Are you a revolutionary seeking to establish an independent Jewish state?" Jesus answered 'you have said so'. That is "You are using the terminology with its political implications not I."[111] Since the people were divided about Jesus and since national unity was at stake, the leaders, after several attempts had to solve the problem once for all. It may be the blasphemy as well as the declaration of messiahship of Jesus might have made them to bring Jesus before Pilate.[112]

The trial before Herod is seen particularly in the gospel of Luke. Probably Luke had contacts with the household of Herod from which he drew this information[113] (cf. 8:3). It seems likely that Pilate would seek to turn over the trail of this embarrassing Galilean to Herod. The sending of Jesus by Pilate from his responsibility to Herod is a clear political skill of Pilate and he had shown respect for Herod's position.[114] Luke is glad to discharge the Roman soldiers for the responsibility, for the outrageous treatment of the prisoner; in his narrative first the priest and then Herod entourage, mock Him.[115]

7.7. The Trial Before Herod (Lk 23:6-12)

Pilate was the governor of the southern kingdom of Judea while Herod was the tetrarch of the northern kingdom of Israel. In the trial before Pilate the blame on him was completely political. When he heard of him as the one from Galilee and was under the jurisdiction of Herod. Pilate took that direction for further judgment. In one sense, Herod is a religious person, because he wanted to see a miracle like many religious people does. Herod never questioned the doctrine or bout the disciples instead he questions were prompted by curiosity. But Jesus did not speak any word to him.[116]

---

[109] Mark Allan Powell, *What are they Saying about Luke*, 85.

[110] Jonathan Knight, *Luke's Gospel* (London: Routledge, 1998), 58.

[111] Malcolm O. Tolbert, *Luke-John,* The Broadman Bible Commentary, 175.

[112] Tibor Horvanth, 'Why was Jesus Brought to Pilate', *Nov. Tes* XI/III (July 1969): 182.

[113] Tibor Horvanth, 'Why was Jesus brought to Pilate?', 182.

[114] G. B. Caird, *Saint Luke,* The Pelican NT Commentaries (Harmondsworth, England: Penguin Books, 1974), 247.

[115] Darrell L. Bock, *Luke*, 367.

[116] Fulton J Sheen, *Characters of the Passion,* 52. The capital of Herod was at Tiberias about fifteen miles from Nazareth and ten miles from Capharnaum, along with the sea of Galilee. There were two things with Herod. Firstly, his divorce from his wife and his

The reason behind the silence of Jesus may be because He considered that the conscience of Herod was dead. Herod was too familiar with religion. He wanted to have miracles but it was just to satisfy his curiosity.[117]

7.8. Sentence of Jesus to Death (Lk 23:13-25)

In Luke 23:13-25, Jesus' sentencing reflects the tragic miscarriage of justice as Pilate, after examining Jesus, finds no basis for the accusations against Him yet succumbs to the demands of the crowd. Despite declaring Jesus' innocence multiple times and acknowledging that neither he nor Herod found any cause for a death sentence, Pilate ultimately capitulates to the pressure of the chief priests, rulers, and a tumultuous crowd. In a moment marked by irony and moral failure, Pilate releases Barabbas—a known insurgent and murderer—instead of Jesus, the innocent. The exchange of Jesus for Barabbas emphasizes the depth of injustice Jesus endures as He is condemned to die on the cross, a sacrifice that fulfills His redemptive mission for humanity.

7.8.1. Enemies Becomes Friends

Jesus' activity had begun in Galilee and it was the home of political upheaval. It was from this place Judas the Galilean had stirred up his revolt[118] and Jesus also came from the land of rebels. Pilate sent Jesus to Herod Antipas, who was the price of Galilee who enjoyed the judicial power. When Jesus was brought before Herod, he was extremely curious to see Jesus and was satisfied.[119] Both Herod and Pilate could not find anything in Jesus. Though they could find anything in Jesus, they could rebuild their friendship. To say it from the study one can say that even in the death of Jesus brought reconciliation into two rulers. "Even though they declare Jesus innocent, these secular powers mock Jesus and ultimately condemn him to death."[120]

---

second marriage to Herodias, who as his brother's wife and the daughter of his half-brother Aristobulus. The other revealing act of Herod was his treatment of John the Baptist. The assassination of John the Baptist Herod when he heard about Jesus he thought that it was John's avenging spirit come back to haunt him (cf. Lk. 9:7-9). With these things Jesus encountered him. Herod had all the vices of his father-cruel, avaricious, and dissipated. He was an Edomite and the Edomites were the descendants of Esau.

[117] Fulton J. Sheen, *Characters of the Passion,* 53.

[118] John L. McKenzie Alois Stoeger, (ed.) *The Gospel According to St. Luke*, vol. 2, NT for Spirituality (London: Burns and Oates, NY), 220. Herod Antipas was the son of Herod the great who was living at the time of Jesus' birth (cf. Lk. 1.5). He was a ruthless, dissolute leader who is intent on destroying Jesus. Herod is seen at first in the beginning of the Gospel (3:1). His reign is noted as coinciding with the beginning of John the Baptist's ministry. Later he imprisoned John.

[119] Donald Senior, *The Passion of Jesus in the Gospel of Luke*, 113.

[120] Donald Senior, *The Passion of Jesus in the Gospel of Luke,* 115.

This was the final, formal encounter between Jesus and the authorities. The narrator of the gospel of Luke narrates the innocence of Jesus from crime, yet his rejection by Israel.[121] "The primary importance of this scene for Luke is not the attitude of the Romans but the choice of the Jews."[122] It is crucial place of decision making in the narrative.

7.8.2. Encounter Between the Innocent and a Murderer

In a court there can be both innocent as well as the guilt. In the case of Barabbas, the choice was left to the people who gathered for the execution of Jesus and for them he was a revolutionist. He may be of those who interested in throwing off the yoke of political tyranny. Politically the whole nation was in palpitating for a deliverer who would deliver them from the bondage of the Romans.[123] In the passion narrative the figure of Barabbas is presented by the narrator as a contrast to Jesus. In contrast to Jesus, he has done something worthy of death. He was a known rebel and he committed murder.[124] He was irrelevant to the accusations made against Jesus and Pilate protests that Jesus is innocent but he releases Barabbas and hands over Jesus to the will of the congregation. Here the narrator never brings a direct encounter of Jesus between Jesus and with Barabbas, instead there is an indirect encounter of Jesus with him. That is "the one who has done no wrong dies in place of the man has been justly convicted as worthy of death."[125] It is a kind of an encounter of salvation for Barabbas, where Jesus offered himself on behalf of him.

In Luke 23:25, by representing the description of Barabbas already given in verse 19, 'the man who had been thrown into prison for instruction and Murder' by adding that Pilate yielded finally to the will of the crowd. Luke forcefully brings out the weakness of Pilate's character, while at the same time indicating that he as a Roman official was inclined not to condemn

---

[121] Donald Senior, *The Passion of Jesus in the Gospel of Luke,* 116.

[122] Donald Senior, *The Passion of Jesus in the Gospel of Luke,* 118.

[123] Fulton J. Sheen, *Characters of the Passion,* 78. Barabbas may be a son of a Rabbi (cf. Mt. 27:16). St. John calls as a robber (Jn 18:40). He was arrested for sedition and for a murder committed on that occasion (Lk 19).

[124] Robert C. Tannehill, *The Narrative unity of Luke-Acts,* 198.

[125] Morna D. Hooker, *Not Ashamed of the Gospel: New Testament Interpretations of the Death of Christ* (Carlisle: The Paternoster Press, 1994), 88. Some thought that it was Jesus who might save them from the yoke of Romans (cf. Mt. 11:3). There were no Judaeus Macchabeus to lead any revolt against Caesar. Barabbas may of the one fill this role and in his enthusiasm for the freedom of his people committed a murder, but for Pilate he was a seditionist. For him both Jesus and Barabbas are two men accused of revolution. Barabbas appealed to national grievances; Christ to conscience. Barabbas would release fetters and ignore sin. Cf. Fulton J Sheen, *Characters of the Passion,* 79.

Jesus to death.[126] But Pilate cannot escape full legal and moral responsibility for his lowered surrender to the Sanhedrin in order to keep his office.

7.9. On the Journey to Calvary (Lk 23:26-32)

Alongside the Roman soldiers, the Pharisees, mounted upon horses, took part in the procession to Calvary. The synagogue leaders desirous of manifesting to the whole community that had succeeded in their arguments, sat proudly upon their horses and still urged on the multitude of the Jews. "Thus, the Jews and the Gentile, representing the world of that time, took their full share of the deadfall responsibility of shedding the blood of the Son of God."[127] Thousands upon thousands of people must have gathered in and around Jerusalem for the feast. Looking on contrast between Jesus and the tormentors. He was not even angry, though he suffered indescribably agonies.

7.9.1. Simon of Cyrene

Fearing the premature collapse of Jesus, the soldiers press into service by Simon of Cyrene[128] (Σίμωνά τινα Κυρηναῖον ἐρχόμενον ἀπ' ἀγροῦ). A Cyrenian on a visit to the city for the feast perhaps or a member of the Jerusalem synagogue of the Cyrenians to relieve him of the load of the heavy burden of the cross-bar of the gibbet which is proving too much for him.[129] May be Simon had lodged courtside the city over night and was coming in for the day's worship and the temple. The guard, seizing him compelled him to carry the cross of Jesus.[130] The attitude of the Cyrenian to help Jesus is theologically significant for the disciples of Jesus as they encounter the social needs of the people around need to keep the same attitude.

---

[126] Maurice Blanchard, *Luke. An Introduction and Commentary* (Madras: The C.L.S., 1969), 140.

[127] [illegible] 19[illegible]), 187.

[128] Ch.23: [26] As they led him away, they seized a man, Simon of Cyrene, who was coming from the country, and they laid the cross on him, and made him carry it behind Jesus.

[129] Laurence E Porter, 'Luke', *The International Bible Commentary*, edited by F.F. Bruce (Michigan: Zondervan Publishing House, 1979), 1225. The details seen in Mk 15:20, that Simon was coming from the field, but the fact that he was the father of Alexander and Rufus. Cyrene in North Africa was major center of Judaism in the first century. In Acts 2: 10 the Jews are present in Jerusalem from Cyrene (cf. also 6:9) and were active as Christian missionaries in Antioch (Acts 11:20; 13:1). The Jews of Cyrene had a synagogue of their own in Jerusalem (Acts. 6:9).

[130] Merrill C Tenny, 'Luke', *The Wycliffe Bible Commentary*, edited by Everett F. Harrison (Chicago: Moody Press, 1962), 1067.

7.9.2. The People

To Luke λαος (τοῦ λαοῦ) with the article, normally refers to Israel as the elect nation which forever retains the specific identity given to them by God.[131] Whenever Luke wished to draw a distinction between the leaders and the people, the narrator regularly used 'the people' for the large group.[132] Luke does not describe the λαος at turning against Jesus and demanding his crucifixion. The term τοῦ λαοῦ may not always had the full theological meaning as the people of God.[133] There is a passing conventional reference to God's wrath on his people (21:23) but much more indicative of Luke's stance is the fact that in the crucifixion the people (τοῦ λαοῦ) is associated with the weeping women (23:27) in the following the condemnation to the place of execution and in beholding the bestial mockery[134] (23:35). The people and its leaders need to be distinguished. In the narrative, the people were not presented as the enemies of Christ and they do not actively mock Jesus.[135]

In 23:48, Luke says that the crowds having come, *for the spectacle* and will indicate that the repent. They returned home beating their breast. The same gesture of beating the breast has appeared once before in the narrative, Chapter 18:13, where the tax collector at prayer shows the same expression. The same gesture here similarly signals repentance rather than conventional sorrow at the death of a fellow Jew. "The repentance implies a requisition

---

[131] P. S. Minear, 'Jesus' Audience, According to Luke', *Nov. Tes* XVI/II (April, 1974): 81.

[132] P. S. Minear, 'Jesus' Audience, According to Luke', 83.

[133] Joseph B. Tyson, "The Jewish Public in Luke-Acts", *NTS* 30 (1984): 576.

[134] P. S. Minear, 'Jesus' Audience, According to Luke', 84. People along with the religious authorities contrast noticeably with both the disciples and the authorities. In contrast to the authorities, the people do not become Jesus' enemies until his trail before Pilate and then only briefly (24:4; 13-25). In contrast to the disciples, who pledge to Jesus their loyalty and become his followers the problem makers no such commitment to him. Jack Dean Kingsbury, *Conflict in Luke: Jesus, Authorities, Disciples* (Minneapolis: Fortress Press, 1991), 29.

[135] Luke also wishes to communicate that the chief priests considered these people a force to reckon with. The people viewed Jesus as a prophet might in word and deed. The Chief Priests and rulers delivered him up to be condemned to death and crucified him. Richard J. Cassidy, 'Luke's Audience, the Chief Priests, and the motive for Jesus' Death', 152. Jesus' trail before Pilate, the people do join with their leaders and call for Jesus' crucifixion (23:4; 13-25) and for this they will suffer punishment in the destruction of Jerusalem (23:27-32). The actions of the people before, during and after Jesus' crucifixion differ noticeably from their leaders. Before Jesus' crucifixion the people follow Jesus in company of the women who bewailed lament him (23:27). During the crucifixion, they watch and proceedings but do not mock him (23:34). After Jesus died, they beat their breasts (23:48) which foreshadows the repentance of large number of the people. The women disciples who make their way to Jesus' tomb at dawn to anoint his body are no strangers to Luke's story. They are the sect same persons who wandered with Jesus in Galilee (8:1-3) witnessed his crucifixion (23:49).

of Jesus' innocence and their own guilt. This contrasts with the centurion in whom there has been no recognition of guilt."[136]

7.9.3. Those Who Were Wailing

There is a funeral procession for Jesus on the way to His death. Women played an important part in the ritual of the Jewish funeral. They were the ones who sang the funeral dirges. Women in the multitude bewailed and lamented for Jesus. This means they beat their breasts, uttered the customary lamentation for Jesus. This went against all customary treatment of a condemned man.[137] The attitude of women those were wailing has a different attitude to Jesus compared to the crowd. Though they cry or lament over Jesus, they also do not escape the communal punishment of Jerusalem. Whereas their mourning could make Jesus to prophecy one last time of the coming destruction of the city, emphasizing that this disaster which may befall the women and their children. They are the most defenseless and least guilty among the Jerusalem's inhabitants who cry out in relation to the death of the suffering of the messiah by depicting a scene of communal mourning now Jesus redirects the morning towards the mourners themselves.[138]

The address of Jesus to the daughters of Jerusalem (Lk 23:27-31) is one of the instances where one could view the presence of women in the passion narrative. They are the real figures who are part of Jesus' general feminine followers and they are actual sympathizers from Jerusalem.[139] The women are said to prove both the historical veracity of the narrative.[140] The role of women in the passion narrative is a story of female power, and it recognizes suffering and reaches out courageously to the suffering and poor.[141] They are faithful followers of Jesus and they deny any association with the Jewish and Roman authorities where the male voices are seems to be voices of denial and condemnation.

The narrative in relation to the trial for the execution and on the way to cross, the narrator mentions the weeping women, the daughters of Jerusalem.

[136] Mark Coleridge, 'You are witnesses' (Luke 24:48)", *ABR* XLV (1997): 4. According to Mk 15:29, "the passers by blaspheming Jesus. In contrast to the people the leaders mocked Jesus Luke adds the mocking and flogging of Jesus by soldiers after his sentencing (cf. Mk 15:16-20; Mt. 27:27-31)

[137] Malcolm O. Tolbert, *Luke-John,* 179.

[138] Robert C. Tannehill, *The Narrative Unity of Luke-Acts,* 165.

[139] Jerome H. Neyrey, 'Jesus' Address to the Women of Jerusalem (Lk 23:27-31) - A Prophetic Judgment oracle', *NTS* (29, January 1983): 74.

[140] Marion L. Soards, 'Tradition, Composition and Theology in Jesus' Speech to the "Daughters of Jerusalem' (Lk. 23:26-32)", *Biblica* (68/2, 1987): 225.

[141] Elaine M. Wainwright, *Towards a Feminist Critical Reading of the Gospel According to Matthew* (Berlin: Werner Hildebrand, 1991), 136.

According to Luke, large number of the people followed him and the women were also with them (cf. 23:27) at times one could find that Luke is fond of crowds and their devotional response to Jesus, especially that of women.[142] In this narrative, the encounter of Jesus with the daughters of Jerusalem describes the women of Jerusalem who beat their chests and lament over Jesus.[143] The prophecy is taken from the Old Testament prophet Hosea (Hos 10:8). The speech of Jesus with these women is very well apt for the situation.

The encounter of Jesus with the women on the way to cross can be interpreted in two ways. It can be a lament of Jesus to the people of Jerusalem in one sense and on the other side, it can mean as a judgment oracle of Jesus to Jerusalem. In this narrative, the narrator uses this occasion to incorporate a lament by the women of Jerusalem but with some revision of the conventional pattern of lamentation.[144] For Jesus, His own death is in no way a tragedy. "Luke seems to sense the horrible parallel between the anarchy and Israel's crucifixion of their own last royal hope"[145] (cf. Lk 23:38).

The women who grieve at His condemnation 'bewailed and lamented him' are favorable to Jesus. The words of Jesus to the women 'do not weep for me (μὴ κλαίετε ἐπ' ἐμέ), but for yourselves' (πλὴν ἐφ' ἑαυτὰς) (23:28) is an expression of the lament of the women is a counter point to the terrible rejection of Jesus by the leaders and the authorities. It is an expression of the grief of the marginalized.[146] The role of women distinguished from the large

[142] Pierre Benoit, *The Passion and Resurrection of Jesus Christ*, tr. Benet Wetherhead (New York: Herder and Herder, 1969), 167.

[143] Pierre Benoit, *The Passion and Resurrection of Jesus Christ*, 167.

[144] Frederick W Danker, *A Commentary on St. Luke's Gospel: Jesus and the New age* (Philadelphia: Fortress Press, 1988), 371.

[145] Frederick W Danker, *A Commentary on St. Luke's Gospel*, 372. Such kinds of proverbial utterance are common among the Jews. There is a contrast between power and weakness- contrasts between fire falls on cedars and hyssop on the wall, the Leviathan (a sea-monster to the Jews) is caught with hook and a fish in shallower water and such kind of proverbs existed among the Jews. In this way by using such proverbs the people could easily be understood and it brings out the truth of the situation.

[146] Donald Senior, *The Passion of Jesus in the Gospel of Lk*, 122. The passage points that if this is what happens to innocent Jesus, what kind of calamity will come upon wicked Jerusalem. Cf. Michael Eaton, *Preaching Through the Bible: Luke 12-24* (Norfolk: CRB Associates, 2000), 147. The great multitude seems to be distinguished from those women to whom Jesus spoke. Luke repeatedly singles out women for special mention. The women who mourned over him were courageous witness that Jesus in no means was a criminal. Herman Hendrickx, *The Passion Narrative* (Manila, Philippians: East Asian Pastoral Institute, 1977), 127. Christ is not rebuking mere sentimentality or sympathetic emotion, as if the meaning were that they ought to lament their own sin rather than His suffering. They are not wrong in weeping for Him. Nevertheless, there is something else for which they may weep with far greater reason. Motherhood, the greatest blessing will prove the greatest curse in the tribulation to come. Burton Scott Easton, *The Gospel According to St. Luke: A Critical and*

crowd the narrator may betraying to bring the attention of the readers of the significance of women as witnesses of Jesus' last days.[147] The encounter of Jesus with these women is a challenge for the present day. The women of Jerusalem consoled Jesus who was condemned to die. They identified with Jesus because they experience the same rejection and marginalization. They are socially, emotionally, politically and legally victimized and now they identify with victimized Jesus. They were socially condemned and treated unjustly by men as in the case of Jesus. They represent the people of Jerusalem and become the recipients of Jesus' final prophecy of the city's destruction.[148]

There are different logical possibilities has been featured for the reference to 'if they do this in the green wood' (εἰ ἐν τῷ ὑγρῷ ξύλῳ ταῦτα ποιοῦσιν 23:31), both the Romans and the Jews as possible choices. Firstly, if the *Romans* treat me, whom they admit to be innocent, in this manner, how will they treat those who are rebellious and guilty? Secondly, if the *Jews* with one chosen has come to save them, what treatment shall they receive themselves for destroying Him?[149] If *God* permits this to happen to one who is innocent, what will be the fate of the guilty?[150] The encounter of Jesus with these women even in the deepest pain of His life, exposes the need of

---

Exegetical Commentary (Edinburgh: T&T Clark, 1926), 346. They are among the women specially honored by Luke and he is the only one who records their effort to comfort Jesus. They were Daughters of Jerusalem, not the women who had followed Jesus from Galilee. Maurice Blanchard, *Luke: An Introduction and Commentary* (Madras: The C.L.S., 1969), 141.

[147] B. Varghese, *Women in the Gospel of Luke: The Role of Women in the Portrayal of Salvation in the Gospel of Luke* (New Delhi: ISPCK, 2005), 178.

[148] Stephen J. Binz, *The Passion and Resurrection Narratives of Jesus: A Commentary* (Minnesota: The Liturgical Press, 1989), 86.

[149] A. Plummer, *A Critical and Exegetical Commentary on the Gospel According to St. Luke*, 529-530, cf also G.H.P. Thompson, *The Gospel According to Luke* (Oxford: Clarendon, 1972), 270.

[150] F. W. Danker, *Jesus and the New Age*, [illegible]. The women who grieve at His condemnation 'bewailed and lamented him' are favorable to Jesus. The words of Jesus to the women 'do not weep for me, but for yourselves' (23:28) is an expression of the lament of the women is a counter point to the terrible rejection of Jesus by the leaders and the authorities. Never the less something is about to fall, for which you will weep with far greater reason, the destruction of your city and the overthrow of your nation. Through the expression of the grief of the Jewish people to Him, some women were sobbing and crying their hearts out over him. Jesus turned and said to them, dear sisters of sooth, no need to cry over me, rather, you should cry for yourself and for your children. See, Clarence Jordan, *The Cotton Patch Version of Luke and Acts: Jesus' Doing and the Happening* (New York: Koinonia Publications, 1969), 84. Jesus did not want to have self-pity, instead his concern habitually was with other. Cf. also Ernest Fremont Tittle, *The Gospel According to Luke: Exposition and Application* (New York: Harper and Brothers Publishers, 1957), 259.

bringing up the marginalized into the forefront. It is also an answer to the constant struggle to whole womanhood.

Galilean Women as Witness (Lk 23:49): Group of Galilean women are pictured as the witnesses of Jesus' crucifixion. It is important to note that Luke identified the women witnesses from all his acquaintances. The women are a linkage between cross (23:39), burial (23:55f.) and resurrection (24:1-10); they makes up the continuity that confirms that it is the crucified and buried Jesus whose tomb is empty. They are also the representatives of the connection from Galilee. "They have their roots in the material common to the synoptics, but as they appear in Luke they have their own special form."[151] The Galilean perspective in Luke is primarily a Lukan *memory* and *retrospect*, the connection backwards.[152] From the narrative, one thing is clear that, these women disciples from Galilee have preserved with Him all the way from Galilee (cf. Lk 23:49, 24:6). These women bring the continuity of the message of the crucifixion and resurrection. Though Jesus did not speak to them anything on the way to cross, they were not carried away. They were confidence that He would win the victory at the end. They were not seen with those women lamenting over Jesus. Instead, they are ready to serve Him until His death and do the necessary things even after the death. They have done the funeral requirements for Him and became the first witness of His victory.

These women were the eye witnesses of Jesus' death; their function was not that of the idle crowds. They not only witnessed the crucifixion but also the resurrection. They are described as 'standing at a distance' not having returned or go away as did the crowds. It emphasizes the commitment and further participation of these women. It evidences the role and active participation of women in Luke's portrayal of the salvific events.[153] They are the faithful disciples who remained with Jesus till the last moments of his life. The role of these women as witnesses and participants in the messianic mission of Jesus is clearly seen.

7.10. Crucifixion (Lk 23:33-43)

While Jesus was on the cross He becomes the victim of mockery as He hanged on the cross and seen by the bystanders. While Jesus was on the cross the people did not join the mockers instead they stood by, watching (23:35).

---

[151] Turid Karlsen Seim, *The Double Message: Patterns of Gender in Luke-Acts* (Nashville: Abingdon Press, 1994), 148.

[152] Turid Karlsen Seim, *The Double Message: Patterns of Gender in Luke-Acts*, 148.

[153] Howard I Marshall, *The Gospel of Luke: A Commentary on the Greek Text* (Exeter: The Paternoster Press, 1978), 895.

"Luke presents at least a portion of the people as responsive to Jesus."[154] Crucifixion was a form of execution by fastening the condemned to two crossed beams. In the Roman style, Crucifixion as the gospels illustrate began with a scourging of the prisoner followed by his carrying[155] (at least the shorter part of it) in which one has to die.[156] A public place may be chosen, often where two or more heavily traveled streets or roads crossed and with a cemetery conveniently nearby.

7.10.1. The Leaders and the Community

The culmination of the way of cross is the crucifixion. There were civil as well as religious authorities in Jerusalem who watched the death of Jesus. It is a kind of two-tier structure of authority. The Roman imperial authority in the upper-tier who was the Roman procurator ruling Judea. This Roman procurator did not live in Jerusalem but made a regular visit and the purpose was to maintain peace and a frequent flow of texts to Rome. When Jesus entered Jerusalem Pilate was the procurator. The religious, civil and the rest of the political authorities of Judean life were under the responsibility of the second-tier of the Jerusalem authorities. These authorities were the chief priests, the teachers of the Law; the scribes and the elders. Their authority was consisted within the Sanhedrin which Luke calls as the 'Council of the elders'[157] (22:66).

---

[154] Donald Senior, *The Passion of Jesus in the Gospel of Luke,* 131.

[155] The upright piece was firmly fastened of the clothing and either tied or nailed to the cross beam, which was off the ground. Sometimes a ledge-like support projected from the upright piece. The feet were tied or nailed. A military guard took charge and remained until death came by exhaustion or heat failure. No vital organs were harmed. The victim was rigidly held in one position unable to deal with heat, cold, muscle cramps, natural body functions, hunger or thirst. Often the crucified died in agony only after a number of days on the cross. After the body was removed, the cross was burned. Both Jesus and Romans as means of healing used nails from crucifixion crosses.

[156] Some people followed Jesus in the way of the cross and grieve at the condemnation of Jesus (23:27). There is also all possibility for the responsibility of the same group for the demand of the crucifixion. But at the end of the narrative, one could easily find that they are driven to repentance by his death (23:48). The mockers demanded him to save himself for he saved others. Here they question the very identity and mission of Jesus. In the mockery, the rulers twisted the major truth about salvation. Salvation comes from God and God would deliver Jesus from the death through resurrection.

[157] Paul Germoned, *Portraits of Jesus: A Contextual Approach to Bible Study: Luke* (London: Collins Liturgical Publications, 1988), 83. The representatives of the aristocracy of Jerusalem which was a body of 72 men had the power for the day-to-day legislation of Jewish affairs was in their hands. The wealthy elite had power over every aspect of Jewish life. They had authority over everything related to the religious and civil life of people with any difference of secular or religious. The Romans appointed the high priests, they also held with power and prestige. At the time of Jesus Caiaphas was the high Priest (43:2). Another

7.10.2. Romans and Jews

There is evidence that the author had detailed knowledge of the Roman siege of Jerusalem (21:20, 22). Romans' military triumph is interpreted as punishment for Israel's rejection of Christ (19:39-44). Roman involvement in the execution of Jesus had been downplay with this gospel and responsibility has been shifted so heavily into Jewish leadership that the impression is given that 'the Jews killed Jesus'[158] (22:54; 23:23-26; 24:20 cf. Acts 2:22-23; 3:17; 7:52-58). According to Luke, the Jewish religious leaders bore primary responsibility for the death of Jesus.[159] Pilate permitted the Sanhedrin to crucify Jesus due to the insistence of the people.[160] In the gospel of Luke τὸν λαόν is used for both Jews (cf. 2:32; 7:16; 20; 1), Gentiles (Lk 2:31 cf. Acts 18:10) and ὄχλος is used as equivalent for crowd (Lk 6:17; 7:24; 29; 9:12; 13; 18:36, 43 cf. Acts 5:12; 13:31). Jerome Kodell, Luke used τὸν λαόν in describing the opposed attitudes of the people and the leaders regarding Jesus.[161]

7.10.3. The People and Crowd

Lukan passion narrative begirds with the arrest of Jesus (22:1-6) and one can find that the chief priests and the scribes seems afraid of the influence and popularity of Jesus among the people (22:2 cf. 19:48; 20:1-8, 19). The legal arm of the Jewish leadership consist of the chief priests, the elders and the captions of the temple comes under the crowd'. It is a crowd and not police or soldiers. They came with 'sticks and knives'. It means that they were not organized police force, but those less status of the Roman army.[162] Among the crowd there were also a group mentioned as 'those who know Him.'[163] They might have known Him from the time of His ministry.

---

powerful community was the Sadducees, they were majority of the ruling class belonged by birth. The Sadducees were urban elite and were large landowners.

158 Jane Schaberg, *Women's Bible Commentary,* 365.

159 R. S. Ascough, "Rejection and Repentance: Peter and the People in Luke's Passion Narrative", 351.

160 R. S. Ascough, Rejection and Repentance, 362.

161 Jerome Kodell, "'Luke's use of Laos, People", especially in the Jerusalem Narrative Lk: 19:28-24: 53", *CBQ* 31/3 (July 1969): 329.

162 Jose Maniparampil, *Reading the Synoptic Gospels*, 576.

163 These characters are present but here it is completely mute and passive. They were neither given name nor faces. They are simply introduced as "those who had known him"(23:49). There is no emphasis of their inner response. The narration remains wholly external in a way it was not with either the centurion of the crowds. Women from Galilee were also may be a part of this group. The mention that they *followed* Jesus from Galilee is a language of discipleship. It implies that they have stayed closer to Jesus and for no longer than any other of *those who know him*. See, Mark Coleridge, 'You are witnesses', 5.

In the crucifixion the crowd are directly involved. They shout three times for Jesus' death. They cried out 'all together. The people not only called out for the crucifixion but also for the release for Barabbas. Especially when the narrator reaches the cruel decision of the death of Jesus the crowd supported their leaders by calling for Jesus' death.[164] "Within the interaction of characters and events of the plot development Luke simply has not provided his readers with an adequate or at least consistent explanation of the *Laos'* demand for Jesus' death."[165] Luke frequently distinguished ὄχλος from λαός, but the former are usually drawn from the latter and represent them. Luke also distinguishes crowds from disciples. According to Luke neither λαός nor ὄχλος bear primary responsibility for the crucifixion. In the narrative of 23:23-25, there is a strong emphasis on the responsibility of both the leaders and the people of Jesus' death.

7.10.4. The Criminal on the Cross

The people with those crucified with Jesus are known as the 'evildoers' (κακοῦργοι) or the 'criminals', executed for misdeeds and crimes. "Jesus is crucified there along with two others in accordance with normal Roman procedures."[166] They can be either Jew or Gentile or a Zealot.[167] "Luke uses the word "criminal" to stress how they represent people who commit the worst type of crimes."[168] One criminal kept insulting him, literally, "Kept blaspheming him" (22:65).[169] Whereas the other pleaded to Him for help.

Jesus hears the request of the repented criminal who asked to remember him in His kingdom. "His request is a plea for a gracious remembrance, for he can do nothing at this point to merit it. Implicitly, his request is an expression of faith in Jesus.[170] It is the last encounter of Jesus with the humanity within his physical body. One of the criminal discovered that Jesus held the key to paradise and that his own death on the cross was no barrier to his entrance upon its joys (23:39-43). "If the first criminal joins the rulers and soldiers in

---

[164] Robert C. Tennyhill, *The Narrative Unity of Luke-Acts*, 164.

[165] David P. Mossner, "'The Leaven of the Pharisees' and 'this Generation': Israel's Rejection of Jesus According to Luke", *JSNT* 34/Oct. (1988): 22.

[166] Richard J. Cassidy, Luke's Audience, 147.

[167] Joseph A. Fitzmyer, 'Today You Shall be with me in Paradise,' *Luke the Theologian: Aspects of his Teaching* (New York: Paulist Press, 1989), 206.

[168] Joseph A. Grassi, *The Five Wounds of Jesus and Personal Transformation* (Mumbai: St. Paul's, 2001), 67.

[169] Joseph A. Fitzmyer, *The Gospel According to Luke (X-XXIV)*, The Anchor Bible (New York: Double Day, 1985), 1509.

[170] Joseph A. Fitzmyer, "Today You Shall be with me in Paradise", 208.

mocking Jesus, the second criminal joins Pilate and Herod in acknowledging Jesus' innocence."[171]

Luke 23:43, 'today you shall be with me in Paradise'(σήμερον μετ' ἐμοῦ ἔσῃ ἐν τῷ παραδείσῳ). The meaning of the verse upon these three expressions. Some elements of 1st century Judaism use the term to describe the heavenly abode of the soul between death and resurrection. Most commentators believe that the promise does refers to an individual heavenly journey but that in common with the Pharisees view of the intermediate state, Jesus is speaking only of the robber's soul.[172] Christ's promise *'today you shall be with me in paradise'* (23:43) implies that within a few hour's time the suffering of both have brought great consolation to His mother, His disciples and other friends who are present, as well as to the thief.[173]

Jesus promised to him a permission to enter into His kingdom which is 'paradise, where the repentant criminal will share in his regal destiny. The idea of 'Paradise' (παραδείσῳ) is originally the place, the old Persian provenience, which means 'enclosed space, precinct', which is translated into Greek language as *paradeisos* (παραδείσως) which means as an 'enclosed park, garden'. It is translated into the LXX as the 'garden of Eden.'[174] One point still remains what is promised to the robber does not alleviate his present suffering, nor make any abatement of his bodily punishment. Instead something which is yet to come.

There is a prayer of forgiveness for those who were His executors (Πάτερ, ἄφες αὐτοῖς 23:34) by Jesus. The first three hours on the cross were in daylight while Jesus suffered the hands of men. During this time Jesus suffered the mocking of the crowds while he encountered to the outcasts at his sides. One criminal responded positively and one rejected his message.[175] One of the characteristics of the Gospel of Luke is the good news of mercy and forgiveness.

Jesus' suffering and death gives access to glory and in relation to the people repentance and faith in Jesus gives forgiveness and salvation. May be the silence of Jesus might have encountered the troublesome heart of the criminal who repented. The thief here acknowledged Jesus to be the Messiah a stupendous act of faith under the circumstances. The Jews who saw Him

[171] Denis McBride, *The Gospel of Luke: A Reflective Commentary*, 308.

[172] E. Earle Ellis (ed.), *The Century Bible: the Gospel of Luke,* Thomas Nelson Pub., 1966, 269.

[173] Maurice Blanchard, *Luke: An Introduction and Commentary* (Madras: C.L.S., 1969), 143.

[174] Joseph A Fitzmyer, 'Today You Shall be with Me in Paradise', 209.

[175] Mark Bailey and Tom Constable, eds, *Nelson's New Testament Survey: Discover the Background, Theology and Meaning of Every Book in the New Testament* (Nashville: Thomas Nelson Pub., 1999), 150.

raising the dead but rejected Him but the thief who saw him hanging with him on the cross did not reject him. The thief apparently expected Christ to rise again and establish his kingdom. Within the scene of the crucifixion stands the centurion[176] who was a silent witness of the death of Jesus.

There are various theological implications of Lukan passion narrative. While stressing the sensitive emotions of Jesus, Luke emphasized His care towards those violated, marginalized and downtrodden people around Him. From the beginning of the narrative itself one could find the non-violence attitude of Jesus when He cured the soldier's ear who came to arrest Jesus with a community. The encounter of Jesus with the soldier is an emphatic statement of the position of Jesus on violence.

The religious authorities as well as the political powers could find nothing in Jesus and they declare the innocence of Jesus. Luke emphasizes the initiative of the leaders in handing over Jesus to the Romans. For Pilate, the only accusation that matters is, whether Jesus is actually presenting himself as an earthly king. It may be the blasphemy as well as the declaration of messiahship of Jesus might have made the religious leaders to bring Jesus before Pilate. According to Luke, this is one of the characterization of Jesus by the way of renewing the mind of the readers that Jesus even in His suffering stands as an apologist for the Christians.

There was an indirect encounter of Jesus between Barabbas and Jesus seen in the gospel of Luke. The figure of Barabbas is presented in the gospel as a contrast to the innocence of Jesus. While suffering unjustly Jesus could save another revolutionist who was an unjust and criminal as per the request of the crowd. The encounter of Jesus with the women on the way to cross exposes the theological significance of the encounter of Jesus with the marginalized, where Jesus speaks to them in public as against the normal

---

[176] The character to whom Luke first pictures as the witness of the crucifixion is a gentile centurion and he was not presented anywhere else in the passion story until then. Here one needs to understand that he was already present among the soldiers in vv. 36-37. Who mocked him and offered him sour wine. Now the centurion saw what had happened and made the conclusion about Jesus that He is the Son of God. 'Like other characters in the Lukan Narrative, the centurion, left to his own devices, has done about as well as he could in the epistemological task. Cf. Mark Coleridge, "You are witnesses', 3. There is a clear irony in the passion of Jesus. The King of Jews died as the death of a slave. The royal dignity of Jesus is completely ignored. He was crucified, stripped, mocked by all and positioned between the criminals. There is mocking from the passersby in relation to the messianic dignity of Jesus, which is questioned at the Jewish trail. The second group of mockers are the Chief Priests in relation to the salvific death of Jesus and asks him to save himself. The third category is the encounter between the criminals. One reviled him and other called out to have mercy. The scandal of the cross as the climax of all suffering. The mockery by the crowds, elites and the robbers depict a total loneliness and isolation of Jesus. Jose Maniparampil, *Reading the Synoptic Gospels,* 588.

custom. The women stand as the liberated ones from their social-cultural boundaries to serve Jesus even when His disciples could not attend Him. When He was treated like a criminal, they did not give up their hope for the liberator who would liberate them from their marginalized condition and bring them to the front to become His witnesses.

The encounter of Jesus with the criminal shows that His encounter as an encounter to the dalit and downtrodden. Though he may be the one of many others who had been crucified for evil doing. This man openly proclaims the innocence of Jesus to his fellow criminal and pleaded to Jesus for deliverance. In every means, he could understand the reality that in no way he could come out of the cross, but here the encounter of Jesus with the criminal brings out the theological significance of the eschatological expectation for its readers.

8. The Resurrection Narrative in Luke

In Luke's Gospel, the resurrection narrative opens with the discovery of the empty tomb by the women who came to anoint Jesus' body. This moment becomes the first concrete sign of Jesus' victory over death and sin, serving as a pivotal event that shifts the disciples' understanding of Jesus' identity and mission. The empty tomb not only fulfills the promises Jesus made about His resurrection but also stands as a powerful testament to the new life offered through Him. Luke's account further emphasizes the physical reality of the resurrection through multiple post-resurrection appearances. Jesus first appears to the women at the tomb, then to the disciples on the road to Emmaus, and finally to the assembled disciples in Jerusalem. These encounters reinforce that the resurrection was not merely a spiritual experience but a bodily one, underscoring Jesus' continued, tangible presence with His followers. Through these appearances, Luke conveys the transformative power of the resurrection, which reorients the disciples' faith and strengthens their commitment.

Additionally, Luke's resurrection narratives focus on the disciples' commission to spread the gospel. In these narratives, Jesus instructs His followers to proclaim repentance and forgiveness to all nations, extending the scope of His ministry universally. This mission, grounded in the resurrection, provides the theological foundation for the disciples' call to spread the message of salvation globally. Luke thereby presents the resurrection not only as the validation of Jesus' messianic identity but as the cornerstone for the church's ongoing mission.

8.1. The Culmination of Salvation

The passion and resurrection narratives in Luke's Gospel signify the culmination of God's salvation plan, in which Jesus' sacrificial death on the cross brings redemption and forgiveness of sins. His resurrection, in turn, confirms His victory over death and promises eternal life to all who believe. These pivotal events encapsulate the essence of the Christian message, showing that through Jesus' suffering and triumph, believers receive the gift of salvation and the hope of life beyond death. These narratives resonate with Luke's broader theme of salvation, consistently emphasized throughout his Gospel as an act of divine grace accessible to all who repent and believe in Jesus Christ. Luke portrays salvation as inclusive and transformative, stressing that it is a freely given gift from God meant to reach people across all nations and backgrounds. By focusing on this theme, Luke reinforces the universal scope of God's redemptive work through Jesus.

The passion and resurrection accounts in Luke form the foundation of the Christian faith, symbolizing the ultimate victory of good over evil, light over darkness, and life over death. These events are a source of hope and assurance for believers, reminding them of Christianity's central message: that through Christ's sacrifice and resurrection, salvation is available to all who accept Him as Lord and Savior. The passion and resurrection narratives in the Gospel of Luke are the climax of the salvation story, emphasizing Jesus' sacrificial death for the forgiveness of sins and His triumphant victory over death through His resurrection. These events are at the heart of the Christian faith, offering hope, redemption, and the promise of eternal life to all who believe.

8.2. Women at the Burial of Jesus (Lk 23:50-56)

This passage deals with how the Galilean women along with Joseph of Arimathea had offered an honorable burial to Jesus. The Galilean women continued to follow Jesus until his burial. They were close witness and participants of Jesus' burial they were not mere eyewitnesses of Jesus' crucifixion. These women are not only witnesses of Jesus' earthly ministry but also authoritative witness of his death, burial and resurrection. Thus, the role and participation of these women in Jesus' life are highly significant.[177] The women were active in participating in preparing costly perfumes and ointments for his burial. Thus, women with all their concerns engaged in the activity of Jesus' burial and thereby one can find that women as active participants on par with men in God's salvific mission.[178]

Luke shows that the women are already to render enormous service to Jesus out of their resources as seen in Luke 8:1-3. Perhaps they may

[177] V. Taylor, *The Passion Narrative of St. Luke A Critical and Historical Investigation* (Cambridge: University Press, 1972), 879.

[178] B. Varghese, *Women in the Gospel of Luke: The Role of Women in the Portrayal of Salvation in the Gospel of Luke*, 109.

surmount Joseph in laying out their resources for a decent burial. These women, in spite of the possible danger from the hostile crowds and officials, proved themselves to be the true followers of Jesus by participating in the preparation for burial through which they assume esteemed roles in the portrait of salvation.[179] The way women are identified with 'having followed' suggests the theological significance of the women followers of Jesus even at the crucial time of Jesus. This theological language is used to describe not only their journey with Jesus from Galilee but their journey with Him until the end of the earthly Jesus. However, their continuous journey with Jesus, their privilege of being eyewitness of his life and ministry climaxing in the death, burial and resurrection. The immediate disciples and other faithful followers are not in the scene but the women were with Jesus in his crucial period of life.

8.3. Women at the Resurrection of Jesus (Lk 24:1-11)

In all four Gospels (Matthew, Mark, Luke, and John), a group of women, including Mary Magdalene and Mary the mother of James, arrive at Jesus' tomb early on the first day of the week, following the Sabbath, to anoint His body with spices according to Jewish burial customs. Their presence at the tomb carries deep significance within the resurrection narrative. First, these women are the first to witness the empty tomb and the resurrection, an extraordinary feature of the Gospel accounts that highlights the importance of their testimony in a time when women's voices were often undervalued in legal and social contexts. Additionally, their actions reflect profound love and devotion, demonstrating their commitment to serve and honor Jesus even after His death. Through their presence, the Gospels emphasize the faith and dedication of these women, positioning them as foundational witnesses to the resurrection event.

Early on the first day of the week, a group of women made their way to the tomb of Jesus with spices, found that the stone at the entrance of the tomb had been rolled away and went in and discovered that his body was not there. Two men appeared to them and reminded that Jesus had risen in accordance with the prophecy, he had made in Galilee. The women then left the tomb to report to the eleven and the other disciples of Jesus what had happened. It was women who came first to the tomb which exposes eagerness of women to see Jesus.[180] They are the link between the crucified and the resurrected Jesus Christ. This proves the epistemological journey of women with Jesus from Galilee till Jerusalem. They were the first group who received the

---

[179] Joseph A. Fitzmyer, *The Gospel According to Luke,* Anchor Bible, vol. 28, edited by David Noel Freedman (New York: Double Day, 1981), 1527.

[180] J. Plevnik, 'The Origin of Easter Faith According to Luke,' *Biblica* (61/4, 1880): 499.

Gospel of the resurrection of Jesus Christ. They were the first missionaries who send by the messengers of God to proclaim the resurrection of Jesus even to those *apostles*. Jesus appeared to the female disciples at first but the tradition of the church ignored it. Liberated Jesus enlightened the life of the powerless and the vulnerable group of the society. The testimony of the women disciples seems to be challenging to their social context. But Jesus made them as the agents in the male dominated society to breakdown the social stigma which isolated and secluded women in the legal position.

8.4. The Angelic Message of Jesus' Resurrection

As the women arrived at the tomb, they were met with a supernatural encounter that transformed their sorrow into awe and wonder. An angel of the Lord appeared to them, described in the Gospel of Matthew as having an appearance like lightning, reflecting the majesty of this heavenly messenger. The angel's presence and the open, empty tomb made it unmistakably clear that something extraordinary had occurred. The angel, aware of the women's purpose, reassures them, saying, "Do not be afraid," knowing that the empty tomb might evoke both fear and confusion. This moment marked the transition from despair to the astonishing news of resurrection, setting the stage for the fulfillment of Jesus' promise.

The angel's announcement to the women is direct and filled with awe-inspiring truth. In Matthew 28:5-7, the angel says, "He is not here; he has risen, just as he said," inviting the women to witness the empty place where Jesus had been laid. Similarly, in Luke 24:5-6, the angelic message addresses their grief and sense of loss by asking, "Why do you look for the living among the dead? He is not here; he has risen!" These words, resonant with hope and victory, remind the women that Jesus' resurrection was not unexpected but part of His divine plan, which He had shared with His followers before His crucifixion.[181] The angel's words, therefore, bring a powerful reassurance that Jesus' promise of life had overcome the darkness of death.

The angel's instruction to the women to go and tell the disciples about the resurrection establishes them as the first messengers of this miraculous news. This directive not only emphasizes the importance of bearing witness but also underlines the significance of the women's role in proclaiming the resurrection. In being the first to carry the message of Jesus' triumph over death, the women become essential participants in the mission of spreading the Gospel. Their testimony, entrusted by the angel, marks the beginning of the Good News that would transform countless lives. Through the angelic message, Jesus' resurrection brings the fulfillment of God's

---

[181] Gary R. Habermas, Michael R. Licona, and Kregel Publications, *The Case for the Resurrection of Jesus* (Kregel Publications, n.d.)., 53.

promise, conquers death, and initiates a new era of hope and eternal life for all believers. The discovery of the empty tomb by the women and the angelic message of Jesus' resurrection are central events in Christian faith. They provide compelling evidence for the truth of the resurrection and serve as a foundation for the Christian belief in the victory of Christ over sin and death.

8.5. The Encounter on the Road to Emmaus

The event of the encounter on the road to Emmaus, recorded in Luke 24:13-35, illustrates a profound moment in which Jesus meets two of His followers on the day of His resurrection. These two disciples, traveling to the village of Emmaus, were weighed down by grief and confusion as they discussed Jesus' crucifixion and the recent, puzzling reports of His resurrection.[182] While they walked, a stranger joined them—unbeknownst to them, it was Jesus Himself. The disciples' inability to recognize Him is a recurring theme in post-resurrection appearances, suggesting that Jesus' resurrected body held a glorified quality or that His identity was divinely veiled until the proper time for revelation.[183]

As they continued on their journey, Jesus, still unrecognized, asked the disciples about their conversation and listened as they recounted the events surrounding His crucifixion and the uncertainty that filled their hearts. Patiently, Jesus then began to explain the Scriptures, showing how the events they witnessed fulfilled the messianic prophecies. He revealed how suffering and death were integral to the Messiah's mission, providing a new perspective on His crucifixion and resurrection. This teaching ignited a sense of hope within them, yet they still did not realize who was speaking to them.

The revelation of Jesus' identity occurs in a moment that mirrors His earlier ministry. As they arrived at Emmaus and sat together to eat, Jesus took bread, gave thanks, broke it, and began to give it to them. At this instant, as described in Luke 24:30-31, "their eyes were opened, and they recognized Him," bringing a powerful recognition that linked this meal with the Last Supper they shared before His crucifixion. Jesus' familiar act of breaking bread was the pivotal moment that opened their eyes, illuminating the connection between the risen Lord and the One they had followed.[184]

Immediately after they recognized Him, Jesus vanished from their sight. His sudden disappearance emphasizes the supernatural and transformed nature of His resurrected body; He was no longer confined by

---

[182] Dennis J. Billy CSsR, *Meeting Jesus on the Road to Emmaus: An Invitation to Friendship, Eucharist and Christian Community* (Wipf and Stock Publishers, 2023), 35.

[183] Cathy Ross and Steve Bevans, *Mission on the Road to Emmaus: Constants, Context, and Prophetic Dialogue* (SCM Press, 2015), 223.

[184] Scott Hahn and Emily Stimpson Chapman, *Hope to Die: The Christian Meaning of Death and the Resurrection of the Body* (Emmaus Road Publishing, 2020), 70.

earthly limitations and did not need to remain physically present in the way He had before.[185] However, the profound impact of His presence lingered. This brief yet powerful encounter allowed the disciples to experience His risen presence, reinforcing their understanding of His divine nature and His fulfillment of God's promises.

The encounter on the road to Emmaus holds significant meaning. It reaffirms Jesus' continued presence with His followers, even when He is not immediately recognized, and underscores the spiritual nourishment found in the breaking of bread.[186] This experience transformed the disciples' grief into joy and reinvigorated their faith, showing that Christ is indeed risen and present, revealed in both familiar acts of fellowship and the unfolding of Scripture. The Emmaus story stands as an encouragement for all believers, reminding them of the abiding presence of Christ in unexpected ways and in every journey of faith.

8.6. The Appearance to the Disciples in Jerusalem

The post-resurrection appearance of Jesus to the disciples in Jerusalem, detailed in both Luke 24:36-49 and John 20:19-23, marks a pivotal moment in the Gospel narratives. The disciples were gathered, likely still fearful of the authorities responsible for Jesus' crucifixion. Suddenly, Jesus stood among them, His presence startling and frightening them. In Luke's account, He offered them reassurance, displaying His hands and feet to confirm His identity as the crucified and risen Lord. He greeted them with, "Peace be with you," providing comfort to dispel their fear. In John's account, Jesus repeated this greeting and showed them His hands and side, filling the disciples with joy as they recognized their resurrected Lord. Both accounts emphasize that Jesus' resurrection was in line with the Scriptures, fulfilling the prophecies of the Messiah's victory over death.

After assuring His disciples, Jesus commissioned them for their future mission. Luke's Gospel records that He identified them as witnesses to His life, death, and resurrection, instructing them to proclaim repentance and forgiveness of sins to all nations, beginning in Jerusalem. Jesus emphasized that the Holy Spirit would empower them for this mission and instructed them to wait in the city for this divine empowerment. In John's Gospel, Jesus breathes on them, saying, "Receive the Holy Spirit," symbolizing their anointing for the ministry ahead.[187] He then gave them the authority to

---

[185] Joan E. Taylor, *What Did Jesus Look Like?* (Bloomsbury Publishing, 2018), 191.

[186] Robert H. Stein, *Luke* (B&H Publishing Group, 1992), 602ff.

[187] George R. Beasley-Murray, *John, Volume 36: Revised Edition* (Zondervan Academic, 2018), 397.

proclaim forgiveness, underscoring the responsibility they carried to share the message of salvation with the world.[188]

This appearance in Jerusalem solidifies the disciples' roles as witnesses to the resurrection, marking the beginning of their mission to spread the Christian message. It reaffirms Jesus' triumph over death, the fulfillment of Old Testament prophecy, and His divine authority. By imparting peace, commissioning the disciples, and introducing the promise of the Holy Spirit, Jesus equips them with both the message and the means to carry out their work, initiating the early movement that would become Christianity.

8.7. Theological Themes and Implications

The Passion and Resurrection narratives in Luke's Gospel carry profound theological themes that form the backbone of Christian faith and discipleship. The Passion underscores themes of atonement, redemption, and forgiveness, revealing Jesus as the innocent, sacrificial Lamb who endures suffering for humanity's sake. In His suffering, believers find both a call to compassion and a model of endurance amid adversity.[189] The Resurrection, meanwhile, embodies the triumph over sin and death, offering hope, victory, and the assurance of eternal life for all who believe. Together, these events reveal God's redemptive plan, affirming Jesus' identity as Messiah and emphasizing the transformative power of His love. These theological insights shape believers' lives, calling them not only to faith but to actively embody the values of sacrifice, service, and witness in their daily walk, mirroring the mission and compassion of Christ.

8.7.1. Theological Significance of the Passion

The Passion of Jesus—His suffering, crucifixion, and death—holds profound theological significance in Christian doctrine, particularly in the areas of atonement, redemption, and forgiveness. Central to this is the concept of *atonement*, which signifies reconciliation between humanity and God. Through His Passion, Jesus provides a pathway for humanity to be "at one" with God, bridging the separation caused by sin. One important aspect of this atonement is *substitutionary atonement*, where Jesus, as the sinless Son of God, takes on the punishment and consequences of human sin.[190] In His suffering and death, He stands as a substitute for humanity, bearing the weight of sin's penalty. This notion echoes Old Testament prophecies like Isaiah 53:4-5, which foretell a suffering servant who bears the sins of others.

---

[188] Mike Licona, *Why Are There Differences in the Gospels?: What We Can Learn from Ancient Biography* (Oxford University Press, 2017), 180.

[189] John Navone and John J. Navone, *Themes of St. Luke* (Gregorian University Press, 1970), 149.

[190] John T. Carroll, *Luke: A Commentary* (Westminster John Knox Press, 2012), 470.

The concept of Jesus as the *sacrificial lamb* further deepens this theological framework. Known as the "Lamb of God," Jesus' death is seen as fulfilling the sacrificial system of the Old Testament, wherein animal sacrifices were offered as a temporary covering for sin. His sacrifice, however, is final and all-encompassing, offering a path to forgiveness and permanent reconciliation with God. Through His death, Jesus bridges the gap between humanity and God, addressing both divine justice and mercy.[191] This act of *reconciliation* demonstrates God's deep love for humanity, restoring a relationship that sin had broken and illustrating the full extent of God's grace and mercy.

The themes of *redemption* and *forgiveness* also run deeply through the narrative of Jesus' Passion. Jesus' death is viewed as a redemptive act in which He "buys back" humanity from the bondage of sin and its separation from God. According to Christian belief, His sacrifice serves as the price for this redemption, as articulated in passages like 1 Peter 1:18-19, which speak of redemption through His precious blood. Furthermore, Jesus' sacrifice opens the door to *forgiveness*, with His shed blood serving as the means by which sin is forgiven. This theme of forgiveness is underscored during the Last Supper when Jesus refers to the wine as "my blood of the covenant, which is poured out for many for the forgiveness of sins" (Matthew 26:28). Thus, the Passion becomes the foundation for humanity's forgiveness, redemption, and ultimate reconciliation with God.

The Passion of Jesus, with its themes of atonement, sacrifice, redemption, and forgiveness, lies at the heart of Christian theology. It serves as the means by which believers are reconciled with God, cleansed from sin, and offered the gift of eternal life.[192] This theological understanding of the Passion is central to Christian faith and is commemorated in the Eucharist or Holy Communion, where believers partake in the symbols of Christ's body and blood, remembering His sacrifice and its implications for their relationship with God.

8.7.2. The Resurrection as Victory Over Death

The resurrection of Jesus is celebrated as the ultimate victory over sin and death, serving as a cornerstone of Christian theology. At its core, the resurrection signifies the *defeat of sin and death*. Theologically, this event is understood as a demonstration of Jesus' triumph over sin, which separates humanity from God. By living a sinless life and subsequently rising from

---

[191] Darrell L. Bock, *A Theology of Luke and Acts: God's Promised Program, Realized for All Nations* (Zondervan Academic, 2015), 389.

[192] N. T. Wright and Patty Pell, *Luke* (InterVarsity Press, 2011), 135.

the dead, Jesus conquers the power of sin.[193] This act not only affirms His identity as the Son of God but also offers forgiveness and reconciliation to all who believe in Him. In this way, the resurrection embodies the hope that, through Christ, believers can overcome the barriers that sin has erected between them and God.

Additionally, the resurrection represents a profound *victory over death*, often regarded as the ultimate consequence of sin. Death, in Christian belief, is seen as the result of humanity's disobedience to God. However, through His resurrection, Jesus transforms death from a final defeat into a gateway to eternal life. As expressed in 1 Corinthians 15:55-57, the resurrection nullifies the sting of death and proclaims that believers can triumph through Christ. This transformative message conveys that Jesus' resurrection is not merely an event but a cosmic shift that redefines humanity's relationship with death. In this context, Jesus' resurrection is referred to as the "firstfruits" of the resurrection of the dead (1 Corinthians 15:20-23). This term emphasizes that Jesus' victory over death is the precursor to the future resurrection of all believers.[194] His resurrection signifies that those who are in Christ will also experience resurrection and eternal life. This assurance provides hope to Christians, affirming that death does not have the final word and that they too will rise in glorified bodies to share in eternal life.

Moreover, the resurrection of Jesus brings believers the *assurance of eternal life*. In John 11:25-26, Jesus declares, "I am the resurrection and the life," affirming that those who believe in Him will live even after death. This promise reassures Christians of their eternal destiny with God, establishing a foundation for their faith and hope.[195] The resurrection instills confidence that, regardless of physical death, believers will enter into a profound and everlasting relationship with their Creator.

Finally, the resurrection signals the beginning of a *new creation*, where the old order characterized by sin and death gives way to a redeemed existence. This new creation is inaugurated through Christ's resurrection, which invites believers to participate in this transformative reality. As they place their hope in Him, they become part of a renewed creation, marked by the glory and life that Jesus embodies. In summary, the resurrection is the centerpiece of Christian faith, affirming victory over sin and death, offering the assurance of eternal life, and ushering in a new creation where believers can fully experience the promise of life beyond the grave. This powerful

---

[193] Joel B. Green, *The Theology of the Gospel of Luke* (Cambridge University Press, 1995), 150.

[194] Justo Gonzalez, *The Story Luke Tells: Luke's Unique Witness to the Gospel* (Wm. B. Eerdmans Publishing, 2015), 93.

[195] Joel B. Green, *The Gospel of Luke* (Wm. B. Eerdmans Publishing, 1997), 22.

message shapes the understanding of salvation and fuels the hope, joy, and confidence of Christians in their daily lives.

Summary of Findings

In exploring the Passion and Resurrection narratives in Luke's Gospel, we uncover profound theological insights that shape the Christian faith. The Passion narrative in Luke details the events leading to Jesus' crucifixion, including betrayal, arrest, trials, and burial. Key moments, such as Jesus' prayer in the Garden of Gethsemane and Peter's denial, highlight human frailty contrasted with divine strength. This narrative illustrates the depth of Jesus' suffering and emphasizes His role as the innocent Lamb of God, offering Himself as a sacrifice for humanity's sins. The Passion, therefore, sets the stage for understanding the significance of Jesus' atoning work and the redemptive purpose behind His suffering.[196]

In contrast, the Resurrection narrative showcases the victory of Jesus over sin and death, a central theme in Luke's Gospel. The discovery of the empty tomb by the women, the angelic proclamation of His resurrection, and the encounters with the disciples—including the transformative experience on the road to Emmaus—underscore the assurance of eternal life and the fulfillment of Jesus' promises. These events not only affirm Jesus' identity as the Messiah but also reinforce the hope of resurrection for all believers. Through these appearances, Luke highlights the continuity between Jesus' suffering and His triumph, reinforcing the idea that death is not the end but rather a transition into eternal life.

The theological significance of these narratives is immense. The Passion highlights key themes of atonement, sacrifice, redemption, and forgiveness, encapsulating the essence of Jesus' mission. Conversely, the Resurrection signifies triumph over sin and death, offering believers the assurance of eternal life. Together, these narratives articulate a cohesive understanding of salvation that encompasses both the necessity of Christ's suffering and the transformative power of His resurrection. They serve as a reminder of God's unfailing love and the lengths to which He goes to restore humanity to Himself.

The Passion and Resurrection narratives are central to Luke's Gospel and the broader Christian message. They form the narrative climax that portrays Jesus' ultimate mission: to save and redeem humanity through His death and resurrection. This centrality is evident in the way these themes are interwoven throughout the Gospel, emphasizing God's redemptive plan. Moreover, they showcase Jesus' compassion and mercy, as He forgives even

[196] Scott Cunningham, *Through Many Tribulations: The Theology of Persecution in Luke-Acts* (Bloomsbury Publishing, 1997), 330.

those who betray and abandon Him. By focusing on these themes, Luke invites readers to reflect on the transformative impact of the Gospel and encourages them to respond in faith and obedience.

Contemporary relevance emerges from the Gospel message of salvation and transformation that these narratives embody. In today's world, marked by suffering, challenges, and existential crises, the hope offered through the Passion and Resurrection remains vital. Believers are reminded that redemption and forgiveness are accessible to all, no matter the depths of their struggles. This hope inspires Christians to remain steadfast in their faith, even in the face of adversity, knowing that God's promise of victory over sin and death stands firm.

Furthermore, the commission given to the disciples to proclaim the resurrected Christ resonates deeply with contemporary believers. Just as the early church was tasked with sharing the message of salvation, modern Christians are called to bear witness to the transformative power of the Gospel in their communities and beyond. This mission emphasizes the ongoing relevance of the Resurrection as a source of hope and a catalyst for personal and communal transformation. As believers engage in acts of service and evangelism, they fulfill the Great Commission, echoing the call to make disciples of all nations.

Lastly, the call to compassion and service in the face of suffering reflects the heart of discipleship. Jesus' example encourages believers to emulate His selflessness and sacrificial love. This aspect of discipleship compels Christians to engage with the marginalized and suffering, showcasing the love of Christ through their actions. The resurrection message further instills an eternal perspective, reminding believers that their efforts in service and compassion have lasting significance in the Kingdom of God. Through these narratives, Luke provides a roadmap for discipleship that intertwines faith with action, love, and a commitment to the well-being of others.

In summary, the Passion and Resurrection narratives in Luke's Gospel are foundational to understanding the Christian faith. They encapsulate themes of suffering, redemption, and hope, inviting believers to embrace their call to discipleship. The implications of these narratives resonate deeply in contemporary contexts, offering assurance, mission, and a model for living that reflects Christ's love and transformative power in the world.

9

Current Discussions in the Gospel of Luke Table Fellowship, Hospitality, Women, and Reversal Themes

Introduction

The Gospel of Luke presents a unique lens on Jesus' ministry, with distinctive themes that illuminate the radical inclusivity and transformation he advocated. Central to Luke's narrative are the themes of table fellowship, hospitality, the role of women, and the principle of reversal, each serving as a profound reflection of Jesus' approach to societal norms and divine priorities. These themes not only reveal the character of Jesus' ministry but also challenge the societal structures of His time, offering a message of inclusivity, justice, and humility. Through Luke's emphasis on these topics, we see how Jesus consistently reaches out to the marginalized and invites everyone into a closer, transformative relationship with God.

Table fellowship is one of the most compelling themes in Luke, showcasing Jesus' intentional association with individuals from various social backgrounds, including tax collectors, sinners, and the poor. Sharing meals with those society deemed unworthy was more than a simple act of kindness; it was a bold statement against the exclusivity and rigidity of social hierarchies. By inviting the marginalized to the table, Jesus underscored the inclusiveness of God's kingdom and broke down barriers that divided people. In Luke's Gospel, table fellowship becomes a powerful symbol of

God's invitation to all people, reflecting the accessibility of salvation and the love of a God who welcomes every person to commune with Him.

Hospitality further enhances this message, as it becomes a central practice that aligns with Jesus' teaching on love, generosity, and openness to others. Luke portrays hospitality not only as a cultural expectation but as a spiritual practice integral to Jesus' mission. The parable of the Good Samaritan, for instance, redefines hospitality by emphasizing compassion and aid to those in need, regardless of their background or affiliation. Through his teachings and actions, Jesus models a hospitality that transcends boundaries and promotes a sense of belonging and mutual care. In Luke, hospitality becomes an act of discipleship, where followers are called to embody God's love through their openness and generosity towards others.

The role of women in Luke's Gospel is notably progressive, highlighting the participation of women in Jesus' ministry and their unique contributions to His mission. Unlike in other Gospel accounts, Luke emphasizes the faith, courage, and discipleship of women, often presenting them as examples of true faithfulness and commitment. Figures such as Mary, the mother of Jesus, Mary Magdalene, and others play prominent roles, not only as recipients of Jesus' ministry but as active participants. Luke's portrayal challenges prevailing cultural norms by recognizing women as significant and valued disciples, affirming their worth and underscoring the inclusive nature of the kingdom of God.

Lastly, Luke's theme of reversal encapsulates the paradoxical values of God's kingdom, where the lowly are exalted, the rich humbled, and the last made first. This theme is apparent from the beginning of Luke, with Mary's Magnificat proclaiming a God who "has brought down rulers from their thrones but has lifted up the humble." Reversal is woven throughout Luke's narrative, highlighting God's justice and mercy. Through parables and interactions, Jesus teaches that societal status, wealth, and power hold no value in God's kingdom; rather, humility, repentance, and compassion define one's standing. Together, these themes present a holistic vision of discipleship that calls believers to embody Jesus' counter-cultural teachings and to live out a faith marked by humility, service, and radical inclusion.

I. Table Fellowship: Meals Scenes with Jesus at the Table in the Gospel of Luke

In the Gospel of Luke, each meal has a far greater significance than simply eating and drinking with others. Meals are a central way of telling a story.[1] The manner in which the meal is eaten and with whom it is eaten

[1] Jerome H. Neyrey, 'Ceremonies in Luke-Acts: The Case of Meals and Table Fellowship,' *The Social World of Luke-Acts: Models for Interpretation,* ed. Jerome Neyrey

symbolize the social system of a group[2] and its values. As John H. Elliott states, "Food and meals encode social relationships, cultural values and norms, and metaphysical worldviews."[3] Therefore, for many first-century Jews and especially purity groups such as the Essenes and Pharisees, the meal was a microcosm of the universe under their God. Jesus' most important teaching moments in Luke's Gospel take place at meals, parties, and celebrations. Jesus and His followers proceeded to overturn three basic boundary markers regarding meals and table fellowships: violating certain laws surrounding food and purity rituals, eating with those who were considered religious outcasts, and giving great importance to include the poor in the proclamation of the kingdom.

There are different conflicts in the Gospel of Luke,[4] which were conflicts between incompatible systems: Jesus, the Roman aristocracy, the Jewish elite, religious leaders, and the Jewish peasantry. Jesus stood against religious abuse, the down-play of women and their social status and the misuse of political structure. This article attempts to highlight the conflict in the meal scenes with Jesus at the table in the Gospel of Luke with the help of the methodological tools related to socio-narrative[5] approach. Narrative

(Peabody: Hendrickson, 1991), 363.

2 Jerome H. Neyrey, 'Ceremonies in Luke-Acts: The Case of Meals and Table Fellowship,' 368.

3 John H. Elliott, "Household and Meals vs. Temple Purity: Replication Patterns in Luke-Acts," *Biblical Theology Bulletin* 21 (Fall 1991): 103.

4 The author's doctoral desertion is also in line with the same pattern of thought. "*Conflict Resolution and Kingdom Values: A Study of Selected Parables in the Gospel According to St. Luke*", D.Th dissertation, Senate of Serampore College, 2014.

5 It is done by an integrative approach employing insights from the literary criticisms particularly narrative criticism and social sciences. This is a growing interest among the New Testament interpreters on literary criticism. The emerging trend in the New Testament studies is its extensive use of insights from social sciences by combining it with literary criticism. Kenneth Ewing Bailey, A Literary Cultural Approach to the Parables in Luke (Michigan: W. B. Eerdmans, 1976); David B. Gowler gives a socio-narratological character analysis of the Pharisees in Luke-Acts in Host, Guest, Enemy and Friend: Portrait of the Pharisees in Luke and Acts, Emory Studies in Early Christianity 2 (New York: Peterlang, 1991); John C. Lentz uses literary criticisms to locate Paul in the socio-historical context of his time in Luke Portrait of Paul, SNTSMS 77 (Cambridge: Cambridge University Press, 1993); Bruce J. Malina and Jerome H. Neyrey paint a portraits of Paul as depicted in Acts using insights from social sciences in Portraits of Paul: An Archeology of Ancient personality (Louisville, Kentucky: Westminster and John Knox Press, 1996); James Malcolm Arlandson also gives a socio-narratological analysis of women in Luke-Acts in Women, Class and Society in Early Christianity: Models from Luke-Acts (Peabody, Massachusetts: Hendrickson, 1997); S. John Roth investigates the characters types in Luke Acts in The Blind, the Lame and the Poor: Character Types in Luke-Acts, JSNT Sup 144 (Sheffield: Sheffield Academic Press, 1997); John D. Darr gives a literary-critical study of Herod the Tetrarch in Luke-Acts, in Herod the Fox: Audience Criticism and Lukan Characterization, JSNT Sup 163 (Sheffield: Sheffield

critical analysis looks at the complex ways in which the Biblical narratives were written. The sociological[6] analysis is to examine the social ethos, values and context of the text. A socio-narrative analysis seeks to shuffle two important tools for biblical studies into a substantial methodology, where a literary perspective of characterization is reinforced by knowledge of the cultural patterns of communication in the 1st century.

Meal scenes and table fellowships are important themes in the Gospel of Luke.[7] Food[8] and meals are the social context in which Lukan concerns are expressed. In the Gospel of Luke, one finds that meals[9] as centers of

---

Academic Press, 1998); and B. J. Syiemlieh, God's Favorites: A Socio-Narrative Analysis of the Characters in the Lukan Infancy Narratives (Lk 1:5-2:52) (Delhi: ISPCK: 2005). One may find helpful reading, Warren Carter, Matthew and the Margins: A Socio-Political and Religious Reading, The Bible Liberation Series (Bangalore: TPI, 2007).

[6] The social situation of the early Christianity directs towards its social conditions as lower and middle strata. To the ancient higher culture, early Christianity stood in a natural opposition, not primarily as Christianity, for it was a movement of the lower social strata. Bengt Holmberg, *Sociology and the New Testament* (Minneapolis: Fortress Press, 1990), 28. In the presentation of Gerd Theissen, *Sociology of Early Palestinian Christianity* tr. by John Bowden (Philadelphia: Fortress Press, 1977) also the same social level of early Christian community has been accepted. Where as in the work of Wayne A. Meeks, *The First Urban Christians: Social World of Apostle Paul* (New Haven: Yale University Press, 1983) finds the urban environment for the early Christian community. Cf. Robert M. Grant, *Early Christians and Society* (San Francisco: Harper and Row, 1977). Sociological Criticism makes its framework of reference to analyze the marginalized groups and its ethos.

[7] John Navone, 'The Parable of the Banquet,' *BT* (Nov, 1964): 923ff. Cf. also John Navone, 'Luke's Banquet Theme,' *BT* 44/4 (July, 2006): 235ff. Cf. Robert L. Kelley, "Meals with Jesus in Luke's Gospel," *HBT* 17/2 (Dec, 1995): 123-131 and Jerome H. Neyrey, 'Meals, Food, and Table Fellowship,' *The Social Sciences and New Testament Interpretation,* edited by Richard Rohrbaugh (MA, Peabody: Hendrickson, 1996), 159-182.

[8] Village set up with peasants and fisherman the people's main diet was bread (4:3; 7:33; 9:13; 11:5; 13:20-21; 14:15; 15:17; 22:19) and fish (9:13; 11:11; 24:42). Meat may be used only for a big celebration (15:23) a lamb for the Passover meal (22:7). Other supplementary food items were wine (1:15), figs (13:6-9); eggs (11:12) grain (6:1). The plenty and hungry are common phenomena (1:53; 6:25; 16:19-21; 15:17) shows the contrast between the rich and needy. There was also famine or hunger in their history (Israel's History) 4:25; 6:3). The basic need for the hungry is to be filled and have enough and sees God as the one who will turn the situation and satisfying the hungry (6:1-5; 21:25; 9:10-17; 15:14-24; 16:19-26).

[9] Meal stories in the gospel are Luke 5:27–39 -In the house of Levi, Luke 7:36–50-In the house of Simon the Pharisee, Luke 9:10–17- At Bethsaida, Luke 10:38–42-In the house of Martha and Mary, Luke 11:37–54- In the house of a Pharisee, Luke 14:1–24-In the house of a Pharisee on a Sabbath, Luke 19:1–10-In the house of Zaccheus, Luke 22:14–38- Jesus' Last Supper with the disciples, Luke 4:13–35, With the risen Lord at Emmaus, Luke 24:36–53- With the risen Lord at Jerusalem. But the reference related to table is found in the narratives which are discussed in this paper.

sociability and of conflicts. Luke evaluates the city culture, patronage[10] and the quest for honor[11] with the presentation of meal scenes in the Gospel.[12] Table fellowship not only shapes community identity but also creates social boundaries.[13] At table, Luke depicts the way God fellowships with Jews, Gentiles and outcasts. In doing so, he is concerned for justice in the treatment of the poor, maimed, lame and blind (Lk 14:13, 21). By eating with outcasts, Jesus provides an 'acted parable' of the Kingdom.[14] In Luke's Gospel, the meals that Jesus ate bridge distinctions between people and include those from different walks of life in a common grouping, gathering people in (to the fold) from the outside (marginalized). Jesus ate with the outsiders, Pharisees and women.[15]

1. 'Jesus at the Table with "Outsiders" or "Sinners" (Lk 5:27-39; 19:1-10)

It includes two scenes, Jesus at the Table at Levi's house (Lk 5:27-39) and Jesus at the Table at Zacchaeus' House (Lk 19:1-10). Both of them were tax-collectors as well as wealthy and the meals motivated conflict.

---

[10] This dependency is evident in various social relationships such as Father-son, God-person, lord-vassal, landlord-tenant, politician-voter and so on. This model of leadership in the Christian community is possible because God is the ultimate patron, and Jesus is depicted as the broker of God's blessings to the people. But in the parable of the Wedding Feast (Lk 12:35-40) a paradox appears: the master (patron) takes the role of a servant (12:37). Jesus here and elsewhere identifies greatness with serving, rather than being served. The result is a transformation of the traditional concept of patronage, and it bypasses the established urban and legal central power of Temple and Torah by proclaiming the immediacy of the kingdom of God.

[11] Bruce J. Malina, *The New Testament World: Insights from Cultural Anthropology* (Atlanta: John Knox Press,1981), discusses in chapter one on *Honor and Shame: Pivotal Values of the First-Century Mediterranean World,* various topics such as understanding honor, how does a person get a grant of honor?, how honor acquired, honor symboled by blood, honor symboled by name, how honor is displayed and recognized, honor and the interpretation of a challenge, honor and [illegible], [illegible] collective honor, honor and the moral division of labor: the double standard toward defining honor and shame etc.

[12] Halvor Moxnes, 'The Social Context of Luke's Community,' *Interpretation* 48/4 (Oct. 1994): 379ff.

[13] James L. Resseguie, *Narrative Criticism of the New Testament: An Introduction* (Grand Rapids: Baker Academic Press, 2005), 110-111.

[14] Cf. Stuart L. Love, 'Women and Men at Hellenistic Symposia Meals in Luke,' *Modeling Early Christianity: Socio-Scientific Studies of the New Testament in its Context,* edited by Philip F. Esler (London: Routledge, 1995), 198.

[15] The basic outline of the article is taken from Richard P. Thompson, "Gathered at the table: Holiness and Ecclesiology in the Gospel of Luke," *Holiness and Ecclesiology in the New Testament,* edited by Kent E. Brower and Andy Johnson, Grand Rapids: Eerdmans, 2007.

1.1. Jesus at the Table at Levi's House (Lk 5:27-39)

Jesus sees Levi sitting at a toll booth.[16] Luke needs no to explain about the toll booth to his audience: everyone knew that tax collectors are undesirables, ridiculed by the rich and hated by the peasant.[17] A visiting Galilean with a reputation for association with tax-collectors (Lk 7:34; 19:1-10) might have been suspected of disloyalty.[18] According to Bruce J. Malina, "As a rule patron-client societies are extensive and extractive; leadership is concerned with plundering rather than developing, and taxation exists for the benefit of elites, not for the common good."[19] A tax-collector[20] is a money-grabbing, cheating and a Roman collaborator. Tax-collectors were Jews empowered by the Roman government and they collected taxes as much as they could. They had permission to collect to any excess above the basic requirement of the government. They were the despised and had no respect among the people.

Jesus calls the tax collector with two words, no explanations: "Follow me." The words of Jesus reverse the expectation and are in conflict with the

[16] During the time of Jesus, Palestine was under the burden of taxation. Rome exacted the tribute directly through its colonial bureaucracy from Judaea and in Galilee, indirectly through their client, Antipas. Two primary taxes collected by the Romans were the poll tax and the land tax. Although the Jews did not always resist taxation by the Romans, taxation was a vexed question among them. Tax-relief was an important issue in the time of the Maccabees. Cf. J. Massyngbaerde Ford, 'Reconciliation and Forgiveness in Luke's Gospel,' *Political Issues in Luke-Acts,* edited by Richard J. Cassidy and Philip J. Scharper (New York: Orbis Books, 1973), 83.

[17] R. Earle, 'Tax-Collector,' *The Zondervan Pictorial Encyclopedia of the Bible*, vol. 5, edited by Merrill C. Tenny (Michigan: Zondervan Publishing House, 1975): 606. Tax-collectors examined goods and collected tolls on roads and bridges. The tax-collectors, whether Jewish or pagan, were ostracized and hated by the Jews and regarded them as the mafia in their contemporary society. The tax-collectors or their families were not allowed to be witness in court and not permitted to give to the charity fund. Even the houses which they entered were declared unclean and no orthodox Jew would dine in their homes because of infringement of the purity and dietary laws.

[18] T. E. Schmidt, 'Taxes,' *Dictionary of Jesus and the Gospels,* edited by Joel B. Green, Scot McKnight and I. Howard Marshall (Downer's Grove, IL: InterVarsity Press, 1992), 800ff.

[19] Bruce J. Malina, *The New Testament World: Insights from Cultural Anthropology* (Louisville: Westminster/ John Knox Press, 1993), 4.

[20] In the Gospel of Luke tax-collectors are carefully placed. Luke recounts John the Baptist's advice to tax collectors. He does not tell them to give up their occupation but merely to exact no more than what was just. Not all Jews received concerted tax collectors back into the community because restitution to those whom they had wronged was so difficult. Luke also records the call to Levi, a tax-collector.

normal judgment of the people concerning the tax-collector.[21] Levi "leaves everything" – a significant Lukan addition to the Markan story – "and follows him." Levi gives a great party in honor of Jesus.[22]

Jesus celebrates with Levi a great feast, inviting other tax collectors into his fellowship, teaching about the new covenant which he is inaugurating (Lk 5:27-39). This meal scene is invitational: Jesus is 'fishing' for people, which he had discussed with Simon (Lk 5:1-11), inviting other tax-collectors, along with Levi, into his new community. This episode lays the groundwork for why the Pharisees accuse Jesus of regularly eating with 'sinners and tax-collectors' (cf. 15:1-2). At this, the first such meal scene, the Pharisees and scribes ask two openly hostile questions: 'Why do you eat with sinners?' (5:30) and 'Why do your disciples not fast?' (5:33). Previously, they had kept their critical reasoning to themselves (5:21-22). Now, however, they voice their hostility and the conflict is clear here. The resolution to the conflict is also made clear in v. 31, 32 with the indirect announcement of Jesus about the repentance of Levi (8: 28=31,32)

Levi cannot be poor for his banquet gathers a great crowd of tax collectors and others who were with them, later to be alluded to as "sinners." The question "Why are you eating and drinking with tax collectors and sinners?" informs the audience that those of Levi's guests who are not only tax collectors but are also "sinners". Jesus is conscious of his divine authority and mission to call sinners for repentance. As the Lukan pericope continues smoothly in Luke 5:33-35, repentance gets close to conversion, it includes faith in Christ.

It seems obvious that Jesus' association with tax collectors, and possibly other disreputable people as well, was later invested with a powerful symbolic meaning. Both Pharisees[23] and sinners become literary vehicles with which to attain his own objectives for Luke.[24] The Lukan story proclaims that Jesus is the Christ and therefore able to save even the dregs of society. By lodging in his house, Jesus gave him back his lost honor by staying in his house and

---

21 Cf. Norman Perrin, *Rediscovering the Teaching of Jesus* (London: SCM Press, 1967), 94,102. In the proclamation of the Kingdom of God, the table fellowship with the tax collectors and sinners is an acted parable of Jesus. It was meaningful for his disciples but offensive to the critics.

22 Eugene LaVerdiere, *Dinning in the Kingdom of God: The Origins of the Eucharist in the Gospel of Luke* (Chicago: Liturgy Training Publications, 1994), 42.

23 There were at least five major sects: Pharisees, Sadducees, Essenes, Herodians and Zealots. Each of these groups had a definite influence on the thinking of the people of that time and each must have come into contact with Jesus on many occasions.

24 Sylvester Johnson, *Jesus and His Parables* (Delhi: ISPCK, 2002), 119.

breaking bread with him and Levi received back his dignity.[25] Finally, Luke has ecclesiastical motives in the controversy of the Gentile Christians and the Jewish Christians.

1.2. Jesus at the Table at Zacchaeus' House (Lk 19:1-10)

These scenes present the ministry of Jesus to the outcasts of Jewish society. Tax-collectors are presented as outsiders and sinners due to their profession. People of the same profession gathered at the table. The Pharisees were grumbling because the disciples of Jesus ate with the tax-collectors and sinners (Lk 5:30). It shows such persons as on the periphery or outside of the community and for the Pharisees. It is the purity regulations that distinguished "insider" from "outsider". The controversy was not over the food that was served but over the people at the table. The conflict in the story is between Jesus and the Pharisees.[26] The resolution for the conflict is seen in v. 8 where Zacchaeus expresses the language of repentance as to share his wealth. The attitude of Jesus redefined pharisaic understanding of holiness, community and the workings of God by including the outcast for the sake of repentance. Jesus' response turned the Pharisees' purity system upside-down. According to Richard P. Thompson "The Pharisees required repentance *before* inclusion within the community where as Jesus ate with the sinners so that they might repent."[27] To what extent this argument can be accepted is in doubt because Jesus went to Levi's house after his repentance (cf. Lk 5:28-29). The story of Zacchaeus is the climax of the Lukan theme of the repentance of tax collectors. This is the last time that tax collectors are mentioned in Luke-Acts. The conversion of a chief tax collector is a model one, with outstanding almsgiving and acts of restitution.

1.3. Jesus at the Table with Pharisees (Lk 7:36-50; 11:37-54; 14:1-24)

This section includes three narratives. They are (1) 'Jesus, Simon the Pharisee and the Sinful Woman' (Lk 7:36-50). (2) 'Jesus, an Unnamed Pharisee and Washing before Dinner' (Lk 11:37-54). (3) 'Jesus, a Leader of the Pharisees, Honored Seating and Dinner Invitations' (Lk 14:1-24).

In the Gospel of Luke, the conflict between Jesus and the Pharisees is concerning how one is to relate to sinners. The pharisaic group arose sometimes after the Babylonian Captivity. They believed in the Law of

---

[25] Jon Sobrino, *Jesus the Liberator: A Historical Theological Reading of Jesus of Nazareth* (New York: Orbis Books, 1993), 97, 98.

[26] Richard P. Thompson, 'Gathered at the table: Holiness and Ecclesiology in the Gospel of Luke,' *Holiness and Ecclesiology in the New Testament,* edited by Kent E. Brower and Andy Johnson (Grand Rapids: Eerdmans, 2007), 81.

[27] Richard P. Thompson, 'Gathered at the table: Holiness and Ecclesiology in the Gospel of Luke,' 81.

Moses and they had developed a significant amount of traditional beliefs or interpretations of the law.[28] "The Pharisees function as rich and powerful patrons of the peasants within the village society and as brokers for the peasants in their relations with the outside world."[29] There are mentions about the Pharisees in the Gospel of Luke (7:36; 11:53; 13:31; 14:1; 16:14; 17:20; 18:10-14), with lawyers and teachers of Law (5:17; 7: 30; 14:3). In the Gospel of Luke, Pharisees are seen with status of respect and as authoritative leaders of Judaism.[30] In Luke, three times Jesus dines with Pharisees. They are presented as community leaders (14:1), involved with wealth (16:14) and politically active and informed (13:31). In the parables, one can find the Pharisees as the opponents of Jesus. "It appears that Luke thinks in terms of two complexes of opposing groups: one gathered around Pharisees, and the other around chief priests, the scribes interacting with both."[31] For Luke, the Pharisees are the natives of Galilee (5:17). Luke preserves conflict stories in which Pharisees encounter Jesus.

Pharisees had important roles in society and were bound together by certain beliefs and practices and had influence for social change.[32] Jesus' attitudes towards Pharisees are expressed in His accusations to them[33] (Lk 11:39-42, 44). In the Gospel of Luke, one finds the Pharisees frequently

---

[28] These were the traditions of the Jews. These were orally passed down from the generation to generation. In the early second century AD, the traditions were gathered together into a collection, now known by the name *Talmud.*

[29] Anthony J. Saldarini, *Pharisees, Scribes and Sadducees in Palestinian Society: A Sociological Approach* (Wilmington, Delaware: Michael Glazier, Inc., 1988), 176.

[30] Robert Lawson Brawley, *Luke-Acts and the Jews: Conflict, Apology and Conciliation* (Atlanta: Scholars Press, 1987), 100.

[31] Halvor Moxnes, *The Economy of the Kingdom: Social Conflict and Economic Relations in Luke's Gospel* (Philadelphia: Fortress Press, 1988), 18.

[32] Antony J. Saldarini, 'Pharisees,' *ABD*, edited by David Noel Freedman, vol. 5 (New York: Doubleday, 1992), 295. In Lucan presentation Pharisees are presented as hosts to Jesus in their houses (7:36-50; 11:37; 14:1-14). There are descriptions about them in the teaching of Jesus too (14:1; 14:15-24; 16:1-9; 16:19-31; 18:10-14). In his discussion of religious teachings and practices that affected everyday life, Luke's focus is on ritual purity, faith in God, and social interaction on a local level (11:37-41; 14:7-14; 16:14-18). The Pharisees are presented in the Gospel as the rich and lovers of money'. Those rich people rejected Jesus, where as the poor accepted Him.

[33] Mathew Black, 'Pharisees,' *IDB*, edited by George Arthur Buttrick, vol.3 (New York: Abingdon, 1962), 777. I. Carrying out the Laws of Purity, while remaining impure inwardly. II. Teaching and paying tithes on green and dry vegetables not required by the Law, while neglecting the religious and moral obligations of the Law. They were considered as the most accurate interpreters of the Law. Believed in fate, believed in resurrection, they had a highly developed angelology and had a greater eschatological expectation.

in conflict with Jesus during His ministry.[34] "Luke takes over the Pharisees in a historical, cultural and religious context in which they demand admiration and assign them a commensurate role."[35] Conflict with Pharisees is consistent and their activity is limited only to Galilee but not connected to the governing circles in Jerusalem. In the Gospel of Luke, Pharisees have definite religious concerns such as hand-washing, Sabbath observance and purity laws (cf. 6:2, 7; 7:39; 11:39; 14:13).

1.3.1. Jesus, Simon the Pharisee and the Sinful Woman (Lk 7:36-50)

In this narrative, the woman, who is known as sinner appears and the following actions crushed the inscribed holiness and purity regulations of the meal for the Pharisees. Jesus articulated and embodied a divine point of view that saw the woman differently, there by affirming her for being not a sinner but someone enjoying the salvific benefits of forgiveness. Here, the reader can understand that Jesus has revealed and challenged the nature of holiness and community.

The story shows Lukan favourite motifs and concerns in dealing with a meal setting, women, humility, love and forgiveness, sinners and Pharisees.[36] The stories of Jesus' anointment (Matt 26:6-13, Mk 14:3-9, Lk 7:36-50, Jn 12:1-8) have inspired scholarly discussions.[37] Luke's anointing story is strikingly different from the other three. In spite of many differences, the basic plot and the point of the stories of Matthew, Mark and John are close to each other. They are set in Bethany shortly before Easter and lead up to the passion narrative: a woman anoints Jesus with a costly perfume, is rebuked by some for her wastefulness but defended by Jesus who claims that the anointing was for his approaching burial. Luke sets the scene in Galilee, in the house of a Pharisee, and in the early days of Jesus' ministry. The woman who enters and anoints Jesus, weeping and kissing his feet, is characterized as a "sinner in the town" (Lk 7:37). Like the other anointing of women, she is defended by Jesus, but in a different way. Finally, He proclaims that her

---

[34] Richard J. Cassidy, *Jesus, Politics and Society: A Study of Luke's Gospel* (New York: Orbis Book, 1978), 50ff.

[35] Robert Lawson Brawley, *Luke-Acts and the Jews: Conflict, Apology and Conciliation*, 105.

[36] Arthur A. Just, *The Ongoing Feast: Table Fellowship and Eschatology at Emmaus* (Minnesota: the Liturgical Press, 1993), 151.

[37] Cf. Kathleen E. Corley, *Private Women, Public Meals: Social Conflict in the Synoptic Tradition* (Peabody: Hendrickson, 1993), 127; Barbara E. Reid, "'Do You See This Women?' Luke 7:36-50 as a Paradigm for Feminist Hermeneutics," *Biblical Research* 40 (1995): 37-39; Evelyn R. Thibeaux, "'Known to be a Sinner': The Narrative Rhetoric of Luke 7:36-50," *Biblical Theology Bulletin* 23 (1993): 152; and David B. Gowler, *Host, Guest, Enemy and Friend: Portraits of the Pharisees in Luke and Acts* (New York: Peter Lang, 1991), 219-20.

sins are forgiven, to the astonishment of everyone present. John and Luke are displaying bewildering similarities and dissimilarities. Strikingly, Luke and John agree in that it is Jesus' feet that the woman anoints and that she dries them with her hair. The conflict is evident in v. 39 … "If this man were a prophet he would know who and what sort of person this woman is…" (cf. Jn. 4: 39 … "He told me *all* the things that I have done"). Here, the conflict is related to the messiahship of Jesus and the resolution is made clear when "He said to the women, "your faith has saved you; go in peace" (v. 50).

It has been claimed that one of the functions of the story was to encourage and defend Christian women who found themselves subject to doubts and misconceptions of their moral integrity because they attended Christian meetings without their male guardians, being widows or wives of unconverted men. As the presence of women at public meals was a subject of social criticism, especially when they were unattended by a husband, joining the Christian movement and attending the meetings in the face of public suspicion would have been emotionally extremely challenging. The action of the women which seems to be disgraceful and shameful to the community, fulfilled the honor and hospitality that the host should have provided for Jesus. The result of the event was the reversal[38] of status, both for Simon and the woman.[39]

1.3.2. Jesus, an Unnamed Pharisee and Washing before Dinner (Lk 11:37-54)

By His teaching, Jesus shows how Pharisees reflect or fail to reflect the Kingdom. This passage contains His harshest criticisms to the Pharisees. In Luke, since his criticisms are made at a meal and are given face to face, they do not mark the end of any relationship with them. There is still a dialogue. Jesus' dealings with the Pharisees were often confrontational, for his approach to purity, which was a major concern of theirs, was quite different from their own. Here, when Jesus is invited to dine with a Pharisee, he does not use the water provided to join in the ritual washing that would have been expected of those who were guests. He meets his host's disapproval with a determined attack upon his group. Their inner attitude does not measure up to their concern for external matters. Tithing laws were complicated but Luke's point is that the Pharisees spend too much energy on little things such as tithing herbs which would have been better spent on more important commandments such as justice and love.

---

[38] Charles H. Talbert, *Reading Luke: A Literary and Theological Commentary on the Third Gospel* (New York: Crossroad, 1982), 170, 171.

[39] Richard P. Thompson, 'Gathered at the Table: Holiness and Ecclesiology in the Gospel of Luke,' 86.

It is the second scene in relation to Pharisees, before being seated for the meal, Jesus had not been washed (11:38), for the Pharisees, it is a violation of the purity regulations. Series of woes to Pharisees are pronounced by Jesus and the outcome of the conflict in this narrative is the increase of conflict (vv. 53, 54). Here in the narrative, the Pharisees held to a narrow understanding of holiness and purity focused on ritual purity and practice while ignoring the social and economic relations. But they had maintained external ritual purity and Jesus accused them of their internal impurity because they upheld a social system that oppressed others. The holiness and ritual purity eventually violated the essential nature of the community itself. There is an alternative understanding of holiness and community that focuses on the needs of others rather than focusing on the inner holiness. Jesus' attitude towards the holiness which is no more theoretical but praxis oriented.[40] The climax of the narrative is the increasing hostility in the hearts of scribes and Pharisees. It led them to plot against Jesus and it ended up in the cross.

1.3.3. Jesus, a Leader of the Pharisees, Honored Seating and Dinner Invitations (Lk 14:1-24)

Throughout the Gospel of Luke one can find the Pharisees are in conflict with Jesus.[41] Jesus, at a meal with a Pharisee,[42] is again critical of the assembly, though this time with far less severity than his previous attack (11:37-53). Here, they watch him not with hostility as in 6:6, but with an interest that rises above mere suspicion. To Jesus' question, 'Is it lawful to cure on the Sabbath or not?' their silence, though not assent, acknowledges the correctness of Jesus' stance. His further question (v. 5) would seems

---

[40] Richard P. Thompson, 'Gathered at the Table: Holiness and Ecclesiology in the Gospel of Luke,' 87.

[41] There are some disagree with such readings. But one can find conflict initiated by the Pharisees in all three episodes (7:39; 11:38; 14:1) but is intensified by Jesus, who responds to the questioning (7:39; 11:38) or hostile observation (14:1) of his Pharisaic meal partners with a barrage of criticism. Cf. Robert C. Tannehill, *The Narrative Unity of Luke-Acts: A Literary Interpretation,* 170, 178.

[42] In the Gospel of Luke, one can find the dynamics of group characterization, especially of Pharisees. Tax-collectors and Pharisee (Lk 5:27-32), feasting and fasting (5:33-39), the grain field incident (6:1-5), the man with withered hand (6:6-11), are you the one who comes? (7:24-35), the Pharisee and the sinful woman revisited (7:24-35), like unmarked graves: Jesus' denunciation of the Pharisees (11:37-54), the hypocrisy of the Pharisees (12:1-3), the Pharisees, Jesus and Herod (13:31-35), Sabbath banquet at the House of a leading Pharisee (14:1-24), the lost sheep, the coin and the son (15:1-32), the Pharisees as lovers of money (16:14-16), the Kingdom of God does not come with observation (17:20-21), the Pharisee and the tax-collector at prayer (18:9-14), Pharisees at the triumphal entry (19:39).

to recognize that. Sabbath meals in particular take on the character of anticipations of those in the Kingdom. Jesus now gives reasons why their meals fail in this respect. They reflect pride rather than humility (he records the same deficiency on the part of the disciples at the last supper (22:24-7). They are exclusive rather than outreaching (vv. 12-14). At this point, a guest proclaims the blessedness of those who will share in the banquet of the Kingdom. Jesus exhibits the concern for the despised and marginalized in the society. It must supersede cultic and religious obligations, a truth evident in Jesus' healing on the Sabbath (Lk 6:6-11; 13:10-17).

In this section, Jesus advocates behavior that contested the social norms of that day and challenged the social concern for seeking honor at the meal tables by instructing them to take the seat of least honor. The text illustrates a crisis of division and reversal within that context that had come as a response to Jesus' ministry of inclusion to outcasts and sinners. The conflict has to do with differences over the nature of community and who were truly invited to the table fellowship. The reversal of status in a different sort is found here, the religious insiders of the story may find themselves outside in the eternal kingdom of God.[43]

1.4. Jesus at the Table with the Disciples (Lk 22:14-38; 24:13-35)

Jesus eating with the disciples includes two segments, Lord's Supper and Emmaus episode. Here Jesus' role as host rather than guest, questions and issues related to conflict still remain. The Last Supper, then, is the theological highlight of Jesus' table fellowship. It is the meal Jesus earnestly longed to share with his disciples (22:15). It is the one meal Jesus has conferred on to His church as His testament. It is the ongoing feast that continues to be repeated in the church in accord with Jesus' instructions. It is the unique meal that conveys to the guests the benefits of Jesus' earthly ministry, His atoning death, and His glorious resurrection. In the Last supper, the conflict is multifaceted. First conflict statement is related to Judas[44] (cf. 22:3; 22) and second is on the theme 'who is greater' (v. 27) and third is with Simon (v. 31-32). The conflict resolution can be found in vv. 28-30 with a

[43] Richard P. Thompson, 'Gathered at the Table: Holiness and Ecclesiology in the Gospel of Luke', 89.

[44] Howard I Marshall, 'Jesus Christ', *The Illustrated Bible Dictionary,* edited by J. D. Douglas (England: IVP, 1980), 767; G. Coleman Luck, *Luke: The Gospel of the Son of Man* (Chicago: Moody Press, 1960), 115; John Dominicrossan, *Who Killed Jesus: Exposing the Roots of Anti-Semitism in the Gospel Story of the Death of Jesus* (New York: Haper San Francisco, 1991), 71 and Darrell L. Bock, *Luke*, IVP New Testament Commentary Series, edited by Grant R Osborne (England: IVP, 1994), 357.

promise for the eternal Kingdom. It is the table of the Kingdom of God.[45] In the Last Supper, the giving of Jesus' body exemplifies the reversal of social expectations and norms that characterizes the community which Jesus advocated. An alternative reading of the text as this, "do this" does not mean specifically to the institution of the Eucharist as a sacrament but to show the gospel embodied and the identification of the mission as seen in the table fellowship.

The meal Jesus had with the two disciples is the meal of the new age.[46] The evangelist's final word on table fellowship in Luke is His meal at Emmaus. Here, He broke bread with two disciples. The conflict in this narrative begins when Jesus met the disciples (24:18) and ends with the resolution made with the meal. The disciples recalled their experience in line with it as "were not our hearts burning within us while he talked with us on the road and opened the scripture to us?" They carried out the same passion to the rest of the disciples in Jerusalem (cf. v. 33ff). This meal was programmatic for Christian worship as Jesus' continued his practice of teaching and eating with his disciples at table, giving the church the pattern for its worship and mission.

2. Theological Implications

The Journey to Jerusalem[47] is the large portion of Jesus' ministry which contributes to the conflict between Jesus and people, and Jesus at the table reflects these conflicts. In the journey section, the narrator makes use of a series of discourses to describe the ideological conflict between Jesus and people,[48] a conflict which revolves around the presence of the kingdom of God, the need for repentance, the correct use of possessions and ritual purity and so on and the kingdom values which give the resolutions to those conflicts. The whole collection of Luke, as he edited it, might have taken on allegorical overtones relating to that conflict,[49] especially in meal scenes. Generally, in the Gospel of Luke, conflict seems to revolve around two

---

[45] Eugene LaVerdiere, *Dining in the Kingdom of God: The Origins of the Eucharist in the Gospel of Luke* (Chicago: Liturgy Training Publications, 1994), 29.

[46] Arthur A. Just, *The Ongoing Feast: The Table Fellowship and Eschatology at Emmaus* (Minnesota: Liturgical Press, 1993), 38.

[47] On travel narrative and its relation to Moses of Deuteronomy and various issues related to it are discussed in David P. Moessner, 'Luke 9: 1-50: Luke's Preview of the Journey of the Prophet Like Moses of Deuteronomy,' *JBL* 102/4 (Dec, 1983): 575-605.

[48] Frank J. Matera, 'Jesus Journey to Jerusalem (Lk 9:51-19:46): A Conflict with Israel,' *JSNT* 51 (Sep, 1993): 77. According to Matera, The journey narrative is the best expression of the why and how Jesus came into conflict with Israel.

[49] Douglas M. Parrott, 'The Dishonest Steward (Luke 16:1-8a) and Luke's Special Parable Collection,' *NTS* 37/4 (1991): 508.

aspects of Jesus' ministry. First, it is about the authority of Jesus. Second, the conflict lies in the message of Jesus.[50]

In the Gospel of Luke, one can find that the religious groups such as the Pharisees, Sadducees, Scribes and Chief Priest are in conflict with Jesus, and sometimes the people and crowd are in conflict with Jesus and at times the disciples are in conflict with Jesus. Luke has presented a theological interpretation of the inescapable enigma that Israel, as a whole, had rejected its messianic fulfiller of salvation.[51] In the Gospel of Luke, one could find that Jesus was opposed by his contemporaries because of the goal and the content of His mission, as well as the way in which they understood His identity. Jesus worked at the margins of society, that is, His actions were seen as going against the grain of accepted societal norms. He mingled with those who were considered outsiders and did not operate in conformity with the goals and interests of his opponents. His identity revealed in his message was an open challenge to the status quo. He challenged the social order by x-raying societal abnormalities such as injustice, oppression, exploitation and racism and stood for an alternative that consisted of justice, love, equality and peace, all virtues of the kingdom. The rich are in a position to relax and enjoy their good fortune. All their responsibilities in life will have now been met, and all the needs of their life will now be satisfied, or so they think.

The church must realize that the work of Christ has broken down the economic barriers that would keep communities apart. The Church must welcome those who are being considered as sinners. The re-drawing of community boundaries does not mean the abandonment to chaos. The church's posture toward sinners, however, should be one of extending forgiveness and welcome. It should also be a position of humility that recognizes its own fallibility in past judgments about who is excluded and who is welcomed. Acting in this way enables the Church to show the healing hospitality that Church has received through the work of Christ. Rather than speaking condemnation to people that are already suffering in bondage to sin, the Church should extend God's love in humility, so that people are given the opportunity to become part of the mutually giving and receiving community that is the Church. When this is done, both people inside and outside the Church community will have their lives and minds changed about what it means to be part of the people of God.

[50] Stevan M. Sheeley, *Narrative Asides in Luke-Acts,* JSNT Supplement Series, 72 (Sheffield: Sheffield Academic Press, 1992), 141, 142. For various aspects related to the literary criticism, narrative elements in particular are discussed in this work. Cf. Jack Dean Kingsbury, 'The Plot of Luke's Story of Jesus,' *Interpretation* 48/4 (Oct, 1994): 369-378.

[51] David P. Moessner, 'The Leaven of the Pharisees' and 'this Generation': Israel's Rejection of Jesus According to Luke,' *JSNT* 34 (Oct, 1988): 42.

In the end, it is God's hospitality toward human, embodied in the life, death, and resurrection of Jesus that enables one to extend that hospitality toward others. As the church break bread together, it reminds us of our common bond to God, to one another, and to the life of this earth. One must continually learn to celebrate the abundance of God's plentiful reign, and overcome hostility with the hospitality of God's welcoming call to all to join in the feast of love. The meals scenes call the disciples of Jesus to constant conversion, reconciliation, and mission. One must learn to see the world as Jesus did, to evaluate it as Jesus does. The Eucharistic mystery is the ritual expression of this transformation. God's new table is all-inclusive and demands a heightened sense of inner readiness. To share the meal is to be in solidarity with Jesus and his mission.

II. Hospitality in Luke

Hospitality is woven throughout Scripture as a fundamental virtue that reflects God's own welcoming nature and care for humanity. In both the Old and New Testaments, hospitality is celebrated as an act of faithfulness, kindness, and compassion, highlighting the responsibility of God's people to welcome strangers and provide for those in need. This theme serves as a bridge between divine love and human action, revealing how believers can manifest God's care in tangible ways. For example, figures like Abraham and Lot in Genesis are commended for their openness and provision for travelers, underscoring how hospitality serves as a practical expression of faith.

In Luke's Gospel, hospitality takes on profound significance, as Jesus models and teaches this virtue within His ministry. Jesus frequently shares meals with people from various backgrounds, including tax collectors, sinners, and religious leaders, each encounter demonstrating hospitality's role in building relationships and challenging social norms. Through these acts of fellowship, Jesus establishes a new paradigm of hospitality that reaches beyond cultural boundaries, emphasizing the inclusiveness of God's kingdom. His meals become symbolic events, reinforcing the value of every individual and illustrating the Gospel's message of love and acceptance for all people.

Moreover, Luke's emphasis on hospitality underscores its importance in the life of faith as more than a mere social courtesy; it is a moral and spiritual imperative. Jesus' parables, such as the Good Samaritan, illustrate that hospitality is about a posture of openness and compassion toward others, even those who may be seen as outsiders. By showcasing hospitality as a response to God's own love, Luke highlights its transformative power, encouraging believers to engage in acts of service and kindness that embody the kingdom's values. In this way, hospitality in Luke is a pathway to deeper discipleship, inviting followers of Jesus to reflect His heart of mercy and inclusion in their daily lives.

The story of Mary and Martha in Luke 10:38-42 reveals a profound lesson about hospitality and discipleship, emphasizing the importance of prioritizing spiritual devotion. When Jesus enters Martha's home, Martha busies herself with preparations to ensure her guest is comfortable, while her sister Mary sits at Jesus' feet, attentively listening to His teachings. Martha's actions reflect a common expression of hospitality, where preparing and serving are central, yet this story introduces an unexpected twist. Martha's preoccupation with tasks becomes a source of frustration, leading her to seek Jesus' intervention, asking Him to tell Mary to assist her. Through this setup, Luke introduces an essential discussion on balancing action and reflection in the context of faith.

Jesus' response to Martha's request is both gentle and insightful. He acknowledges her worry and frustration, saying, "Martha, Martha, you are worried and upset about many things, but few things are needed—or indeed only one. Mary has chosen what is better, and it will not be taken away from her." In this moment, Jesus reframes the value of Martha's well-intentioned service, suggesting that while her dedication to hospitality is meaningful, there is something even more essential—being present with Him.[52] Jesus' affirmation of Mary's choice subtly challenges the conventional view of hospitality, emphasizing that true hospitality includes attentiveness to the presence of God and prioritizing moments of spiritual engagement over tasks.

This encounter between Mary and Martha is often seen as a portrayal of the tension between service and contemplation, underscoring the value of balancing practical responsibilities with the importance of spiritual devotion. While Martha's actions reflect a sincere desire to honor Jesus, Mary's choice to sit and listen exemplifies a focus on relational closeness with Him.[53] This story ultimately highlights that genuine hospitality goes beyond physical preparations; it invites believers to seek presence with God as the foundation for all acts of service.[54] By prioritizing time with Jesus, even amidst responsibilities, disciples are reminded of the need to cultivate a heart that remains centered on Him, allowing acts of hospitality to flow from a place of spiritual abundance.

In the Lukan parables, Luke appears keen to foster, in particular, a strong sense of the life of faith that Jesus requires of his followers in the context of the Journey with the Lord Jesus to Jerusalem. In this relationship perspective,

---

[52] R. Q. Ford, *The Parables of Jesus: Recovering the Art of Listening,* 105.

[53] Jerome H. Neyrey, *The Social World of Luke-Acts,* 74.

[54] R. Q. Ford, *The Parables of Jesus: Recovering the Art of Listening,* 109.

the life of faith can be divided into three categories. In the first place, the relationship of the Christians with neighbours is presented as love and forgiveness. Luke has a prominent emphasis on the need to love and forgive all people. Christians should love and forgive their neighbours, including enemies and sinners.[55] It is the appropriate attitude that all the Christians should have towards their neighbours. One after the other, it is emphasized that Christians should properly use their own material possessions which are entrusted to them for service of God and the poor. The Lukan Jesus repeatedly warns of the danger of attachment to riches as an obstacle to discipleship, and calls for the positive use of wealth, especially in the form of giving alms to the poor.

After all, it is the right use of wealth that Christians should pursue in relationship with material possessions. Lastly, it is especially faith and repentance that the Christians in relationship with God must bear in mind. Two prayer parables convey that prayer itself is an expression of faith towards God. Indeed, the evidence of faithfulness must be seen in prayer which presents itself as constant fellowship with God. As regards repentance, the parables related to repentance call for urgent repentance with a warning of imminent judgment, and still more describe that repentance means honestly acknowledging that one has broken the relationship between oneself and God, and fervently desiring the restoration of that relationship.

1. Teaching to Love Others

In the Lukan parables, the relationship of the Christians with neighbours is presented as love and forgiveness. First of all, it is obvious that the Parable of the Good Samaritan (10:25-37) teaches us to love our neighbour, and that this love is to be unconditional and unqualified, emphasizing that we must put love of neighbour into action. Regardless of ethnic or social ties, the people of God must show mercy to all, even one's enemies.[56] None of us must limit boundaries of care and obligation. The parable firmly rejects all prejudice and discrimination, namely, racial, intellectual, financial, religious and nationalistic prejudice, or anything else that would restrict doing acts of love. The teaching of the parable harmonizes well not only with Jesus' concern of the outcasts of the society, but also with Jesus' emphasis on loving one's enemies. The parable reminds us of the sermon on the plain where the love command is so central (6:27-36).

In this respect, the Samaritan is indeed a practical example of the teaching of Jesus. Just as Jesus sees and has compassion on the widow at Nain (7:13), so the Samaritan sees and has compassion on the injured man.

---

55 Frederick Houk Borsch, *Many Things in Parables: Extravagant Stories of New Community* (Philadelphia: Fortress, 1988), 34.

56 Robert F. Capon, *The Parables of the Kingdom* (Grand Rapids: Eerdmans, 1991), 54.

Compassion with divine quality enables one to feel deeply the suffering of others, and still more to move from the world of observer to the world of helper. The commandment of practice, "Go and do likewise" not only seeks to turn a man with a mania for creeds and anemia for deeds into a man of practice, but also teaches that it is our task too which we must all tenaciously pursue and combats against.[57] Even though loving our neighbour as oneself is difficult, there is no alternative for followers of Jesus. The purpose of the Parable of the Prodigal Son (15:11-32) lies in the father's love and compassion. At the heart of the parable is the father's love towards his sons in which the father deals impartially with his sons. His love not only enables repentance for the younger son, but could also, demolish the elder son's hostility and grievances, and enable his participation in the celebration.

The story, as J. R. Donahue mentions, is really a story of the 'Prodigal father'- lavish in love-who shatters the servile self-understanding of both sons and wants both to be free. Along this line of analogy, God, who Jesus represents in his ministry is identified with the forgiving and merciful father presented in the parable. Particularly in relation to the introduction of vv. 1-2, the parable functions as a defense of Jesus' association with sinners.[58] Like the instruction of the parable, if Jesus' receiving sinners and eating with them reveal God's mercy and forgiveness, then the Pharisees and the scribes' grievances must cease. The point, in relation to the story between the elder son and his father, lies in understanding grace rather than partiality and envy. If the elder son continuously clings to self-righteousness and the mind of merit and reward, he will never understand his father's generous and unmerited actions. In the end, his obstinacy prevents him from feeling his father's love, even the fact that he has been living in the shade of his father all this time, Son, you are always with me.[59]

But if, having discarded his own standpoint, he stands in his father's position with love and compassion towards the younger son, he will finally understand the grace offered without any cost and unconditional forgiveness. In the case of the preceding two parables, he is to treasure the mind of the shepherd and the woman, who place tremendous value on their lost one.[60] Jesus' aim is not to rebuke, but to persuade. That is to say, according to the father's love and forgiveness towards his sons, those who are grumbling in 15:1-2 must be willing to accept as a token of forgiveness, and love the return of sinner. In addition, The Pharisee and The Tax-Collector (18:9-14) implicitly can be mentioned in that the parable also provides an instruction

---

[57] R.Q. Ford, *The Parables of Jesus: Recovering the Art of Listening*, 55.

[58] K. Bailey, *Poet and Peasant: A Literary Cultural Approach to the Parables of Luke,* 56.

[59] K. Bailey, *Poet and Peasant: A Literary Cultural Approach to the Parables of Luke,* 60.

[60] K. Bailey, *Poet and Peasant: A Literary Cultural Approach to the Parables of Luke,* 66.

about justification.[61] That is to say, there is no justification before God without love of neighbour, for example, the Pharisee in 18:9-14 who despises one's own neighbour, and at the same time, there is justification before God within the humble admission of sins and the plea for forgiveness, whilst fully relying on God's mercy. By means of Lukan parables, Luke conveys a strong call for the need to love and forgive all people. According to Jesus' teaching in Lukan parables, the Christians, thus, should love and forgive our neighbours, including enemies and sinners. This is a right attitude that all the Christians should have towards their neighbours.

2. The Teachings of Jesus on Hospitality

The relationship of the Christians with material possessions is the right use of wealth. The Rich Fool (12:13-21) not only teaches us about attitudes towards wealth and possessions, but the right use of one's wealth for others. The parable betrays the planning of the rich and his attitude towards wealth and possessions, by means of the narrative device of soliloquy. That is to say, the rich denotes that one's life consists in the abundance of his possessions through his plan to tear down his barns and build bigger ones, and his monologue, "Soul, you have ample goods laid up for many years; take your ease, eat, drink, be merry" (v. 19).[62] But the plan of the rich man is shattered by the abrupt intrusion of God in v. 20. God calls him a fool because he believed that he controlled his own destiny. In conclusion, the main instruction of the parable is that one's life does not consist in the abundance of possessions, but rather in God.[63] It is reminiscent of the Jewish heritage where the Torah requires that gleanings from a harvest be left for the poor, the widow, the orphan, and the immigrant (Lev 19:9-10, 23:22, Deut 24:21).

As a result, his wealth became an idol which blinded him. It is difficult to discard the wrong attitude towards wealth, like the rich in our modern acquisitive society that tempts us to believe that one's security and pleasure are found in possessions.[64] The parable of the Unjust Steward (16:1-13) is a crisis parable, and a "how much more" parable.[65] The audience is faced with the radical demands of the kingdom that is begun by Jesus' preaching and ministry. The concerns between a proper attitude to wealth and eschatological crisis should not be separated, since the eschatological awareness influences how one sees material possessions. Just as the steward acted in the worldly crisis for his safety, how much more in eschatological crisis should Jesus'

---

[61] R.Q. Ford, *The Parables of Jesus: Recovering the Art of Listening,* 56.

[62] K. Bailey, *Poet and Peasant: A Literary Cultural Approach to the Parables of Luke,* 70.

[63] R. Q. Ford, *The Parables of Jesus: Recovering the Art of Listening,* 58.

[64] R. Q. Ford, *The Parables of Jesus: Recovering the Art of Listening,* 60.

[65] K. Bailey, *Poet and Peasant: A Literary Cultural Approach to the Parables of Luke,* 73.

followers act for their safety? Prudence means both preparedness for one's safe future, with right awareness of a crisis and the proper use of wealth in view of the presence of the kingdom and of coming judgment, just as the steward did in his crisis.

Despite listening, engaging, debating and complaining about Jesus, the Pharisees, like the rich man in the next parable do not realize that the eschatological crisis has arisen from Jesus' preaching and ministry. In addition, the correct use of worldly wealth focuses in particular on almsgiving, which is also a main teaching in the next parable that exposes mammon's powerful force which can enslave people. "You cannot serve both God and Mammon" (v. 13). The closing saying may be a warning against being unfaithful in God's service and a warning against being enslaved by mammon. Jesus here seems to personify mammon as an evil, powerful, cosmic force diametrically opposed to God's plan to set at liberty those who are oppressed. The pursuit of wealth and wholehearted allegiance to God are mutually exclusive. V. 13 makes it clear that unfaithfulness in the use of worldly wealth reveals ultimate loyalties and heart attitudes. If the disciples use their worldly wealth faithfully, it is to express that they serve God with wholehearted love. Whereas, if the disciples use their worldly wealth unfaithfully, it is to express that they do not serve God.

In conclusion, the disciples' use of wealth is tied to their future in heaven. Given this, the disciples must manifest their own position in the eschatological perspective without hesitation. On the whole, the parable not only functions as a challenge to evaluate correctly the nature of present time and take necessary action, but also teaches the proper use and attitude towards material possessions. The Rich man and Lazarus (16:19-31) is the converse of the preceding parable that for one's safe future the steward uses wealth as prudence under right awareness of his crisis. It is addressed to the Pharisee, whose love of money hinders them from their duty under God's law to give to the poor.[66] According to the description of the parable, the rich man, in contrast to the misery of Lazarus in front of his gate, dresses himself with the most expensive garment to signify either royalty or wealth, as well as throwing a splendid feast every day that is reminiscent of guests participating in a celebration.[67] To put it another way, the rich man has spent excessive resources on his own desires rather than redistributed it to those in need, by almsgiving. In this respect, the parable serves to warn the rich who use wealth only for themselves, while neglecting the needs of the poor.

The parable also addresses private charity in its modern form, in that it teaches the correct use of one's own wealth in responsibility to God and

---

[66] R. Q. Ford, The Parables of Jesus: Recovering the Art of Listening, 61.

[67] K. Bailey, *Poet and Peasant: A Literary Cultural Approach to the Parables of Luke,* 75.

other people. Of course, the parable conveys the theme of repentance that is represented as the proper use of possessions, and concern for the poor as one aspect of it, and also the idea of the sufficiency of the Scripture, thereby demonstrating the fact that Moses and the prophets have permanency and abiding validity (vv. 16-18).[68] Even so, it is self- evident that the proper use of possessions is one of the main themes of the parable. The parable gives the audience a lesson in generous almsgiving and to caring for one's neighbour in need. In this world, Christians should properly use their own material possessions that are entrusted to them for service of God and the poor. The rich fool in 12:13-21 and the rich man in 16:19-31 show a negative example in the use of their wealth only for their complacency, whereas the steward in 16:1-13 indicates a positive example of the proper use of possessions with a right awareness of his crisis.

3. Restoring Spirituality to Empower Society

According to the instruction of the Lukan parables, it is faith and repentance that Christians in relationship with God must bear in mind. The Lukan parables below disclose either explicitly or implicitly how Christians should live in relationship with God. The parables of prayer in the Lukan parables are properly related to faith in God. In the first place, the Friend at Midnight (11:5-8) teaches in effect the certainty of a prayer response on the basis of the character of God. All prayer should approach God boldly, by throwing away all the rising disturbances in relation to one's prayer, such as time, place, content of prayer, or doubting the response to prayer and so on. This is stressed in 11:1-4 (in terms of "our Father") and 11:9-13 (in a certainty of a prayer response).[69] Here is a parable contrasting God who is not like the sleeper.

The parable thus encourages the believer to be confident of their prayer on grounds of the character of God. The parable ends with the sleeper's standpoint, which is compared to God willingly granting the request, beginning with the petitioner's viewpoint, with the emphasis on boldness of the petitioner, and having no hesitation and discouragement in the face of opposition.[70] In other words, the point of view of the parable shifts naturally from the attitude of prayer towards the character of God. The Judge and the Widow (18:1-8) not only makes two main points from one of the characters in the story, that is, the certainty of God's hearing prayer and persistence in prayer, but also tightly interweaves the two points in the application (v. 1 and vv. 6-8).

---

[68] K. Bailey, *Poet and Peasant: A Literary Cultural Approach to the Parables of Luke,* 79.

[69] K. Bailey, *Poet and Peasant: A Literary Cultural Approach to the Parables of Luke,* 86.

[70] K. Bailey, *Poet and Peasant: A Literary Cultural Approach to the Parables of Luke,* 87.

The first point drawn from the character of the judge, after telling the parable, appears in *a fortiori* argument, that if an unjust judge will finally grant the request of a widow, how much more will God vindicate his people who cry to him day and night? There is at the same time a contrast between the judge and God: The contrast is that God, as opposed to the judge, is mercifully patient with the requests of the people, but also will vindicate quickly, unlike the judge's delay.[71] The second point, persistence in prayer, is derived from the widow who kept coming to the judge saying, "vindicate me against my adversary" (v. 3, 5b, 7a and 1). It is entirely based on the confidence of being vindicated by God (vv. 7-8a), and goes further to have the faith (v. 8b) to always pray and not lose heart, until the coming the Son of the Man. The evidence of faithfulness and alertness is seen in prayer itself, which reveals constant fellowship with God.[72] The matter of how we remain faithful until the coming of the Son of the Man, is certainly persistence in prayer. As a result, it seems safe to say that confident faith in God is what the prayer is all about.

Two prayer parables teach that prayer itself is an expression of faith of the Christians towards God. Indeed, the evidence of faithfulness must be seen in prayer that presents constant fellowship with God. With regards to repentance, we can enumerate the following parables: The Barren Fig Tree, The Parable of the Prodigal Son and The Pharisee and the Tax-Collector, including implicitly The Rich Man and Lazarus, the Great Feast (14:15-24) and the parable of the Unjust Steward. Chiefly, in The Barren Fig Tree, there are three main points: the figs that the farmer expects, cutting the tree without fruit down according to commandment of the farmer, and a potential additional year by suggestion of the vinedresser, namely the fruit as God's people, judgment and mercy. "Cut it down; why does it use up the ground?" It is a warning of judgment on Israel as the Israelite community because of their lack of productivity. The delay here becomes a call for repentance like Rom 2:4 where the riches of God's kindness and forbearance and patience lead to repentance. The parable is clearly a warning of [illegible] of judgment and a merciful call for the repentance of Israel offered for a short while.

In The Parable of the Prodigal Son, the younger son who lost all his property is confronted with the bigger problem, a severe famine, which he could not have anticipated. As he recognizes his desperate need, he begins to seek employment among the citizens of that country, and gets a job from a Gentile, feeding pigs.[73] After all, he is personally as well as financially spent. Therefore the scene focuses on his low and miserable life, more than

[71] R. Q. Ford, *The Parables of Jesus: Recovering the Art of Listening,* 96.

[72] K. Bailey, *Poet and Peasant: A Literary Cultural Approach to the Parables of Luke,* 90.

[73] R. Q. Ford, *The Parables of Jesus: Recovering the Art of Listening,* 58.

on the abandonment of his religious customs. "But when he came to himself he said, How many of my father's hired servants have bread enough and to spare, but I perish here with hunger I will arise and go to my father, and I will say to him, 'Father, I have sinned against heaven and before you; I am no longer worthy to be called your son; treat me as one of[74] our hired servants.' and he arose and came to his father" (15:17-20). Here, a question arises as to whether the younger son's confession and return are sincere acts of repentance. Concerning this question, there is, as seen in the preceding part, an argument that rather than being a euphemism for repentance, the expression simply reveals his desire to get himself out of his horrible situation.

Even though there is certainly no mention of repentance in his monologue, it must be recognized that his confession and change are at least sincere. The expression is nonetheless something of a prelude, leading him to repentance. What is more, it is even more likely to be a prelude to repentance, given the fact that such situations as reallife boundary situations not only can grow true religion, but also can allow him to let God in. Even though the parable of the Pharisee and Tax Collector (18:9-14) directly instructs on both the manner and content of prayer which occur in comparing the Pharisee's and the tax collector's prayer, the parable still has sub-themes.[75] The Tax collector in the parable plays a role as models of prayer, repentance, conversion and belief in Jesus, through the contrasting between tax collectors and Pharisees. The Pharisee may insist that his many good deeds, often exceeding even the demands of the Law, should bring him justification.[76] Yet justification before God is pertinently expressed by a repentant heart of straightforward confession, entrusting himself to the mercy and grace of God, not by external piety as the confession of the Pharisee that "I thank thee that I am not like other men, extortioners, the unjust, adulterers, or even like this tax collector. I fast twice a week, I give tithes of all that I get (vv. 11-12)." Repentance, therefore, means honestly acknowledging that one has broken the relationship between oneself and God, and fervently desiring the restoration of that relationship. In addition, in the second part of the parable of the Rich and Lazarus (16:19-31) with metanohvsousin in v. 30, the theme of repentance is explicit to some extent. It is here presented as the proper use of possessions, and concern for the poor.

---

[74] K. Bailey, *Poet and Peasant: A Literary Cultural Approach to the Parables of Luke,* 91.

[75] K. Bailey, *Poet and Peasant: A Literary Cultural Approach to the Parables of Luke,* 92.

[76] R.Q. Ford, *The Parables of Jesus: Recovering the Art of Listening,* 97.

III. Women in Luke's Gospel

The New Testament presents a transformative view of women, particularly in the way Jesus interacts with them, challenging the patriarchal norms of His time.[77] Through His teachings and actions, Jesus affirms the dignity, worth, and role of women, offering a counter-cultural perspective that elevates their position in religious and social contexts. This section will explore how Jesus treated women with respect and inclusion, specifically focusing on women as disciples, His counter-cultural attitude, and the central role of women in the resurrection narratives.[78] By examining these themes, we will gain a deeper understanding of the theological significance of women in the New Testament and the early Christian community.[79]

1. Women as Significant Figures

In the Gospel of Luke, women hold a distinct and honored place in Jesus' ministry, emphasizing their active and faithful roles in His mission. Unlike the societal norms of the time, where women were often relegated to the background, Jesus includes women as essential figures in His ministry, recognizing their faith, dedication, and contributions. Women are portrayed not merely as bystanders but as disciples and witnesses who play crucial roles in proclaiming and supporting Jesus' work. From the healing of women, like the woman with the issue of blood (Lk 8:43-48), to Mary and Martha's close relationship with Jesus, Luke's narrative demonstrates the inclusivity and honor Jesus extends to women. This portrayal challenges existing social boundaries, underlining women's importance in the early Christian community and as followers of Christ.

2. The Annunciation and Mary's Magnificat (Luke 1:26-56)

The Annunciation and Mary's Magnificat hold significant theological and social implications, particularly regarding themes of humility, reversal, and divine purpose. When the angel Gabriel visits Mary, she responds to God's call with obedience and humility, embodying the posture of a servant willing to fulfill God's will. Her response reveals her deep faith and willingness to embrace her role in God's redemptive plan, even when it demands personal sacrifice. The Magnificat, Mary's song of praise, captures the prophetic and subversive nature of God's kingdom, with its declarations that the proud will be scattered, the mighty brought down, and the humble

---

[77] Mary Ann Getty-Sullivan, *Women in the New Testament* (Collegeville, MN: Liturgical Press, 2017), 32.

[78] Bonnie Bowman Thurston, *Women in the New Testament: Questions and Commentary* (Eugene, OR: Wipf and Stock Publishers, 2004), 44.

[79] Shirley Stephens, *A New Testament View of Women* (Authors Book Nook, 1980), 7.

exalted. Through Mary, Luke presents a vision of divine justice that reverses societal expectations, suggesting that God's kingdom values humility, mercy, and justice. Mary's actions and words thus set a powerful example of courage and faith, and her Magnificat resonates as a timeless proclamation of God's transformative power.

3. Lessons from Women in Luke for Contemporary Gender Equality

Luke's portrayal of women holds valuable insights for contemporary discussions on gender equality, especially within faith communities. Women in the Gospel of Luke demonstrate leadership, devotion, and courage, qualities that serve as a model for inclusive ministry. From the women who follow and support Jesus financially to those who stand by Him at the cross, they embody a commitment that challenges traditional limits on women's roles. This portrayal invites reflection on the theological implications of gender equality in church leadership, encouraging communities to recognize and value women's contributions in ministry and discipleship. By revisiting these stories, modern believers can affirm the Bible's recognition of women's roles, helping foster faith communities that embody the principles of justice, mutual respect, and shared spiritual responsibility.

3.1. Jesus' Treatment of Women

One of the most distinctive features of Jesus' ministry is His revolutionary approach toward women. In a culture where women were often marginalized, Jesus not only welcomed them but also engaged with them in meaningful ways, treating them as valuable individuals capable of spiritual understanding and leadership.[80] His interactions with women, often highlighted in the Gospels, reveal His intention to dismantle societal barriers and affirm women as integral to His ministry and the coming Kingdom of God.[81]

3.2. Women as Disciples (e.g., Mary Magdalene, Martha, and Mary of Bethany)

Contrary to the typical exclusion of women from formal religious education in first-century Judaism, Jesus consistently included women in His circle of disciples. Notably, women such as Mary Magdalene, Martha, and Mary of Bethany are depicted as devoted followers and learners of

[80] Elizabeth A. McCabe, *Women in the Biblical World: A Survey of Old and New Testament Perspectives* (University Press of America, 2011), 39.

[81] Luise Schottroff, Silvia Schroer, and Marie-Theres Wacker, *Feminist Interpretation: The Bible in Women's Perspective* (Minneapolis: Fortress Press, 1998), 60.

Jesus.[82] Mary of Bethany is celebrated for sitting at Jesus' feet, a posture traditionally associated with discipleship, indicating her desire to learn from Him (Luke 10:39). Jesus' response to Martha's complaint about Mary's focus[83] on spiritual matters— "Mary has chosen what is better, and it will not be taken away from her" (Luke 10:42, NIV)—reveals His affirmation of women's capacity for theological reflection and discipleship.[84]

Mary Magdalene, often referred to as a devoted follower of Jesus, is another significant figure. She not only supported His ministry but was also present at His crucifixion and the first to witness the resurrected Christ (John 20:11-18). Her role as the first witness to the resurrection underscores her importance in the early Christian movement, affirming the place of women as primary participants in the unfolding of the Gospel message.[85]

3.3. Women in the Resurrection Narratives

The role of women in the resurrection narratives is both profound and pivotal to the Christian faith. All four Gospels record that women were the first to witness the empty tomb and the resurrected Christ.[86] Mary Magdalene, along with other women such as Mary the mother of James and Salome, went to anoint Jesus' body and found the tomb empty (Mark 16:1-8).

In John's Gospel, Mary Magdalene's encounter with the risen Jesus marks a key moment where she is commissioned[87] by Christ to "go to my brothers and tell them" (John 20:17, NIV), effectively making her the first apostle of the resurrection. This moment is radical given the cultural context, where women's testimony was often devalued.[88] By entrusting the news of His resurrection to women, Jesus further underscores their central role in the Gospel story and the spread of the Christian message.

---

[82] Helen Bond and Joan Taylor, *Women Remembered: Jesus' Female Disciples* (London: Hodder & Stoughton, 2022), 70.

[83] Benjamin Galan, *Women of the Bible: New Testament* (Tustin, CA: Rose Publishing Inc, 2014), 20.

[84] Satoko Yamaguchi, *Mary and Martha: Women in the World of Jesus* (Eugene, OR: Wipf and Stock Publishers, 2006), 78.

[85] Adriana Valerio, *Mary Magdalene: Women, the Church, and the Great Deception* (Europa Editions UK, 2021), 99.

[86] David R. Catchpole, *Resurrection People: Studies in the Resurrection Narratives of the Gospels* (Macon, GA: Smyth & Helwys Publishing, Inc., 2002), 22.

[87] Liz Curtis Higgs, *The Women of Easter: Encounter the Savior with Mary of Bethany, Mary of Nazareth, and Mary Magdalene* (New York: Random House Publishing Group, 2017), 50.

[88] Richard Buckham, *Gospel Women: Studies of the Named Women in the Gospels* (Wm. B. Eerdmans Publishing, 2002), 13.

In conclusion, Jesus' treatment of women, His inclusion of them as disciples, and their essential presence in the resurrection narratives challenge prevailing norms of gender and hierarchy, illustrating a theological vision where women are integral to the mission of God's kingdom.[89]

Women were expected to remain unobserved in public. "Women were regarded as inferior to men. They could not appear in Public as a witness before a court or take an active part in the cults."[90] The rules forbade a man to be alone with a woman and even to look at a married woman or even to greet her. The position of woman in the house compared to man was lower. Preference was given to sons and the education of girls were only learning domestic arts and looking after their smaller brothers and sisters. Father had all power over the girls and they had no rights of possessions. A girl had no right to refuse a marriage decided by her father and she could be sold by her father as a slave.[91]

The first duty of a wife is the household care: such as cooking, washing, taking care of children, prepare bed for husband, spinning, weaving and washing the face, head and feet of the husband. There was polygamy and husband had all authority to divorce his wife.[92] Women had limited religious duties and rights. Birth of a male child gave her few moments of happiness and received a female child with sorrow. The encounter of Jesus with the daughters of Jerusalem in the passion story, He said them that bareness to be a blessing at the time of persecution with the back up of such sociological framework.

Gospel of Luke is the favorite gospel for large community due to its special characteristics. It gives so much of importance for individuals. Donald Guthrie says that "Luke as a gentile, would know much of the degradation of women and would be concerned to emphasize all he had heard of the Lord towards them."[93] According to those who view a positive

---

[89] Francis J. Moloney, *The Resurrection of the Messiah: A Narrative Commentary on the Resurrection Accounts in the Four Gospels* (Mahwah, NJ: Paulist Press, 2013), 30.

[90] Eduard Lohse, *The New Testament Environment*, 149.

[91] Joachim Jeramias, *Jerusalem in the Time of Jesus*, 364. Joachim Jeramias, *Jerusalem in the Time of Jesus*, 364. They were not seen in the public instead had to stay indoors and to live in retirements, limited by the middle door for young girls and outer door for married women were appreciated.

[92] Joachim Jeramias, *Jerusalem in the Time of Jesus*, 370. Though women were population group living on the margins in Roman antiquity, particular attention were given to woman in Luke's Gospel (4:16-20; 7:11-17; 18:1-8; 21:1-4; 20:45-47). It is interesting to note that women are placed alongside men in sayings and stories. (1:10-20, 26-38; 2:25-38; 4:31-39; 7:1-7; 13:10-17; 14:1-6; 15:4-10). There is a strong male-female parallelism in the gospel of Luke.

[93] Donald Guthrie, *New Testament Introduction* (England: InterVarsity Press, 1985), 91.

attitude of Luke towards widows finds that all through out the Gospel this distinguished character can be seen. It may be part of his broader interest in reference to the marginalized. The status of women in Roman antiquity also marks the population group as living on the margins.[94] Luke has referred to widows in keeping the Old Testament instructions to care for widows and consistent with the early Church's support of widows (cf. Acts 6:1-6; 1 Tim. 5:3-6). Such as Anna the prophetess (Lk. 2:36-38), the widow at Zarephath (4:25-26), the widow at Nain (7:11-15), the parable of the widow and the unjust judge (8:1-8) and widows on whom the scribes prayed (20:45-47).

The Gospel of Luke shows the greatest interest in women in the life and ministry of Jesus, including numerous accounts and stories[95] about women unique to its presentation. Luke also gives the specific names of more women in Jesus' life than do the other Gospels. This interest is continued in Acts (cf. Acts 1:14). Luke relates stories about the healing (Lk 4:38–39; 8:1–3, 40–56; 13:11–17; 17:11–17) and faith (Lk 4:26; 7:36–50; 8:48; 18:1–8; 21:1–4) of women, many of which are unique to Luke. Women are important in two parables unique to Luke (Lk 15:8–10; 18:1–8) and are mentioned in two stories about the kingdom of God (Lk 13:20–21; 17:35). "In the gospel of Luke both men and women are mentioned as pairs,[96] with some exceptions, this is not done by way comparison or contrast, but rather to suggest a measure of equality that was unexpected in the time of Jesus.[97]

On the way to cross, He identifies with the marginalized group, the women, and prophesied to them. Jesus in His struggles identified with those

---

[94] Stählin, "ch,ra," *TDNT*, edited by Gerhard Friendrich (Michigan: Wm. B. Eerdmans Publishing Company, 1994), 441.

[95] The place of women in discipleship is particularly stressed by Luke, both in general statements (Lk 8:19–21; 11:27–28), in the story of Mary and Martha (Lk 10:38–42) and in the reports of the female disciples who traveled with Jesus (Lk 8:1–3) and are described in the passion and resurrection narratives (Lk 23:49; 23:55–24:12). Again, some of these accounts are unique to Luke (Lk 8:1–3; 10:38–42; 11:27–28).

[96] cf. Zacharia and Elizabeth, Joseph and Mary, Simon and Hannah (2:25-38), widow of Zarephath and Naaman (Lk. 4:25-28), Healing of Peter's mother-in Law and demoniac (Lk. 4:3). Centurion of Capernaum and widow of Nain (Lk. 7:1-7), Simon the Pharisee and the sinful women (Lk 13:18 21), Good Samaritan and Mary/Martha (Lk. 10:29-42), man with a hundred sheep and women with ten pieces of silver (Lk. 15:4-10). Unfortunate widow and the publican (Lk. 18:1-14), women at the tomb and Emmaus disciples (Lk 23:58-24:35), sleeping man and women at the grinder (Lk. 17: 34-35), Jairus and women with issue of blood (Lk 8:40-41; 49-56; 43-48). Men healed on Sabbath and woman healed on Sabbath (Lk.14:1-6; 13:10-17). Abraham's daughter (Lk. 19:9; 13:16). Peter at the tomb and women at the tomb (Lk 24:12, 1-11).

[97] Constance Parvey, 'The Theology and Leadership of Women in the New Testament,' *Religion and Sexism,* edited by Rosemary R. Ruether, Simon and Shurter (NewYork). Cited by Jane Kopas, 'Jesus and Women,' *Theology Today,* 46/2 (July, 1986): 193.

marginalized women in the society. The poor are seen all through the gospel as being rejected in the society. In the passion narrative, one could find the consideration of Jesus with those on the way with Him to the cross. In His trail, execution, on the way to cross, and in the tomb, the women faithfully followed Jesus.

All through the life and ministry of Jesus, one could find Jesus placed women by regarding as equal to men. He also recognized the intrinsic value of women. In the passion narrative, women are overshadowed by a host of other witness.[98] In the first century Mediterranean world, women were not accepted nor did they were given any dignity in the society. But in the passion narrative, even though Jesus was in a deep pain He extended tender words to the women who followed him, the daughters of Jerusalem. Those women were from the lower level of the social scale. Their low social status is intensified by the characterization as the daughters of Jerusalem. They are those who weep now and they will be ultimately consoled (7:13; 8:52).

There were also women from Galilee who followed Him all through His ministry and did not leave Him even when all His disciples left Him. The women from Galilee also represent a new group within the people who followed Jesus on the way to Cross. They give the continuity of the crucifixion, burial and resurrection of Jesus. It may be one of the qualifications of the women being the witness of His victory from death. With courage, they followed Jesus and became the witness of His victory. They were with Jesus not just because of the affection-oriented experience but must be seen from the view point of the apostolic community. Their ecclesial and ministerial significance must be accepted. Women disciples are not to be seen less important than male disciples. The role of women in the passion narrative remains us the liberation of women from any bondage and her role in the ministry is to be socialized.

Though women were not given any priority in the social life of the 1st century, in the passion narrative they are seen as actively participating with the suffering of Jesus or can be said that they are identified with the struggles of Jesus. The narrator portrays these women as faithful disciples. Jesus showed His concern for women by identifying Himself with their plight. Women's affectionate attitude to Jesus and His concern for them is represented by the encounter of Jesus with them. Passion narrative is a place where one finds women with greater spiritual dynamic which liberate anyone who is marginalized, powerless, voiceless, unacknowledged and crushed on the basis of gender. They are the symbols of the voiceless, treated unjustly by the male dominated legal tradition identified with the voicelessness of

[98] Barbara E Reid, *Choosing the better Part? Women in the Gospel of Luke* (Minnesota: The Liturgical Press, 1969), 200.

Jesus.[99] The resurrection of Jesus is the place of liberation, liberation from all the bondage and the experience of personal transformation for women. The women being the link between the passion and resurrection must be seen from the ecclesiastical point of view. The role of women in the resurrection narrative highlights the equal role of women in the mission and it calls for the revitalization of women in the local congregations so that they may be liberated from their social situation. Passion narrative is the voice of women's liberation from any external powers to transformation.

The Gospel of Luke gives prominence to the role of women in Jesus' ministry, highlighting them as integral figures who challenge societal expectations of their time and contribute significantly to God's unfolding plan. Through various narratives, Luke emphasizes women's faith, compassion, and dedication, underscoring their place within the story of Jesus. Women such as the woman with the issue of blood display remarkable faith, finding healing and compassion in their encounters with Jesus (Lk 8:43-48). These stories highlight Jesus' sensitivity to their needs and His willingness to engage with women as individuals of value, making them pivotal examples of healing and compassion.

Women also play a practical role in supporting Jesus' ministry. Luke mentions Mary Magdalene, Joanna, and Susanna, among others, who provide for Jesus and His disciples from their own resources (Lk 8:1-3). Their support demonstrates a form of hospitality that goes beyond mere provision, reflecting a partnership in Jesus' mission. Similarly, in the story of Mary and Martha, Luke shows women as both learners and followers, with Mary taking the posture of a disciple by sitting at Jesus' feet (Lk 10:38-42). This act, traditionally reserved for male disciples, symbolizes an inclusive approach to discipleship, where women, too, are welcomed into the fold as learners and followers of Jesus.

The resurrection narrative further elevates the role of women as they are the first to witness the empty tomb and receive the angelic message of Jesus' resurrection (Lk 24:1-10). These women become the first proclaimers of the resurrection, entrusted with sharing this transformative news with the disciples. Through these accounts, Luke presents women as faithful disciples who engage deeply with Jesus' ministry, modeling discipleship and devotion. In portraying women in these significant roles, Luke's Gospel sends a powerful message about the inclusive nature of Jesus' ministry, affirming the value of women as active participants in God's redemptive plan, whose faith and witness are essential to the unfolding Gospel narrative.

---

[99] Gillard D, *Deconstructing the Bible: A Consideration of the Interpretive Possibilities Inherent in Deconstructionist Readings of the Biblical Text such as those Offered by Feminist Hermeneutics*.

In summary, the lessons from women in the Gospel of Luke have profound implications for contemporary gender equality within faith communities. They challenge traditional gender roles, promote the inclusion of women in leadership roles, and encourage theological reflections that affirm the equality of all individuals in God's sight. These lessons inspire contemporary faith communities to work toward greater gender justice and equality within their religious contexts.

IV. Reversal Themes in Luke

In Luke's Gospel, the Beatitudes and woes serve as profound expressions of reversal, where Jesus blesses those often overlooked by society and issues warnings to those who may be complacent in wealth and privilege. The Beatitudes (Lk 6:20-23) offer comfort to the poor, the hungry, and the sorrowful, with promises like, "Blessed are you who are poor, for yours is the kingdom of God." These blessings reveal God's special concern for those who face hardship and exclusion, upending traditional ideas of happiness and success. Instead of wealth or social standing, God's kingdom is promised to those who suffer and who rely on Him, highlighting the ultimate reversal where the lowly are elevated.

Conversely, the woes (Lk 6:24-26) address the wealthy, the satisfied, and the highly regarded, offering a sobering reminder that material comfort and social approval do not equate to divine favor. For instance, Jesus warns, "Woe to you who are rich, for you have already received your comfort," emphasizing the precariousness of relying on wealth and societal status. These woes suggest that those who prioritize personal wealth over compassion may experience a drastic reversal, losing the very comfort and security they value. This message is particularly potent in a world where prosperity often leads to self-sufficiency, leaving little room for dependence on God or for acts of mercy and justice.

The Beatitudes and woes invite readers to reimagine societal values, challenging cultures that prioritize affluence, recognition, and power over humility, justice, and compassion. These passages are a call to action, urging believers to care for the vulnerable and reassess priorities in line with God's kingdom values. In contemporary contexts, they resonate with issues of social justice and economic equity, prompting followers of Christ to advocate for the marginalized and confront societal structures that perpetuate inequality. Through these teachings, Luke's Gospel presents a powerful vision of divine justice, where God's grace lifts the oppressed and the complacency of privilege faces divine scrutiny.

In the Gospel of Luke, the reversal theme has been widely known.[100] One sentence, which appears several times in the Gospel, sums up this view: 'the last will be first and the first will be last' (Lk 13:30). The admonition to be like a child (Lk 18:15-17) parallels the parable of Lazarus and the rich man: Lazarus, who has an exceptionally hard life, prospered in the world to come, while the fortunes of the rich man were reversed (Lk 16:19-31). The parable of the prodigal son is also another example to it. This concept of reversal is well evident in the parable of the Pharisee and the tax-collector.[101]

The Gospel of Luke "brings about a *reversal* of previously held human values, and certainly a strong condemnation of any attempt to establish or enhance one's own honour in the sight of others."[102] Therefore, the Gospel is not only good news for those who are economically poor, but also for those without honor in society, in proclaiming the reversal of such human values in the sight of God. "It is self-justification that makes persons and groups to deal with their enemies cruelly, disregarding their humanity,"[103] and the oppressed are to experience the reversal of the present human values.

In the reversal situation, by bringing the high and mighty down to the level of the lowly or exalting the lowly to a mock status with the lofty. Luke addresses both the rich and poor and he never glorifies poverty, but the overriding concern is to foster a community in which the rich and poor alike can hear the word of Jesus and respond appropriately.[104]

---

[100] Narrative parables present unexpected twists in plot. Examples of such conflict are: the enemy (Samaritan) is the one who saves the one in need, an oriental potentate is compassionate beyond measure to a slave. The prodigal son is treated as successful son returning home, outcasts become the guests of the wealthy man at a feast. There are also reversals in which the characters receive that which they don't deserve: the improperly attired guest is cast out from the wedding, the negligent servants (virgins) are excluded from the wedding, the rich man, who neglected the Torah, is in hell and the guests with other concerns exclude themselves from the feast. Cf. Pheme Perkins, *Hearing the Parables of Jesus*, 134.

[101] For more details see E. P. Sanders, *The Historical Figure of Jesus* (London: The Penguin Press, 1993), 196.

[102] Christopher M. Tuckett, *Luke* (Sheffield: Sheffield Academic Press, 1996), 108. In [illegible] value system, the whole set of criteria for attributing honor/shame (for example in the parable of the Pharisee and the tax-collector) and how far Luke's Jesus is simply adopting the current criteria to critique just selfishness.

[103] M. M. Thomas, *Jesus God's Anointed (Lk. 9-19): Contextual Theological Bible Commentary*, 122.

[104] Walter E. Pilgrim, *Good News to the Poor. Wealth and Poverty in Luke Acts* (Minneapolis: Augsburg Pub. House, 1981). And Robert J. Karris, 'The Gospel According to Luke,' *The New Jerome Biblical Commentary,* edited by Raymond E. Brown, Joseph A. Fitzmyer and Roland E. Murphy (Bangalore: TPI, 2004).

The parable also plays an apologetic resolution of the conflict between Jesus and Pharisees on the messiahship of Jesus. The parable of Good Samaritan involves an important moral implication of the preaching of the kingdom of God. It is also true that the parable is true-to-life apology by means of which Jesus defends himself and justifies his mission. Through the parable Jesus formulates and sustains his messianic claims by identifying himself with the Samaritan.[105] The parable of the Good Samaritan is a parable of reversal, where the arrival of the kingdom upturns existing conventions. For the Jewish audience including the Pharisees, this involves a re-evaluation of their opinions of Samaritans. While demonstrating the compassion of the Samaritan, the parable depicts the kingdom value.[106]

The Parable of the rich fool is an interesting parable which is addressed to a spokesman of the multitudes. The parable is set in the context of conflict between brothers on the division of inheritance. The kingdom value presented in the parable calls one to be rich towards God. Through the parable, the request to share the inheritance between brothers is dismissed with a question. The concern of Jesus is not about sharing the inheritance instead the covetousness which comes out of a tendency to identify life with the abundance of possessions.

Through the parable Jesus opposes all kinds of covetousness and maintains that human life does not consist in the surplus of wealth. The rich man in the parable fails to maintain his relation with God and therefore, he is addressed a 'fool'. He is with the self-promotive tendency. The kingdom value of the parable suggests the importance of proper setting of priorities in life. The conflict within an individual to be richer is brought down with the kingdom value to set one to be rich towards God. This is the resolution to the conflict between the brothers who wished to divide the inheritance between them as well as to all those who are greedy and tries to store surplus wealth. But the kingdom value presented in the parable is a challenge to all those with the same attitude to store one's wealth towards God.

The parable of the rich man and Lazarus gives a detailed description of the deprivation and misery of the poor man and luxurious life-style of the rich man. The rich man, till the end of his life in this world has enjoyed the

---

[105] Time and again the life and teaching of Jesus led to a conflict situation. His opponents resented and rejected his authority and his concern for the people of his time. This conflict situation made Jesus to defend himself. Cf. Jan Lambrecht, *Once more Astonished: Parables of Jesus* (New York: Crossroad, 1981), 73.

[106] This is frame work of the Gospel. John Dominic Crossan, 'Parable and Example in the Teaching of Jesus,' *NTS* 18 (1971): 285-307; John Dominic Crossan, *In Parables: The Challenge of the Historical Jesus* (New York: Harper and Row Publishers, 1973), 55-64; and Robert W. Funk, *Parables and Presence: Forms of the New Testament Tradition* (Philadelphia: Fortress Press, 1982), 24-29.

same luxury and the poor man is deliberately contrasted with the rich man.[107] This parable is to be seen as an indictment of the social institution in which one content to be in luxury while the other at the door was in deprivation and misery.[108] According to P. A. Sampath Kumar, there are three dimensions concerning the poor, the rich and the wealthy, firstly, God of Jesus is the God of the poor and lowly, secondly, eschatological reversal and thirdly, the promise of the present.[109]

The parable of the rich man and Lazarus gives a detailed description of the deprivation and misery of the poor man and luxurious life-style of the rich man. The rich man, till the end of his life in this world has enjoyed the same luxury and the poor man is deliberately contrasted with the rich man.[110] This parable is to be seen as an indictment of the social institution in which one content to be in luxury while the other at the door was in deprivation and misery.[111] According to P. A. Sampath Kumar, there are three dimensions concerning the poor, the rich and the wealthy, firstly, God of Jesus is the God of the poor and lowly, secondly, eschatological reversal and thirdly, the promise of the present.[112]

Reversal of Expectations best seen in the parable of Pharisee and Tax-collector where they represent two social hierarchies. They are in the temple to pray. Temple is the conjecture for the religious standard and it highlights symbolic distance between the secular and sacred space and it gives value to both the characters. The Pharisee is socially honored and religiously accepted. He is a representation of the religious ideal; pious and devout and rigorous in observing the law. The Pharisee was self-satisfied and his ride in his goodness blocked the way to God. In conflict with this attitude, the tax-collector was resented as marginalized and hatred by all. They were despised and had no respect among the people and it shows the conflict between the characters. According to the occupation, one is noble and other is base. As to the bearing one is proud and other is shameful. When the self evaluation is made, one is self-confident and other is cringing.

The parable of Jesus reverses the expectations and are in conflict with the normal judgment of the people concerning the tax collector. In the parable, the tax-collector is justified by God and not the Pharisee. The

---

107 Sam P. Mathew, 'The Poor and the Rich in Luke's Gospel,' 55.

108 Sam P. Mathew, 'The Poor and the Rich in Luke's Gospel,' 55.

109 P. A. Sampathkumar, 'The Rich and Poor in Luke-Acts,' *Bible Bhashyam* 22/4 (Dec. 1996): 187. The parable of the rich man and Lazarus is an example for it.

110 Sam P. Mathew, 'The Poor and the Rich in Luke's Gospel,' 55.

111 Sam P. Mathew, 'The Poor and the Rich in Luke's Gospel,' 55.

112 P. A. Sampathkumar, 'The Rich and Poor in Luke-Acts,' *Bible Bhashyam* 22/4 (Dec. 1996): 187. The parable of the rich man and Lazarus is an example for it.

differences between these two characters are their attitudes and approach towards God. The prayer of the tax-collector (God, be merciful to me a sinner) is accepted before God. This is considered to be the essential genuine religious insight for anyone in the presence of God. The character of Pharisee is in conflict with the straight forward, genuine directness of the prayer of the tax-collector, the perfect example of simplicity and repentance. God's sovereignty and his execution of judicial functions and powers are also highlighted through the parable. God as a righteous judge, merciful towards the poor and the humble and inflicts the self-righteous and proud.

The reversal and surprise of fortune is one of the familiar themes in the Gospel of Luke. The humble receives the recognition that the prideful seek (Lk 14:11; 18:14); the pious poor will finally receive reward (Lk 6:19-31); the outsider teaches the insider what the insider should have known (Lk 10:29-37). In this parable, the conflict between the Pharisee and the tax-collector is evident both in the position of their prayers and climax of the parable in which the pious Pharisee can learn from the sinner on the outskirts of Jewish society what it means to be righteous.

Conclusion

As we conclude our exploration of the Gospel of Luke, it is essential to reflect on the profound insights gained from each chapter of this book. Each section not only illuminates the distinctive aspects of Luke's narrative but also underscores the relevance of its teachings for contemporary readers. The Gospel of Luke presents a compelling narrative that transcends its historical context, inviting readers into a transformative journey through the life and teachings of Jesus Christ. As we have explored throughout this book, Luke's account is marked by its profound theological depth and its unique emphasis on social justice, compassion, and the inclusive nature of God's Kingdom. The threads woven throughout this Gospel not only recount the events of Jesus' life but also challenge us to reflect on our understanding of discipleship, community, and our role in the ongoing mission of the Church.

In the first chapter, we examined the **distinctive features of the Lukan infancy narratives**. Luke's account presents a rich portrayal of Jesus' birth that emphasizes themes of humility, joy, and divine purpose. By spotlighting figures like Mary and the shepherds, Luke highlights the significance of God's intervention in human history, setting the stage for a Savior who embodies hope for the marginalized and the humble.

The second chapter focused on **the ministry of John the Baptist**. John's call to repentance and his radical lifestyle serve as a powerful precursor to Jesus' ministry. This chapter emphasizes the need for an alternative lifestyle that challenges the status quo, urging readers to embrace a transformative relationship with God that reflects in their everyday lives.

In the third chapter, we provided an overview of **recent studies on Luke's Gospel**. This critique highlights how scholars have engaged with Luke's unique theological emphases, such as social justice and the inclusive nature of the Kingdom. Understanding these contemporary discussions enriches our interpretation of the text and invites ongoing dialogue about its implications for faith communities today.

The fourth chapter delved into **the Beatitudes and Woes** found in Luke's account. These teachings challenge prevailing attitudes toward wealth and poverty, advocating for a radical rethinking of societal values. The stark contrasts between the blessed and the woe-ridden call us to align our lives with Kingdom principles that prioritize compassion, equity, and justice for the marginalized.

In the fifth chapter, we explored the **characteristics of Lukan parables**. These stories, with their memorable imagery and profound moral lessons, serve to convey deep theological truths about the Kingdom of God. Luke's parables challenge readers to reflect on their own lives and relationships, encouraging active engagement with the Gospel message in everyday contexts.

The sixth chapter focused on the **theology of miracles** within Luke's narrative. Miracles are not merely extraordinary events; they serve as signs of God's Kingdom breaking into the world. This chapter emphasizes the importance of faith and the transformative power of Jesus' actions, encouraging readers to recognize the divine in their own lives and communities.

In the seventh chapter, we examined **Luke's model of discipleship and leadership**. Jesus' example of servant leadership redefines traditional notions of authority and power. This chapter calls readers to embrace humility and service as central tenets of their faith, inspiring a model of leadership that fosters community, compassion, and mutual support.

The eighth chapter discussed the **passion and resurrection narratives**. These events encapsulate the heart of the Gospel message, revealing God's ultimate plan for redemption through suffering, death, and resurrection. This chapter serves as a reminder of the transformative power of Christ's sacrifice, inviting believers to live in the light of His resurrection hope.

Finally, in the ninth chapter, we addressed **current discussions in the Gospel of Luke** regarding table fellowship, hospitality, and the role of women. Luke's emphasis on inclusion and community challenges contemporary readers to reflect on their practices and attitudes. This chapter urges us to create spaces that embody the welcoming spirit of Christ, fostering relationships that reflect God's love and grace for all.

In conclusion, the Gospel of Luke is a rich narrative that invites readers to engage deeply with its themes and teachings. Each chapter of this book has sought to illuminate the complexities and nuances of Luke's message, offering insights that are both timeless and relevant. May this exploration inspire readers to live out the values of the Kingdom, embodying compassion, justice, and hospitality in their lives as they follow the example of Jesus Christ. Through our understanding of Luke's Gospel, we are called not just to knowledge, but to action—a transformative journey that aligns our hearts and lives with the mission of Christ in our world today.

Finally, as we reflect on the **implications** of Luke's Gospel for our lives today, it becomes clear that the message of Jesus is as radical and transformative now as it was in the first century. The call to live out Kingdom values—justice, mercy, and love—remains a challenge for Christians everywhere. In a world fraught with division, inequality, and suffering, Luke's teachings invite us to actively participate in God's redemptive work. This involves not only personal transformation but also a commitment to social justice and community engagement. It is a call to embody the essence of the Gospel in our actions, reflecting the character of Christ in a world longing for hope and healing.

As we conclude this exploration of the Gospel of Luke, it is essential to remember that this narrative is not merely a historical account but a living document that calls each of us to action. The themes of compassion, justice, and discipleship woven throughout Luke's Gospel are timeless and continue to resonate in our current context. They invite us to engage with our world with the same love and commitment that Jesus demonstrated, empowering us to be agents of change and ambassadors of His Kingdom.

In a world grappling with division, inequality, and despair, Luke's Gospel offers hope and a blueprint for a different way of living—one rooted in the teachings and example of Jesus Christ. May this study inspire you to not only deepen your understanding of the Gospel of Luke but also to actively embody its message in your daily life. As we journey forward, let us commit ourselves to the values of the Kingdom, living out the call to love, serve, and extend grace to all, thereby participating in the unfolding story of God's redemptive work in the world.

This study serves not only as a comprehensive exploration of the Gospel of Luke but also as an encouragement for readers to delve deeper into the rich theological and historical dimensions of this text. By engaging with the distinctive features of Luke's narrative, the various themes presented, and the contemporary discussions surrounding it, readers may feel inspired to undertake further academic research or personal study in areas such as Lukan theology, the socio-political context of Luke's writings, or the implications of his teachings on modern discipleship and community life. Such further exploration can enrich understanding and foster a more profound engagement with the text, ultimately contributing to the broader conversation about the relevance of the Gospel message in today's world. Through continued scholarship, we can uncover new insights and applications that resonate with the challenges and opportunities facing faith communities in the contemporary landscape.

Bibliography

Adams, Dwayne H. *The Sinner in Luke*. Eugene, OR: Wipf and Stock Publishers, 2008.

Adolf Harnack. *What is Christianity*. Escondido: Book Tree, 2006.

Aland, Barbara, Johannes Karavidopoulos et al. *The Greek New Testament*. Fourth Revised Edition. Edmonds, WA: United Bible Societies, 2001.

Allen, Charles L. *The Touch of the Master's Hand*. USA: Fleming H. Revell Company, n.d.

Anderson, Garwood P. "Seeking and Saving What Might Have Been Lost: Luke's Restoration of an Enigmatic Parable Tradition." *CBQ* 70, no. 4 (October 2008): 729–43.

Andrews, Edward D. *The Bible as History: A Historical Journey Through the Bible*. Christian Publishing House, 2023.

Arn, Win, and Charles Arn. *The Master's Plan for Making Disciples*. 2nd Ed. Grand Rapids, MI: Baker Books, 1998.

Arndt, William F., and F. Wilbur Gingrich. *A Greek-English Lexicon of the New Testament and Other Early Literature*. Chicago: The University of Chicago Press, 1957.

Athompson, G. H. P. *The Gospel According to Luke*. Oxford. The Clarendon Press, 1972.

Augsburger, D. W. *Dissident Discipleship: A Spirituality of Self-Surrender, Love of God, and Love of Neighbor*. Grand Rapids, MI: Brazos Press, 2006.

Augsburger, Myron S. *The Expanded Life*. New York: Abingdon Press, 1972.

Aune, David E. *The New Testament in its Literary Environment*. Edited by Wayne A. Meeks. Philadelphia: The Westminster Press, 1997, 122.

B. J. Malina. "Reading Theory Perspective: Reading Luke-Acts." In *The Social World of Luke-Acts: Models of Interpretation*. Edited by J. H. Neyrey, 99. Peabody, MA: Hendrickson Publishers, 1991.

Bailey, Kenneth Ewing. *Poet and Peasant: A Literary Cultural Approaches to the Parables in Luke.* Michigan: W. B. Eerdmans Publishing *Company*, 1976.

Bailey, Mark L. "Guidelines for Interpreting Jesus' Parables." *Bibliotheca Sacra* 155 (January–March 1998): 30.

Bailey, Mark, and Tom Constable, eds. *Nelson's New Testament Survey: Discover the Background, Theology and Meaning of Every Book in the New Testament.* Nashville: Thomas Nelson Pub., 1999.

Baird, William. "The Gospel According to Luke." *The Interpreter's One Volume Commentary on the Bible.* Edited by Charles M. Laymon. Nashville: Abingdon, 1971.

Barclay, William. *The Gospel of Luke.* Philadelphia, PA: Westminster Press, 1956.

Barrera, Albino. *Biblical Economic Ethics: Sacred Scripture's Teachings on Economic Life.* New York: Lexington Books, 2013.

Barrett, C. K. *Luke the Historian in Recent Study.* London: The Epworth Press, 1961.

Baxter, Margaret. *Jesus Christ: His Life and His Church.* Delhi: ISPCK, 2003.

Beasley-Murray, George R. *John.* Volume 36, Revised Edition. Grand Rapids: Zondervan Academic, 2018.

Beavis, Mary Ann. "Parable and Fable." *Catholic Biblical Quarterly 52.* No. 3, July 1990: 480.

Beck, D. M. "Passion." *The Interpreter's Dictionary of the Bible.* Vol. 3. Edited by George Arthur Buttrick. New York: Abingdon Press, 1962.

Benedict XVI, Pope. *Jesus of Nazareth: The Infancy Narratives.* London: A&C Black, 2012.

Bengt Holmberg. *Sociology and the New Testament.* Fortress Press, 1990.

Benoit, Pierre. *The Passion and Resurrection of Jesus Christ.* Translated by Benet Wetherhead. New York: Herder and Herder, 1969.

Beresford, Anna. *Before You Were Born, I Anointed You: Uncovering Scripture's "Hidden" Female Prophets.* Eugene, OR: Wipf and Stock Publishers, 2022.

Best, W. E. *Studies in the Person and Work of Jesus Christ.* USA: South Belt Assembly of Christ, 1975.

Betz, Hans Dieter. *The Sermon on the Mount: A Commentary on the Sermon on the Mount, Including the Sermon on the Plain (Matthew 5:3-7:27 and Luke 6:20-49).* Minneapolis, MN: Fortress Press, 1995.

Billy, D. J. *Meeting Jesus on the Road to Emmaus: An invitation to Friendship, Eucharist and Christian Community.* Wipf and Stock Publishers, 2023.

Binz, Stephen J. *The Passion and Resurrection Narratives of Jesus: A Commentary*. Minnesota: The Liturgical Press, 1989.

Binz, Stephen J. *The Infancy Narratives of Jesus*. Minnesota: Liturgical Press, 2020.

Binz, Stephen J., and Little Rock Scripture Study Staff. *The Infancy Narratives of Jesus*. Liturgical Press, 2020.

Black, Matthew. *The Gentiles and Gentile Mission in Luke-Acts.* Cambridge: Cambridge University Press, 1973.

Blanchard, Maurice. *Luke: An Introduction and Commentary*. Madras: C.L.S., 1969.

Blinzler, Josef. *The Trial of Jesus. Translated by Isabel and Florence Mc Hugh*. Cork: The Mercier Press, 1959.

Blomberg, Craig L. *Interpreting the Parables.* Downers Grove, IL: InterVarsity Press, 1990.

Bloomberg, Craig. *The New American Commentary,* Volume 22: Matthew. Nashville: Broadman Press, 1992.

Bock, Darrell L. *A Theology of Luke and Acts: God's Promised Program, Realized for All Nations.* Grand Rapids: Zondervan Academic, 2015.

Bock, Darrell L. *Luke. IVP New Testament Commentary Series*. Edited by Grant R. Osborne. England: IVP, 1994.

Bock, Darrell L. *Luke: Baker Exegetical Commentary on the New Testament.* 2 Volumes. Grand Rapids, MI: Baker Academic, 1996.

Bock, Darrell L., et.al. *The Luke Commentary Collection: An All-In-One Commentary Collection for Studying the Book of Luke*. Grand Rapids, MI: Zondervan Academic, 2016.

Bonhoeffer, Dietrich. *The Cost of Discipleship*. New York: Touchstone, 1995.

Borgman, Paul. *The Way According to Luke: Hearing the Whole Story of Luke-Acts.* Grand Rapids: Eerdmans, 2006.

Bornkamm, Günther. *Jesus of Nazareth. Translated by Irene Fraser Mc Luskey and James* M. Robinson. London: Harper and Row Publishers, 1973.

Boucher, Madeleine I. *The Parables: A Biblical Theological Commentary.* New Testament Message, vol. 7. Edited by Wilfrid Harrington and Donald Senior. Wilmington, Delaware: Michael Glazier Inc.

Bovon, François. *Luke 1: A Commentary on the Gospel of Luke 1:1–9:50.* Tr. By Christine M. Thomas. Hermeneia; Minneapolis: Fortress Press, 2002.

Bovon, François. *Luke the Theologian: Fifty-Five Years of Research (1950–2005),* 2nd edition. Waco, Tex.: Baylor University Press, 2006.

Bowman, Richard G. "Narrative Criticism: Human Purpose in Conflict with Divine Purpose." In *Judges and Method: New Approaches in Biblical Studies*, edited by Gale A. Yee, 30. Minneapolis: Fortress Press, 1985.

Brandon, S.G.F. *The Trial of Jesus of Nazareth.* London: B.T. Batsford Ltd., 1968.

Braun, Willi. *Feasting and Social Rhetoric in Luke 14.* Cambridge: Cambridge University Press, 1995.

Brawley, R. L. *Luke-Acts and the Jews: Conflict, Apology and Conciliation.* Atlanta: Scholars Press, 1987.

Bromiley, Geoffrey William, Ed. *The International Standard Bible Encyclopaedia.* Grand Rapids, MI: Wm. B. Eerdmans Publishing, 1979.

Brown, Michael L. *Israel's Divine Healer.* Michigan: Zondervan Publishing House, 1995.

Brown, Raymond E. Crucified Christ in Holy Week: Essays on the Four Gospel Passion Narratives. Collegeville, Minnesota: The Liturgical Press, 1986.

Brown, Raymond E. *The Death of Messiah: From Gethsemane to the Grave: A Commentary on the Passion Narratives in the Four Gospels*, vol. 1. New York: Doubleday, 1994.

Brown, Raymond E. *Crucified Christ in Holy Week: Essays on the Four Gospel Passion Narratives.* Collegeville, Minnesota: The Liturgical Press, 1986.

Brown, Raymond E. *The Birth of the Messiah: A Commentary on the Infancy Narratives in the Gospels of Matthew and Luke.* New Updated Edition. New York: Doubleday, 1993.

Brown, Raymond E., et.al., eds. *Mary in the New Testament.* New York/ Mahwah, 1978.

Bruehler, Bart B. *A Public and Political Christ: The Social-Spatial Characteristics of Luke 18:35–19:43 and the Gospel as a Whole in Its Ancient Context.* Eugene, OR: Wipf and Stock Publishers, 2011.

Buckwalter, H. Douglas. *The Character and Purpose of Luke's Christology.* Society for New Testament Studies Monograph Series 89. Cambridge: Cambridge University Press, 1996.

Bultmann, Rudolf. *History of the Synoptic Tradition.* Translated by John Marsh. Revised Edition. New York: Harper and Row, 1963.

Bultmann. "πενθεῖν/πενθος." *Theological Dictionary of the New Testament.* Vol. VI. Edited by Gerhard Friedrich. Grand Rapids: William B. Eerdmans Publishing Company, 2006.

Burge, Gary M., and Gene L. Green. *The New Testament in Antiquity. 2nd Edition: A Survey of the New Testament within Its Cultural Contexts*. Grand Rapids, MI: Zondervan Academic, 2020.

Burkett, Delbert. *An Introduction to the New Testament and the Origins of Christianity.* Cambridge: Cambridge University Press, 2019.

Buttrick, George Arthur. "Health, Healing." *The Interpreter's Dictionary of the Bible*. Nashville: Abingdon Press, 1962.

Buttrick, George Arthur. "Matthew." *The Interpreter's Bible*, Vol. VII. New York: Abingdon Press, 1951.

Caird, G. B. *Saint Luke: The Pelican New Testament Commentaries.* Middlesex, England: Penguin Books, 1963 c. 1985.

Card, Michael. *Luke: the Gospel of the Amazement.* Downers' Grove: IVP, 2011.

Carlston, Charles E. "Reminiscence and Redaction in Luke 15:11-32." *Journal of Biblical Literature* 94, no. 3 (September 1975): 368ff.

Carroll, John T. *Luke: A Commentary*. Louisville: Westminster John Knox Press, 2012.

Carson, D. A. *The Pillar New Testament Commentary*. Michigan: W.E. Eerdmans, 2015.

Carter, W. *Matthew and the Margins: A Socio-political and Religious Reading*. The Bible Liberation Series, 2007.

Cassidy, R. J. *Jesus, Politics and Society: A Study of Luke's Gospel*. New York: Orbis Books, 1978.

Cassidy, Richard J. "Luke's Audience, the Chief Priests, and the Motive for Jesus' Death." *Political Issues in Luke-Acts*, Edited by Richard J. Cassidy and Philip J. Scharper. New York: Orbis Books, 1983.

Cassidy, Richard J. and Philip J. Scharper. Ed. *Political Issues in Luke-Acts.* NewYork: Orbis Books, 1983.

Cassidy, Richard J. *Jesus, Politics, and Society. A Study of Luke's Gospel.* Wipf and Stock Publishers, 2016.

Castellino, Robert. "Is India Really Shining?" *Indian Current*, vol. XXII, no. 33 (August 2010). 33.

Cauchi, Tony. *Healing in the Gospel*. Revival Library, 2011

Chan, Francis. *Forgotten God: Reversing our Tragic Neglect of the Holy Spirit*. Colorado Springs: David C. Cook, 2009.

Charles Homer Giblin. "Structural and Theological Considers on Luke 15." *Catholic Biblical Quarterly* 24, No. 1 (January 1962): 15-31.

Chenevix Trench, Richard. *Notes on the Miracles of Our Lord*. Grand Rapids: Baker Book House, 1949.

Cherian, M. T. *Hindutva Agenda and Minority Rights: A Christian Response*. Bangalore: Centre for Contemporary Christianity, 2007.

Clark, Ron. *Jesus Unleashed: Luke's Gospel for Emerging Christians*. Eugene, OR: Wipf and Stock Publishers, 2014.

Coleman, Rachel L. *The Lukan Lens on Wealth and Possessions: A Perspective Shaped by the Themes of Reversal and Right Response*. Leiden: Brill, 2019.

Coleridge, Mark. "You Are Witnesses (Luke 24:48)." *Australian Biblical Review* 45 (1997): 4.

Coleridge, Mark. *The Birth of the Lukan Narrative: Narrative as Christology in Luke 1-2*. London: A&C Black, 1993.

Collins, Raymond F. "Beatitudes." *The Anchor Bible Dictionary*, vol. 1. Edited by David Noel Freedman. New York: Doubleday, 1992.

Constable, T. (Ed.). *Nelson's New Testament Survey: Discover the Background, Theology and Meaning of Every Book in the New Testament*. Thomas Nelson Pub, 1999.

Conzelmann, Hans. *The Theology of St. Luke*. Translated by Geoffrey Buswell. London: Faber and Faber, 1960.

Copeland, Gloria. *God's Will for your Healing*. KCP Publication, 1987.

Corley, K. E. *Private Women, Public Meals: Social Conflict in the Synoptic Tradition*. Peabody: Hendrickson, 1993.

Coser, L. A. *The Functions of Social Conflict*. Glencoe: The Free Press, 1956.

Crossan, J. D. "Parable and Example in the Teaching of Jesus." *NTS, 18*, 285-307, 1971.

Crossan, J. D. *In Parables: The Challenge of the Historical Jesus*. New York: Harper and Row Publishers, 1973.

Crossan, J. D. *Who Killed Jesus: Exposing the Roots of Anti-Semitism in the Gospel Story of the Death of Jesus*. New York: Harper San Francisco, 1991.

Crossan, John Dominic. "Parable and Example in the Teaching of Jesus." In *A Structuralist Approach to the Parable*, edited by Robert W. Funk. *Semeia* I (1974): 63ff.

Crossan, John Dominic. "Parable and Example in the Teaching of Jesus." Religious Studies Review 4, July 1978: 78.

Crossan, John Dominic. "Parables." In The Anchor Bible Dictionary, vol. 5, Edited by David Noel Freedman. New York: Doubleday, 1992.

Crossan, John Dominic. "The Parables of Jesus." *Interpretation* 56/3 (July 2002): 258.

Culas, Laurence. *Good News Amidst Crises Antioch and the Gospel of Matthew*. New Delhi: ISPCK, 2010.

Culpepper, R. A. "The Gospel of Luke: An Introduction, Commentary and Reflections." In The New Interpreter's Bible Commentary, vol. 9, Edited by Neil. Nashville: Abingdon Press, 1995, 10.

Cunningham, Scott. "*Through Many Tribulations?*": *The Theology of Persecution in Luke-Acts*. JSNTSup 142. Sheffield: Sheffield Academic Press, 1997.

Cunningham, Scott. *Through Many Tribulations*: *The Theology of Persecution in Luke-Acts*. London: Bloomsbury Publishing, 1997.

Curkpatrick, Stephen. "Parable Metonymy and Luke's Kerygmatic Framing." *JSNT* 25/3 (2003): 289-307.

Daft, R. L. *Leadership: Theory and Practice*. Orlando: The Dryden Press, 1999.

Dan O. Via. "Parable and Example Story: A Literary-Structuralist Approach," 107, 118. Cf. Mark Allan Powell, "Toward a Narrative Critical Understanding of Luke." *Interpretation* 48, no. 4 (October 1994): 341-46.

Danker, Frederick W. *Jesus and the New Age: A Commentary on St. Luke's Gospel*. Philadelphia: Fortress Press, 1988.

Dapaah, Daniel S. *The Relationship Between John the Baptist and Jesus of Nazareth: A Critical Study*. Lanham, MD: University Press of America, 2005.

Darr, J. D. *Herod the Fox: Audience Criticism and Lukan Characterization* (JSNT Sup 163). Sheffield Academic Press, 1998.

David B. Gowler. "Characterization in Luke: A Socio-Narratological Approach." *Biblical Theology Bulletin* 19, no. 2 (1989): 56.

Davis, Noah Knowles. *The Story of the Nazarene in Annotated Paraphrase*. Revell, 1903.

Dayton, W.T. "Teaching of Jesus." *The Zondervan Pictorial Encyclopedia of the Bible*, Vol. 5, Edited by Merrill C. Tenny. Michigan: Zondervan Publishing House, 1975.

De Lai, Gaetano Cardinal. The Passion of Our Lord. Boston: The Pilot Pub. Co., 1923.

Deboer, W. P. "Beatitudes." *The International Standard Bible Encyclopedia*, Edited by Geoffrey W. Bromiley. Michigan: William B. Eerdmans Publishing Company, 1979.

Dennert, Brian C. *John the Baptist and the Jewish Setting of Matthew*. Tübingen: Mohr Siebeck, 2015.

Derrett, J. Duncan M. "Law in the New Testament: The Parable of the Unjust Judge." *NTS* 18 (1971): 178ff.

Desjardins, M. *Peace, Violence and the New Testament*. Sheffield: Sheffield Academic Press, 1997.

Diamond, G. J. “Reflections Upon Recent Developments in the Study of Parables in Luke.” *ABR* 29 (Oct 1981): 3.

Doble, Peter. *The Paradox of Salvation: Luke's Theology of the Cross*. Society for New Testament Studies Monograph Series 87. Cambridge: Cambridge University Press, 1996 .

Dodd, C. H. *Historical Tradition in the Fourth Gospel*. Cambridge: Cambridge University Press, 1976.

Dodd, C. H. *The Parables of the Kingdom*. London: Nisbet, 1961.

Doerksen, Vernon D. “The Interpretation of the Parables.” *Grace Journal* 11 (Spring 1970): 11.

Donahue, Bill, and Russ Robinson. *The Seven Deadly Sins of Small Group Ministry*. Grand Rapids: Zondervan, 2002.

Donahue, J. R. “Passion Narrative.” *The Interpreter's Dictionary of the Bible, Supplementary Volume*. Edited by Keith Crim. Nashville: Abingdon Press, 1976.

Donahue, John R. “The Parable of Luke.” *BT* 41, no. 5 (September 2003): 283.

Douglas M. Parrott. “The Dishonest Steward (Luke 16:1-8a) and Luke's Special Parable Collection,” 510.

Douglas, J. D. “Disease and Healing.” *The New Bible Dictionary*. Michigan: William B. Eerdmans Publishing Company, 1962.

Downing, Gerald, F. “The Ambiguity of “The Pharisee and the Toll-Collector” (Luke 18: 9-14) in the Greco Roman World of Late Antiquity.” *CBQ* 54/1 (January 1992): 80-99.

Doyle, Alan. *Meeting Jesus: A New Approach to Faith*. Eugene, OR: Wipf and Stock Publishers, 2019.

Drane, John. *Introducing the New Testament*. Revised Edition. Oxford: Lion Publishing, 1999.

Driscoll, Mark, and Gerry Breshears. *Doctrine: What Christians Should Believe*. Wheaton: Crossway, 2010.

Drury, John. *The Literary Guide to the Bible*. Edited by Robert Alter and Frank Kermode. London: Fortress Press, 1989, 428.

Drury, John. *The Parables in the Gospels: History and Allegory*. New York: Crossroad, 1985, 124.

Drury, John. *Tradition and Design in Luke's Gospel: A Study in Early Christian Historiography*. London: Darton, Longman and Todd, n.d.

Dunn, James D. G. *The Evidence for Jesus*. Kentucky: The Westminster Press, 1985. Dunstan, Richard. Lukan Theology and the Parables of Jesus. Eugene, OR: Wipf and Stock Publishers, 2013.

Durber, Susan. “The Female Reader of the Parables of the Lost.” *Journal for the Study of the New Testament* 45 (March 1992): 59-78.

Dutt, Samuel P. “Pontius Pilate: In Search of Truth.” *The Trial of Jesus*. Edited by Satish C. Gyan. Raipur: Guru Sadan, Nd.

Easton, Burton Scott. *The Gospel According to St. Luke: A Critical and Exegetical Commentary*. Edinburgh: T&T Clark, 1926.

Edmiston, John. *Healing*. AIBI International Publishers, 2010.

Edwards, O. C. *Luke's Story of Jesus*. Philadelphia: Fortress Press, 1981.

Eims, Leroy. *The Lost Art of Disciple Making*. Grand Rapids, MI: Zondervan, 1980.

Elliott, James Keith. *A Synopsis of the Apocryphal Nativity and Infancy Narratives: Second Edition, Revised and Expanded*. BRILL, 2016.

Ellis, E. Earle, Ed. *The Century Bible: The Gospel of Luke*. Nashville: Thomas Nelson Pub., 1966.

Ellis, E. Earle. *The Gospel of Luke:* New Century Bible Commentary. Michigan: W.B. Eerdmans, 1980.

Elsner, Jas', and Ian Rutherford. Eds. *Pilgrimage in Graeco-Roman and Early Christian Antiquity: Seeing the Gods*. Oxford: OUP Oxford, 2007.

Elwell, Walter A. “Heal, Healing.” *Evangelical Dictionary of Theology*. Michigan: Baker Books House Company, 2001.

Emswiler, Thomas and Sharon Neufer. *Wholeness in Worship*. New York: Harper and Row, 1980.

Eric Franklin. *Luke: Interpreter of Paul, Critic of Matthew.*. Michigan: JSOT Press, 1994.

Erniakulathil, John. “Kingdom of God in the Teaching of Jesus.” *Bible Bhashyam* 23, no. 2 (June 1997): 90-101.

Ernst R. Wendland. “A Tale of Two Debtors: On the Interaction of Text, Context, and Context in a New Testament Dramatic Narrative (Luke 7: 36-50).” In *Linguistics and New Testament Interpretation: Essays on Discourse Analysis*, Edited by David Alan Black, 101. Nashville, TN: Broadman Press, 1992.

Esler, Philip F. “The Socio-Redaction Criticism of Luke-Acts”. *Social-Scientific Approaches to New Testament Interpretation*. Edited David G. Horrell. Edinburgh: T&T Clark, 1999.

Esler, Philip F. *Community and Gospel in Luke-Acts: The Social and Political Motivations of Lucan Theology*. Cambridge: Cambridge University Press, 1987.

Estep, William R. *Renaissance and Reformation*. Grand Rapids: William B. Eerdmans Publishing Company, 1986.

Evans, Craig A. *Luke: New International Biblical Commentary*. Peabody: Hendrickson, 1990.

Evans, G. R. *A History of Pastoral Care*. London: A&C Black, 2000.

Fallon, Michael. *The Gospel According to Saint Luke: An Introductory Commentary*. Bangalore: ATC, 1997.

Fallows, Samuel. "Heal." *The Popular and Critical Bible Encyclopedia and Scriptural Dictionary*. Chicago: The Howard-Severance Company, 1908.

Farris, Stephen. *The Hymns of Luke's Infancy Narratives: Their Origin, Meaning and Significance*. London: Bloomsbury Publishing, 2015.

Fausset, A. R. "Jesus Christ."*Fausset's Bible Dictionary*. 14th print. Michigan: Zondervan Pub. House, 1949.

Fee, Gordon D., and Stuart D. *How to Read the Bible for All Its Worth*. 3rd Ed. Grand Rapids, MI: Zondervan, 2003.

Ferda, Tucker S. *Jesus, the Gospels, and the Galilean Crisis*. London: Bloomsbury Publishing, 2018.

Fernando Mendez-Moratalla. *The Paradigm of Conversion in Luke*. London: A&C Black, 2004.

Fitzmyer, J. A. *The Gospel According to Luke* (Vol. 28). Anchor Bible, 1981.

Fitzmyer, Joseph A. "Today You Shall Be with Me in Paradise." *Luke the Theologian: Aspects of His Teaching*. New York: Paulist Press, 1989.

Fitzmyer, Joseph A. *Luke the Theologian: Aspects of his Teaching*. London: Geoffrey Chapman, 1989.

Fitzmyer, Joseph A. *The Gospel According to Luke* (2 vols.). Garden city: Doubleday, 1981, 1985.

Fitzmyer, Joseph A. *The Gospel According to Luke* (X-XXIV). The Anchor Bible. New York: Doubleday, 1985.

Fitzmyer, Joseph A. *The Gospel of Luke I-IX*. AB 28. New York: Doubleday, 1985.

Fleddermann, Harry T. "Mid-Level Techniques in Luke's Redaction of Q." ETL (Ephemerides Theologicae Lovanienses) LXXIX/1 (April 2003): 53-71.

Flender, Helmut. *St. Luke: Theologian of Redemptive History*. Tr. by Reginald H. and Ilse Fuller. London: SPCK, 1967.

Flynn, Leslie B. *Four Faces of Jesus: The Uniqueness of the Gospel Narratives*. Michigan: Kregal Publications, 1993, 84.

Forbes, Greg W. *The God of the Old: The Role of the Lukan Parables in the Purpose of Luke's Gospel*. Sheffield: Sheffield Academic Press, 2000.

Ford, J. M. "Reconciliation and forgiveness in Luke's Gospel." In R. J. Cassidy & P. J. Scharper (Eds.), *Political issues in Luke-Acts*. New York: Orbis Books, 1973.

Foreman, C. Lee. *Luke's Use of the Old Testament in His Infancy Narrative*. Portland, OR: Western Conservative Baptist Seminary, 1979.

France, R. T. *Jesus the Radical: A Portrait of the Man They Crucified.* Leicester: IVP, 1990.

France, R. T. *Luke*. Grand Rapids: Baker Books, 2013.

France, R. T. *New International Commentary on the New Testament: The Gospel of Matthew.* Grand Rapids: Baker Books, 2013.

France, T. *The Gospel of Matthew. The New International Commentary on the New Testament*. Grand Rapids: William B. Eerdmans Publishing Company, 2007.

Freed, Edwin D. "The Parable of the Judge and the Widow (Luke 18:1-8)." *New Testament Studies* 33, no. 1 (1987): 38ff.

Fuller, R. H. *Luke's Witness to Jesus Christ.* London: Lutterworth Press, 1963.

Fuller, Reginald H. "Jesus Christ." *Oxford Companion to the Bible*. Edited by Bruce M. Metzger and Michael D. Coogan. New York: Oxford University Press, 1993.

Fung, Benjamin Wing Wo. *A Defense for the Chronological Order of Luke's Gospel: The Meaning of "Orderly" (Kathexes) Account in Luke 1:3*. Eugene, OR: Wipf and Stock Publishers, 2019.

Funk, R. W. *Language, Hermeneutic, and the Word of God: The Problem of Language in the New Testament and Contemporary Theology*. New York: Harper and Row, 1966.

Funk, Robert W. *Parables and Presence: Forms of the New Testament Tradition*. Philadelphia: Fortress Press, 1982.

G. H. P. Thompson. *The Gospel According to Luke*. Oxford. Clarendon, 1972.

Garrison, Winfred E., and Yehuda Harry Levin. "Palestine." In *The World Book Encyclopedia*, vol. 14. Chicago: Field Enterprises Educational Corporation, 1962.

Garwood P. Anderson. "Seeking and Saving What Might Have Been Lost: Luke's Restoration of an Enigmatic Parable Tradition." *Catholic Biblical Quarterly* 70, no. 4 (October 2008): 729f, 731, 735, 737, 743.

Geldenhuys, J. N. 1962. "Jesus Christ, Teaching of." *The New Bible Dictionary*. Edited by J. D. Douglas, 629. London: InterVarsity Press.

Germoned, Paul. *Portraits of Jesus: A Contextual Approach to Bible Study: Luke*. London: Collins Liturgical Publications, 1988.

Giblin, Charles Homer. "Structural and Theological Considers on Luke 15." *CBQ* 24, No. 1 (January 1962): 15–31.

Gillmann, John, *Possessions and the Life of Faith: A Reading of Luke-Acts.* Collegeville: The Liturgical Press, 1991.

Glean, J. Stanly. *The Parables of Conflict in Luke.* Philadelphia: The Westminster Press, 1952.

Godet, F. *The Gospel of St. Luke: The Foreign Theological Library: A Commentary*. Edited by M.D. Cusin. 5th Edition. Edinburgh: T&T Clark, 1976.

Gonzalez, Justo. *The Story Luke Tells: Luke's Unique Witness to the Gospel.* Grand Rapids: Wm. B. Eerdmans Publishing, 2015.

Gooding, David. *According to Luke: A New Exposition of the Third Gospel.* Michigan: W. B. Eerdmans, 1987.

Gowler, D. B. "Characterization in Luke: A Socio-Narratological Approach." *BTB* 19 (1989): 54-62.

Gowler, David B. "Characterization in Luke: A Socio-Narratological Approach." *BTB* 19, no. 2 (1989): 56.

Gowler, David B. *What Are They Saying About the Parables?* New Jersey: Paulist Press, 2000.

Grant, Frederick C. "Beatitudes." *The Encyclopaedia Americana*, Vol. 3. Danbury: Grolier Incorporated, 1983.

Grant, R. M. *Early Christians and Society*. London: Harper and Row, 1977.

Grassi, Joseph A. *The Five Wounds of Jesus and Personal Transformation.* Mumbai: St. Paul's, 2001.

Grassi, Joseph. *Peace on Earth: Roots and Practices from Luke's Gospel.* Collegeville, Minn.: Liturgical Press, 2004.

Graves, Mike. "Preaching Lukan Parables: A Socio-Rhetorical Approach." *Southwestern Journal of Theology 40*. No. 1 (Fall 1997): 21.

Graves, Mike. "Preaching Lukan Parables: A Socio-Rhetorical Approach." *SWJT* 40/1 (1997): 19.

Green, J. B. *The Gospel of Luke*. Wm. B. Eerdmans, 1997.

Green, J. B. *The Theology of the Gospel of Luke*. Cambridge University Press, 1995.

Green, Joel B. 1998. "Death of Jesus." *Dictionary of Jesus and the Gospels.* Edited by Joel B. Green, Scot McKnight, and Howard I. Marshall, 161. Downers Grove, IL: InterVarsity Press.

Green, Joel B. *The Gospel of Luke.* New International Commentary on the New Testament. Grand Rapids: Eerdmans, 1997.

Green, Joel B. *The Theology of the Gospel of Luke.* New Testament Theology. Cambridge: Cambridge University Press, 1995.

Green, Joel B., and Scot McKnight. "Healing." *Dictionary of Jesus and the Gospels*. Illinois: Inter Varsity Press, 1992.

Griffiths, Jonathan, and Rhonda Harrington Kelley. Eds. *Women's Evangelical Commentary: New Testament.* Nashville, TN: B&H Publishing Group, 2011.

Griffiths, Jonathan. *Preaching in the New Testament: An Exegetical and Biblical-Theological Study*. London: SPCK, 2017.

Griggs, Donald L. and Paul W. Walaskay, *Luke's Gospel from Scratch: The New Testament for Beginners.* Louisville: Westminster John Knox Press, 2011.

Grobel, Kendrick. "Beatitudes." *Encyclopaedia Britannica*. Vol. 3. Chicago: William Benton Publisher, 1971.

Gundry, Robert H. *Luke, A Commentary on His Literary and Theological Art.* Grand Rapids, MI: William B. Eerdmans, 1982.

Gushee, David P. *The Moral Teachings of Jesus: Radical Instruction in the Will of God.* Eugene, OR: Wipf and Stock Publishers, 2024.

Guthrie, D. "Jesus Christ." *The Zondervan Pictorial Encyclopedia of the Bible*. Vol. 3, Edited by Merrill C. Tenny. Michigan: Zondervan Pub. House, 1977.

Guthrie, Nancy. *Biblical Theology in Discipleship*. Carol Stream, IL: Tyndale Publishing House, 2007.

Habermas, Gary R., Michael R. Licona, and Kregel Publications. *The Case for the Resurrection of Jesus*. Grand Rapids: Kregel Publications, n.d.

Hagee, John. *The Power to Heal*. Dallas: Hagee Ministries, 1991.

Harnack, Adolf. *What is Christianity*. Escondido: Book Tree, 2006.

Harpur, James. *The Miracles of Jesus*. New York: The Reader's Digest Association, Inc., 1997.

Harrington, Daniel J., and James F. Keenan. *Jesus and Virtue Ethics: Building Bridges Between New Testament Studies and Moral Theology.* United States of America: Rowman & Littlefield Publishers, 2002.

Hastings, Adrian, Alistair Mason, and Hugh S. Pyper. Eds. *The Oxford Companion to Christian Thought.* Oxford: Oxford University Press, USA, 2000.

Hauck. "μακάριος." *Theological Dictionary of the New Testament*, 362-369.

Hauerwas, Stanley, et al. *The Wisdom of the Cross*: Essays in Honor of John Howard Yoder. Eugene, OR: Wipf and Stock Publishers, 2005.

Hays, Christopher M. *Luke's Wealth Ethics: A Study in Their Coherence and Character.* Tübingen: Mohr Siebeck, 2010.

Hendrickx, Herman. *The Parables of Jesus: Studies in the Synoptic Gospels*. 2nd ed. 1994.

Hendrickx, Herman. *The Passion Narrative*. Manila, Philippines: East Asian Pastoral Institute, 1977.

Hendriksen, William. *Luke: New Testament Commentary, Exposition of the Gospel According to Luke.* Michigan: Baker Book House, 1978.

Heney, Dave. *Luke 10 Leadership: How to Succeed at Parish Ministry*. Notre Dame, IN: Ave Maria Press, 2020.

Henrich, Sarah. "Embedded in the 1st Century Elite in Our Own: Recent Research on Luke's Gospel." *Currents in Theology and Mission* 33/6 (Dec 2006): 483.

Hiers, Richard H. *The Kingdom of God in the Synoptic Tradition*. Gainesville: University of Florida Press, 1970.

Hirsch, Alan, and Debra Hirsch. *Untamed: Reactivating a Missional Form of Discipleship*. Grand Rapids, MI: Baker Books, 2010.

Holgate, David A. *Prodigality, Liberality and Meanness in the Parable of the Prodigal Son: A Greco- Roman Perspective on Luke 15:11-32*. JSNTSup 187. Sheffield: Sheffield Academic Press, 1999.

Hollar, Larry. *Hunger for the Word: Lectionary Reflections on Food and Justice.* Collegeville, MN: Liturgical Press, 2004.

Holman, Susan R. Wealth and Poverty in Early Church and Society. Grand Rapids, MI: Baker Academic, 2008.

Holmås, Geir Otto. *Prayer and Vindication in Luke-Acts: The Theme of Prayer within the Context of the Legitimating and Edifying Objective of the Lukan Narrative.* London: T&T Clark, 2011.

Holmberg, B. *Sociology and the New Testament*. Fortress Press, 1990.

Hooker, Morna D. Not Ashamed of the Gospel: *New Testament Interpretations of the Death of Christ*. Carlisle: The Paternoster Press, 1994.

Hoskyns, Edwyn, and F. Noel Davey. *The Riddle of the New Testament*. London: Faber and Faber, 1947.

Houston, J. M. "An Environmental Background to the New Testament." *In The Layman's Bible Commentary*. Vol. 1, Edited by G. C. D. Howley, F. F. Bruce, and H. L. Ellison. Grand Rapids: Zondervan Publishing House, 1979.

Hull, Bill. *The Complete Book of Discipleship: On Being and Making Followers of Christ*. Colorado Springs: NavPress, 2006.

Hultgren, Arland J. *The Parables of Jesus: A Commentary*. Grand Rapids, Michigan: W.B. Eerdmans, 2002.

Hunter, A. M. *The Work and Words of Jesus.* Delhi: ISPCK, 1969.

Hunter, Archibald. *Interpreting the Parables*. Philadelphia: Westminster Press, 1960.

Irwin, Kevin W. *Sunday Worship, a Planning Guide to Celebration*. Boulder, CO: Pueblo Publishing Company, 1983.

J. B. Tyson. "Conflict as a Literary Theme in the Gospel of Luke." In *New Synoptic Studies*. Edited by W. Farmer, 320-26. Macon, GA: Mercer University Press, 1983.

J. D. Kingsbury. *Conflict in Luke: Jesus, Authorities, Disciples*. Minneapolis: Fortress Press, 1991.

Jacobus, Melancthon W. "Health." *Funk and Wagnall's New Standard Bible Dictionary*. New York: Funk and Wagnall's Company, 1936.

James L. Resseguie. "Literature, New Testament as." *Eerdmans Dictionary of the Bible*, 817.

Jarvis, Cynthia A., and E. Elizabeth Johnson. *Feasting on the Gospels--Luke, Volume 1: A Feasting on the Word Commentary.* Louisville, KY: Presbyterian Publishing Corp, 2014.

Jensen, Robin. *Living Water: Images, Symbols, and Settings of Early Christian Baptism*. Leiden: Brill, 2010.

Jeremias, J. *The Parables of Jesus*. New York: Charles Scribner's Sons.

Jervell, Jacob. *Luke and the People of God.* Minneapolis: Augsburg, 1972.

Jill, Amy, Levine and Marianne Blickenstaff (Eds). *A Feminist Companion to Luke: Feminist Companion to the New Testament and Early Christian Writings.* Sheffield: Sheffield Academic Press, 2002.

John R. Donahue. "The Parable of Luke." *Bible Today* 41. No. 5 (September 2003): 283.

Johnson, Luke Timothy. *Prophetic Jesus, Prophetic Church: The Challenge of Luke-Acts to the Contemporary Christians.* Cambridge: W.B. Eerdmans, 2011.

Johnson, Luke Timothy. *The Gospel of Luke*: Sacra Pagina. Edited by J. Harrington. Minnesota: The Liturgical Press, 1991.

Johnson, S. *Jesus and his parables.* Delhi: ISPCK, 2002.

Jordan, Clarence. *The Cotton Patch Version of Luke and Acts*: Jesus' Doing and the Happening. New York: Koinonia Publications, 1969.

Judge, M. "Passion of Christ (In the Bible)." *In New Catholic Encyclopedia.* Vol. x. Edited by John P. Whalen. New York: McGraw Hill Book Company, 1967.

Juel, Donald. Luke-Acts. London: SCM Press, 1984.

Juel, Donald. *Luke-Acts: The Promise of History.* Atlanta: John Knox Press, 1973.

Jülicher, Adolf. Die *Gleichnisreden Jesu*, 2 Vols. Tübingen: Mohr, 1888.

Jung, Chang-Wook. *The Original Language of the Lukan Infancy Narrative*. London: A&C Black, 2004.

Just, A. A. *The Ongoing Feast: Table Fellowship and Eschatology at Emmaus*. Minnesota: Liturgical Press, 1993.

Karris, R. J. "The Gospel according to Luke." In R. E. Brown, J. A. Fitzmyer, & R. E. Murphy (Eds.), *The New Jerome Biblical Commentary* (Bangalore: TPI, 2004).

Karris, Robert J. "Poor and Rich: The Lukan Sitz im Leben." *Perspectives on Luke-Acts*. 9 Edited by Charles H. Talbert. Edinburgh: T&T Clark, 1978, 112ff.

Karris, Robert J. "The Gospel According to Luke". *The New Jerome Biblical Commentary*. Edited by Raymond E. Brown, Joseph A. Fitzmyer and Roland E. Murphy. Bangalore: TPI, 2004.

Karris, Robert J. *Invitation to Luke: A Commentary on the Gospel of Luke with Complete Text from the Jerusalem Bible*. Garden City, New York: A Division of Doubleday & Company, 1991.

Keck, Leander E. and J. Louis Martyn. Ed. *Studies in Luke-Acts*. London: SPCK, 1968c.1966.

Kee, Howard C. *Jesus in History: An Approach to the Study of the Gospels*. Second Edition. New York: Harcourt Brace Jovanovich Publishers, 1977, 76ff.

Keener, Craig S. "Matthew." *The IVP New Testament Commentary Series*. Downers Grove, IL: InterVarsity Press, 1987.

Kelley, R. L. "Meals with Jesus in Luke's Gospel." *HBT*, 17(2), 123–131, 1995.

Kent, Homer A. "Matthew." *The New Testament and the Wycliffe Bible Commentary*. New York: The Iverseb-Norman Associates, 1980.

Khiangte, Vanlalchhawna. *Matthean Beatitudes in Socio-Historical Context: Their Implications for Contemporary Christian Discipleship*. New Delhi: Christian World Imprints, 2016.

Kilgallen, John J. "Parables in the Gospel of Luke." Chicago Studies 38/3 (Fall/Winter 1999): 273.

Kim, Kyoung-Jin. *Stewardship and Almsgiving in Luke's Theology*. JSNTSup 155. Sheffield: Sheffield Academic Press, 1998.

Kim, Sehyun. *The Kingship of Jesus in the Gospel of John*. Wipf and Stock Publishers, 2018.

Knight, Jonathan. *Luke's Gospel*. Psychology Press, 1998.

Knight, Matthew A. *The Book of Luke: Physician and Historian*. Xlibris Corporation, 2018.

Kingsbury, Jack Dean. "The Developing Conflict between Jesus and the Jewish Leaders in Matthew's Gospel: A Literary-Critical Study." *CBQ* 49. No. 1 (1987): 57–73.

Kingsbury, Jack Dean. "The Plot of Luke's Story of Jesus." *Interpretation* 48. No. 4 (October 1994): 369–78.

Kittel, Gerhard. "νΙαομια." *Theological Dictionary of the New Testament*. Michigan: Wm. B. Eerdmans Publishing Company, 1965.

Kjargaard, Mogens Stiller. *Metaphor and Parables: A Systematic Analysis of the Specific Structure and Cognitive Function of the Synoptic Similes and Parables qua Metaphors*. Leiden: E. J. Brill, 1986.

Klutz, Todd. *The Exorcism Stories in Luke-Acts: A Sociostylistic Reading*. Society for New Testament Studies Monograph Series 129. Cambridge: Cambridge University Press, 2004.

Knight, Amy-Jill, Dale C. Allison Jr., and John Dominic Crossan. Eds. *The Historical Jesus in Context*. Princeton, NJ: Princeton University Press, 2009.

Knight, Matthew A. *The Book of Luke: Physician and Historian*. Bloomington, IN: Xlibris Corporation, 2018.

Kodell, J. "'Luke's Use of Laos, People' Especially in the Jerusalem Narrative (Lk 19:28-24:53)." *CBQ, 31*(3), 329–340, 1969.

Koet, Bart J. *Dreams and Scripture in Luke-Acts: Collected Essays*. Contributions to Biblical Exegesis and Theology 42. Leuven: Peeters, 2006.

Kramer, Mark A. *A Stir in the Waters*. Maitland, FL: Xulon Press, 2011.

Kruschwitz, Robert B. "Introduction." *Parables: Christian Reflection*, A Series in Faith and Ethics, edited by Robert B. Kruschwitz. Waco: Baylor University Press, 2006.

Kuhrt, Stephen, and Gordon Kuhrt. *Believing in Baptism: Understanding and Living God's Covenant Sign*. London: Bloomsbury Publishing, 2020.

Kuske, David P. *Biblical Interpretation: The Only Right Way*. Milwaukee, WI: Northwestern Publishing House, 1995.

La Verdiere, Eugene. Luke: *New Testament, A Biblical-Theological Commentary*. Veritas Pub.: Dublin, 1980.

Lambrecht, J. *Once More Astonished: Parables of Jesus*. New York: Crossroad, 1981.

Lame, G. W. H. "Luke." *Peake's Commentary on the Bible*. Edited by Matthew Black. Nairobi, Kenya: Thomas Nelson, 1977.

Lane, William L. "The Gospel of Mark." *The New International Commentary of the New Testament*. Grand Rapids, MI: Eerdmans, 1974.

LaVerdiere, Eugene, *Luke: New Testament Message; Biblical-Theological Commentary.* Vol. 5. Edited by Wilfrid Harrington and Donald Senior. Wilmington, Delaware: Michael Glazier, 1980.

Lenski, R. C. H. *The Interpretation of St. Luke's Gospel: Commentary on the New Testament.* Peabody: Hendrickson, 1946 c. 2001.

Lensky, R. C. H. *The Interpretation of St. Matthew's Gospel.* Minneapolis: Augsburg Publishing House, 1964.

Lentz, J. C. *Portrait of Paul.* SNTSMS 77. Cambridge University Press, 1993.

Léon-Dufour, Xavier. "Passion of Christ." *Dictionary of the New Testament.* Translated by Terrence Prendergast. London: Geoffrey Champion, 1980.

Letter and Hill. "Christian Healing." *New Catholic Encyclopedia.* Grand Rapids: Zondervan Publishing House, 2003.

Levin, Yehuda Harry, and Winfred E. Garrison. "Palestine." *The World Book Encyclopedia,* vol. 14. Chicago: Field Enterprises Educational Corporation, 1962.

Levine, Amy-Jill, Dale C. Allison Jr., and John Dominic Crossan. Eds. *The Historical Jesus in Context.* Princeton, NJ: Princeton University Press, 2009.

Licona, M. *Why are There Differences in the Gospels?: What we Can Learn from Ancient Biography.* Oxford University Press, 2017.

Licona, Michael R. *Why Are There Differences in the Gospels?: What We Can Learn from Ancient Biography.* Oxford: Oxford University Press, 2016.

Lieu, Judith M. *The Gospel of Luke: Epworth Commentaries.* Eugene, OR: Wipf and Stock Publishers, 2012.

Litwak, Kenneth Duncan. *Echoes of Scripture in Luke-Acts: Telling the History of God's People Inter-textually.* JSNT Supp. Series 282. London: T&T Clark, 2005.

Longenecker, Richard N. *Patterns of Discipleship in the New Testament.* Grand Rapids, MI: Eerdmans, 1996.

Louis, Ndekha. *Identity and Socio-Economic Relations in Luke's Gospel*: The Sermon on the Plain (Lk 6:20-49) and Greco-Roman Panegyrics, 62.

Luck, G. Coleman. Luke: The Gospel of the Son of Man. Chicago: Moody Press, 1960.

M. Desjardins. *Peace, Violence and the New Testament.* Sheffield: Sheffield Academic Press, 1997.

Mac Pherson, Duncan. "Luke." *Scripture Discussion Commentary.* Vol. 8. Edited by Laurence Bright. London: Sheed and Ward, 1971.

Maddox, Robert. *The Purpose of Luke-Acts.* Edinburgh: T&T Clark, 1982.

Malina, B. J. "Reading Theory Perspective: Reading Luke-Acts." In *The Social World of Luke-Acts: Models of Interpretation*. Edited by J. H. Neyrey. Peabody, MA: Hendrickson Publishers, 1991.

Malina, B. J. *The New Testament World: Insights from Cultural Anthropology*. Westminster/ John Knox Press, 1993.

Malina, Bruce and Richard L. Rohrbaugh. *Social Science Commentary on the Synoptic Gospels*. Minneapolis: Fortress Press, 1992.

Malphurs, Aubrey. *A New Kind of Church: Understanding Models of Ministry for the 21st Century*. Grand Rapids: Baker Books, 2007.

Malphurs, Aubrey. *Planting Growing Churches for the Twenty-First Century*. Grand Rapids, MI: Baker, 1992.

Maniparampil, Jose. *Reading the Synoptic Gospels*. Bangalore: Clavetian Publications, 2004.

Manson, William. *The Gospel of Luke: The Moffatt New Testament Commentary*. London: Hodder and Stoughton, 1930.

Marcus, Joel. *John the Baptist in History and Theology*. Columbia, SC: University of South Carolina Press, 2018.

Mark Allan Powell. *What Are They Saying About Luke?* New York: Paulist Press, 1989.

Marshall, H. I. "Jesus Christ." In J. D. Douglas (Ed.). *The Illustrated Bible Dictionary*. England: IVP, 1980.

Marshall, Howard I. The Gospel of Luke: A Commentary on the Greek Text. Exeter: The Paternoster Press, 1978.

Marshall, I. Howard. *The Gospel of Luke: A Commentary on the Greek Text.* New International Greek Testament Commentary. Michigan: W.B. Eerdmans and Exeter: The Paternoster Press, 1978.

Marshall, I. H. Millard, A. R Packer, J. I Wiseman, D. J. Eds., *New Bible Dictionary, Third Edition*. Hyderabad: Authentic Books, 1996.

Marshall, Thomas E. *The New Testament: Its Background, Setting & Content*. Cincinnati, OH: Christian Publishing House, 2023.

Martin, John A. Luke. *The Bible Knowledge Commentary:* An Exposition of the Scriptures. Edited by John F. Walvoord. Canada: Victor Books, 1983.

Martin, Ralph P. *New Testament Foundations: A Guide for Christian Students*. Vol. 1, revised Edition. Michigan: W.B. Eerdmans, 1985, 30.

Martin, Ralph P., and Carl N. Toney. *New Testament Foundations: An Introduction for Students*. Eugene, OR: Wipf and Stock Publishers, 2018.

Martinez, Roberto. *The Question of John the Baptist and Jesus' Indictment of the Religious Leaders: A Critical Analysis of Luke 7:18-35*. Cambridge: James Clarke & Company Limited, 2012.

Mary Ann Tolbert. *Perspectives on Parables: An Approach to Multiple Interpretation*. Philadelphia: Fortress Press, 1979.

Massey, James. *The Gospel of Luke.* Dalit Bible Commentary-New Testament. Vol. 3. New Delhi: CDS, 2007.

Matera, Frank J. "Jesus' Journey to Jerusalem (Lk 9:51-19:46): A Conflict with Israel." *JSNT* 51 (Sep 1993): 77.

Matera, Frank J. 1985. "The Death of Jesus According to Luke: A Question of Source." Catholic Biblical Quarterly 47 (3): 90.

Mathai, Samuel. *A Guide to Church Ministry*. Bhopal: SSM, 2008.

Matson, Mark A. *In Dialogue with Another Gospel? The Influence of the Fourth Gospel on the Passion Narrative of the Gospel of Luke.* Atlanta: Society of Biblical Literature, 2001.

McArthur, H., and R. Johnson. *They Also Taught in Parables*. New York: Abingdon Press.

McBride, Denis. The Gospel of Luke: *A Reflective Commentary*. Dublin: Dominican Publications, 1997.

McDonald, J. Ian H. *The Crucible of Christian Morality*. New York: Routledge, 2016.

McFague, Sallie. Metaphorical Theology: Models of God in Religious Language. Philadelphia: Fortress Press, 1982.

McGee, J. Vernon. *Moving Thru Matthew.* California: Thru the Bible Books, 2006.

McGrath, James F. *John of History, Baptist of Faith: The Quest for the Historical Baptizer*. Grand Rapids, MI: Wm. B. Eerdmans Publishing, 2024.

Mckenna, Megan. *Blessings and Woes: The Beatitudes and the Sermon on the Plain in the Gospel of Luke.* Maryknoll, NY: Orbis Books, 1999.

McKenzie, John L., Ed. "Passion." *Dictionary of the Bible*. Milwaukee: The Bruce Publishing Company, 1965.

Meadors, Edward P. "The 'Messianic' Implications of the Q Material." *JBL* 118/2 (Summer 1999): 253-277.

Meagher, Paddy. *Paddy Fields and a Grain of Rice.*

Meehan, Bridget. *The Healing Power of Prayer*. Mumbai: St Paul's, 2005.

Mendez-Moratalla, Fernando. *The Paradigm of Conversion in Luke.* London: A&C Black, 2004.

Metzger, James A. *Consumption and Wealth in Luke's Travel Narrative.* Leiden: Brill, 2007.

Michaels, J. Ramsey. *Servant and Son: Jesus in Parable and Gospel*. Eugene, OR: Wipf and Stock Publishers, 2017.

Miller, D. G. Luke. *Layman's Bible Commentaries*. London: SCM Press, 1963.

Minear, P. S. "Jesus' Audience, According to Luke." Nov. Tes XVI/II (April 1974): 81.

Moessner, David P. "Luke 9:1-50: Luke's Preview of the Journey of the Prophet Like Moses of Deuteronomy." *JBL* 102. No. 4 (December 1983): 575–605.

Moessner, David P. "The Leaven of the Pharisees' and 'This Generation': Israel's Rejection of Jesus According to Luke." *JSNT* 34 (October 1988): 42.

Moessner, David P. *Lord of the Banquet: The Literary and Theological Significance of Lukan Travel Narrative.* Minneapolis: Fortress, 1989.

Montgomery Boice, James. Christ's Call to Discipleship. Chicago, IL: Moody Press, 1986.

Moore, Michael S. *Wealth Wise: A Study of Socio-economic Conflict in Hebrew Wisdom.*

Moore, Stephen D. *Mark and Luke in Poststructuralist Perspectives: Jesus Begins to Write.* London: Yale University Press, 1992.

Morgan, M. Gwyn. "Hellenism and Persecution: Antiochus IV and the Jews." In *Hellenistic History and Culture*. Edited by Peter Green. London: University of California Press, 1993.

Morris, Leon. *New Testament Theology.* Grand Rapids, MI: Zondervan Academic, 2011.

Morris, Leon. *The Gospel According to Luke: An Introduction and Commentary.* Michigan: WB Eerdmans Publishing Company, 1974.

Mounce, William D. *The Analytical Lexicon to the Greek New Testament.* Grand Rapids: Zondervan Publishing House, 1993.

Moxnes, Halvor. *The Economy of the Kingdom: Social Conflict and Economic Relation in Luke's Gospel.* Philadelphia: Fortress Press, 1988.

Murphy, Frederick James. *An Introduction to Jesus and the Gospels.* Nashville, TN: Abingdon Press, 2005.

Myers, Allen C. "Beatitude." *The Eerdmans Bible Dictionary*. Grand Rapids: William B. Eerdmans Publishing Company, 1987.

Nadella, Raj. *Dialogue Not Dogma: Many Voices in the Gospel of Luke.* London: T&T Clark international, 2011.

Nave, Guy D. *The Role and Function of Repentance in Luke-Acts*. Atlanta: Society of Biblical Literature/ Leiden: Brill, 2002.

Navone, J. "The Parable of the Banquet." *BT* (Nov), 923ff, 1964.

Nelson, Peter K. *Leadership and Discipleship: A Study of Luke 22:24-30.* Atlanta, GA: Scholars Press, 1994.

Neusner, Jacob. "Types and Forms in Ancient Jewish Literature: Some Comparisons." *History of Religions* 11 (1972): 376.

Newberry, Julie. *Lukan Joy and the Life of Discipleship: A Narrative Analysis of the Conditions That Lead to Joy According to Luke*. Mohr Siebeck, 2023.

Newton, Gary C. *Growing Toward Spiritual Maturity*. Wheaton, IL: Evangelical Training Association, 1999.

Neyrey, Jerome H. "Jesus' Address to the Women of Jerusalem (Lk 23:27-31) - A Prophetic Judgment Oracle." NTS 29 (January 1983): 74.

Neyrey, Jerome H. Ed. *The Social World of Luke-Acts*: *The Models for Interpretation*. Peabody: Hendrickson, 1991.

Neyrey, Jerome H. *The Passion According to Luke: A Redaction Study of Luke's Soteriology*. New York: Paulist Press, 1985.

Nichols, David R. *The Healing Presence of Jesus*. Hyderabad: A.P Bible College, 2003.

Nickelsburg, George W. E. 1992. "Passion Narrative." *The Anchor Bible Dictionary*. Vol. 5. Edited by David Noel Freedman, 172. New York: Doubleday.

Nolland, John. "Luke 1-9." In *Word Biblical Commentary*, vol. 35A. Edited by Bruce M. Metzger and Others. Dallas: Word Books, 1989.

Nolland, John. *Luke. Word Biblical Commentary*. 3 Vols. Dallas: word Books, 1993.

O. C. Edwards, *Luke's Story of Jesus*. Philadelphia: Fortress Press, 1981.

Oak, John H. *Called to Awaken the Layman*. Seoul: Tyrannus Press, 1984.

Ogden, Greg. *Transforming Discipleship*. Downers Grove, IL: InterVarsity Press, 2003.

Ogg, George. "The Central Section of the Gospel According to St. Luke." *NTS* 18 (1971): 39.

Orr, James. "Heal." *International Standard Bible Encyclopedia*. Grand Rapids: Wm.B. Eerdmans Publishing Co., 1915.

Osborn, T. L. *Biblical Healing*. Tulsa: Global Publishers, 2004.

Osborne, Grant R. The Hermeneutical Spiral: *A Comprehensive Introduction to the Biblical Interpretation*. Downers Grove, Illinois: IVP, 1991.

Osburn, Carroll D. *Essays on Women in Earliest Christianity, Volume 1*. Eugene, OR: Wipf and Stock Publishers, 2007.

Palmer, Donald S. K. *The Kingdom of God*. Welwyn: Evangelical Press, 1986.

Parrott, Douglas M. "The Dishonest Steward (Luke 16:1-8a) and Luke's Special Parable Collection." *NTS* 37/4 (1991): 506.

Parsons, Mikeal C. "Land Marks Along the Way: The Function of the 'L' Parables in the Lukan Travel Narrative." SWJT 40/1 (Fall 1997): 34f.

Parsons, Mikeal. *Luke: Storyteller, Interpreter, Evangelist.* Peabody: Hendrickson, 2007.

Parvey, C. "The Theology and Leadership of Women in the New Testament." In R. R. Ruether Ed. *Religion and sexism*. New York: Simon and Schuster, 1986.

Patella, Michael F. *The Gospel according to Luke.* New Collegeville Bible Commentary. Collegeville: Liturgical Press, 2005.

Paterson, W. P. "Jesus Christ." Hastings' *Dictionary of the Bible*. Edited by James Hastings. 3rd Printing. New York: Hendrickson Publishers, 1996.

Patey, Edward H. A Doctor's Life of Jesus: St. Luke's Gospel. London: SCM Press, 1965.

Patterson, Dorothy Kelley, Rhonda Kelley, and Rhonda Harrington Kelley. *Women's Evangelical Commentary: New Testament*. B&H Publishing Group, 2011.

Paul Ricoeur. "Biblical Hermeneutics." *Semeia* 4 (1975): 65.

Pennington, Jonathan T. *The Sermon on the Mount and Human Flourishing: A Theological Commentary*. Grand Rapids: Baker Academic, 2018.

Perrin, N. *Rediscovering the Teaching of Jesus*. London: SCM Press, 1967.

Peters, George W. *A Biblical Theology of Missions*. Chicago: Moody Press, 1972.

Pfeiffer, Charles F. "Healing, Health." *Wycliffe Bible Encyclopedia*. Chicago: Moody Press, 1975.

Phillips, Thomas E. "Reading Recent Reading of Issues of Wealth and Poverty in Luke-Acts". *Currents in Biblical Research* 1 (2003): 231-269.

Phillips, Thomas E. *Reading Issues of Wealth and Poverty in Luke-Acts.* Lewiston, NY: Edwin Mellen Press, 2001.

Pilgrim, W. E. *Good News to the Poor: Wealth and Poverty in Luke-Acts*. Minneapolis: Augsburg Publishing House, 1981.

Pinckaers, Servais. *The Pursuit of Happiness God's Way*. Translated by Mary Thomas Noble. Oregon: Wipf and Stock Publishers, 1998.

Plevnik, J. "The Origin of Easter Faith According to Luke." *Biblica, 61*(4), 499–509, 1980.

Plummer, A. A *Critical and Exegetical Commentary on the Gospel According to St. Luke*. Edinburgh: T&T Clark, 1914.

Porter, Stanley E. *Hearing the Old Testament in the New Testament.* Grand Rapids, MI: Wm. B. Eerdmans Publishing, 2006.

Poter, Laurence E. "Luke." *The International Bible Commentary*. Edited by F. F. Bruce, 1225. Michigan: Zondervan Publishing House, 1979.

Powell, Mark Allan. "The Religious Leaders in Luke: A Literary-Critical study." *JBL* 109/1 (1990): 93-110.

Powell, Mark Allan. *Introducing the New Testament: A Historical, Literary, and Theological Survey*. Grand Rapids, MI: Baker Books, 2018.

Powell, Mark Allan. *What Are They Saying About Luke*. New York: Paulist Press, 1989.

Powell, Mark Allan. *What Is Narrative Criticism?* Minneapolis: Fortress Press, 1953.

Prime, Derek. *Jesus His Life and Ministry*. London: Thomas Nelson Publishers, 1995.

Purves, George Tybout. "Jesus Christ." *Davis Dictionary of the Bible*. 4th Revised Edition, Edited by John D. Davis. Michigan: Baker Book House, 1980.

R. H. Stein. *An Introduction to the Parables of Jesus*. Philadelphia: Westminster Press, 1981.

R. T. France. *Jesus the Radical: A Portrait of the Man They Crucified.* Leicester: IVP, 1990.

Radford Ruether, Rosemary and Eleanor McLaughlin. *Women of Spirit: Female Leadership in the Jewish & Christian Traditions*. New York: Simon & Schuster, 1979.

Ragg, Lonsdale. *St. Luke*. London: Methuen and Co., 1922.

Raj, Daniel Monika. *The Inheritors of the Basileia Tou Tqeou*: *According to Lucan Perspective*. Delhi: ISPCK, 2008.

Raja, R. J. "'Rich Towards God:' Bhakti in the Gospel of Luke I." *VJTR* 59/4 (April 1995): 233.

Raja, R. J. "'Rich Towards God:' Bhakti in the Gospel of Luke III." VJTR 59/6 (June 1995): 389-399.

Raja, R. J. "'Rich Towards God': Bhakti in the Gospel of Luke." *The Gospels With an Indian Face.* Madrass, CLS, 1996.

Ramsperger, Frank. *The Literary Form and Theological Content of Luke's Infancy Narratives*. Toronto: Regis College, 1965.

Reid, B. E. "'Do You see this Woman?' Luke 7:36-50 as a Paradigm for Feminist Hermeneutics." *Biblical Research, 40*, 37-39, 1995.

Reid, B. E. *Choosing the Better Part? Women in the Gospel of Luke.* Minnesota: The Liturgical Press, 1969.

Reid, Barbara E. "Luke's Mixed Message for Women." Chicago Studies 38. No. 3, Fall/Winter 1999: 287ff.

Reid, Barbara E. Choosing the Better Part? Women in the Gospel of Luke. Grand Rapids: Eerdmans, 1996.

Reid, Barbara E. *Choosing the Better Part?: Women in the Gospel of Luke.* Collegeville: Liturgical Press, 1996.

Resseguie, James L. "Literature, New Testament as." *Eerdmans Dictionary of the Bible.* Edited by David Noel Freedman, Grand Rapids, Michigan: W.B. Eerdmans, 2000.

Riches, John. *The World of Jesus: First-Century Judaism in Crisis.* Cambridge: Cambridge University Press, 2001.

Rick Warren. The Purpose Driven Church: Growth Without Compromising Your Message and Mission. Grand Rapids, MI: Zondervan Publishing House, 1995.

Ricoeur, Paul. "Biblical Hermeneutics." *Semeia* 4 (1975): 65.

Ringe, Sharon H. *Luke, Westminster Bible Companion.* Louisville: John Knox Press, 1995.

Robertson, A. T. *Luke the Historian in the Light of Research.* Michigan: Baker Book House, 1977.

Robertson, Arther. *Matthew*. Chicago: Moody Press, 1983.

Robinson, Anthony B., and Robert W. Wall. *Called to Be Church: The Book of Acts for a New Day*. Grand Rapids, MI: Wm. B. Eerdmans Publishing, 2006.

Rogan, Wil. *Purity in the Gospel of John: Early Jewish Tradition, Christology, and Ethics*. Bloomsbury Publishing, 2023.

Ross, C., & Bevans, S. *Mission on the Road to Emmaus: Constants, Context, and Prophetic Dialogue*. SCM Press, 2015.

Ross, Cathy, and Steve Bevans. *Mission on the Road to Emmaus*: Constants, Context, and Prophetic Dialogue. London: SCM Press, 2015.

Rothschild, Clare K. *Baptist Traditions and Q*. Tübingen: Mohr Siebeck, 2003.

Rowe, C. Kavin. *Early Narrative Christology: The Lord in the Gospel of Luke*. Berlin: Walter de Gruyter, 2012.

Ruffini, Giovanni. *Life in an Egyptian Village in Late Antiquity: Aphrodito Before and After the Islamic Conquest*. Cambridge: Cambridge University Press, 2018.

Ryan, Judith M. "Luke's Infancy Narrative." *The Bible Today* 35 (1997): 342.

Ryle, J. C. *Expository Thoughts on the Gospels: Luke*, vol. 2. Edinburgh: The Banner of Truth Trust, 1858.

Ryrie, Charles C. *The Miracles of Our Lord*. 175.

Saldarini, A. J. "Pharisees." *ABD*. Ed. by D. N. Freedman Vol. 5. New York: Doubleday, 1992.

Saldarini, A. J. *Pharisees, Scribes and Sadducees in Palestinian Society: A Sociological Approach*. Wilmington, Delaware: Michael Glazier, Inc., 1988.

Sam, L. R. Arul. *The Love Commandments of Jesus in the Gospel of Luke and its Implication in the Indian Context.* Delhi: ISPCK, 2008.

Sampathkumar, P. A. "The rich and poor in Luke-Acts." *Bible Bhashyam, 22*(4), 187, 1996.

Samra, James G. *A Biblical View of Discipleship*. Bibliotheca Sacra 160 (2003): 219-220.

Sander, Jack. "The Salvation of the Jews in Luke Acts." *Luke-Acts*-New Perspectives From the Society of Biblical Literature Seminar. NewYork: Cross Road, 1984.

Sander, Jack. *The Jews in Luke-Acts*. Philadelphia: Fortress Press, 1989.

Sanders, E. P. *The Historical Figure of Jesus*. London: The Penguin Press, 1993.

Sarma, B. A. *Hermeneutics of Mission in Matthew: Israel and the Nations in the Interpretative Framework of Matthew's Gospel*. Eugene, OR: Langham Monographs, 2015.

Schaberg, Jane. "Luke". *The Women's Bible Commentary.* Edited by Carol A. Newsom and Sharon H. Ringe. London: SPCK, 1992.

Schmidt, T. E. "Taxes." In J. B. Green, S. McKnight, & I. H. Marshall (Eds.), *Dictionary of Jesus and the Gospels* (pp. 800ff). InterVarsity Press, 1992.

Schreiner, Thomas R., Shawn Wright, and E. Ray Clendenen. *Believer's Baptism: Sign of the New Covenant in Christ*. Nashville, TN: B&H Publishing Group, 2007.

Schweizer, Eduard. *The Good News According to Luke.* Louisville, KY: Westminster John Knox Press, 1984.

Schweizer, Edward. *The Good News According to Luke*. Trans. by David E. Green. Atlanta: John Knox Press, 1984.

Schweizer, Edward. *The Good News According to Luke.* Tr. By David E. Green. Atlanta: John Knox Press, 1984, c.1913.

Scott, B. B. "Lost Junk, Found Treasure." *Biblical Theology* 26. No. 1 (January 1988): 31-34.

Scott, Bernard Brandon. *Hear Then the Parable: A Commentary on the Parables of Jesus*. Minneapolis: Fortress Press, 1989.

Seim, Turid Karlsen. *The Double Message: Patterns of Gender in Luke-Acts.* Edinburgh: T&T Clark, 1994.

Seim, Turid Karlsen. *The Double Message: Patterns of Gender in Luke-Acts.* Nashville: Abingdon Press, 1994.

Sellew, Philip. "Interior Monologue as a Narrative Device in the Parables of Luke." *Journal of Biblical Literature* 111. No. 2 (1992): 239–253.

Selvanayagam, Israel. "The Parable of the Prodigal Son: A Contextual Reflection". *Light on Our Dusty Path: Essays for a Bible Lover*. Edited by Israel Selvanayagam. Bangalore: BTESSC/SATHRI, 2008.

Senior, Donald, and Caroll Stuhlmueller. *The Biblical Foundations for Mission.* New York: Orbis Books, 1983.

Senior, Donald. *The Passion of Jesus in the Gospel of Luke*. Delaware: Michael Glazier Wilmington, 1988.

Seo, Pyung-Soo. *Luke's Jesus in the Roman Empire and the Emperor in the Gospel of Luke*. Cambridge: James Clarke & Company Limited, 2015.

Sheeley, Stevan M. *Narrative Asides in Luke-Acts.* Sheffield: Sheffield Academic Press, 1992.

Sheeley, Stevan M. *Narrative Asides in Luke-Acts*. JSNT Supplement Series, 72. Sheffield: Sheffield Academic Press, 1992.

Sheen, Fulton J. *Characters of the Passion*. New York: Garden City Books, 1953.

Shellard, Barbara. *New Light on Luke: Its Purpose, Sources and Literary Context.* London: Sheffield Academic Press, 2002.

Shoemaker, Mel. *The Theology of the Four Gospels*. Nashville, TN: WestBow Press, 2011.

Sloyan, Geard S. *Jesus on Trial: The Development of the Passion Narratives and their Historical and Ecumenical Implications*. Philadelphia: Fortress Press, 1973.

Smither, Edward. *Augustine as Mentor: A Model for Preparing Spiritual Leaders.* Nashville: B&H Publishing Group, 2008.

Snodgrass, K. R. "Parable." *Dictionary of Jesus and the Gospels.* Edited by Joel B. Green, Scot McKnight, and I. Howard Marshall. Downer's Grove: IVP, 1998.

Soards, Marion L. "Tradition, Composition and Theology in Jesus' Speech to the 'Daughters of Jerusalem' (Lk. 23:26-32)." *Biblica 68*. No. 2 (1987): 225

Soards, Marrion L. 2000. "Passion Narratives." *Eerdmans Dictionary of the Bible.* Edited by David Noel Freedman, 1011. Michigan: W.B. Eerdmans Publishing Company.

Soares-Prabhu, George M. *The Kingdom of God*: Jesus' Vision of a New Society. Theology of Liberation: An Indian Biblical Perspective.

Collected Writings of George M. Soares-Prabhu. Vol. 4. Edited by F. X. D'Sa. Pune: Deepa Vidyapeett Theological, 2001, 239.

Sobrino, J. *Jesus the liberator: A Historical Theological Reading of Jesus of Nazareth*. New York: Orbis Books, 1993.

Sprinkle, Joe M. 1996. "Death of Christ." *Baker Theological Dictionary of the Bible*. Edited by Walter A. Elwell, 156. Michigan: Baker Books.

Stählin, G. "ch,ra." In G. Friedrich (Ed.), *TDNT* (pp. 441). Michigan: Wm. B. Eerdmans Publishing Company, 1994.

Stanton, Graham N. *The Gospels and Jesus*. The Oxford Bible Series. Oxford: Oxford University, 1992.

Stark, Rodney. *The Rise of Christianity: A Sociologist Reconsiders History*. New Jersey: Princeton University Press, 1996.

Stein, Robert A. *Luke: An Exegetical and Theological Exposition of Holy Scripture*. Nashville, TN: B&H Publishing Group, 1993.

Stein, Robert H. *Luke*. Nashville, TN: B&H Publishing Group, 1992.

Stern, David. "Jesus' *Parables from the Perspective of Rabbinic Literature*: The Example of the Wicked Husbandmen." In *Parable and Story in Judaism and Christianity*, edited by Clements Thoma and Michael Wyschogrod, 43. New York: Paulist Press, 1989.

Strauss, Mark L. *The Davidic Messiah in Luke-Acts: The Promise and Its Fulfillment in Lukan Christology*. JSNTSup 110. Sheffield: Sheffield Academic Press, 1995.

Strauss, Mark. *The Davidic Messiah in Luke-Acts: The Promise and Its Fulfilment in Lukan Christology*. London: Bloomsbury Publishing, 1995.

Strecker, Georg. *Theology of the New Testament: German Edition Edited and Completed*. Berlin: Walter de Gruyter, 2012.

Strelan, Rick. *Luke the Priest: The Authority of the Author of the Third Gospel*. Ashgate Publishing Company, London 2008.

Strong, Augustus H. *Popular Lectures on the Books of the New Testament*. Chicago: The Judson Press, 1914.

Strong, James. *A Concise Dictionary of the Words in the Greek Testament: With Their Rendering in the Authorized English Version*. New Jersey: Madison, 1890.

Stronstad, Roger. *Charismatic Theology of St. Luke*. Grand Rapids, MI: Baker Publishing Group, 1990.

Syiemlieh, B. J. *God's Favorites: A Socio-narrative Analysis of the Characters in the Lukan Infancy Narratives (Luke 1:5-2:52)*. ISPCK, 2005.

Szkredka, Slawomir. *Sinners and Sinfulness in Luke: A Study of Direct and Indirect References in the Initial Episodes of Jesus' Activity*. Tübingen: Mohr Siebeck, 2017.

Takatemjen, *The Banquet is Ready: Rich and Poor in the Parables of Luke.* Delhi: ISPCK, 2003.

Talbert, C. H. *Reading Luke: A Literary and Theological Commentary on the Third Gospel*. New York: Crossroad, 1982.

Talbert, Charles H. *Reading Luke: A Literary and Theological Commentary on the Third Gospel.* NewYork: Crossroad, 1989.

Talbert, Charles H. "Promise and Fulfillment in Lucan Theology." *Luke-Acts-* New Perspectives From the Society of Biblical Literature Seminar. NewYork: Cross Road, 1984.

Talbert, Charles H. *Literary Patterns, Theological Themes and Genre of Luke-Acts.* Montana: SBL and Scholars Press, 1974.

Talbert, Charles H. *Perspectives on Luke-Acts.* Edinburgh: T&T Clark, 1978.

Talbert, Charles H. *What is a Gospel: The Genre of Canonical Gospels*. London: SPCK, 1978.

Tannehill, R. C. *The Narrative Unity of Luke-Acts: A Literary Interpretation*. Minneapolis: Fortress Press, 1994.

Tannehill, Robert C. *The Narrative Unity of Luke-Acts: A Literary Interpretation.* Vol.1. The Gospel of Luke. Philadelphia: Fortress Press, 1986.

Tasker, R. V. G. "Parable." *The New Bible Dictionary*. Edited by J. D. Douglas. London: IVP, 1962.

Tasker, R. V. G., and I. Howard Marshall. "Parable." *New Bible Dictionary*, 869.

Tatum, W. Barnes. *John the Baptist and Jesus: A Report of the Jesus Seminar*. Santa Rosa, CA: Polebridge Press, 1994.

Taylor, V. *The Passion Narrative of St. Luke: A Critical and Historical Investigation*. Cambridge University Press, 1972.

Taylor, Vincent. *The Formation of the Gospel Tradition*. London: Macmillan and Co., 1933, 93.

Taylor, Vincent. *The Passion of St. Luke: A Critical Historical Investigation*. Edited by O.E. Evans. SNTSMS 19, 1972.

Tenney, Merrill C. *New Testament Survey*. Michigan: Wm. B. Eerdmans Publishing Co., 1961.

Tenny, Merrill C. "Luke." *The Wycliffe Bible Commentary*. Edited by Everett F. Harrison. Chicago: Moody Press, 1962.

The Greek New Testament, Edited by Barbara Aland, Johannes Karavidopoulos et al. Fourth Revised Edition. Edmonds, WA: United Bible Societies, 2001.

Theissen, G. *Sociology of Early Palestinian Christianity* (J. Bowden, Trans.). Fortress Press, 1977.

Theoharis, Liz. *Always with Us? What Jesus Really Said About the Poor.* Michigan: Wm. B. Eerdmans Publishing Company, 2017.

Thibeaux, E. R. "'Known to be a Sinner': The Narrative Rhetoric of Luke 7:36-50." *Biblical Theology Bulletin, 23*, 152, 1993.

Thomas, C. T. *Jesus and His Good News: A Lay Perspective*. Delhi: ISPCK, 2001, 109.

Thompson, R. P. "Gathered at the Table: Holiness and Ecclesiology in the Gospel of Luke." In K. E. Brower & A. Johnson (Eds.), *Holiness and Ecclesiology in the New Testament* (pp. 81). Grand Rapids: Eerdmans, 2007.

Thrailkill, Phillip C. *Following Jesus: Discipleship in the Gospel of Luke and Beyond*. Eugene, OR: Wipf and Stock Publishers, 2022.

Tinsley, E. J. *The Gospel According to Luke.* Cambridge: Cambridge University Press, 1969.

Tittle, Ernest Fremont. *The Gospel According to Luke: Exposition and Application.* New York: Harper and Brothers Publishers, 1957.

Tolbert, Malcolm O. Luke-John. *The Broadman Bible Commentary*. Edited by Clifton J. Allan. Nashville: Broadman Press, 1970.

Tolbert, Mary Ann. *Perspectives on Parables: An Approach to Multiple Interpretation*. Philadelphia: Fortress Press, 1979.

Topel, John. "On Being Parabled." *Biblical Theology* (December 1976): 1010-1017.

Torrance, T. F. *Service in Jesus Christ*. Grand Rapids: Eerdmans Press, 1975.

Trites, Allison A., and William J. Larkin. *Luke, Acts*. Carol Stream, IL: Tyndale House, 2016.

Troemé, Etienne. *The Passion as a Liturgy: A Study in the Origin of the Passion Narratives in the Four Gospels.* London: SCM Press, 1983.

Tucker, Jeffrey T. *Example Stories: Perspectives on Four Parables in the Gospel of Luke*. Journal for the Study of the New Testament Supplement Series 162. Sheffield: Sheffield Academic Press, 1998.

Tuckett, Christopher M. *Luke.* Sheffield: Sheffield Academic Press, 1996.

Turner, David L. *Baker Exegetical Commentary on the New Testament: Matthew*. Grand Rapids: Baker Academic, 2008.

Turner, Nigel. *The Gospel of Luke*. Cambridge: Cambridge University Press, 1976.

Twelftree, Graham H. *People of the Spirit*. Grand Rapids, MI: Baker Academic, 2009.

Tynan, John Dominic. Who Killed Jesus: *Exposing the Roots of Anti-Semitism in the Gospel Story of the Death of Jesus*. New York: Harper San Francisco, 1991.

Tyson, J. B. "Conflict as a Literary Theme in the Gospel of Luke." In *New Synoptic Studies*. Edited by W. Farmer and Macon. GA: Mercer University Press, 1983.

Tyson, Joseph B. "The Jewish Public in Luke-Acts." *New Testament Studies* 30 (1984): 576.

Tyson, Joseph B. "The Lukan Version of the Trial of Jesus." Novum Testamentum 3/4 (October 1959): 258.

Tyson, Joseph B. Ed, *Luke-Acts and the Jewish People*: *Eight Critical Perspectives.* Minneapolis: Augsburg Publishing House, 1988.

van Harn, Roger. "Peter's Denials—How Many? To Whom?" CBQ 52/3 (July 1990): 472.

van Linden, Philip. *The Gospel of Luke and Acts*. Wilmington: Michael Glazier, 1970.

Varghese, B. *Women's in the Gospel of Luke*: *The Role of Woman in the Portrayal of Salvation in the Gospel of Luke.* Delhi: ISPCK, 2005. Via, Dan O. Parable and Example Story: A Literary-Structuralist Approach. Philadelphia: Fortress Press, 1967.

Via, E. Jane. 1983. "According to Luke, Who Put Jesus to Death." *Political Issues in Luke-Acts.* Edited by Richard J. Cassidy and Philip J. Scharper, 130. New York: Orbis Books.

Vincent, Marvin R. *Word Studies in the New Testament*. Massachusetts: Hendrickson Publishers, 2009.

Vine, W. E. "Mourn." In *Vine's Expository Dictionary of Old and New Testament Words*. Iowa: World Bible Publishers, 1981.

Vine, W. E. *An Expository Dictionary of New Testament Words*. New Jersey: Fleming H. Revell Company, 1966.

Vollmer, Philip. *New Testament Sociology*. New York: Fleming H. Revell Company, 1923.

Wainwright, Elaine M. *Towards a Feminist Critical Reading of the Gospel According to Matthew*. Berlin: Werner Hildebrand, 1991.

Walvoord, John F. 1975. "Jesus Christ." *Wycliffe Bible Encyclopedia*. Vol. 1. Edited by Charles F. Pfeiffer, Howard F. Vos, and Jon Rea, 335. Chicago: Moody Press.

Walvoord, John F., and Roy B. Zuck. *The Bible Knowledge Commentary Gospels*. Colorado Springs, CO: David C Cook, 2018.

Warren, Rick. *The Purpose Driven Church: Growth Without Compromising Your Message and Mission*. Grand Rapids, MI: Zondervan Publishing House, 1995.

Watson, David. *Called and Committed: World-Changing Discipleship*. Wheaton, IL: Harold Shaw Publishers, 1982.

Webb, Robert L. *John the Baptizer and Prophet: A Sociohistorical Study*. Eugene, OR: Wipf and Stock Publishers, 2006.

Wehrill, Eugene S. *Exploring the Parables: Let Him Hear*. Philadelphia: Boston, 1963.

Wendland, Ernst R. "A Tale of Two Debtors: On the Interaction of Text, Context, and Context in a New Testament Dramatic Narrative (Luke 7:36–50)." In *Linguistics and New Testament Interpretation: Essays on Discourse Analysis*. Edited by David Alan Black. Nashville, Tennessee: Broadman Press, 1992.

Wenham, David. *The Parables of Jesus*. London: Hodder & Stoughton, 1989.

Wenk, Matthias. *Community-Forming Power*. Bloomsbury Publishing, 2004.

Westfall, Cynthia Long, and Bryan R. Dyer. *The Bible and Social Justice: Old Testament and New Testament Foundations for the Church's Urgent Call*. Eugene: Wipf and Stock Publishers, 2015.

White, Ellen G. *Steps to Christ*. Mountain View, CA: Pacific Press, 1956.

White, Ellen G. *Testimonies for the Church*. 9 Vols. Mountain View, CA: Pacific Press, 1949.

White, Ellen Gould. *Thoughts from the Mount of Blessing*. Germany: Jazzybee Verlag, 2014.

Wiersbe, Warren W. *Be Loyal: Discover the Excitement of Knowing and Serving the King of Glory.* England: Victor Books, 1987.

Wilder, Amos N. *Early Christian Rhetoric: The Language of the Gospel.* New York: Harper and Row, 1964.

Wilkins, Michael J. "Matthew." *The NIV Application Commentary*. Grand Rapids, MI: Zondervan, 2004.

Wilkins, Michael J. *The Concept of Disciple in Matthew's Gospel As Reflected in the Use of the Term Mathetes*. Novum Testamentum Supplements 59. Leiden, The Netherlands: Brill Academic Publishers, 1988.

Williams, Robert E. *The Trial of Jesus: A Historical and Legal Analysis*. New York: Random House, 1993.

Wilson, Stephen G. *The Gentiles and the Gentile Mission in Luke-Acts*. Cambridge: Cambridge University Press, 1973.

Wing Wo Fung, Benjamin. *A Defense for the Chronological Order of Luke's Gospel: The Meaning of "Orderly" (Kathexes) Account in Luke 1:3*. Eugene, OR: Wipf and Stock Publishers, 2019.

Winter, P. "Some Observation on the Language in the Birth and Infancy Stories of the Third Gospel." *NTS* 1 (1954): 111.

Wintle, Brian C. *Synoptic Studies: A Primer*. Bangalore: Theological Book Trust, 2007.

Work, Telford. *Living and Active: Scripture in the Economy of Salvation*. Grand Rapids, MI: Wm. B. Eerdmans Publishing, 2004.

Wright, N. T. *Simply Jesus*. London: SPCK, 2011.

Wright, N.T., and Patty Pell. *Luke*. Downers Grove: InterVarsity Press, 2011.

Yamasaki, Gary. *John the Baptist in Life and Death: Audience-Oriented Criticism of Matthew's Narrative*. A&C Black, 1998.

Yamauchi, Edwin. *Harper's World of the New Testament*. Philadelphia: Harper & Row Publishers, 1981.

Yinger, Kent L. *The Pharisees: Their History, Character, and New Testament Portrait*. Eugene, OR: Wipf and Stock Publishers, 2022.

Young, Brad H. *Jesus and His Jewish Parables: Rediscovering the Roots of Jesus' Teaching*. New York: Paulist Press, 1989.

Zuck, Roy B. *The Gospel of Luke: A New Perspective on Its Purpose and Message*. Nashville: Broadman Press, 1990.